A DICTIONARY OF
PHILOSOPHY

A DICTIONARY OF
PHILOSOPHY

THIRD REVISED EDITION

A. R. LACEY

BARNES
&NOBLE
BOOKS
NEW YORK

Preface to the
___ first edition

This book aims to give the layman or intending student a pocket
encyclopaedia of philosophy, one with a bias towards explaining
terminology. The latter task is not an easy one since philosophy is
regularly concerned with concepts which are unclear. It is one main
part of philosophy to clarify them rather than use them. What I
have tried to do is to take some of the commonest terms and
notions in current English-speaking philosophy and to give the
reader some idea of what they mean to the philosopher and what
sort of problems he finds associated with them.

A work of this size cannot do justice to individual philosophers.
The entries devoted to them offer only the barest outlines of their
work, followed by the most philosophically important of their publications or, occasionally, those of other interest. Where possible, the
original title and publication date is given, sometimes followed by
the standard title of an English translation, or by a brief indication
of the work's topic. Where applicable, each of these entries ends
with cross-references to all other entries where the philosopher is
mentioned unless cross-references are already given in the text of
the entry. It is important to remember that both the description
of a philosopher's activity and the list of his writings are by no
means exhaustive. The choice of eighty or so philosophers represents, with some inevitable arbitrariness, a compromise between
importance and popularity.

In the book as a whole, epistemology and logic occupy far more
space than, say, ethics, politics or aesthetics. This is because the
former subjects are the central ones. Terms and concepts from
them are constantly used in discussing the latter subjects, while the
opposite process occurs rarely, of at all. Mathematical logic needs

Preface

a dictionary to itself, and only those terms are included which occur widely in philosophical and traditional logic. Much the same applies to linguistic theory. I have also generally avoided terms associated with only one author, for which a standard edition or commentary is best consulted.

Many philosophical terms, such as CONFIRMATION, also have a meaning in ordinary language and a technical meaning associated with a particular outlook. I have only occasionally mentioned the ordinary language one and I have not mentioned certain fairly obvious ambiguities of a kind common to many words. 'Entailment' may mean the relation of entailment, a proposition entailed, and a proposition saying that something entails something else. More important, many words are too complex for even the philosophically significant ambiguities to be covered completely. I have tried to give the dominant sense or senses in current, or currently studied, philosophy, and especially those senses which are technical, or reflect or give rise to philosophical problems. The short definitions that begin many of the longer entries should be taken only as attempts at giving the general character of the term in question.

The wide-ranging reader must be prepared to find almost any term used in ways I have not mentioned. In particular, it can only mislead to offer brief and precise definitions of philosophical ' –isms'. I have thus tried instead to bring out something of the general spirit of such terms, which often refer to features or aspects rather than to people or systems. Precision is similarly inapposite in recommending the use of a term like 'the causal theory of meaning' rather than 'causal theories of meaning'. Context or even whim will often decide whether one talks of different theories, or of variants of a single theory. Words like 'principle', 'law', 'rule', 'thesis', 'axiom', again, are usually used almost indifferently in phrases like 'the principle of . . .'.

The cross-references are denoted by small capitals (italic type simply picks terms out), and are of two kinds, within entries and self-standing. The former are given only when they seem useful. The term referred to is often mentioned in an approximate or abbreviated, but obvious, form. For example, the entry called 'conversion' might be referred to as 'converse'. The self-standing cross-references are not a guarantee that a term is treated fully, but they may be thought of as forming a sort of index. Terms with more than one word normally appear only once. RUSSELL'S PARADOX appears under R but not under P, and the discussion of innate ideas can be traced through IDEA. Cross-references which occur, preceded by 'See also', at the ends of articles may refer to the article as a whole, not just the last paragraph.

No single principle underlies the bibliographies. An item may be

Preface

the original source of a notion, or a good, elementary, or accessible discussion, or a recent discussion from which previous ones can be traced, or a bibliographical source. I have mentioned certain reprintings of articles, but have not tried to be exhaustive, because space forbids and they are constantly being added to. I do not claim to have read everything mentioned, though I hope I have not mentioned things without adequate reason. The absence of a work is not of course a point against it. It may mean no more than that I have not come across it. Readers lucky enough to have access to P. Edwards (ed.), *The Encyclopaedia of Philosophy*, 8 vols, 1967, will no doubt use it anyway, so I have hardly ever referred to it, though I am immensely indebted to it myself. J. O. Urmson (ed.), *The Concise Encyclopaedia of Western Philosophy and Philosophers*, 1960, and D. Runes (ed.), *Dictionary of Philosophy*, 1942 (mainly its logical entries) have considerably helped me, and may also help the reader. The intermittent 'recent work in . . .' surveys in the *American Philosophical Quarterly* may also be mentioned.

Finally it is a pleasure to acknowledge the great help I have received from my friends and colleagues, Mr D. A. Lloyd Thomas, Dr D. M. Tulloch and Dr. J. L. Watling have between them offered detailed comments on the entire manuscript, and each has made very significant contributions to both the merits of the work and the morale of its author. For similar comments on smaller portions I am greatly indebted to Dr W. A. Hodges, Miss R. L. Meager, Mr. J. D. Valentine and Professor P. G. Winch. Many other colleagues have helped me by answering queries and discussing individual points. I am also of course indebted to many philosophical publications, especially those mentioned in the bibliographies. The following among my non-philosophical colleagues have gone to great trouble in assisting me to communicate comprehensibly: Mrs J. H. Bloch, Prof. D. F. Cheesman, Dr G. Darlow, Dr D. R. Dicks, Dr M. R. Hoare, Dr E. Jacobs, Mr T. B. Taylor, Miss E. C. Vollans, Dr G. H. Wright. None of these, naturally, is responsible for what I have said, especially as I have occasionally gone my own way, and have made many alterations since they saw it. Mrs Helen Marshall has helped me to make a considerable number of improvements in my style and Dr Ted Honderich has been of great assistance to me in various ways in the later stages. I am also grateful to the Philosophy Department of Bedford College for allowing me two sabbatical terms to work on this book. And I am grateful to numerous typists and secretaries who have come to my aid in time of need.

Preface

Preface to second edition

This edition contains twenty-five new entries: Abstraction, Agglomeration, Ancestral, Cambridge change, Charity (principle of), Determinates and determinables, Dualism, Functionalism, Genidentity, Goldbach's conjecture, Heap (paradox of), Hermeneutic, Holism, Materialism, Memory, Newcomb's paradox, Polish notation, Prisoner's dilemma, Quale, Qualities (primary and secondary), Relativism, Santayana, Satisfice, Whewell, Zombie. Twenty-four cross-references have been added and two deleted. I have made various corrections, amendments and additions throughout, and have added to many of the bibliographies.

My main debt of gratitude is to Dr J. L. Watling for discussing in detail with me substantial parts of the new material. I am also grateful to many of my philosophical colleagues, especially Dr D. M. Edgington, Dr S. Guttenplan, Prof. D. W. Hamlyn, Dr W. A. Hodges, Dr C. Hughes, Dr R. M. Sainsbury, Mr A. B. Savile, Dr. R. Spencer-Smith, and to Mrs M. Blackburn of the University of London Library, for help on smaller portions or points of detail, and I have tried to benefit from the many points made by reviewers and private correspondents.

Finally I am grateful to King's College Philosophy Department for allowing me a sabbatical term part of which was devoted to this work.

Preface to third edition

This edition contains sixty-six new entries (as well as a handful of new cross-references): Abstract, Actualism, Algorithm, Analysis (paradox of), Armstrong, Chinese room argument, Chisholm, Closure, Cognitivism, Combinatorialism, Connectionism, Consciousness, Content, Davidson, Dialetheism, Disposition, Doxastic, Dummett, Egocentric predicament, Emergence, Folk psychology, Foundationalism, Frege argument, Generality constraint, Haecceity, Idiolect, Imagery, Individualism, Innate, Internalism and externalism, Intrinsic and extrinsic, Kripke, Language of thought, Lewis, Mach's Principle, Mereology, Methodological solipsism, Numbers, Original position, Paraconsistency, Particularism, Perdurance, Perspectivism, Possible worlds, Primitive, Process philosophy, Psycholinguistics, Psychosemantics, Putnam, Ramsey sentence, Reflective equilibrium, Scientism, Superassertible, Supervaluation, Supervenience, Synechism, Tacit and implicit knowledge, Thick and thin concepts, Third man argument, Tracking, Trope, Turing machine,

Preface

Turing test, Vagueness, Veil of perception, Virtue. A few other entries have been substantially rewritten (notably A priori, Belief, Burali-Forti's paradox, Cognitive psychology, Excluded middle, Feeling, Good, Psychologism, Satisfy), and the rest revised and updated in varying degrees where necessary. One entry (Beauty) has been completely dropped. The bibliographies have been substantially expanded and updated, and sometimes cut (though I have retained a fair amount of older material, sometimes despite advice to cut it: being now past retirement age I might perhaps be allowed the thought that 'old' is not synonymous with 'bad'). But I have tried throughout to represent the change in philosophical outlook that has occurred since the first edition, written still under the influence of the 'linguistic philosophy' era. An asterisk in a bibliography signifies a relatively elementary starting-point, though not all such items have one.

My greatest debts for this edition are to Dr T. Crane and Prof. J. Cargile, each of whom sent me both general and detailed comments on the whole of the second edition. Dr Crane also sent similar comments on my initial revisions, and suggested a hundred or more bibliographical additions, virtually all of which I have adopted. I am indebted for very substantial help on individual entries to Dr K. Hossack, Prof. M. Machover, Dr C. Hughes, Mr J. Hopkins and Dr G. Segal, and also for various individual points and references to Dr S. Botros, Dr D. M. Edgington, Prof. D. A. Gillies, Mr D. A. Lloyd Thomas, Prof. D. Papineau, Prof. R. M. Sainsbury, Prof. A. B. Savile, Prof. P. Simons, Dr L. Siorvanes and Dr A. Thomas. I have also used a number of valuable suggestions from Mr P. Wesley, who translated the second edition into Dutch. Since so many of whatever merits this edition has are due to all these people, it would be nice to add that the remaining faults must be due to them as well; but unfortunately I cannot do this, as I have in some cases not followed their advice or followed it only in part, and none of them has seen the final version.

Finally I am grateful to Gale Research International Ltd for letting me re-use some of the material I contributed for their *Dictionary of Theories*, 1993, and to the sources mentioned in the Acknowledgements to that volume.

A Dictionary of
PHILOSOPHY

Abelard (Abailard), Pierre. 1079–1142. Born near Nantes, he lived and worked in France writing mainly on theology, logic and metaphysics, and ethics. His theology is sometimes thought to be rationalistic, subordinating faith to reason, though interpretations differ. He steered a middle course between realism and nominalism over UNIVERSALS, and his ethics particularly emphasized intention. His writings are of uncertain date, but include in theology *Theologia Christiana* and *Sic et Non*, in logic and metaphysics *Logical Ingredientibus* and *Dialectica*, and in ethics *Ethica* (or *Scito Teipsum*).

About. See REFERRING.

Absolute. See IDEALISM.

Abstract. An abstract entity may be one constructed by the mind through the process of ABSTRACTION. But the term is also sometimes used for entities regarded as being outside space and time, as, e.g. numbers are for a Platonist philosopher of MATHEMATICS. When applied to properties, ideas, etc., 'abstract' usually has the former sense, though the criteria for when a property counts as abstract in that sense are various, such as being a universal rather than a TROPE, or being mind-dependent in a certain way. But certain spatiotemporal things are also sometimes called abstract particulars, such as actions and events and tropes (where tropes are distinct from other tropes they belong within a concrete object.)

K. Campbell, *Abstract Particulars*, Blackwell, 1990. (Constructs a metaphysics taking tropes as basic.)

1

Abstraction

N. Cartwright and R. Le Poidevin, 'Fables and models', *Proceedings of the Aristotelian Society*, supplementary vol., 1991. (A symposium containing some discussion of the abstract/concrete contrast.)

B. Hale, *Abstract Objects*, Blackwell, 1987. (Uses 'abstract' in second sense and defends Platonist view of abstract objects.)

R. Teichmann, *Abstract Entities*, St. Martin's Press and Macmillan, 1992 (Nominalist approach.)

Abstraction. Process by which allegedly we form concepts on the basis of experience or of other concepts. On being confronted with red things, each of which has many other properties, we abstract the redness and so form a concept of red. Having done the same with blue, yellow, etc., we then abstract from these concepts themselves the concept of colour, and so on. Empiricists like Locke use abstraction to help specify how we build up our concepts on the basis of experience. It is unclear, however, that Locke properly distinguishes such things as forming a concept on the basis of repeated presentations of a quality, abstracting genera from species, abstracting determinables from DETERMINATES. *Abstractionism* is the view that the mind does operate in this way.

D. Bell, 'Objects and concepts', *Proceedings of the Aristotelian Society*, supplementary volume, 1994, § 1. (Defends abstractionism.)

P. T. Geach, *Mental Acts*, 1957, pp. 18–44. (Criticizes abstractionism.)

J. Locke, *An Essay concerning Human Understanding*, 1690, e.g. 2.11.9–10, 2.12.1, 2.32.6–8, 3.3.9.

J. R. Weinberg, *Abstraction, Relation, Induction*, 1965. (Historical).

Acceptance, acceptability. See CONFIRMATION, LOTTERY PARADOX.

Access. It has often been held that we alone have access to our own thoughts and sensations (*private* or *privileged access*). See also PRIVATE LANGUAGE, and (for a different use of 'access') POSSIBLE WORLDS.

W. Alston, 'Varieties of privileged access'. *American Philosophical Quarterly*, 1971, reprinted in R. M. Chisholm and R. J. Swartz (eds), *Empirical Knowledge*, Prentice-Hall, 1973.

J. Heil, 'Privileged access', *Mind*, 1988, with discussions by N. Georgalis and A. Brueckner in *Mind*, 1990. (B. Brewer in *Mind*, 1992 is also relevant.)

N. Malcolm. 'The privacy of experience', in A. Stroll (ed.) *Epistem-*

ology, Harper and Row, 1967. (Discusses an ambiguity, and then the issue itself.)

Achilles paradox. See ZENO'S PARADOXES.

Acrasia (Akrasia). See INCONTINENCE.

Action. The doing of something or what is done. Problems about actions concern first of all what they are, and how they relate to things like trying, choosing, willing, intending (cf. also basic action); and how are persons related to their actions, and how do they know about them? We talk of the action of rain, and of reflex actions, but action of the central kind is what is done by rational beings. Only they can *perform* actions. Acting usually involves moving in some way, or at least trying to move, so how are actions related to movements? How is my raising my arm related to my arm's rising? What one intends is relevant here, and this involves the ways in which what happens can be viewed (cf. INTENSIONALITY.) Consider (as relating to one occasion): making certain neurones in the brain fire, tightening one's arm-muscles, flexing one's finger, moving a piece of iron, pulling a trigger, firing a gun, heating a gun-barrel, shooting a man, shooting an ex-farmer, shooting the President, assassinating the President, earning a bribe, grieving a nation, starting a war.

Are all these descriptions of one action, or of an action and its consequences, or what? Two substantive questions are connected with this. First, since an action cannot cause itself, how is action related to causation? Indeed is an action the sort of thing that can be caused at all? Second, what bearing has this on responsibility?

Further problems, which also bear on responsibility, concern omissions, inaction, negligence, and also unintentional actions, as when one frightens a bystander, or involuntary ones, as when one unwillingly reveals one's feelings by gasping, but perhaps something can only be an action when it is something an agent *could* set out to fulfil, even if indirectly (firing neurones by flexing one's finger).

A historically important contrast, deriving from Aristotle, lies between action, as what someone or something does, and 'passion', in the sense of what is done to it.

The relations between acts and actions are complex and disputed. 'Act' seems more of a technical term, especially in phrases like 'mental act' and SPEECH ACT, and less connected to responsibility, etc. Sometimes it was the sense of 'actuality', contrasting with potentiality rather than with state or condition. See also EVENT.

Action (philosophy of)

M. Brand and D. Walton (eds), *Action Theory*, Reidel, 1980. (Specially written essays on various relevant issues.)

W. Cerf, Review of J. L. Austin, *How to Do Things with Words, Mind*, 1966, pp. 269–76, reprinted in K. T. Fann (ed.). *Symposium on J. L. Austin*, RKP, 1969, pp. 359–68. W. D. Ross, *The Right and the Good*, Clarendon, 1930, pp. 6–7. G. H. von Wright, *Explanation and Understanding*, RKP, 1971, p. 69. J. L. Mackie, 'The grounds of responsibility', in P. M. S. Hacker and J. Raz (eds), *Law, Morality, and Society*, Clarendon, 1977, p. 176. (Different views of act/action distinction.)

A. B. Cody, 'Can a single action have many different descriptions?', *Inquiry*, 1967. (Cf. R. E. Dowling's discussion and Cody's reply, ibid.)

D. Davidson, *Essays on Actions and Events*, Clarendon, 1980. (Reprinted articles discussing *inter alia* action and causation, reasons, persons, and intentions.)

L. H. Davis, *Theory of Action*, Prentice-Hall, 1979. (General discussion of relevant issues.)

J. H. Hornsby, *Actions*, RKP, 1980. (Discuss many of the questions above, though harder than Langford.)

A. Kenny, *Action, Emotion and Will*, RKP, 1963. (Chapter 7 distinguishes actions from relations.)

*G. Langford, *Human Action*, Macmillan, 1971. (Elementary discussion. Extensive bibliography.)

A. I. Melden, *Free Action*, RKP, 1961. (Raising one's arm, etc.)

D. Owens, *Causes and Coincidences*, Cambridge UP, 1992, chapter 8. (Action and causation.)

I. Thalberg, *Perception, Emotion and Action*, Blackwell, 1977. (Attempts common approach to various problems in these areas.)

Action (philosophy of). See MIND.

Actualism. View that only what is actual exists, as against *possibilism*, which allows mere possibilities to exist. Actualism is a view about POSSIBLE WORLDS.

In ethics, 'actualism' has been used for the view that whether we ought to do X depends on what would happen if we did it, while possibilism tells us to do whatever action is best. Suppose X would be best but only if we also did Y, which we shall not in fact do (whether or not we ought to): then possibilism says Do X, while actualism says Don't do X.

F. Jackson and R. Pargetter, 'Oughts, options and actualism', *Philosophical Review*, 1986 (reprinted in P. Pettit (ed.), *Consequentialism*, Dartmouth Publishing Co., 1993). (Ethical sense.)

Aesthetics

M. J. Loux (ed.), *The Possible and the Actual*, Oxford UP, 1979. (See its index.)

A. McMichael, 'A problem for actualism about possible worlds', *Philosophical Review*, 1983. (See first two sections for relations between actualism and possibilism, with references.)

E. Prior, *Dispositions*, Aberdeen UP, 1985. (Chapter 2 discusses different versions of actualism.)

Aesthetics. Also called *philosophy of art*. Roughly, that branch of philosophy concerned with the creation, value and experience of art and the analysis and solution of problems relating to these. The primary topic is the appreciation of art, and major problems centre on what makes something a work of art. Must it exhibit certain formal e.g. geometrical, properties (*formalism*), or express certain emotions, attitudes, etc. (*expressionism*), or do other things? What in fact is the role of pleasure and emotion, and are special types of them involved? Is there a special kind of value involved? Does the work of art embody special properties, like beauty, sublimity, prettiness, and if so, how are these related to its other properties? How relevant are the object's function, the context of production and the artist's intentions? Does it matter how a work was produced, whether difficulties had to be overcome, and whether it was a forgery? These latter questions, involving the artist, are balanced by questions about the appreciation of beauty, and other qualities, in nature, and how this relates to appreciation of art.

Many problems in aesthetics are parallel to problems in ethics. How are aesthetic terms and judgments to be analysed? Can such judgments be true or false, and how, if at all, can they be justified? Are there objective canons of taste? The relations between art and morality are especially relevant in literature, which can portray moral situations, and which has, like other arts, moral or psychological effects. Questions about the moral justification of producing works of art belong to ethics. Aesthetics, however, can ask whether a work's moral or psychological content is relevant to its aesthetic merit, and whether any subject-matters, such as pornography, are intrinsically inimical to aesthetic merit. Further questions cover the relations of art to wit and humour.

Metaphysical issues arise over the nature of a work of art. Is it a UNIVERSAL, or a paradigm, or a particular object, or is the answer different for different arts? Must a work of art be unique, or could it be created independently by different artists? And how is a work of art related to performances of it, where these are relevant? Philosophy of mind introduces questions about emotion, enjoyment, etc., and also about imitation or representation in the various arts: e.g. to what extent does fiction 'imitate' life? Fiction also raises

Aesthetics

questions of meaning and reference, which involve philosophy of language. What am I referring to when I mention Mr Pickwick? Can statements in fiction be true or false? Other questions concern phrases like 'merry tune', 'imaginative portrait': are the adjectives being used literally here?

Judgments on particular works of art do not properly belong to aesthetics, but general questions, like those about the 'golden section', concerning ways of achieving aesthetic value, may. It is, however, no longer as obvious as it once seemed that positions on general aesthetic theory and judgments on particular works are independent of each other. (Cf. ETHICS for some considerations analogous to those in this paragraph.

Aesthetics also discusses various aesthetic values, such as beauty, asking, e.g. how central it really is.

M. Budd, *Values of Art: Pictures, Poetry and Music*, Lane (Penguin), 1995. (General discussion of nature of aesthetic value, and of problems arising in these three arts. Cf. also his *Music and the Emotions*, Routledge, 1985, which claims music is autonomous and its value must be intrinsic, while no satisfactory relation between it and the emotions has yet been proposed.)

E. F. Carritt, *The Theory of Beauty*, 1914. (Introduction from point of view of what makes something a work of art.)

W. Charlton, *Aesthetics: An Introduction*, Hutchinson, 1970. (General introduction, with some emphasis on metaphysical issues.)

R. G. Collingwood, *The Principles of Art*, Clarendon, 1938.

E. H. Gombrich, *Art and Illusion*, Phaidon, 1960. (Emphasizes problems about representation.)

*J. Hospers (ed.), *Introductory Readings in Aesthetics*, Free Press, 1969. (Aimed at non-philosophers.)

D. Hume, 'Of the standard of taste', 1757, reprinted in his *Essays Literary, Moral and Political*, Routledge, n.d. (Applies his general philosophical outlook to aesthetics. Useful also for comparison with his ethics).

I. Kant, *Critique of Judgment*, 1790. (Kant's main work on aesthetics. See part 1, § 16, for distinction between two kinds of beauty, 'free' and 'dependent'.)

C. Radford, 'Fakes', *Mind*, 1978. (Relevance of forgery.)

R. L. Saw, *Aesthetics: An Introduction*, Macmillan, 1972. (Rather discursive. Emphasizes more purely aesthetic issues.)

K. L. Walton, *Mimesis as Make-Believe: On the Foundation of the Representational Arts*, Harvard UP, 1990. (Aims to bring under one focus aesthetic, metaphysical and semantic problems about representation. For a summary by Walton, followed by discussions and his reply, see *Philosophy and Phenomenological Research*, 1991, pp. 379–431, and also R. Moran, 'The expression of feeling in imagination', *Philosophical Review*, 1994.

R. Wollheim, *Art and its Objects*, Cambridge UP, 1968, 2nd edn with additions, 1980.

Affirming the consequent. Fallacy of arguing that if the consequent of a conditional statement is true, so is the antecedent, e.g., 'If all cats are black, Tiddles is black; and Tiddles *is* black; so all cats are black.' Sometimes, however, such an argument may be acceptable if regarded as inductive.

Agglomeration. If I can go out and I can stay in, the conjunction 'I can go out and I can stay in' must be true, but 'I can go out and stay in' does not follow. 'Can' is therefore not agglomerative. An important ethical issue concerns whether 'ought' is agglomerative.

B. A. O. Williams, R. F. Atkinson, 'Consistency in ethics', *Proceedings of the Aristotelian Society*, supplementary vol., 1965.

D. Owens, *Causes and Coincidences*, Cambridge UP, 1992, pp. 11–15. (Uses the notion to show why coincidences cannot be explained.)

Albert the Great. (Albertus Magnus) c. 1200–80. Born in Germany, he worked mainly there and in Paris (and taught AQUINAS in the 1240s). He contributed to empirical science, and was a pioneer in reconciling Greek and Arabic science and philosophy with Christianity. He also translated Aristotle from Greek to Latin. He studied PLATO and ARISTOTLE partly through the eyes of the Neoplatonists and the Arabs. He wrote, among other things, commentaries on Aristotle and other Greek authors, and on the *Sentences* of Peter Lombard and at the end of his life a *Summa Theologiae*.

Algorithm. Procedure for answering a given problem or type of problem by the properly disciplined applying of certain already established steps which are guaranteed to yield the answer. The procedures for long division and for extracting a square root are algorithms in arithmetic. See also DECIDABLE, HEURISTIC, RECURSIVE.

Alienans. See ATTRIBUTIVE.

Aliorelative. See REFLEXIVE.

Alternation. See CONJUNCTION.

Ambiguity

Ambiguity. The property, had by some terms, of having two or more meanings. Ambiguity is not the same as VAGUENESS. 'Bald' is vague (how many hairs can a bald man have?) but not ambiguous. An ambiguous term can be quite precise in each of its senses. Also it can be argued that ambiguity applies to terms, vagueness to concepts. 'How ambiguous is "ambiguous"?' is a favourite philosophical question. Ambiguity may apply to words, phrases and sentences, considered in the abstract, or to utterances considered as uttered on a given occasion.

'Bank', connected with rivers and money, may be treated as two words with the same sound but different meanings or as one word with different meanings. Philologists would call 'bank' two words if its uses have different etymologies, but philosophers often arbitrarily treat it as one word or two. Such words, especially when treated as one word with different meanings, are often called *equivocal*, or *homonyms*.

Phrases or sentences can be ambiguous while none of the words in them is so. In 'little girls' camp' either the girls or the camp may be little. This is sometimes called *amphiboly*.

The ambiguity of 'Jack hits James and Jill hit him' depends not on the *meaning* of 'him' but on who is being referred to by 'him' on the particular occasion of utterance; 'him' here has *ambiguity of reference*. Where the ambiguity depends on the structure of the sentence or expression, as here and with amphiboly, we have *syntactical ambiguity*. Where it depends on the meanings of individual words or expressions we have *semantic ambiguity*. 'Pretty little girls' is a mixed example, where the semantic ambiguity of 'pretty' affects its syntactic role according as 'pretty' qualifies 'girls' or modifies 'little'. *Pragmatic ambiguity* is ambiguity in what is done *in* saying something, as 'You're a fine fellow!' may be sincere or sarcastic. 'Ambiguity' itself is sometimes used in wider, sometimes in narrower, senses.

Some words seem to have senses which differ, but are related. A healthy body is a flourishing one, while a healthy climate produces or preserves health and a healthy complexion is a sign of it. 'Healthy' is therefore often said to have *focal meaning* (Owen). It senses 'focus' on one dominant sense. Words like 'big', which are syncategorematic (see CATEGORIES), have something like focal meaning, in that it makes a difference what standards we use in applying them. A big mouse is not a big animal, so that to call something 'big' without further ado, can be ambiguous; see ATTRIBUTIVE.

When the ambiguities of an expression can be predicted according to a rule the expression has *systematic ambiguity*. On the theory of TYPES words like 'class' are systematically or *typically ambiguous* because their meaning varies according to the type to which they belong.

Other kinds of ambiguity, or related notions, include analogical and metaphorical uses of expressions, e.g. God is sometimes called 'wise' in a sense different from, thought analogous to, that in which men are wise. Since many terms are ambiguous in this way when applied to God and men, this can be regarded as a case of systematic ambiguity; it is also related to focal meaning.

Some pervasive ambiguities are given special names, such as *process/product ambiguity* of words like 'vision' which can mean power of seeing or something seen, or 'statement' which can mean act of stating or what is stated. Many philosophically important terms have this ambiguity. See also OPEN TEXTURE.

W. Leszl, *Logic and Metaphysics in Aristotle*, Editrice Antenore, Padua, 1970, part II, chapter 1. (Kinds of ambiguity in Aristotle.)

G. E. L. Owen, 'Logic and metaphysics in some earlier works of Aristotle', in I. During and G. E. L. Owen (eds), *Aristotle and Plato in the Mid-Fourth Century*, Almquist and Wiksell, Göteborg, 1960, and 'Aristotle on the snares of ontology', in R. Bambrough (ed.), *New Essays on Plato and Aristotle*, RKP, 1965. D. W. Hamlyn, 'Focal meaning', *Proceedings of the Aristotelian Society*, 1977–8. (Discussions of focal meaning and its significance in Aristotle (small amount of Greek in Owen). Cf. esp. § 2 of latter, and also (for a related concept) R. Robinson, 'The concept of knowledge', *Mind*, 1971, p. 20.)

W. V. O. Quine, *Word and Object*, Wiley, 1960, §§ 27–9. (Various kinds of ambiguity, § 216 discusses vagueness.)

Amphiboly. See AMBIGUITY.

Analysis. See PHILOSOPHY.

Analysis (paradox of). The paradox which arises when we attempt to analyse, say, the concept *brother* into the concept *male sibling*. If they are the same concept differently named, no analysis has occurred; if different concepts, how can one analyse the other? Hence the analysis must apparently be either trivial or wrong. This raises the question, among others, of what CONCEPTS are.

C. H. Langford, 'Moore's notion of analysis', in P. A. Schilpp (ed.), *The Philosophy of G. E. Moore*, Northwestern UP, 1942. (Analysis in Moore. See p. 323 for the paradox, and pp. 660ff. for Moore's reply.)

Analytic. The analytic/synthetic distinction is first explicitly made

Analytic

by Kant. A proposition is analytic, on Kant's view, if the predicate is covertly contained in the subject, as in 'Roses are flowers'. A proposition where the predicate is attached to the subject but not contained in it is synthetic, as in 'Roses are red'. The contradictory of a synthetic proposition is always synthetic whereas the contradictory of an analytic proposition is usually called 'analytically false'. Kant's distinction was partly anticipated by Leibniz, who distinguished 'truths of reasons' from 'truths of fact', and had the idea of containment, and by Hume, who distinguished 'relations between ideas' from 'matters of fact'.

Kant's distinction can easily be extended to conditional propositions, which are analytic if the consequent is contained in the antecedent, e.g. 'If this is a rose, it is a flower', and otherwise synthetic. Some other kinds of propositions raise difficulties, for instance, existential propositions like 'There exist black swans', where containment does not seem to apply, and the notion of containment is anyway hard to analyse. In general in 'Red roses are red' the containment is straightforwardly verbal. But in what sense precisely is the predicate 'contained' in the subject in 'Roses are flowers', or the consequent in the antecedent in 'If all men are mortal and Socrates is a man, then Socrates is mortal'?

Because of this difficulty Kant himself proposed an alternative definition now often adopted: a proposition is analytic if its negation is, or is reducible to, a contradiction or inconsistency; otherwise the proposition is synthetic. A proposition which is true because it exemplifies a certain logical FORM, as 'Bachelors are bachelors' exemplifies the form 'x's are x's', can be called *explicitly analytic*. A proposition which is true because of certain definitions, as 'Bachelors are male' is true because of the definition of 'bachelor', is *implicitly analytic* or *true by definition*. Explicitly analytic propositions, and sometimes implicitly analytic ones too, can be called *logically true* or *logically necessary*.

A proposition like 'Nothing is both red and green all over' seems to be true in virtue of the meanings of the words involved, but not true by definition: 'red' is not *defined* in terms of 'not green', nor 'green', in terms of 'not red'. This proposition therefore must be called analytic, if at all, in a sense even wider than that of 'implicitly analytic'.

Recently the analytic/synthetic distinction has been attacked, especially by Quine, who argues that any clear account of the implicitly analytic would require notions like meaning, definition and synonymy, which themselves presuppose the implicitly analytic. He also alleges that the point of calling something analytic is to give a reason why is cannot be revised in the light of experience, and then claims that no statements are immune to such revision.

Analytic

Some statements are revisable with little effect on others (suppose 'I see a cat' is taken as true: it could be revised, i.e. rejected as false, by simply dismissing the experience as a hallucination). The rejection of other statements, such as the laws of logic, would profoundly affect our whole way of talking, but Quine thinks it is still possible. Scientific laws form an intermediate case. Thus Quine ends by saying that 'analytic' even in the narrow sense of 'explicitly analytic' cannot be applied absolutely, but at best as a matter of degree to those statements we are least willing to revise. Controversy still rages over this, especially concerning the laws of logic: is it simply that any sentence now expressing such a logical truth could one day change its meaning and fail to do so, or is there more to it than this? Cf. LOGIC (on deviant logics), PARACONSISTENCY.

The distinction has also been attacked, in a less fundamental way, by Waismann, who claims that it is not a sharp one, and that statements such as 'I see with my eyes' and 'space has three dimensions' cannot be unambiguously classified in accordance with it.

A further problem about the analytic/synthetic distinction, for those who accept it, is how it relates to the A PRIORI/empirical and necessary/contingent (see MODALITIES) distinctions. It is usually assumed that nothing can be both analytic and empirical, or both analytic and contingent, and in fact Kripke defines 'analytic' as what is both a priori and necessary, though he makes an important related claim (for which see A PRIORI). Kant, though he took 'analytic' in the wider sense, as 'implicitly analytic', treated analytic propositions as trivial and uninformative, like TAUTOLOGIES. He and others have claimed that the propositions of mathematics, etc., must be synthetic a priori, while logical positivists and others have vigorously denied that anything can be both synthetic and a priori. Often the synthetic a priori, which before Kripke was generally assumed to coincide with the synthetic necessary, is defended merely by interpreting 'analytic' in a narrow sense. Thus the issue at least partly depends on distinguishing senses of 'analytic' and giving reasons for preferring one to another. It is still disputed whether a substantial notion of synthetic a priori is needed for statements like 'Nothing can be red and green all over', or 'If A exceeds B and B exceeds C then A exceeds C'; and also whether the laws of logic themselves can properly be called analytic. How too should we classify the statement itself that no synthetic statement is a priori? (Cf. POSITIVISM for the objection to the verification principle that it cannot account for its own status.)

Certain problems concern the relation between sentences and the statements they are used to make. Does 'The fat cow which I see is fat' make an analytic statement, although it apparently implies the synthetic statement that I do see a cow? And does 'I exist',

Analytical hypothesis

since it cannot be uttered to make a false statement, make an analytic statement?

All the above must be distinguished from the question of the analytic and synthetic *methods*, deriving from Greek mathematics. See also SENTENCE.

T. Burge, 'Philosophy of language and mind', *Philosophical Review*, 1992. (See pp. 4–11 for three senses of 'analytic', with discussion.)

R. Descartes, *Reply to Second Objections* (to his *Meditations*), last few pages. (Analytic and synthetic methods.)

H. P. Grice and P. F. Strawson, 'In defense of a dogma', *Philosophical Review*, 1956. (Defence of analyticity against Quine. See also A. Sidelle, *Necessity, Essence and Individuation: A Defense of Conventionalism*, Cornell UP, 1989 (see its index).)

*J. F. Harris and R. H. Severens (eds). *Analyticity*, Quadrangle Books, 1970 (Readings. Includes Quine, Grice and Strawson, and bibliography.)

I. Kant, *Critique of Pure Reason*, Introduction, § 4.

S. Kripke, *Naming and Necessity*, Blackwell, 1980 (original version, 1972). (See especially pp. 39, 122, n. 63.)

H. Putnam, 'The analytic and the synthetic' in H. Feigl and G. Maxwell (eds), *Minnesota Studies in the Philosophy of Science* III, Minnesota UP, 1962, reprinted in his *Mind, Language and Reality: Philosophical Papers* vol. 2, Cambridge UP, 1975. (Claims that the distinction does exist but should not be overestimated.)

W. V. O. Quine, 'Two dogmas of empiricism', in *From a Logical Point of View*, Harper and Row, 1953, chapter 2.

*A. Quinton, 'The a priori and the analytic', *Proceedings of the Aristotelian Society*, 1963–4. (Distinguishes several senses of 'analytic' and rejects synthetic a priori for each of them.)

L. Resnick, 'Do existent unicorns exist?', *Analysis*, 23, 1963, pp. 128 ff. ('Fat cow' example. Cf. J. J. Katz, *Linguistic Philosophy*, 1972, pp. 146–73; pp. 156–7 claim analytic sentences are not always true.)

R. Robinson, 'Analysis in Greek geometry', *Mind*, 1936, reprinted in his *Essays in Greek Philosophy*, Clarendon, 1969. (Greek origins of analytic and synthetic methods).

F. Waismann, 'Analytic-synthetic' (in six parts). *Analysis*, 10, 11, 13, (1949–1953); reprinted in his *How I See Philosophy*, Macmillan, 1968.

Analytical hypothesis. See TRANSLATION.

Ancestral relation. If a relation connects every two adjacent terms in a series there must be a relation which connects any two terms in the series. This relation is the ancestral of the original one. 'Ancestor of' is the ancestral of 'parent of', but a better example (since people have two parents) is that 'greater than' among whole numbers is the ancestral of 'greater by one than'. See also DEFINITION

And. See CONJUNCTION.

Angst, Angoisse. See EXISTENTIALISM.

Anselm, St. 1033–1109. Born in Aosta, he studied in France and became archbishop of Canterbury in 1093. He originated the 'ONTOLOGICAL ARGUMENT' for God's existence in his *Proslogion* (his *Monologian* contains related proofs of God's existence). He also wrote on truth (*De Veritate*) and on logic and problems such as that of universals (*De Grammatico*).

D. P. Henry, *The Logic of St Anselm*, Clarendon, 1967. (Henry has also translated the *De Grammatico*, 1964.)

Antilogism. An inconsistent set of three propositions. The two premises of a valid SYLLOGISM with the CONTRADICTORY of its conclusion, or more generally three propositions, any two of which entail the contradictory of the third. Also called *inconsistent triad*. The *principle of antilogism* says that if two propositions together entail a third, then either of them and the contradictory of the third together entail the contradictory of the other, e.g. if 'All men are mortal' and 'Socrates is a man' together entail 'Socrates is mortal', then 'All men are mortal' and 'Socrates is not mortal' together entail 'Socrates is not a man'.

Antirealism. See REALISM.

Apodictic. See MODALITIES, IMPERATIVES.

Aporetic. Raising and discussing problems without solving them.

A posteriori. See A PRIORI.

Apperception. In Leibniz, reflective consciousness rather than mere passive perception. In Kant, consciousness of oneself as a unity, on the empirical or transcendental level. Other writers use the term in fairly similar senses. Perhaps the unifying thread in its main senses is awareness of the self as that which judges. It plays little part in contemporary philosophy.

A priori

A priori. A priori knowledge is that which has its justification independently of experience, though it may presuppose experience from which we can get the concepts it involves; many philosophers (though not all: see Lehman) regard mathematical knowledge as a priori, though children can't acquire it until they have experience of the world. Knowledge which can only be justified by at least some appeal to experience (basically the five senses, and perhaps introspection) is called *a posteriori* or *empirical*. A proposition, judgment, etc. is a priori or empirical according as knowledge of it is one or the other. Originally, in Aristotelian philosophy, a proposition was a priori if it was based on, or inferred from, something prior to it in the sense of being its cause or ground. A proposition was a posteriori if it was inferred from its effects. When it was later assumed that the main way of knowing a proposition through its effects was to know it through sense-experience, 'empirical' largely replaced 'a posteriori', and 'a priori' took on the meaning given above.

The philosophical and epistemological question of how our claims to knowledge can be justified is different from the psychological question how we in fact came to our knowledge. Some of it we may be born with, but this will only be innate *knowledge* if it could be justified, whether a priori, as above, or empirically, through experience, though innate empirical beliefs, whether true or not, are likely to be called instinctive, especially if they manifest themselves only in action rather than in conscious awareness. However, these philosophical and psychological questions have often been conflated, sometimes through confusion, but sometimes through the thought that the psychological question should properly replace the philosophical one, as in naturalized EPISTEMOLOGY (cf. NATURALISM). Also the way we acquire a belief, especially if we acquire it by reasoning or intuitive insight, may well coincide with the way we could justify it – but not always: we know that a belief we 'acquire' by its being innate may well be false (for more on this see INNATE). Kant, in particular, usually talks of our a priori, rather than innate knowledge, meaning knowledge which we cannot get by experience because only if we already have it can we make any sense of experience. Innate ideas or concepts are also often called a priori, and a proposition can be regarded as *absolutely a priori* if all the concepts in it are a priori e.g. 'No proposition is both true and false', and as *relatively a priori* if they are not, e.g. 'Nothing can be simultaneously red and green all over'. 'Relatively a priori' could also apply to the everyday sense in which an empirical proposition is knowable independently of a given context, as when a detective says, 'I haven't yet found any clues, but I know a priori that money is a motive for murder'.

A priori

It has usually been assumed that for any given sense of 'a priori' and the corresponding sense of 'empirical' every proposition is either a priori or empirical. But sometimes a proposition is not justified by experience, nor known a priori, but simply postulated. Those postulated as regulative principles to guide scientific procedure can be called *non-empirical*, though they are often classed as a priori, or sometimes, 'weak' a priori. 'Non-empirical can also cover the a priori in general. The term *pragmatic a priori* (C. I. Lewis) has been applied to propositions we decide by fiat to make immune to falsification by experience, e.g. 'Through a point not on a given straight line infinitely many straight lines parallel to the given one can be drawn', as a postulate of a non-Euclidean geometry.

The epistemological a priori/empirical distinction has often been thought to coincide with the metaphysical necessary/contingent distinction (see MODALITIES) and the logical ANALYTIC/synthetic distinction (concerning the structure of propositions). Kant, however, split the third distinction from the other two, calling some a priori and necessary propositions synthetic, while more recently Kripke has split the first two distinctions, arguing that some propositions are both a priori and contingent ('The standard meter rod is one metre long'), while others are both empirical and necessary ('Water is H_2O'). See also INNATE, RATIONALISM, INTUITION.

Aristotle, *Posterior Analytics* I. 1, 2.

D. Bostock, 'Necessary truth and a priori truth', *Mind*, 1988. (Complex but often illuminating defence of claim that a priori/empirical and necessary/contingent distinctions come apart, though for different reasons than Kripke gives.)

D. W. Hamlyn, *Theory of Knowledge*, Macmillan, 1970, chapter 9. (General discussion of a priori knowledge.)

I. Kant, *Critique of Pure Reason*, 2nd edn, 1787, B1–6.

J. J. Katz, 'What mathematical knowledge could be', *Mind*, 1995. (Defends a priori knowledge in maths etc. as not requiring causal or quasi-perceptual contact with abstract objects.)

P. Kitcher, 'A priori knowledge', *Philosophical Review'*, 1980. (Offers analysis of a psychologistic or materialistic kind. For criticism, and defence of a moderate version of a more traditional type, see D. M. Summerfield, 'Modest a priori knowledge', *Philosophy and Phenomenological Research*, 1991.)

S. Kripke, *Naming and Necessity*, Blackwell, 1980 (originally published 1972).

H. Lehman, *Introduction to the Philosophy of Mathematics*, Blackwell, 1979. (Part II defends an empiricist view of mathematics. Cf. also I. Lakatos, 'A renaissance of empiricism in the recent philosophy of mathematics', *British Journal for the Philosophy of Science*, 1976, tracing reactions to various unsettling developments like GÖDEL'S THEOREMS.

C. I. Lewis, 'The pragmatic conception of the a priori', *Journal of Philosophy*, 1923, reprinted in H. Feigl and W. Sellars (eds), *Readings in Philosophical Analysis*, Appleton-Century-Crofts, 1949.

*P. Moser (ed.), *A Priori Knowledge*, Oxford UP, 1987. (Reprinted selections.)

A. Quinton, *The Nature of Things*, RKP, 1973, pp. 132–4 ('A priori' and 'instinctive'.)

M. Thompson, 'On a priori truth', *Journal of Philosophy*, 1981. (Argues that it concerns our thinking itself, not any subject-matter it has.)

Aquinas, St Thomas, c. 1224–74. He came from Aquino, near Naples, and worked at the University of Paris and elsewhere. His work largely consisted in continuing the efforts of his teacher ALBERT THE GREAT to reconcile Greek philosophy with Christianity, and he was similarly influenced by the Arabs. He went beyond Albert in the extent to which he created a full-blooded philosophy, based on that of ARISTOTLE but developed so as to fit in with Christian dogma; this involved original treatments of notions like BEING and analogy. He wrote prolifically, but his philosophical work is largely contained in monographs on particular questions, e.g. *De Ente et Essentia* (c.1253), *Quaestiones Disputatae de Potentia Dei* (c.1265), and in more general works like *Quaestiones Disputatae de Veritate* (1256–9), and in commentaries on Aristotle's main philosophical writings. It is summed up in the *Summa de Veritate Catholicae Fidei contra Gentiles* (c. 1259–64) and the *Summa Theologica* (c.1265–73). He is also known for his 'five ways' of proving God's existence (see RELIGION). His philosophy, with that of his followers, is called Thomism. See also AUGUSTINE, COSMOLOGICAL, MARITAIN, METAPHYSICS, OCKHAM, ONTOLOGICAL ARGUMENT, PHILOSOPHY, SCOTUS, SUBSTANCE.

R. Goodwin (ed. and tr.), *Selected Writings of St Thomas Aquinas*, Macmillan, 1965. (Metaphysics etc. Includes *De Ente et Essentia* and three other short works.)

A. C. Pegis (ed.), *Basic Writings of Saint Thomas Aquinas* (2 vols), Random House, 1945. (Theology. Vol. 1: *God and the Order of Creation*, vol. 2: *Man and the Conduct of Life*.)

Argument. See FUNCTION

Aristotle. 384–22 BC. Pupil of PLATO, after whose death he travelled round the Aegean (and was tutor to Alexander the Great), and then founded Lyceum in Athens (355 BC; also called Peripatos; hence 'Peripatetics'). His interests were encyclopaedic, and he contributed to most of the main branches of philosophy and natural science, as well as initiating the systematic study of logic. His major works of current interest included the *Organon* (set of treatises mainly on logic), *Metaphysics, Physics, De Anima (On the Soul), Nicomachean Ethics, Politics, Poetics* (fragmentary). See also ALBERT, AMBIGUITY, A PRIORI, AQUINAS, AUGUSTINE, BACON, BRENTANO, BEING, CATEGORIES, CAUSATION, COSMOLOGICAL, DIALECTIC, DIFFERENTIA, ELENCHUS, ENTELECHY, ETHICS, EXPLANATION, FORM, FREEWILL, GOOD, INCONTINENCE, LOGIC, MEANING, METAPHYSICS, MIND, MODALITIES, NEO-PLATONISTS, OCKHAM, PLEASURE (bibliography), PLENITUDE, POLITICAL, PROPERTY, REASON, SCOTUS, SENSES, SOCRATES, SPACE, SUBSTANCE, SYLLOGISM, THIRD MAN ARGUMENT, TRANSCENDENTAL ARGUMENTS, TRUTH, UNIVERSALS, ZENO'S PARADOXES.

J. Barnes (ed.), *Oxford Translation of Aristotle*, 2nd edn, Princeton UP, 1984.

Armstrong, David M. 1926–. Born in Melbourne, he has worked mainly at Sydney, and is a leading representative of Australian materialism, which he combines with a moderate realism. After some early work on epistemology, he has written mainly on philosophy of mind and metaphysics. His publications include *Perception and the Physical World*, 1961; *Bodily Sensations*, 1962; *A Materialist Theory of Mind*, 1968 (2nd edn, 1993); *Universals and Scientific Realism*, vol. 1: *Nominalism and Realism* (critical), vol. 2: *A Theory of Universals* (positive), 1978; *What is a Law of Nature?* 1983; *Universals: an Opinionated Introduction*, 1989 (partly revised 1978, vol. 2); *A Combinational Theory of Possibility*, 1989.

Arrow paradox. See ZENO'S PARADOXES.

Arrow's paradox. See VOTING PARADOX.

Art (philosophy of). See AESTHETICS.

Assertion sign. The Symbol '⊢' invented by Frege, who drew its two parts from a complex system of symbols. It means either that what follows it is being asserted and not merely mentioned for consideration, or, more usually, that what follows can be asserted as a truth of logic, or as a theorem in a system (see AXIOM SYSTEM), 'p, q⊢r'

Assertoric

normally means that proposition r is assertible if propositions p and q are given as true.

Assertoric. See MODALITIES.

Attributive. An adjective stands in *attributive* position if it goes with its noun. ('A *red* house'), and in *predicative* position if it occurs after a verb ('The house is *red*'). It is grammatically attributive if it can only occur attributively ('veritable'), and grammatically predicative if it can only occur predicatively ('well', 'over', meaning 'finished'). It is logically attributive if a significant noun or equivalent must always be understood after it. 'That mouse is *large*' means. 'That mouse is a large mouse' – it need not be a large animal. 'Logically predicative' has no use.

Attributives are of different kinds. A large mouse is large for a mouse, but a mere child is not mere for a child. Adjectives like 'bogus' or 'alleged', which repudiate or cast doubt on the application of the following noun, occasionally called *alienans*, may or may not be called attributive. See also CATEGORIES, GOOD.

J. Brentlinger, 'Incomplete predicates and the two-world theory of the *Phaedo,' Phronesis*, 1972, p. 71 note 13. (Brief discussion, with references.)

P. T. Geach, 'Good and evil', *Analysis*, vol. 17, 1956–7. (Explains distinction and claims 'good' is always logically attributive.)

W. V. O. Quine, *Word and Object*, MIT Press, 1960. (See p. 103 for 'mere child' example.)

Augustine, St. 354–430. Born in North Africa, he was converted to Christianity in his early thirties, and became bishop of Hippo in 395 or 396. His philosophical interests turned progressively into theological ones, and he strongly influenced medieval thought, in ways somewhat contrasting with the current represented by ARISTOTLE and AQUINAS. His personal religious experience urged him to extricate himself from scepticism, and led him to study the types of knowledge (perception, reason, etc.). He tried to work out the nature of man in a Christian framework, and studied problems concerning the universe and its creation, the mind/body problem, freewill, and, now often regarded as his most lasting philosophical contribution, the nature of time (see SPACE). He also discussed ethical and (in the *City of God*) political topics. He started from a generally PLATONIC and NEOPLATONIC base. His important writings containing philosophical material include the *Confessions* (400), *De Libero Arbitrio* (freewill, and proof of God's existence), *City of*

God (late in life and largely theological), *De Genesi ad Litteram* (late; a commentary on Genesis).

W. J. Oates (ed.) *Basic Writings of Saint Augustine* (2 vols), Random House, 1948. (Vol. 1 has *Confessions* and other works; vol. 2 has *The City of God* and *On the Trinity.*)

Austin, John L. 1911–60. British philosopher who worked in Oxford where he was one of the leaders of 'linguistic PHILOSOPHY' after the Second World War. He emphasized the philosophical significance of the nuances of ordinary language, and is mainly noted for his theory of SPEECH ACTS. 'Ifs and Cans', 1960. 'A Pleas for Excuses', 1956. (Two lectures relevant to FREEWILL, and reprinted in his *Collected Papers*, 1961.) *Sense and Sensibilia*, 1962 (attacks SENSE-DATUM theory of AYER). *How to Do Things with Words*, 1962 (main source for speech act theory). See also CONDITIONALS, EPISTEMOLOGY, LANGUAGE (PHILOSOPHY OF), MEANING, SCEPTICISM, TRUTH.

John Austin (1790–1859) was a legal philosopher noted mainly for his theory that the law is the command of the sovereign. *The Province of Jurisprudence Determined*, 1832.

Autological. See HETEROLOGICAL.

Avowals. Certain first-person utterances, like 'I am in pain', which when sincere seem to be infallible. Another person saying 'He is in pain' about oneself could be mistaken. Problems arise about whether avowals can, or need, be justified, and whether they are assertions.

D. Gasking, 'Avowals', M. E. Lean, 'Mr Gasking on avowals', in R. J. Butler (ed.), *Analytical Philosophy*, 1st series, 1962. (Relation of avowals to justification and fallibility.)

F. E. Sparshott, 'Avowals and their uses', *Proceedings of the Aristotelian Society*, 1961–2. (Avowals and their relations to similar utterances.)

Axiology. See ETHICS.

Axiom system. Any system wherein certain expressions are derived in accordance with a given set of rules from a decidable initial set of expressions taken as given (and called *axioms*). The axioms themselves of such a system form an *axiom* set. 'Axiom system' is often used for 'axiom set'. The *formation rules* specify what elements or symbols the system is going to use and what combinations of them are to count as expressions which can serve as axioms or be tested to see whether they can be derived from the axioms. These expressions are called *well-formed formulae* or *wff*, for short, and those of them which can be derived from the axioms are called *theorems*. The formation rules are analogous to rules of grammar, and the wff analogous to meaningful sentences. The axioms themselves will count as theorems if, as in most systems, they are trivially derivable from themselves. For reasons of economy and elegance the axioms should be *independent*, i.e. not derivable within the given system from each other. The axioms may be infinite in number, provided rules for selecting them are given. Such a rule will define an *axiom scheme* by saying 'All wff of such and such a kind are to count as axioms'. The *transformation rules* say what wff can be derived from others, and so govern what the theorems of the system will be, given the axioms.

In an abstract axiom system the expressions are simply symbols, or marks on paper. But if the system is applied to a certain subject-matter we have a MODEL or *interpretation* of the system, and the subject-matter is said to be *axiomatized*. To axiomatize a subject is thus to systematize it, and show how most of it can be derived if certain selected axioms and transformation rules are taken for granted. These are so selected that the system shall be CONSISTENT and, where possible, COMPLETE. The axioms are therefore either true propositions, which need not be simple or obvious, or propositions which can be postulated as true without leading to contradiction, as in non-Euclidean geometries (see SPACE). The transformation rules are related to VALIDITY as the axioms are to truth. See also MODELS, BOOLEAN ALGEBRA.

C. Glymour, *Thinking Things Through*, MIT Press, 1992.

Ayer, Sir Alfred J. 1910–89. British philosopher, born in London, who has worked mostly in Oxford and London. He introduced logical POSITIVISM to Britain in 1936, and has since then defended an empiricist outlook, writing mainly on perception and meaning, as well as on various historical issues. *Language, Truth and Logic*, 1936, 2nd edn (with important new 'Introduction') 1946. *The Foundations of Empirical Knowledge*, 1940 (the book criticized by AUSTIN). *Philosophical Essays*, 1954. *The Problem of Knowledge*, 1956, *Probability and Evidence*, 1972. *The Central Questions of Philosophy*, 1973, See also BASIC STATEMENTS, NEGATION, PHENOMENALISM, PRAGMATISM, PROBABILITY, SENSE DATA, SENTENCES.

B

Bacon, Francis. 1561–1626. Philosopher, essayist and politician, he was born and lived in London, was created Lord Verulam and Viscount St Albans, and appointed Lord Chancellor. His main philosophical work lay in philosophy of science, where he tried to replace what he saw as the a priorism of the Aristotelian tradition by a new and thoroughgoing empiricism. His political writings rely heavily on the scientific optimism which he thought this method justified. *Essays*, 1597, expanded later. *The Proficience and Advancement of Learning*, 1605 (later revised as *De Dignitate et Augmentis Scientiarum* 1623), *Novum Organum*, 1620 (the title contrasts with ARISTOTLE's *Organon*, This and the *De Dignitate et Augmentis* form part of the projected *Instauratio Magna*.) *New Atlantis*, 1627 (a scientific Utopia.) See also MILL.

Roger Bacon (died 1292) was a student of sciences and languages, who wrote commentaries on various works of Aristotle and tried to institute a 'universal science'.

P. Urbach and J. Gibson (eds and trs), *Novum Organum*, Open Court, 1994.

Bad faith. In Sartre a kind of self-deception, where this involves behaving as a mere thing rather than realizing, in acts of authentic choice, the true type of being for a human being (what Sartre calls 'existence', or being 'pour soir' and not merely 'en soi'). This distinction is metaphysical, but has moral effects, for in 'bad faith' we evade responsibility and 'anxiety' by 'not noticing' possibilities of choice, or by behaving in a role others expect of us. A famous example is Sartre's 'waiter'. See also EXISTENTIALISM, INCONTINENCE.

Bald man (paradox of)

H. Bergson. *Laughter*, Macmillan, 1911, French original, 1900. (Bergson's theory of the comic has some affinity to Sartre's view of bad faith, though Bergson and Sartre wrote quite independently.)

H. Fingarette, *Self-Deception*, 1969. (Self-deception in general. Cf. D. W. Hamlyn, H. O. Mounce, 'Self-deception', *Proceedings of the Aristotelian Society*, supplementary vol. 1971.)

J.-P. Sartre, *Being and Nothingness*, 1943, transl. 1956, part 1, chapter 2. (See also his *Essays on Existence* (ed. W. Baskin), Citadel Press, Secaucus NJ, 1965 (selections from his writings. For writer example see pp. 167ff.).)

Bald man (paradox of). See HEAP.

Barber paradox. Does a barber who shaves all and only those not shaving themselves shave himself? Less important than RUSSELL'S PARADOX, etc., because there is no reason to assert the existence of such a barber.

Basic action. Action not involving further action as its cause, or which we do not perform by performing another action; e.g. moving our hands but not steering our car, which we do *by* moving our hands.

A. Baier, 'The search for basic actions', *American Philosophical Quarterly*, 1971. (Develops and criticizes the notion, giving references.)

S. Candlish, 'Inner and outer basic actions', *Proceedings of the Aristotelian Society*, 1983–4 (Further development and references.)

L. H. Davis, *Theory of Action*, Prentice-Hall, 1979. (Mainly on action in general, but see its index.)

Basic statements. Also sometimes called *protocol statements (sentences)* or (by Carnap) *primitive protocol statements*. Statements which, according to logical POSITIVISTS in particular, are needed as the basis for the rest of our empirical knowledge. But the various conceptions of them have little else in common. Their subject-matter varies, with different writers, from immediate personal experience to the common world. Their role may be to give a foundation for the individual's own knowledge (Ayer), or for INTERSUBJECTIVELY testable knowledge (O. Neurath). In a variant of the latter role they provide tools for testing universal hypotheses, and are therefore themselves mainly singular existential statements, saying that something exists or occurs at a certain place and date

Behaviour

(Popper; e.g. the statement 'There is a black swan in Sydney now' could be used to test the hypothesis 'All swans are white').

A. J. Ayer, *Language, Truth and Logic*, Gollancz, 1936. (See 2nd edn 1946, p. 10.)

R. Carnap, *The Unity of Science*, Kegan Paul, Trench, Trubner, 1934, esp. pp. 43–4.

O. Neurath, 'Protocol sentences', in A. J. Ayer (ed.), *Logical Positivism*, Free Press, 1959 (trans. from German original in *Erkenntnis*, vol. 3, 1932–3).

K. R. Popper, *The Logic of Scientific Discovery*, Hutchinson, 1959 (German original, 1934), esp. §§ 28–9.

Bayes's Theorem. Theorem of PROBABILITY calculus, variously formulated and developed by and after T. Bayes (1702–61). Briefly, where p and q are propositions, the probability of p, given q, is that of q, given p, multiplied by the prior probability of p and divided by the prior probability of q. The prior probability of a proposition is the probability it has by itself, not its probability 'given' another proposition. 'Bayesian' inductive procedures take the theorem to imply that the increase in probability which a hypothesis gains when its consequences are verified is proportional to the improbability of those consequences. The theorem's validity is undisputed, but its applications and usefulness are controversial (cf. CONFIRMATION). One form of the law of large NUMBERS, unrelated to the above, is also sometimes called 'Bayes's theorem'. 'Bayesian' is also often used by adherents of the subjectivist theory of PROBABILITY for the process which they think ought to govern changes in degrees of belief. A *Bayesian* approach to probability allows hypotheses etc. to have probabilities, while a *frequentist* approach, using the frequency theory of PROBABILITY, confirms probabilities to repeatable events.

H. E. Kyburg, *Probability and Inductive Logic*, Macmillan, 1970. (See its index.)

Beauty. See AESTHETICS.

Bedeutung. See MEANING.

Behaviour. What an object, particularly a living creature, does. There are problems and ambiguities: is intention, or at least controllability, needed for behaviour? Are heart-beats behaviour? Must behaviour affect the outer world and be publicly observable? Is silent thinking behaviour? Must behaviour described in one way (e.g. waving one's arms) also be behaviour when described in another (accidentally breaking a vase)? Can the utterances of a

Behaviourism

parrot be called verbal behaviour? Should an uncontrollable reflex action, like a knee-jerk, be called behaviour of the knee but not of the person? See also ACTION.

D. Davidson, 'Psychology as philosophy' in S. C. Brown (ed.), *Philosophy of Psychology*, Macmillan and Barnes and Noble, 1974, with comments and replies, reprinted with replies but without comments in Davidson's *Essays on Action and Events*, Oxford UP, 1980. (One view of behaviour, causation, and rationality.)

D. W. Hamlyn, 'Behaviour', *Philosophy*, 1953. (Revised on one point in his 'Causality and human behaviour', *Proceedings of the Aristotelian Society*, supplementary vol. 1964.)

G. H. von Wright, *Explanation and Understanding*, RKP, 1971, p. 193, n. 8 (Knee-jerk.)

Behaviourism. Doctrine or policy of reducing mental concepts to publicly observable BEHAVIOUR. In psychology it involves an experimental, and often physicalist and operationalist approach (see POSITIVISM), which rejects introspection, and is concerned with prediction and control rather than understanding. *Logical* or *analytic behaviourism* defines mentalistic terms using only behavioural or physiological terms. *Metaphysical* or *philosophical behaviourism* refuses to see more than physical behaviour where claims for mentality are made. *Methodological behaviourism* insists on behavioural tests but is neutral on the philosophical implications. *Radical behaviourism*, is similar, but more rigorous; it rejects hypothetical constructs and intervening variables (see LOGICAL CONSTRUCTIONS). See also COGNITIVE, PSYCHOLOGISM.

N. Block (ed.), *Readings in the Philosophy of Psychology*, vol. 1, Harvard UP and Methuen, 1980. (Includes section on behaviourism.)

G. Ryle, *The Concept of Mind*, Hutchinson, 1949. (Classic work, usually taken to support analytical behaviourism.)

Being. Being seems at first to be a property of everything, or at least of everything there is, for how can anything have a property unless it is there to have it? Do unicorns have, say, the property of being vegetarian? Or is it only that they would have it if there were any unicorns? But if we accept this latter view, being cannot be a property after all, for anything which was to have it would have to have it already in order to do so, which is absurd; to say that something exists is not to say something *about* it. This point, that being is not a property, or, as it is commonly expressed, that 'exists' is not a (logical as against grammatical) predicate, was insisted on by Kant who used it to attack the ONTOLOGICAL

Being

ARGUMENT, though others have disagreed (see Strawson). It raised the question: what counts as being a property or (logical) predicate?

A position to some extent like Kant's is that of Aristotle, who insisted that being could not be an all-embracing genus (as *animal* is the genus of *horse, cow*, etc.), and that to call something existent is not to add to its description. (He said the same about unity and, for a different reason, about goodness.) Out of this arose the medieval doctrine of *transcendentals*. Aquinas listed 'being', 'one', 'true', 'thing', 'something', 'good' as transcending the CATEGORIES and applying to everything. Some other writers, e.g. Duns Scotus, use 'transcendentals' rather more widely, and Aristotle said of 'good' not, with Aquinas, that everything real was somehow good, but that 'good' was predicable in all the categories – a substance, quality, relation, etc. could be good. These transcendentals are usually included among the syncategorematic terms (see CATEGORIES (end)). They were intended to delineate the characteristics of *being qua being*, another notion originating in Aristotle, who made it the subject matter of metaphysics. In English, 'being' can be a participle ('Being fat, I ate less') or a gerund ('Being fat is unhealthy'), but Greek distinguishes, and Aristotle uses the participle, sometimes in the plural ('beings qua beings'). Interpretations of it differ. It may refer to everything that is, considered just as being, or to something which somehow accounts for the being of everything else. This may be substance in general or the highest kind of substance like God, or the movers of the cosmic spheres. On this latter view God and the movers account for the being of other substances, and substance accounts for that of qualities, relations, etc.

Despite the difficulties in supposing that there are things which do not exist, philosophers have often been reluctant to put into one basket all the things that in some sense have being. Aristotle shows this reluctance in his doctrine of CATEGORIES (see *Metaphysics*, Book 4, chapter 2), but more recently, different kinds of being have been distinguished in another way. Existence is sometimes distinguished from subsistence and other notions. Meinong, for instance, evidently thinking that a thing must in some sense be there for us to talk about it at all, thought that material objects in space and time *exist*, along with other things in space and time like shadows and gravitational fields, while things like UNIVERSALS, numbers and the difference between red and green, *subsist*. Fictional or imaginary objects, which can be concrete (unicorns) or abstract (the prime number between eight and ten), are sometimes said to subsist, but for Meinong they neither exist nor subsist; he says simply that they 'are objects' and have *Sosein* which means, literally, being so, or essence. But 'exist' and 'subsist', like 'existent' and 'subsistent', are often used interchangeably, especially when it

Being

is said that certain things, such as universals, do have being in some sense, and are not, as *nominalism* holds, analysable in terms of mere words.

Existence and subsistence, etc. can here be regarded as different grades or kinds of being. One strand of idealism treats being rather as having different degrees. Reality as a whole, the 'absolute', exists fully, while its parts derive their reality from their relations to it and to each other, and exist, but less fully, in proportion to their comprehensiveness.

Carnap divided questions of existence into those internal and external to a given system, e.g. that of arithmetic. 'Is there a prime number between six and nine?' is an internal question and belongs to arithmetic. 'Do numbers exist?' is an external question and belongs to philosophy, along with similar questions about universals, propositions, etc.

These various problems about fictional and timeless objects connect metaphysics with philosophical logic, and two further questions arise here. First, how do we tell to what ontology (i.e. list of things that are) a philosopher has committed himself? What counts as holding that, e.g. universals do or do not exist? Quine introduced this question to replace the traditional question, 'What is there?' He answered with the slogan, 'to be is to be the value of a variable'; i.e. we are committed to the reality of a thing or kind of things if and only if we cannot state our views in formal (i.e. logical) language without using affirmative statements where VARIABLES ranging over the thing or things in question are bound by the existential quantifier (see QUANTIFICATION). The second question is what the laws of logic themselves commit us to. In particular can we prove by logic alone that there must be at least one object? By the predicate CALCULUS (let *F* stand for some predicate and *a* for any arbitrary individual) the seemingly undeniable logical truth 'Everything is *F* or not *F* implies '*a* is *F* or not *F*.' This in turn implies 'At least one thing is *F* or not *F*', and therefore that there is at least one thing. Various attempts to avoid this have been made. Both these questions are bound up with the interpretation of 'is' in the existential quantifier. Does it signify existence in a substantial sense, and if not, then what does it signify?

Many philosophers, especially the medievals and the existentialists, have contrasted a thing's essence, or what it is, with its existence (though in the case of God, these have been thought by Aquinas to coincide – but the sense of 'existence' ('esse') here is controversial). Some forms of existentialism contrast being or essence with existence. Being belongs to animals and inanimate things, and existence only to humans, who can create themselves and are not products of the environment.

Being

A linguistic question concerns the different senses often ascribed to the verb 'to be'. The main senses are: existential ('These things shall be', 'There is . . .'), predicative or copulative ('This is red'), classifying ('This is a shoe'; often subsumed under predicative), identifying ('This is Socrates', 'Tully is Cicero'). In ancient Greek it seems to have had also a veridical sense ('. . . is true'). Other senses, some rather technical, have been suggested, including constitutive ('This house is bricks and mortar') and presentational ('The meaning of "bald" is: *hairless*'). Sometimes 'is' signifies the present tense as in 'He is hot', but sometimes it is timeless as in 'Twice two is four' or 'Chaucer is earlier than Shakespeare'. What makes these senses different is that different things can be inferred from statements made by sentences containing them. 'Tully is Cicero' implies 'Cicero is Tully', but 'This book is red' does not imply 'Red is this book', where 'red' is the subject. But these differences are complex and controversial in detail, and so is the question what, if anything, links the senses together. (Aristotle thought at least some senses were linked by 'focal meaning'; see above, and AMBIGUITY.) Some think the attempt to distinguish definite senses is mistaken (Kahn). See also SUBSTANCE, REFERRING, ESSENCE, CATEGORIES.

Aristotle, *Metaphysics*, 998b22–7 (being not a genus; cf. *Topics*, 144a32–b4); 1003b26 ('one' and 'existent' not descriptive; cf. 1045a36–b8); book 4, chapters 1–3, book 6, chapter 1 (being qua being). *Nicomachean Ethics*, 1096a19–29 ('good').

J. Barnes, *The Ontological Argument*, Macmillan, 1972, chapter 3. (Also has bibliography, to which add S. Read, ' "Exists" is a predicate', *Mind*, 1980 (watch for misprints), discussed by L. Chipman, 'Existence, reference and definite singular terms', *Mind*, 1982.)

R. Carnap, *Meaning and Necessity*, 2nd edn, Chicago UP, 1956, supplement, A, § 2, reprinted in C. Landesman (ed.), *The Problem of Universals*, Basic Books, 1971. (External and internal questions.)

L. J. Cohen, *The Diversity of Meaning*, Methuen, 1962, § 33. (Does logic prove the universe cannot be empty?)

P. T. Geach, 'Form and existence', *Proceedings of the Aristotelian Society*, 1954–5, reprinted in A. Kenny (ed.), *Aquinas*, Doubleday, 1969, Macmillan, 1970. (Essence and existence in Aquinas.)

C. H. Kahn, 'The Greek verb "to be" and the concept of being'. *Foundations of Language*, 1966. (Attacks rigidity of distinction into senses.) See also his *The Verb 'Be' in Ancient Greek*, part 6 of J. W. M. Verhaar (ed.), *The Verb 'Be' and its Synonyms*, Reidel, 1973.

Belief

I. Kant, *Critique of Pure Reason*, 1781, revised 1787, B626–9. (Classic attack on existence as predicate.)

L. Linsky, *Referring*, RKP, 1967. (Discusses theories of Meinong and later writers, playing down the metaphysical extravagance often attributed to Meinong.)

E. J. Lowe, *Kinds of Being: A Study of Individuation, Identity and the Logic of Sortal Terms*, Blackwell, 1988. (Distinguishes uses of 'is', and claims mutual dependence of individuals and kinds.)

A. Meinong, 'The theory of objects', transl. in R. Chisholm (ed.), *Realism and the Background of Phenomenology*, Free Press, Glencoe, 1960.

Plato. Relevant passages include *Republic*, 476e ff., *Timaeus*, 27d.

W. V. O. Quine, 'On what there is', in *Review of Metaphysics*, 1948, reprinted in his book *From a Logical Point of View*, Harper and Row, 1953, in L. Linsky (ed.), *Semantics and the Philosophy of Language*, Oxford UP, 1952, in Landesman (above), and (with comments and contributions from others on the same theme) in *Proceedings of the Aristotelian Society*, supplementary vol. 1951. ('To be is to be the value of a variable'. Cf. also his defence of this in 'Ontology and ideology revisited', *Journal of Philosophy*, 1983.)

W. Sellars, 'Grammar and existence: a preface to ontology', *Mind*, 1960, reprinted in Landesman (above). (Rather more technical criticism of Quine.)

P. F. Strawson, 'Is existence never a predicate?', *Critica*, 1967, reprinted in his *Freedom and Resentment*, Methuen, 1974.

J. J. Valberg, 'Improper singular terms', *Proceedings of the Aristotelian Society*, 1970–1, p. 132. (Presentational being.)

G. J. Warnock, 'Metaphysics in logic', in A. Flew (ed.), *Essays in Conceptual Analysis*, Macmillan, 1956. (Criticizes Quine's use of logic to solve ontological problems.)

D. Wiggins, *Sameness and Substance*, Blackwell, 1980. (Constitutive 'is'; see index.)

Belief. Assent to or acceptance of the truth of propositions, statements or facts (but see CONFIRMATION (end).). The proposition forms the content of the belief, and to believe is usually regarded as in some sense involving, and perhaps as standing in a certain relation to, the relevant proposition, so that belief is a *propositional attitude* (cf. SENTENCES). Belief is rather like JUDGMENT except for being a state rather than a mental act. It is often regarded as a DISPOSITION, and as such need not be constantly manifesting itself: we have many beliefs we are not currently thinking of, and sometimes may not even be aware of having. But presumably it must manifest itself sometimes, or at least be able to do so (though the REALISM/antire-

Belief

alism debate raises difficulties here), and this raises problems in some cases: can we believe TAUTOLOGIES, and even contradictions? Where *p* is a proposition, can we believe *p* and believe not-*p* (to be distinguished from not believing *p*). And does this entail believing *p* and not-*p*? Also, can we believe what we know is false (or regard as improbable), and can we be mistaken about whether we believe something? When are beliefs justified? These questions link belief with knowledge and rationality (see EPISTEMOLOGY).

A belief may be *de dicto* or *de re* (see MODALITIES) according as it matters, or does not, how what it is about is described. Suppose I believe a certain spy should be hanged, without realizing that the spy is my sister. Then I believe de re, but not de dicto, that my sister should be hanged – I believe it *of* her. See INTENSIONALITY AND INTENTIONALITY. But the distinction is controversial.

Further problems concern how belief relates to other notions, such as desires, actions, inner experiences and language. In fact, difficulties in isolating activities in the brain that could correspond to belief have even led some people to say there is no such thing as belief. Like meaning and thinking, belief also raises the sort of problems discussed under INTERNALISM. Also how far is belief, assuming it does exist, voluntary, and can we have a duty to believe something (the *ethics of belief*)? Often, however, 'believe' is a *parenthetical verb*, in the sense that 'I believe it's raining' or 'It's raining (I believe)', is meant to be about the weather, not about the speaker. See also Moore's PARADOX about belief.

Finally, we can 'believe in' the existence, occurrence, truth, validity, or value of something, or in something we think ought to be or occur. We often use 'believe in' for what is good rather than bad; we 'believe in' Smith's generosity but not his malevolence.

R. M. Chisholm, 'Firth on the ethics of belief', *Philosophy and Phenomenological Research*, 1991. (Relations between ethical and epistemological requirements.)
D. Dennett, 'Beyond belief' in A. Woodfield (ed.), *Thought and Object*, Clarendon, 1982, reprinted with afterthoughts and other relevant items in his *The Intentional Stance*, MIT Press, 1987. General problems about belief (see especially pp. 54ff. (pp. 168ff. in reprint) on de re/de dicto distinction).
*A. P. Griffiths (ed.), *Knowledge and Belief*, Oxford UP, 1967. (Articles and bibliography, with introduction. See article by Braithwaite for a dispositional account.)
J. Heil, 'Believing what one ought', *Journal of Philosophy*, 1983. (Can it ever be reasonable or right to believe against the evidence? See also his 'Doxastic incontinence', *Mind*, 1984, and A. Michalos, 'The morality of cognitive decision-making', in

Belief

M. Broad and D. Walton (eds), *Action Theory*, Reidel, 1980. For classic discussion see W. K. Clifford, 'The ethics of belief' in his *Lectures and Essays*, vol. 2, Macmillan, 1879, and see P. Helm, *Belief Policies*, Cambridge UP, 1994, for discussion of this and related issues.)

W. G. Lycan, 'Tacit belief', in R. J. Bogdan (ed.), *Belief: Form, Content and Function*, Clarendon, 1986.

R. B. Marcus, 'A proposed solution to a puzzle about belief', *Midwest Studies in Philosophy*, vol. VI, 1981. (Presents and discusses a puzzle raised by Kripke and also discusses belief and assent. See also her 'Rationality and believing the impossible', *Journal of Philosophy*, 1983. For Kripke's puzzle see his article in N. Salmon and S. Soames (eds), *Propositions and Attitudes*, Oxford UP, 1988, reprinted from A. Margalit (ed.), *Meaning and Use*, Reidel, 1979, where a comment by Putnam is added.)

D. H. Mellor (ed.) *Prospects for Pragmatism*, Cambridge UP, 1980. (Essays in honour of F. P. Ramsey (1903–30), many of which are relevant to belief. Mellor's own contribution, on 'Consciousness and degrees of belief', develops a theory of conscious belief, linking it to the subjectivist theory of probability, and is reprinted in his *Matters of Metaphysics*, Cambridge UP, 1991.)

J. Perry, 'The problem of the essential indexical', *Nous*, 1979, reprinted in N. Salmon and S. Soames (eds), *Propositional Attitudes*, Oxford UP, 1988. (Difficulties raised by the fact that some beliefs seem to involve indexicals or TOKEN-REFLEXIVES essentially.)

H. H. Price, 'Belief "in" and belief "that" ', *Religious Studies*, 1965, reprinted in B. Mitchell (ed.), *The Philosophy of Religion*, Oxford UP, 1971.

S. P. Stich, *From Folk Psychology to Cognitive Science: the Case Against Belief*, MIT Press, 1983. (Discusses how COGNITIVE science has tried to rehabilitate FOLK PSYCHOLOGY from the ravages of BEHAVIOURISM, but expresses 'reluctant scepticism' (p. 5) over whether this will be ultimately possible. Cf. critical discussion by T. Crane in 'The language of thought: no syntax without semantics', *Mind and Language*, 1990 and also J. A. Fodor, *Psychosemantics*, MIT Press, 1987.)

Bentham, Jeremy. 1748–1832. Moral, political and legal philosopher, who was born in London and worked mainly there. He is generally regarded as the first major UTILITARIAN thinker, though he also had some interest in the theory of meaning, where he held a nominalist position, treating abstract entities as 'fictions'; this position underlay his treatment of moral and legal notions. He also devoted much of his writing to working out the practical applications of his theoretical views, in such fields as prison reform and the writing of constitutions. *A Fragment on Government*, 1776 (attacks the then fashionable legal theorist W. Blackstone). *An Introduction to the Principles of Morals and Legislation*, 1789).

Bergson, Henri L. 1859–1941. Worked mostly in his native Paris. He is perhaps most famous for his doctrine of 'creative evolution', which tried to supplement Darwinism by postulating an *élan vital* which causes variations as species develop. He combined this with a double view of time, as time in physics and time as experienced (*durée*), of which only the latter was continuous and flowing. He also made a famous study of laughter and the comic. *Essai sur les données immédiates de la conscience*, 1889 (*Time and Free Will*). *Matière et mémoire*, 1896. *Le Rire*, 1900. *L'Evolution créatrice*, 1907. *Les Deux Sources de la morale et de la religion*, 1932. See also INTUITION, MARITAIN, METAPHYSICS.

Berkeley, George. 1685–1753. Born in Kilkenny, Ireland, he mainly stayed in Ireland, though with visits abroad, including one to America, and he became bishop of Cloyne. He is considered one of the 'British EMPIRICISTS', and his philosophy starts from LOCKE's 'new way of ideas', but rejects abstract ideas and the possibility of real existence outside perception. This slogan 'esse est percipi' ('to be is to be perceived') sums up much of his philosophy, which is commonly known as 'subjective IDEALISM', though he himself called it 'immaterialsm'; cf. PHENOMENALISM. However, among percipients Berkeley included God. *An Essay towards a New Theory of Vision*, 1709. *A Treatise concerning the Principles of Human Knowledge*, 1710. *Three Dialogues between Hylas and Philonous in Opposition to Sceptics and Atheists*, 1713. *De Motu*, 1721 (on motion). *Alciphron, or the Minute Philosopher*, 1732 (largely theological, but with philosophical passages). See also SENSATION, SENSE DATA, SUBJECTIVISM.

A. A. Luce and T. E. Jessop (eds), *The Works of George Berkeley*, 9 vols, Nelson, 1948–57.

Bernoulli's theorem. See NUMBERS (LAW OF LARGE).

Berry's paradox. The phrase 'the least integer not nameable in fewer than nineteen syllables' seem to name a number. But the number concerned must be not nameable in fewer than nineteen syllables since the phrase does name it, yet nameable in fewer since the phrase itself has only eighteen. The paradox is of the kind

Bertrand's box paradox

sometimes called semantic (see PARADOX, and also RUSSELL'S PARADOX, TYPES).

E. Teensma, *The Paradoxes*, Van Gorcum, 1969, pp. 34–5. (Exposition with brief discussion.)

Bertrand's box paradox. Three boxes hold respectively two gold coins, two silver, one of each. A coin drawn randomly is gold. What is the probability that the other coin in the same box is gold? The box chosen must be double gold or mixed, so the probability is a half. Yet the coin must be the first or second in the gold box, or the gold in the mixed box; two of these three alternatives makes the other coin gold, so the probability is two-thirds. The paradox affects the classical theory of PROBABILITY, by suggesting that it is indefinite what the alternatives are.

Bertrand's paradox. What is the probability that a random chord of a circle exceeds the side of an inscribed equilateral triangle? It is longer if its midpoint lies on the inner half of the radius bisecting it, so, since the midpoint may lie anywhere on this radius, the probability is a half. It is also longer if its midpoint lies within a concentric circle with half the original radius, so, since the area of this inner circle is a quarter that of the original circle, the probability is a quarter. Other answers exist, and the paradox has many variants. It affects the classical theory of PROBABILITY, by showing a difficulty in dividing up infinitely many alternatives.

Best (principle of). See SUFFICIENT REASON.

Better. Not always the comparative of 'good'. Something can be 'better but not yet good', and it may be easier to decide whether one thing is better than another than whether either is good.

S. Hallden, *On the Logic of 'Better'*, 1957. (Full formal treatment.)
A. Sloman, 'How to derive "better" from "is" ', *American Philosophical Quarterly*, 1969. (Makes 'better' more fundamental than 'good', and defines it in logical terms.)
G. H. von Wright, *The Varieties of Goodness*, RKP, Humanities Press, 1963, p. 26. ('Better' as non-TRANSITIVE.)

Between. Two main senses: (i) That in which a term lies between two other terms in some ordering. (ii) That in which a relation holds between two terms, as in 'difference between' and 'resemblance between'. In 'The Rhine passes between France and Germany' we have (i), but some cases seem less clear; 'The Rhine stretches between Switzerland and Holland'. 'The Rhine is the link between Switzerland and Holland', 'the link between these events is such-and-such'. The analysis of 'distance between' is relevant to questions about empty space.

A. N. Prior, 'On a difference between "betweens" ', *Mind*, 1961.

Biconditional. The connective (see CONJUNCTION) 'if and only if' (often abbreviated to 'iff') or a sentence comprising two clauses connected by it. Where p and q are propositions, 'p iff q' stands for 'If p then q and if q then p'.

Bivalence (principle, law of). See EXCLUDED MIDDLE.

Boolean algebra. Algebra or, strictly, set of algebras, invented by G. Boole (1815–64) for the CALCULUS of classes; later developed further and given other applications, e.g. to electrical circuits, computing, etc. It resembles ordinary numerical algebra limited to one and zero (so that $x^2 = x$), but differs from it because classes are not confined to the universal and null CLASSES.

C. Glymour, *Thinking Things Through*, MIT Press, 1992, chapter 4.
G. E. Hughes and M. J. Cresswell, *An Introduction to Modal Logic*, Methuen, 1968, chapter 17 (beginning).
P. H. Nidditch, *The Development of Mathematical Logic*, RKP, 1962, chapter 6.

Bracketing. See PHENOMENOLOGY.

Bradley, Francis H. 1846–1924. Born in Clapham (London), he worked in Oxford, and is usually considered the main British objective IDEALIST. He developed a MONISTIC system whereby the Absolute is the only subject of predicates, and the only fully true proposition would be one completely describing it. No other propositions can be more than partly true. He argued that relations were always internal to their terms (an argument MOORE criticized) – though he also thought that they were illusory. He criticized the psychologism of empiricists like MILL in their use of terms like 'IDEA'. His logic is now particularly known for his views on negation, and his ethics for the anti-utilitarian stance of his essay on 'My Station and its Duties'. *Ethical Studies*, 1876 (contains 'My Station . . .'). *Logic*, 1883 (2nd edn, revised especially on negation, 1922),. *Appearance and Reality*, 1893. *Essays on Truth and Reality*, 1914. See also HEGEL, NATURALISM, OUGHT, UNIVERSALS.

Brain process theory. See IDENTITY THEORY OF MIND.

Brentano, Franz C.

Brentano, Franz C. 1839–1917. Born near Boppard (Germany) he worked mainly in Würzburg and Vienna and retired to Florence. He was a Catholic priest for a short period. He is particularly remembered for his claim that mental phenomena can be identified as those which are 'intentional' in nature (see INTENSIONALITY). He also studied certain interrelations between ideas, judgments, and emotions of love and hatred, and elaborated a theory of truth which based it on 'evidence' in the sense of evidentness. His analysis of mental phenomena was especially influential on PHENOMENOLOGISTS like HUSSERL, and on MEINONG, and on English-speaking writers such as CHISHOLM, and less directly on the recent concern with intentionality (see MIND). He was himself much concerned with the study of ARISTOTLE. *Psychologie vom empirischen Standpunkt (Psychology from an Empirical Standpoint)*, 1874, *Ursprung sittlicher Erkenntnis (The Origin of Our Knowledge of Right and Wrong)*, 1889. *Grundlegung und Aufbau der Ethik (The Foundation and Construction of Ethics)*, 1952 (more elaborate than previous item). *Wahrheit und Evidenz (The True and the Evident)*, 1930.

Broad, Charlie D. 1887–1971. Born in Harlesden (London) he worked mainly in Cambridge. Broad's contribution lay chiefly in his systematic exposition and thorough examination of a large number of philosophical theories in widely different spheres, and in his refusal to be browbeaten by current fashions into rejecting unpopular views. Like RUSSELL he appreciated the importance of modern science, and he also, like SIDGWICK, took psychical research seriously. His views were often unfashionable as compared with those of his more POSITIVIST contemporaries on topics such as causation and induction, perception, and the synthetic a priori, but they were elaborated to take account of current scientific and philosophical thought. Other topics to which he contributed in this way include time, substance, determinism, the body/mind problem, and certain ethical issues. *Perception, Physics, and Reality*, 1914. *Scientific Thought*, 1923. *The Mind and Its Place in Nature*, 1925. *Five Types of Ethical Theory*, 1930. *Examination of McTaggart's Philosophy*, 2 vols, 1933, 1938. See also PROBABILITY, SELF-REGARDING, SPACE.

Burali-Forti's paradox. See NUMBERS. The class of ordinals less than a given ordinal has that ordinal as its ordinal. (For the reasons for this see Fraenkel in bibliography to NUMBERS, especially foot of p. 197.) Therefore the ordinal of the class of all ordinals is greater than any ordinal in that class, and so is not an ordinal. One of the logical PARADOXES, it was published by C. Burali-Forti in 1897. The usual modern way out is to distinguish CLASSES from sets and say that an 'ordinal' is only defined for well-ordered sets; what Burali-

Forti shows is then that the class of ordinals is not a set, because if it were, it would have an ordinal greater than all ordinals, including itself. Cf. RUSSELL'S PARADOX, TYPES.

Butler, Joseph. 1692–1752. Natural theologian and moralist who was born at Wantage and became bishop of Bristol and then of Durham. His contribution to moral philosophy consists in his examination of moral psychology, including the roles of self-love and benevolence, and his treatment of conscience as a principle having overriding authority. In natural theology he claims to see an analogy between the course of events in nature and what religion teaches, and so to derive confirmation of the latter, and he emphasizes the 'progressive' rather than 'static' nature of the afterlife. He also discusses personal identity with reference to LOCKE. *Fifteen Sermons*, 1726 (his moral philosophy). *The Analogy of Religion, Natural and Revealed, to the Constitution and Course of Nature*, 1736 (including appendix on personal identity).

C

Calculus. A general name, applied to a subject, for the body of principles governing reasoning in the subject. One can talk of *an* AXIOM SYSTEM for *the* propositional calculus, etc. Sometimes such systems are themselves called calculi.

The *propositional calculus* (also called the *sentential calculus, calculus of unanalysed propositions, calculus of truth values,* or *calculus of truth functions*) concerns truth FUNCTIONS of propositions, but with the restriction that the propositions are regarded as either the same as each other or completely different. Partial similarities like that between 'All cats are black' and 'Some cats are black' are ignored. Its theorems are the relevant TAUTOLOGIES. When the restriction is lifted and the structure of propositions is taken into account, we have the *functional* or *predicate calculus,* or the *calculus of relations.* When the predicates are limited to MONADIC predicates we have the *monadic predicate calculus.* The predicate calculus is called *extended* or *second-order* when predicates are quantified over (see QUANTIFICATION). When only INDIVIDUALS are quantified over, it is called *restricted* or *first-order.* There is also an *extended propositional calculus,* where propositions are quantified over.

The *calculus of classes* concerns classes and their members. It is structurally the same as the monadic predicate calculus. ('*x* is red' is interchangeable with '*x* belongs to the class of red things, – though RUSSELL'S PARADOX raises a difficulty for the view that every predicate defines a class.) It is the elementary nucleus of *set theory,* which treats problems arising out of the calculus of classes and goes beyond it by treating, for example, classes whose members are ordered, and problems specific to infinite classes. The relations

Cancelling-out fallacy

between set theory and logic are important in connexion with logicism (see philosophy of MATHEMATICS).

The *calculus of individuals* concerns the part/whole relationship, and is linked to MEREOLOGY.

For the *calculus of chances* see PROBABILITY.

The *hedonic calculus*, or *calculus of pleasures*, is the set of principles which would govern any system claiming that pleasures can be measured, added, and in general systematically compared. But whether such a calculus could be constructed is controversial.

N. Goodman, *The Structure of Appearance*, Harvard UP, 1951, chapter 2. (Calculus of individuals.)

D. Hilbert and W. Ackermann, *Principles of Mathematical Logic*, 1928; 2nd edn 1938, trans. Chelsea, NY, 1950. (A standard account of the main logical calculi. Elementary introductions to symbolic logic, covering similar ground, are legion.)

D. C. Makinson, *Topics in Modern Logic*, Methuen, 1973, chapter 5. (Set theory and logic. Cf. also Introduction to P. Benacerraf and H. Putnam (eds), *Philosophy of Mathematics*, Cambridge UP, 1964).

Cambridge change. Something undergoes a Cambridge change whenever any predicate starts or stops being true of it, including predicates like 'is an uncle', which do not seem to involve any real or intrinsic change in the subject itself. Similarly if I stay the same while you grow bigger than me, we both undergo Cambridge changes, though only you would be said to undergo a real change. Normally, however, the term 'Cambridge change' is reserved for changes which are not real but are properly speaking 'mere' Cambridge changes, so that I but not you would be said to undergo a Cambridge change in the above example, i.e. 'Cambridge change' normally means 'mere Cambridge change'. So called from alleged popularity of 'mere' Cambridge change among some early twentieth-century Cambridge philosophers.

S. Shoemaker, *Identity, Cause, and Mind*, Cambridge UP, 1984, pp. 207–9. (Develops the notion further.)

Cancelling-out fallacy. The assumption that where two partially identical expressions mean the same, one can cancel out the identical parts and the remaining parts will mean the same as each other, e.g., if 'Socrates killed Socrates' means the same as 'Socrates was killed by Socrates', then 'killed Socrates' means the same as 'was killed by Socrates'.

Cantor's paradox

P. T. Geach, *Reference and Generality*, Cornell UP, 1962. (See index.)

Cantor's paradox. It is provable that any class has more subclasses than members. Suppose there were a class of all classes. Its subclasses, being classes, would *be* members of it. So there can be no class of all classes (and also no greatest cardinal NUMBER, not even among infinite numbers).

Carnap, Rudolf. 1891–1970. German logical POSITIVIST, born in Ronsdorf, and a member of the Vienna Circle. He migrated to America where he worked mainly in Chicago and Los Angeles. He tried to show that METAPHYSICS arose through our confusing talk about the world with talk about language (cf. FORMAL MODE). He sought to apply his positivism to scientific method by his physicalism (see POSITIVISM), and later in an elaborate examination of CONFIRMATION and probability. *Der logische Aufbau der Welt (The Logical Structure of the World)*, 1928. 'Die physicalische Sprache als Universalsprache der Wissenschaft', *Erkenntnis*, 1932 (transl. separately as *The Unity of Science*, 1934; physicalism). 'Testability and Meaning', *Philosophy of Science*, 1936–7. *Meaning and Necessity*, 1947, enlarged 1956. *Logical Foundations of Probability*, 1950. *The Continuum of Inductive Methods*, 1952. See also BASIC STATEMENTS, BEING, EXPLANATION, FUNCTION, ISOMORPHIC, MEANING, MEANING POSTULATES, PROBABILITY, REDUCTION SENTENCES, SENTENCES, TRUTH, TYPES.

Cartesian. Connected with Descartes, or his ideas.

Casuistry. See ETHICS.

Categorematic. See CATEGORIES.

Categories. Ultimate or fundamental divisions or kinds. For much of its history the search for categories has wavered between seeking distinctions among things in the world and distinctions among our ways of thinking or talking about the world. Much of the difficulty in each case has lain in knowing what distinctions to count as sufficiently fundamental. It is mainly by being ultimate or fundamental that categories differ from mere classes.

This wavering appears in Aristotle, who first explicitly introduced categories. His 'official' list contains ten categories, but the most important are SUBSTANCE, quantity, relative and quality, and his main interest seems to lie in distinguishing substance from the others. The list is clearly derived from different kinds of question that can be asked about a person, like 'How big is he?', 'What is he doing?'

Sometimes Aristotle seems to take a 'metaphysical' view, treating categories as the highest genera into which things in general can be divided, so that the world contains substances, qualities, etc., and anything one picks out such as a horse, or red, can be classed under one of these headings. He sometimes lets categories overlap, so that the same item appears in more than one (end of chapter 8 in his *Categories*). At other times he seems to take a 'logical' view and to be classifying the things one can say about something, and in particular about a substance, such as what it is, what qualities it has, how it is related to other things. Here he might be described as classifying predicates, but he often seems to regard predicates themselves as things in the world and not as linguistic expressions, so that the 'metaphysical' and 'logical' approaches are not clearly separate. Aristotle's classification is not very exhaustive. The terms 'one', 'good', 'being', he said, did not belong to any one category. These were later called transcendentals (see BEING). There are many others, some of which he discussed, which have no obvious place, including 'surface', 'sound', 'chance', 'proposition', 'necessity', and complex terms like 'multiple of three', 'knowledge of French'. Aristotle also argues that there cannot be a single all-embracing genus like *being* or *unit*.

Many writers have followed Aristotle in elaborating sets of categories, usually more systematic than his. The Stoics had a set of four and they apparently wanted to classify at least some of the world's contents by examining the questions one can ask about a thing.

Among modern writers the most important contribution is that of Kant, who had a system of four groups of three. He intended these as a classification, whose correctness and exhaustiveness he claimed to prove, of the ways in which any mind recognizably like the human mind necessarily had to perceive and think about the appearances it was presented with. The categories were not a classification of things in themselves (NOUMENA), for Kant thought we could never know these and so never apply categories to them. The categories could only be applied to material given by experience, but they could not themselves be derived from experience, since all use of experience presupposes them. Kant's general idea is that we can only make sense of the world by imposing some structure originating from the mind upon it, e.g. to choose two of his categories, by seeing it as a set of *substances* in *causal* relationships. Many who accept this general idea reject the particular list he gave, and deny that there is some one list valid for all people and times. There is still much dispute about such related questions as whether

Categories

there are certain features every language must share (cf. philosophy of LANGUAGE, INNATE).

In this century two converging streams of thought have aroused interest in categories. First there are the logical PARADOXES, which led Russell to construct his theory of TYPES. This theory divides the world up by insisting that things of different 'types' cannot be put together into a single class. It leads to corresponding divisions in language, e.g. two sentences of which one refers to the other are on different 'levels', and cannot be joined into a single sentence by 'and'. In fact 'type' and 'category' are sometimes used synonymously. Secondly, thinkers like Husserl and Ryle, among others, have tried to construct a doctrine of categories in order to systematize the ways in which a sentence can go wrong, and in particular the distinction between the false and the meaningless. Roughly speaking, the ideal of this approach would be to divide things into non-overlapping groups so that what could be said truly or falsely, but not nonsensically, of the members of one group differed radically from what could be said of the members of another, rather as most of the things that can be said of a cat differ from what can be said of a wish, or of a day of the week. Sentences which say about a subject in one category something that can only be sensibly said about a subject in another category, are called *category mistakes* or type confusions, e.g. 'Saturday is in bed'. Such a doctrine cannot tell us when a sentence makes sense if we must already know this before constructing the doctrine. But the doctrine could systematize the situation, and throw useful light on individual cases through comparisons.

Many difficulties arise concerning categories. It sometimes seems to be thought that, if they exist at all, they must belong to the world and not language, because they must be found out and not created by us. But even if we create a language, we can still *discover* things about it. We may choose what our sentences shall mean, but once we have chosen we are committed to the implications of our choice, and we do not choose these implications. The main difficulties seem to be of two kinds. First, to think of subjects and predicates that will not go together is perhaps too easy for we may reach so many categories that the doctrine becomes rather trivial, and 'category' becomes a pompous name for 'class' as often happens in ordinary speech. Are spoons and forks in different categories because 'This fork has lost one of its prongs' becomes nonsensical when 'fork' is replaced by 'spoon'? A distinction between absolute and relative categories has been found necessary in facing this problem (Strawson).

The second kind of difficulty, connected with the first, centres round the notion of meaninglessness. There are many ways in which something might be meaningless, nonsensical or absurd, as the following examples illustrate: 'Horse whether the', 'Twice two is five', 'My wish has whiskers', 'I have found', 'I have any apples', 'He sleeps like milk'. Some of these may be given senses in special cases, but which of them serve to distinguish categories? One can ask how clearly in fact is the meaningless distinct from the false? 'Absurd' can cover both. And is *every* kind of predicate relevant? Are two things in the same category merely because the predicate 'being thought about by me now' can apply to both of them? One controversy arising out of all this is whether categories can be ultimately founded on grammatical distinctions (called *syntactical* in logic), or whether considerations of meaning independent of mere grammar must be used (in which case categories will have a *semantic* basis; cf. SEMIOTIC).

Categorial means 'having to do with categories'. *Categorical*, though often misused for 'categorial', has something like its ordinary meaning of 'definite' or 'downright', but refers to a certain *form* of proposition, one which says something is the case without reference to conditions or alternatives. 'That's a cat' is categorical, 'If that's a cat, it's an animal' is *hypothetical*. 'That's either a cat or a dog', is *disjunctive*. *Mongrel categorical* is Ryle's name for a statement overtly categorical but covertly including a hypothetical statement; e.g. 'He drove carefully' says, for Ryle, not only that he did something but that he would have done certain things if certain events had occurred. See also categorical IMPERATIVE.

Categorematic, rarely used, refers to words or phrases naming things in categories, especially the Aristotelian categories, substance, quality, etc. *Syncategorematic* applies to words or phrases that somehow link or go 'together with' the categories. Basically, syncategorematic words are all those which are not categorematic, and they have often been regarded as not having meaning independently. The commonest examples are words like 'all', 'if', 'the', which do not name substances, qualities, etc., and are often known as logical words although many other examples are often given, including most adverbs. Also some words which behave grammatically like ordinary categorematic ones, yet which are somehow incomplete in meaning, are sometimes included. Some adjectives, especially, only apply to things when the things are described in certain ways. A big mouse is not a big animal. A thing cannot be big (unqualified) as it can be red (cf. ATTRIBUTIVE). A philosophically important case is GOOD. Bigness and goodness, etc., are therefore sometimes called *syncategorematic properties*, because they only apply to an object when taken together with categorematic terms ('mouse' or 'animal' in the above example). Cf. transcendentals, under BEING.

Causation

Aristotle, *Categories*, transl. with comentary by J. L. Ackrill in Clarendon Aristotle series, 1963, reprinted (without the commentary) in the 2nd edition of the *Oxford Translation of Aristotle*, ed. by J. Barnes, Princeton UP, 1984. (See also his *Topics*, Bk I, chap. 9, and for argument that being is not a genus see *Metaphysics*, 998b22–7.)

K. Campbell, *Abstract Particulars*, Blackwell, 1990. (Uses tropes as basis of a one-category metaphysical system, in contrast to Aristotle's.)

A. D. Carstairs, 'Ryle, Hillman and Harrison on categories', *Mind*, 1971. (Discusses some of their recent work.)

R. Grossmann, *The Categorial Structure of the World*, Indiana UP, 1983. (Discusses categorial status of individuals, properties, relations, classes, numbers, and facts. Full table of contents.)

Kant, *Critique of Pure Reason*, 1781, trans. by N. Kemp Smith in 1929. (See its index.)

S. Körner, *Categorial Frameworks*, Blackwell, 1970. (Discusses basic frameworks of our thinking, allowing that these may legitimately change.)

*J. Passmore, *Philosophical Reasoning*, Philosophical Reasoning, 1961, chapter 7. (Somewhat sceptical approach.)

J. M. Rist, 'Categories and their uses', in A. A. Long (ed.). *Problems in Stoicism*, Athlone, 1971. (Stoic categories.)

*G. Ryle, 'Categories', *Proceedings of the Aristotelian Society*, 1938–9, reprinted in A. Flew (ed.), *Logic and Language*, 2nd series, Blackwell, 1953. (Attempts to construct theory of categories on semantic basis, resulting in so many category differences that the notion seems in danger of becoming trivial. See also his *The Concept of Mind*, Hutchinson, 1949, esp. p. 16 (p. 17 in Peregrine edn), for category mistakes, and esp. p. 141 (p. 135 in Peregrine edn) for mongrel categoricals.)

F. Sommers, 'Types and ontology', *Philosophical Review*, 1963. (One of several articles by Sommers elaborating a semantic theory of categories more rigorous than Ryle's.)

T. L. S. Sprigge, *Facts, Words and Beliefs*, RKP, 1970, pp. 70–2. (Syncategorematic properties. Cf. N. Griffin, *Relative Identity*, Oxford UP, 1977, pp. 10–11 on 'polymorphous predicates'.)

P. F. Strawson, 'Categories', in O. P. Wood and G. Pitcher (eds), *Ryle*, Doubleday, 1970. (General discussion of possibility and usefulness of categories, starting from Ryle. See p. 199 (Papermac edn, 1971) for absolute and relative categories.)

Causation. Roughly, the relation between two things when the first is thought of as somehow producing or responsible for the second. But to elaborate this intuitive idea is difficult, since it seems impossible to find or even conceive of any active production going on in nature. Why then do we think in terms of such production? Where do we get the 'idea of causation' from, and when in fact is it correct to apply it? Modern discussions of causation stem primarily from Hume's claim that our idea of causation cannot be gained in any simple way from either reason or observation: it cannot come from reason because reason can only tell us of logical relations, and if the cause and effect were logically related, i.e. if the occurrence of the cause *entailed* (see IMPLICATION) that of the effect, they would not be 'distinct existences' as Hume thought they should be; one proposition ('This has shape') can entail a distinct one ('This has size'), but there it does not make sense to suppose the first true and the second false, whereas it should *make sense* to suppose a cause exists without its effect. All this is not to deny that causal statements can be ANALYTIC, like 'Whatever causes cancer causes cancer'. If something correctly described as the cause of cancer exists, then cancer must exist – otherwise the first thing could not be called its cause. Hume thought observation can only tell us that some things regularly follow on other things. It cannot reveal that special 'force' or 'necessity' that we feel a causal situation must contain.

Causation may involve regularities (though this is disputed; see Alexander), but is that all it involves? Regularities may be causally significant or they may be accidental, and in trying to distinguish these we meet problems about natural laws and counterfactual CONDITIONALS. Furthermore what regularities are relevant? Perhaps, in the case of singular causal statements, i.e. those about given occasions, to say that *a* caused *b* is to say that *a* was followed by *b*, and that *a*-like things are regularly followed by *b*-like things; but how like *a* and *b* must the things in question be? If I say that striking that match caused it to light, am I saying that all matches light when struck, or only that all dry matches do, or what? One view (Davidson) is that in saying '*a* caused *b*' we imply that there exists some true non-accidental generalization of the form 'Things like *a* in certain respects are followed by things like *b* in certain respects', but we need not know what generalization.

Since the world is an interlocking whole, so that exact repetition of all circumstances is presumably impossible, and the course of events leading to a given event is enormously complex, a looser view of causes has often been taken. On one view an event's cause is some condition, or set of conditions, which is either necessary or sufficient, or both, for the event (see NECESSARY AND SUFFICIENT CONDITIONS). This condition is singled out because it is rare or striking in some respect, or is amenable to human control. If matches were usually wet, and so did not light when struck, we

Causation

might call its dryness the cause when some particular match did light when struck. As things are, we call the striking the cause because it is controllable and matches are usually dry.

We could tighten this up by calling an event's cause the set of those things which are separately necessary and together sufficient for its occurrence, perhaps with a proviso that general background conditions (the stars in their courses, etc.) can be excluded as irrelevant. But two difficulties arise. First, this would not distinguish causal from logical relations (see NECESSARY AND SUFFICIENT CONDITIONS). Secondly, if a is a necessary condition of b, b is a sufficient condition of a, and vice versa. So if a is a necessary and sufficient condition of b, so is b of a. But then if a causes b we must say that b causes a, which seems absurd. (Variants of this 'tightening up' procedure are possible, but with similar disadvantages.)

There are problems about how causation in related to time. We often feel that a cause should precede its effect, but since time is continuous this seems to imply that there must be a gap between cause and effect. But when 'cause' is being used strictly, and not just to pick out what is striking or unusual, such a gap, whether temporal or spatial ('action at a distance'), seems mysterious. As Hume observed, once the total cause exists, how can it not have its effect there and then? Yet if cause and effect are simultaneous everything should happen at once. It seems no better to say, alternatively, that the gap is filled by a chain of infinitely many causes. Some kinds of causes, however, do seem simultaneous with their effects, e.g. forces or objects: 'Gravity caused him to fall', 'The dog caused the accident'. It has even been suggested that an effect could precede its cause (Dummett).

One way of explaining why causation seems to be a one-way relation, so that things cannot cause each other (though they can sustain each other, like the stones in an arch) is to derive the idea of causation from our experience of our own activity. To cause something is then to bring it about, and we call causes those things that could serve us, at least in principle, as recipes for producing their effects. On a primitive version of this view nature itself does the bringing about, but we need not assume this. Even things clearly outside our control, like stellar processes, can be viewed *as if* they were in our control, and we need not attribute activities to nature. Why we refuse to allow effects to precede their causes may then be because we cannot make sense of bringing about the past, because we have no experience of it in our own activities. We could always explain the case where the later event seems to cause the earlier (Dummett) by saying the earlier causes the later but by a process that has escaped us; but cf. von Wright (under DUMMETT).

Causation

Heisenberg's uncertainty principle (1927) says that we cannot in principle discover both the momentum and the position of a fundamental particle, because the process of discovery will always affect what is being discovered. (Whether the particle *has* both a momentum and a position is disputed.) Also the behaviour of individual particles is often unpredictable in quantum mechanics. We can, however, attribute probabilities to the behaviour of such particles, and then use PROBABILITY theory to predict with virtual certainty the behaviour of swarms of particles, i.e. of ordinary objects. This, coupled with the fact that physicists usually talk in terms of equations rather than one-way relations, raises three questions: Has physics abandoned or even undermined causation? Does it make sense to suppose that individual sub-atomic movements are caused, even though we cannot in principle discover their causes? Can there be ultimate causal *tendencies*, i.e. cases where a cause is followed by its effect, say, 90 per cent of the time and where this cannot be explained by pointing to an underlying 100 per cent generalization? (If 90 per cent of matches light when struck, this might be because 100 per cent of dry matches light when struck.) Clearly the answers will depend on how we view causation. The 'recipe' view might say causation is irrelevant for physics, not undermined by it, and that *virtual* certainty is all that causation requires. Alternatively we may say that a cause is simply something which makes its effect more probable.

A further important question about causation, which may affect the answers to some of the above questions, is how far it is really a metaphysical notion connected with necessitation and how far an epistemological notion connected with explanation, and how causation is related to coincidences (see Sorabji and Owens). How are causation and causal explanation related? (See e.g., Owens, p. 23.)

What sort of things can be causes? Objects, events, forces, facts, states, processes, even absences ('The absence of oxygen caused his death'), can be described as causes. Which, if any, of these has the prior claim to the title of cause is disputable. No doubt the 'strikingness' mentioned above can explain much here. But sometimes what appear to be near synonyms have been explicitly distinguished, notably 'effects', 'results' and 'consequences'.

An important question in recent philosophy of mind concerns whether actions can be caused, and if so, whether this affects our notion of responsibility (see FREEWILL). Obviously the word 'because', which we use in giving reasons for our actions, need not be causal. It can, e.g., signify logical relations, as in '141 cannot be a prime number because the sum of its digits is divisible by 3'. But even 'cause' may imply causality less than 'causal' does. We might

Causation

accept 'My wife's profligacy caused me to sell my house', while rejecting 'The relation between my wife's behaviour and my action was a causal one.'

Aristotle's *four causes*, here illustrated by reference to a man, are the *material cause*, (flesh, etc.), *formal cause* (FORM of man), *efficient cause* (father), *final cause* (end or purpose, e.g. to live in a certain way). The notions are, however, less clearcut than this suggests, and the Greek word is wider than 'cause'. It means something like 'responsible factor'. An *exemplary cause* is a pattern or exemplar playing the role of Plato's 'FORMS'. God was sometimes called the exemplary cause when these Forms were regarded as IDEAS in His mind.

P. Alexander, P. B. Downing, 'Are causal laws purely general?', *Proceedings of the Aristotelian Society*, supplementary vol., 1970.

G. E. M. Anscombe, 'Causality and determination' in Sosa, and in Sosa and Tooley, and also, with other items on causation, in her *Collected Philosophical Papers*, vol. 2, Blackwell, 1991. (Insists that causality need not involve regularity.)

Aristotle, *Physics*, book 2. (Four causes.)

B. Blanshard, *The Nature of Thought*, Allen and Unwin, 1939, chapter 32, §§ 10–21. S. Shoemaker, *Identity, Cause, and Mind*, Cambridge UP, 1984, chapter 10, esp. pp. 222ff. (Both these connect causation with logical necessity. E. Nagel, *Sovereign Reason*, Free Press, 1954, pp. 387–95, criticizes Blanshard.)

M. Brand (ed.), *The Nature of Causation*, 1976. (Readings.)

F. Copleston, *A History of Philosophy*, vol. 2, 1950. (Exemplary causes. See its index.)

D. Davidson, 'Causal relations', *Journal of Philosophy*, 1967, reprinted in his Essays on *Actions and Points*, Clarendon, 1980, and in Sosa and Tooley, below. (Singular causal statements.)

M. Dummett, 'Bringing about the past', S. Gorovitz, 'Leaving the past alone', *Philosophical Review*, 1964. Cf. G. H. von Wright, *Explanation and Understanding*, RKP, 1971, chapter 2, § 10, and S. Waterlow, 'Backwards causation and continuing', *Mind*, 1974, which also contains a bibliography, to which add P. B. Downing, 'Subjunctive conditionals, time order and causation', *Proceedings of the Aristotelian Society*, 1958–9.)

E. Fales, *Causation and Universals*, Routledge, 1990, esp. part I. (Defends realist view of causation as relation between universals.)

D. Gasking, 'Causation and recipes', *Mind*, 1955, reprinted in A. Sesonske and N. Fleming (eds), *Human Understanding*, Wadsworth, 1965, and in Brand (above). (Cf. von Wright (above), chapter 2, §§ 8, 9.)

C-Function

H. L. A. Hart and A. M. Honoré, *Causation in the Law*, Clarendon, 1959. (Standpoint of philosophy of mind.)

J. Heil and A. Mele (eds), *Mental Causation*, Oxford UP, 1994. (Specially written essays.)

D. Hume, *Treatise*, 1739, I 3, §§ 2, 3, 7. (Classic statement of problem. Cf. his *Enquiry concerning Human Understanding*, 1748, §§ 4, 7.)

*J. L. Mackie, *The Cement of the Universe*, Oxford UP, 1974. (Basically empiricist treatment but taking full account of directionality, necessity, etc. For extended summary see preface to paperback edition (1980).)

D. H. Mellor, 'The singularly affecting facts of causation' in P. Pettit *et al.* (eds), *Metaphysics and Morality*, Blackwell, 1987, reprinted in Mellor's *Matters of Metaphysics*, Cambridge UP, 1991. (Causation primarily links facts, not events. Cf. also his *The Facts of Causation*, Routledge, 1995.)

D. Owens, *Causes and Coincidences*, Cambridge UP, 1992. (General discussion, defining causation in terms of coincidences and linking it to explanation.)

D. Papineau, 'Probabilities and causes', *Journal of Philosophy*, 1985. (Discusses various views connecting these notions.)

B. Russell, *Analysis of Mind*, Allen and Unwin, 1921, chapter 5, esp. beginning. (Can a cause precede its effect? Cf. his *Our Knowledge of the External World*, Allen and Unwin, 1914, chapter 8.)

R. Sorabji, *Necessity, Cause and Blame*, Duckworth, 1980, chapters 1 and 2. (Causation, necessitation, explanation, coincidences.)

*E. Sosa and M. Tooley (eds), *Causation*, Oxford UP, 1993. (Readings.)

Z. Vendler, 'Causal relations', *Journal of Philosophy*, 1967. (Criticizes Davidson and treats causes as facts. Also discusses effects, results and consequences, on which see also Hart and Honoré (above), pp. 25–6, and symposium in R. J. Butler (ed.), *Analytical Philosophy*, 1st series, Blackwell, 1962; Vendler's contribution to this is revised in his *Linguistics in Philosophy*, Cornell UP, 1967. On results and consequences see also S. Candlish, 'Inner and outer basic actions', *Proceedings of the Aristotelian Society*, 1983–4, esp. pp. 86–7.)

G. J. Warnock in A. Flew (ed.), *Logic and Language*, 2nd series, Blackwell, 1953. (Discusses 'Every event has a cause'.)

Central state materialism. SEE IDENTITY THEORY OF MIND.

C-Function. See CONFIRMATION.

Charity (principle of)

Charity (principle of). Principle that when interpreting an unknown language one should make the most favourable assumptions possible about the speaker's intelligence, knowledge, sense of relevance, etc., so as to make as much as possible of what is said come out true. Important in connexion with radical interpretation (see TRANSLATION). However, it has come to be replaced, more realistically, by the *principle of humanity*, that one takes account of the speaker's desires as well as beliefs, interpreting these, unless there is reason to do otherwise, as being similar to one's own, so that one will have less need to attribute inexplicable errors to the speaker.

I. Hacking, *Why Does Language Matter to Philosophy?*, Cambridge UP, 1975, pp. 146–50. G. Sundholm, 'Brouwer's anticipation of the principle of charity', *Proceedings of the Aristotelian Society*, 1984–5, pp. 264–8. (Both discuss with historical references. Hacking is easier. Cf. also S. Evnine, *Donald Davidson*, Polity/Blackwell, 1991, chapter 6.)

Chinese room argument. Argument offered by Searle against the claim he attributes to supporters of what he calls 'Strong AI' (artificial intelligence), that to instantiate a computer program is enough to constitute intentionality, i.e. 'that feature of certain mental states by which they are directed at or about objects and states of affairs in the world' (cf. INTENSIONALITY AND INTENTIONALITY). Searle argues that something could always instantiate a program, and thereby simulate understanding, without duplicating it, and without itself actually understanding. To illustrate this he imagines that, knowing no Chinese, he is locked in a room and presented with Chinese characters together with rules for correlating the characters and producing some in response to others. These rules might be such that the characters he produced could serve as meaningful answers to questions represented by the characters presented to him. Yet however far this process was elaborated, Searle claims, he would not be understanding Chinese. What the argument in fact shows has been much disputed.

*T. Crane, *The Mechanical Mind: an Introduction to Minds, Machines and Mental Representation*, Penguin, 1995, chapter 3. (Contains elementary introduction.)
J. R. Searle, 'Minds, brains and programs', *The Behavioral and Brain Sciences*, vol. 3, 1980, pp. 413–57. (Includes discussions and Searle's reply. For quotation see p. 424 n. 3.)

Chisholm, Roderick M. 1916–. Born in Maryland, he has worked mainly at Brown University, Rhode Island. His work covers the central areas of philosophy, and is distinguished by an attempt

Class paradox

to bring the insights of the Austrian phenomenologists, especially Brentano and Meinong, to bear on modern analytical philosophy, whose interests and methods he largely adheres to; he has been instrumental, for instance, in focusing our attention on intentionality (see INTENSIONALITY AND INTENTIONALITY). His publications include *Perceiving*, 1957; *Theory of Knowledge*, 1966 (substantially revised in 1977 and again in 1989); *Person and Object*, 1976; *The First Person*, 1981; *Brentano and Meinong Studies*, 1982; *Brentano and Intrinsic Value*, 1986; *On Metaphysics*, 1989.

Church's theorem. See DECIDABLE.

Class. Loosely, a group of objects or things. In many non-technical contexts (including most of this entry) 'class' and 'set' are synonymous. But there are technical reasons, associated with J. von Neumann, K. Gödel and P. Bernays, who hoped to avoid RUSSELL'S PARADOX, for saying some classes are not members of any other classes (as the class of cats *is* a member of the class of animal-classes). 'Set' is then limited to those classes which *are* members of other classes, the rest being called *proper classes*. The terms 'set theory' and 'CALCULUS of classes' are conventional, irrespective of this variation in usage.

Roughly, but only roughly, a class is *closed* if it has finitely many members and these are theoretically enumerable. It is *open* if it has infinitely many members, or if its membership is indeterminate (e.g. the class of horses, if it is indeterminate how many there will be).

It is important to distinguish *class-inclusion* from *class-membership*. A class is included in any class containing at least the same members. The class of cats is included in, but is not a member of, the class of animals for it is not an animal. It is a member of, but is not included in, the class of animal-classes for cats are not animal-classes. Class-inclusion is TRANSITIVE, but class-membership is non-transitive. Smith may be a member of a union, and the union a member of the TUC, without Smith being a member of the TUC. For extensional and intensional definitions of classes see UNIVERSALS.

A *unit class* (or *singleton*) is a class with exactly one member. The *universal class* is the class containing everything, or everything in a given sphere.

The *null*, or *empty, class* is the one class with no members '[*a*, *b*]' means the class whose members are *a* and *b*. '<*a*, *b*>' means the ordered class whose members are *a* and *b*, in that order.

Class paradox. see RUSSELL'S PARADOX.

Closure

Closure. A notion easiest to explain by example. Let *p* etc. be propositions, and suppose that whenever *p* is true, so is '*p* or *q*' (as indeed is the case in classical logic). Then truth is said to be 'closed under' disjunction (the or-relation: see CONJUNCTION). The idea is presumably that when *p* is true the truth of '*p* or *q*' is no longer an open question but is settled or closed. Closure is not limited to truth, however. The principle of *epistemic closure* says that someone who knows that *p*, and knows that *p* entails *q*, also knows that *q*; in this case knowledge is closed under known entailment. It is not closed under plain entailment, since we cannot know the infinitely many things entailed by what we know, but even allowing it to be closed under known entailment can lead to scepticism, by suggesting that quite modest claims to knowledge can commit us to false claims, and so must themselves be rejected.

R. Nozick, 'Knowledge and scepticism', in J. Dancy (ed.), *Perceptual Knowledge*, Oxford UP, 1988. (Extracted from his *Philosophical Explanations*, Harvard UP, Oxford UP, 1981. Argues that knowledge is not closed under known entailment. For discussion, see J. Dancy, *An Introduction to Contemporary Epistemology*, Oxford, UP, 1985. See its index.)

Clusters. see UNIVERSALS.

Cognitive psychology. The psychology of the cognitive processes involved in thinking. When extended to cover the study of artificial intelligence and areas bordering on cybernetics and other sciences it becomes *cognitive science*. One form it takes is that of *computational psychology*, which grew up as an attempt to mediate between purely behavioural and purely introspective approaches to the mind by postulating and studying events in the brain which 'represent' inferences etc. in the way in which computer programs can represent things. Sometimes also 'cognitive science' itself is regarded as an alternative term for computational psychology.

M. A. Boden and D. H. Mellor, 'What is computational psychology?' *Proceedings of the Aristotelian Society*, supplementary vol., 1984, (Critical discussions.)

C. E. M. Dunlop and J. H. Fetzer, *Glossary of Cognitive Science*, Paragon House, 1993. (Brief explanations of cognitive science terms and relevant philosophical ones.)

J. Heil, 'Does cognitive psychology rest on a mistake?', *Mind*, 1981. (Yes. Treats 'cognitive psychology' as a synonym for 'computational psychology'. See also his *Perception and Cognition*, California UP, 1983, esp. chapter 7.)

Combinatorialism

A. I. Goldman (ed.), *Readings in Philosophy and Cognitive Science*, MIT Press, 1993. (Wide-ranging anthology. Cf. also his *Philosophical Applications of Cognitive Science*, Westview Press, 1993.)

Cognitivism. Knowledge, belief, thinking, and intellectual processes are called cognitive, and cognitivism can be any theory which appeals to such processes. In ethics especially, there has been since the days of logical POSITIVISM (with premonitions in the eighteenth century) a debate between *cognitivism*, which treats ethics as concerned with truths, which by one means or another are accessible to human knowledge, and *non-cognitivism*, which treats ethics rather as concerned with emotions, prescriptions, or similar attitudes. However, in the last third of the twentieth century the sharpness of the distinction has become blurred, in keeping with complex treatments of notions like truth and objectivity. See also NATURALISM, SUBJECTIVISM.

F. Jackson, G. Oppy and M. Smith, 'Minimalism and truth aptness', *Mind*, 1994. (Attacks the attempt to defend cognitivism in ethics and elsewhere by watering down the notion of truth.)
J. Dancy, *Moral Reasons*, Blackwell, 1993. (Includes defence of cognitivism in the context of discussing moral motivation.)

Coherentism. See FOUNDATIONALISM.

Collingwood, Robin G. 1889–1943. Philosopher and archaeologist who was born at Coniston and worked mostly in Oxford. Most of his philosophical work concerns aesthetics, philosophy of mind, philosophy of history and metaphysics. His theory of art, influenced by CROCE, bases art on expression and imagination, which leads him to a treatment of language. In philosophy of history he treats the historian's task as that of reconstructing the thoughts that lay behind or were embodied in historical actions. His later metaphysics is rather similar in nature, in that he sees its task as limited to the reconstruction of the 'absolute presuppositions' of an epoch in the history of thought (see IMPLICATION). *The Principles of Art*, 1938. *Autobiography*, 1939. *An Essay on Metaphysics*, 1940. *The New Leviathan*, 1942 ('an attempt to bring the *Leviathan* [of HOBBES] up to date' (preface)). *The Idea of History*, 1946.

Combinatorialism. The view that POSSIBLE WORLDS can be regarded as different combinations of elements taken from the actual world. This avoids having to postulate the existence of entities other than what is actual. An initial objection is that the elements themselves

Complete

might have been different from what they are, not just differently arranged.

D. M. Armstrong, *A Combinatorial Theory of Possibility*, Cambridge UP, 1989. (Elaborates and defends such a view.)

M. J. Loux (ed.), *The Possible and the Actual*, Cornell UP, 1979. (See p. 60 for the basic idea, and its index for some critical discussion.)

Complete. An AXIOM SYSTEM, in the sense of a set of axioms and rules of inference, is complete in a weak sense if all the truths of the kind it caters for can be derived within the system. It is complete in a strong sense if the addition of any other proposition of the relevant kind as an independent axiom makes the system inconsistent. There are further refinements. In particular, formalizations of the propositional CALCULUS can be complete in both senses; formalizations of the first-order predicate CALCULUS can only be weakly complete. Also a set of axioms in a formal language is called complete if for every sentence S in the language either S or not-S follows from the axioms. In this sense no explicitly definable set of axioms rich enough for elementary arithmetic is complete (see GÖDEL'S THEOREMS); in fact no such set is complete in any sense mentioned above.

A. H. Basson and D. J. O'Connor, *Introduction to Symbolic Logic,* 3rd edn, University Tutorial Press, 1959. (See its index.)

E. J. Lemmon, *Beginning Logic*, Nelson, 1965. (See its index.)

A. N. Prior, *Formal Logic*, Clarendon, 1955. (See its index.)

Composition and division. 'Someone sitting could walk' might be interpreted in the *composite sense (sensus compositus)* to mean 'Someone could walk while sitting', or in the *divided sense (sensus divisus)* to mean 'Someone sitting could walk instead'. In a fairly intuitive sense the former puts *walking* and *sitting* together, while the latter keeps them apart. To wrongfully infer the expression interpreted in the composite sense from the same expression interpreted in the divided sense is to commit the *fallacy of composition*. The converse *fallacy of division* occurs if, e.g. we are given 'Everyone is male or female' in the composite sense, that each person is male-or-female, and take it in the divided sense, that everyone is male or everyone is female.

Other forms of the fallacy occur when we infer that what holds of a whole must hold of its parts, or what holds of a class must hold of its members (division), or vice versa in each case (composition); e.g. that if a solid made of atoms is coloured each part must be coloured, or that if X is an aggressive country X-ians

Concept

must be aggressive individuals (division), or that if each vote fails to elect the candidate all the votes fail to do so, or that if each citizen is not numerous the citizens are not numerous (composition).

In modal contexts 'composite' and 'divided' have been thought to correspond respectively to 'de dicto' and 'de re' (see MODALITIES). 'All cats may be black' can mean 'Possibly all cats are black' or 'Any given cat may be black'. In the former (de dicto, composite) *cats* and *black* go together, with the modal term ('possibly') outside. In the latter (de re, divided) the modal term comes essentially between *cat* and *black*.

I. M. Copi, *Introduction to Logic*, Macon NY, 6th edn, 1982 (1st edn. was 1953), chapter 3 § 3.

A. N. Prior, *Formal Logic*, Clarendon, 1955. (See 'composition' in index.)

Comprehension. See INTENSIONALITY AND INTENTIONALITY.

Computational psychology. See COGNITIVE PSYCHOLOGY.

Comte, I. Auguste M. F. X. 1798–1857. Born in Montpellier, he lived mainly in Paris, holding various minor academic posts. From 1817 he was secretary for some years to the social reformer C. H. de Saint-Simon (1760–1825) and was influenced by him. His main work consisted in the development of POSITIVISM. *Cours de philosphie positive*, 6 vols, 1830–42. *Discours sur l'esprit positif*, 1844 (popular exposition). *Système de politique positive, ou traité de sociologie, instituant la religion de l'humanité*, 4 vols, 1851–4. (Comte also applied the title *Système de politique positive* to the second edition (1824) of a small work published in 1822.)

A. Comte, *Introduction to Positive Philosophy*, Bobbs-Merrill, 1970, Haskett, 1988. (Transl. of first two chapters of *Cours de philosophie positive*.)

Concept. 'Concept' has taken over some uses of the ambiguous term 'IDEA', perhaps partly because 'idea' suggests images etc.; but 'concept' is ambiguous between a logical sense, associated with Frege, and a (more usual) psychological sense, where it is the content of a thought (see Newman), or the mode of presentation of a property (Peacocke). Concepts, however, are connected with UNIVERSALS, and on one view concepts are 'of' universals, so that to have a concept of, say, dog, is to be related to a non-material object like a Platonic FORM. But 'concept of dog' is perhaps best

Concept

taken as a single linguistic unit, like 'dog-concept', so that one is not tempted to seek some entity that 'dog' stands for.

A closely related view, *conceptual realism*, makes the concept itself a substantial entity, to which one is somehow related when one 'has' the concept. This leads to the 'paradox of ANALYSIS'.

Whereas conceptual realism says in effect that concepts are universals, *conceptualism* says that universals are concepts, but leaves open what concepts in the psychological sense are. They seem to be mind-dependent but common to many minds.

It may be that to have a concept is to have a means for classifying together things of a certain kind, and in some way thinking or reasoning about them, though some would insist that to have a concept of something one must also know what that thing is. This perhaps suggests that concepts are abilities, so that to have a concept of dog is to be *able* to think about dogs. How much the ability must cover is disputed. Has an animal, or a machine, a concept of dog if it reacts differentially to dogs? Can a man blind from birth have a concept of red? Does having a concept involve being able to use a word? Perhaps 'having a concept' is ambiguous in these respects. We must distinguish between the public concept of dog, or the concept *dog*, and an individual's concept of dog (though perhaps 'conception' might be used here: see below). An individual may include foxes, or think that dogs must by definition have tails; but if he diverges too far his concept will no longer be one of dog.

For Frege 'concept' is a logical term, contrasted with OBJECT. 'A concept is the referent of a predicate', while only an object can be the referent of a subject. Concepts can indeed he talked about, but only rather obliquely, in the way that 'There is at least one square root of four' talks about the concept *square root of four*. In 'Arkle is a horse' 'Arkle' introduces an object while 'is a horse' introduces a concept. Concepts are thus somehow incomplete: 'Arkle' can stand by itself, as a name, in a way that 'is a horse' cannot. Frege expressed this by calling objects *saturated* and concepts *unsaturated* (but cf. Dummett, pp. 31–3). Frege in fact defined a concept as 'a FUNCTION whose value [see VARIABLE] is always a TRUTH-VALUE'. Since what is referred to by a subject-term is automatically an object, Frege concluded paradoxically that ' the concept *horse* is not a concept' since we are referring to it. For Peacocke concepts are modes of presentation of properties.

Concepts are normally general (the concept *dog* covers dogs in general), but there can be *individual concepts* (e.g. the concept of the Atlantic; cf. also HAECCEITY).

Conception normally has only its everyday senses, perhaps tightened up a little, in philosophy (but see Woodfield). For *conceptual scheme* see RELATIVISM. See also POLAR CONCEPTS.

Conditionals

P. T. Geach, *Mental Acts,* RKP, 1957. (Discusses nature and acqui- sition of concepts. Sometimes difficult.)

P. T. Geach and M. Black (eds), *Translations from the Philosophical Writings of Gottlob Frege,* Blackwell, 1952. (Contains his 'Con- cept and Object'. See also p. 30 for 'concept' and 'function', pp. 47–8 for concept as reference of predicate; for discussion of 'horse' paradox see J. Valberg, 'Improper singular terms', *Pro- ceedings of the Aristotelian Society,* 1970–1, and D. Wiggins, 'The sense and reference of predicates', *Philosophical Quarterly,* 1984, reprinted in C. Wright (ed.), *Frege: Tradition and Influence,* Blackwell, 1984. Also see M. Dummett, *Frege: Philosophy of Language,* Duckworth, 1973.)

A. Newman, 'The material basis of predication and other concepts', *Australasian Journal of Philosophy,* 1988. (See esp. pp. 334, 341, for psychological/logical ambiguity.)

C. Peacocke, *Sense and Content,* Oxford UP, 1983. (See p. 89.)

K. R. Popper, *The Logic of Scientific Discovery,* Hutchinson, 1959 (German original, 1934), §14. (Individual concepts. See also Leib- niz, e.g. *Discourse on Metaphysics,* §8.)

A. Woodfield, 'Conceptions', *Mind,* 1991. (See esp. pp. 548–50 for concepts and conceptions, and also D. Wiggins, *Sameness and Substance,* Blackwell, 1980, p. 79 n.1 and R. Shiner in *Journal of the History of Philosophy,* 1979, pp. 71–2).

Conceptualism. See UNIVERSALS, CONCEPT, IDENTITY.

Conditionals. 'Conditional' and 'hypothetical' are normally used synonymously before terms like 'proposition' or 'statement'. Stan- dardly a proposition of the conditional form. 'If p then q', is taken to entail its CONTRAPOSITIVE, 'If not-q then not-p'. There are cases, however, whatever their ultimate analysis, which seem not to be of this kind, e.g. 'If you want it, there's some bread here' does not entail 'If there's no bread here, you don't want it'. Austin uses this concerning freewill. Also an antecedent may be followed by a question or command as in 'If it rains, stay in'.

As there is a problem about relating entailment to strict IMPLICATION and its 'paradoxes', so there is one about relating the standard 'if' of ordinary thought to material implication and its 'paradoxes'. One cannot truly say 'If p then q' when p is true and q is false, i.e. when p does not materially imply q. But can one say it in all other cases? or must p and q be somehow relevant to each other? Or must some other condition be fulfilled? Some say that relevance has nothing to do with the *meaning* if 'If p then q', but that general conventions forbid us to utter it when p and q are mutually irrelevant. 'If that's so, I'm a Dutchman' may be an excep-

Conditionals

tion to these conventions, relying for its effect on contrast to the normal case (Strawson; see IMPLICATION (last paragraph)). Also should we distinguish between asserting a conditional and conditionally asserting its consequent? Perhaps in saying 'If p then q' we are simply asserting q conditionally, in which case when p is false, 'If p then q' is neither true nor false but simply inapposite.

A particular source of difficulty lies in *subjunctive* and *counterfactual conditionals* or *counterfactuals* (also called *contrafactual* (Quine), *contrary-to-fact, unfulfilled*). Strictly subjunctive conditionals and counterfactuals are not the same. Counterfactuals may be conditionals with a false antecedent. Or they may be conditionals interpreted as entailing or presupposing that their antecedents are false. Or other analyses may be offered. (In the first case they will not have a special analysis, for the analysis of something should not depend on whether it or part of it is true or false; but the fact that a conditional can have a false antecedent will then affect the analysis of conditionals in general.) Subjunctive conditionals are those normally expressed in the subjunctive in English or related languages, and may include some *open conditionals*, which leave open whether or not the antecedent is taken as true ('Were it to rain tomorrow we should get wet'). However, the relevant problems are largely common to counterfactuals and subjunctive conditionals, and so are often expressed in terms of either. '□→' and '>' are sometimes used as symbols for counterfactual implication.

An important analysis of counterfactuals is offered by Lewis in terms of POSSIBLE WORLDS. Roughly, the idea is that a counterfactual is true if in the nearest possible world in which the antecedent is true the consequent is also true. More strictly (since there may not be a 'nearest' possible world) a counterfactual is true if any possible worlds in which the antecedent is true and the consequent false are further from the actual world than some possible world in which the antecedent is true and the consequent also true. How worlds are to be compared in terms of 'nearness' (i.e. similarity) raises problems, especially when we try to balance changes in initial conditions against breaching laws of nature. Counterfactuals and subjunctive conditionals seem even more remote from material implication than ordinary conditionals. They also provide problems for the verification theory (POSITIVISM) and the correspondence theory of TRUTH, and have a puzzling element of indefiniteness. After 'If Bizet and Verdi had been compatriots' should we put 'Bizet would have been Italian' or 'Verdi would have been French'?

Counterfactuals are also important in connexion with LAWS of nature, PHENOMENALISM, and dispositional statements like 'This glass is brittle', which seems to imply that had it been struck it would have broken. Some writers distinguish natural laws from

56

accidental generalizations ('All the coins in my pocket are silver', 'All ruminants are, as it happens, cloven-hoofed') by saying laws entail counterfactuals (or *'sustain'* them, a looser term used in case counterfactuals are not, properly speaking, statements, and because on some views laws of nature do not make, and so cannot entail, assertions about the world). Counterfactuals have also, however, been divided into 'purely hypothetical' ones of the Bizet/Verdi type and 'nomological' ones which we accept only if they accord with laws or similar acceptable statements. We accept 'If it were snowing it would be cold (since snow is always cold)' rather than 'If it were snowing snow would be hot (since today is in fact hot)' (Rescher). But obviously one cannot, without circularity, explain natural laws in terms of counterfactuals and explain counterfactuals in terms of natural laws.

Other views about conditionals say that they state relations between propositions. They state that the antecedent proposition implies, in some sense, the consequent. Alternatively, conditionals may be condensed arguments (Mackie), or rules or sets of instructions for making inferences. See also CAUSATION.

P. Alexander and M. Hesse, 'Subjunctive conditionals', *Proceedings of the Aristotelian Society*, supplementary vol., 1962. (Connection between them and natural laws.)

J. L. Austin, 'Ifs and cans' in his *Philosophical Papers*, 1961, reprinted in B. Berofsky (ed.), *Free Will and Determinism*, Harper and Row, 1966. (Relevance of senses of 'if' to freewill problem.)

J. Bennett, 'Counterfactuals and temporal direction', *Philosophical Review*, 1984. (Full discussion of some different kinds of counterfactuals.)

R. B. Braithwaite, *Scientific Explanation*, Harper, 1953, p. 295. (Distinguishes 'conditional' from 'hypothetical'; cf. also P. Edwards (ed.), *Encyclopedia of Philosophy*, 1967, 4, p. 128.)

D. Edgington, 'On conditionals', *Mind*, 1995. (Long survey and discussion of various modern views, esp. on indicative conditionals. See also J. Bennett, 'Classifying conditionals' in same volume.)

N. Goodman, *Fact, Fiction and Forecast*, Athlone Press, 1954, revised in later editions. (Difficulties in using material implication to analyse counterfactuals.)

S. Hampshire, 'Subjunctive conditionals', *Analysis*, vol. 9, 1948, reprinted in M. Macdonald (ed.), *Philosophy and Analysis*, Blackwell, 1954. (Problems raised by subjunctive conditionals.)

F. Jackson, *Conditionals*, Blackwell, 1987. (Full treatment.)

*F. Jackson, G. Oppy and M. Smith, 'Minimalism and truth aptness',

Confirmation

Mind, 1994. (Claims that one cannot defend the status of if/then statements as true or false by watering down the notion of truth.)

D. Lewis, *Counterfactuals*, Blackwell, 1973. (Offers extended analysis. See especially chapters 1, 3, 4. For discussion of some issues see W. A. Davis, 'Indicative and subjunctive conditionals', *Philosophical Review*, 1979. Cf. also E. J. Lowe, 'Indicative and counterfactual conditionals', *Analysis*, vol. 39, 1979.)

J. L. Mackie, 'Counterfactuals and causal laws', in R. J. Butler, (ed.), *Analytical Philosophy*, 1st series, Blackwell, 1962. (Counterfactuals as argument forms. Develops Rescher.)

N. Rescher, 'Belief-contravening suppositions', *Philosophical Review*, 1961. (Differences among counterfactuals.)

G. Ryle, ' "If", "so" and "because" ', in M. Black (ed.), *Philosophical Analysis*, Cornell UP, 1950, Prentice-Hall, 1953. (Conditionals as instructions for inferences.)

*E. Sosa (ed.), *Causation and Conditionals*, Oxford UP, 1975. (Readings. The items on conditionals reprinted with some extra items in F. Jackson (ed.), *Conditionals*, Oxford UP, 1991.)

*P. F. Strawson, *Introduction to Logical Theory*, Methuen, 1952, chapter 2 §7, chapter 3 §9. (Distinguishes 'if' and material implication. For 'Dutchman' see p. 89.)

D. Wilson, *Presuppositions and Non-Truth-Conditional Semantics*, Academic Press, 1975, pp. 120–3. (Nature of counterfactuals.)

Confirmation. A weak form of verification. To verify something is to show that it is true, or else to test it in a way that will reveal its truth if it *is* true. Often, however, we can only show that something is more likely to be true than it was, or was thought to be. This is one sense of confirmation. In logic 'confirmation' usually lacks its everyday senses of verifying or making definite ('I confirmed the booking', 'The facts confirmed my hypothesis'). The opposite of confirmation is usually called *disconfirmation*, occasionally *infirmation*.

Confirmation is closely related to PROBABILITY, though both terms are used in various senses. Speaking only generally, confirmation is the process by which probability is conferred on a hypothesis, and probability is what is conferred by confirmation. The problems in this area therefore, especially in earlier writings, concern the two notions in this way: Problems about confirmation concern the methods that can make a hypothesis more probable, while problems about probability concern what it is that we are saying about something when we say that it is probable. The two sets of problems overlap, however, and the difference is not clearcut. *Probability* means 'make probable to some degree' (not necessarily more probable than not), and so is synonymous with *one* sense (see below) of 'confirm'.

So far we have taken 'confirmation' to cover any process by which a scientific hypothesis is made more probable. In this sense its problems approximate to those of INDUCTION. One way to support a hypothesis is to eliminate its rivals, and through much of its history induction has been viewed as an eliminative process. But a hypothesis can only be established in this way, if *all* its rivals are eliminated, which in practice is seldom possible. It is difficult even in theory, unless it can be shown that its rivals are finite in number. Eliminating merely some of them will help only if there is some way of assigning probabilities to those that remain. Only if there is such a way can we talk of confirming by partial elimination. In fact confirmation has sometimes been contrasted with elimination and confined to some real or alleged process of giving positive support to a hypothesis – a process not dependent on eliminating any of its rivals. To find such a process is one aim of confirmation theory. Another aim is to account for how it is we can talk, as we do, of evidence being favourable even to a hypothesis we know to be false. These aims, especially the second, have led recently to technical notions of confirmation as a logical relation holding between a set of evidence propositions and a conclusion. ('*Support*' is often then used for the original notion, though it has other uses too.) One such relation (according to Carnap and Hempel) holds whether or not the conclusion is true, and even if we know it is false.

Confirmation is here a relation between some evidence and a conclusion, and holds irrespective of any other evidence. (Whether a conclusion is 'probable' in the ordinary sense depends on how far it is confirmed by all the available evidence.) Confirmation in this sense resembles entailment (see IMPLICATION), but is weaker, and the conclusion is not (as with entailment) contained in the premises. (There are further differences, e.g. where p, q and r are propositions, if p entails q then, normally, p-and-r entails q; this does not hold for confirmation.) For other writers (Popper, Swinburne) the confirmation given to a conclusion by some evidence is not the probability the conclusion acquires, but the ratio between that probability and the probability the conclusion had previously, usually on the basis of all the available evidence. Here confirmation is *increase* in probability.

An enquiry into confirmation can ask three main questions (Hempel). First, what is confirmation? Second, when is one conclusion more highly confirmed by some evidence than another? Third, can numerical values be given to degrees of confirmation?

In treating the second problem Carnap, like most of those who elaborate a logic of induction, relies on the calculus of chances

Confirmation

(PROBABILITY) and BAYES'S THEOREM. He considers a finite model, which can later be extended to an infinite one. He imagines a world containing a definite number of objects and a definite number of properties, and considers the various states that world might be in according to how the properties were distributed among the objects; e.g. if the objects were Tom and Bill and the properties tall and short, four *state-descriptions* could be given of the world, namely 'both tall', 'both short', 'Tom tall, Bill short', 'Tom short, Bill tall'. The confirmation given to a conclusion by evidence is then expressed in terms of a ratio between the number of state-descriptions compatible with the evidence and conclusion together and the normally larger number compatible with the evidence considered by itself. An important complication, however, is that not all state-descriptions need be treated equally, and part of the task is to devise a 'measure' which will give a certain weighting to any given state-description. A favoured way is to give equal weight to different *structures* in the world. In the above example 'both tall' and 'one tall, one short' represent two structures and have equal weight. They are *structure-descriptions* ('both tall' is also a state-description). 'Tom tall, Bill short' and 'Tom short, Bill tall' share the structure-description 'one tall, one short', and so each has half the weight of 'both tall'. The resulting formula by which confirmations are worked out is called a *confirmation-function* or *c-function* (in particular, c^*, which is based on structure-descriptions, as opposed to $c\dagger$, which is based on state-descriptions).

What ultimately justifies a given c-function is presumably that it gives results that tally with our intuitions of what should confirm what. But there is a difficulty about applying c-functions. If a proposition is entailed by something we know, we can assert it, but if it is only confirmed it may be absurd to assert it. That Smith is twenty no doubt confirms that he will live another forty years, but we would not assert that he will if we knew also that he had acute heart disease. Carnap therefore insisted on the *requirement of total evidence*, that we should not apply a confirmation argument unless the premises represent our total knowledge. This naturally raises practical difficulties over what can be excluded as irrelevant.

It is disputable how far Carnap has cut confirmation adrift from elimination, especially when we turn to the first of Hempel's three problems of confirmation and ask what confirmation is, and when one proposition confirms another.

Two *paradoxes of confirmation* arise here, associated with Hempel and Goodman, Hempel's paradox begins from *Nicod's criterion* of confirmation. This says that 'All ravens are black' is confirmed by a black raven (strictly, by a sentence asserting the existence of one) and refuted by a non-black one, other objects

Confirmation

being irrelevant. But it is plausible to say that whatever confirms a hypothesis in one formulation should confirm it in any logically equivalent formulation (the *equivalence condition*). A sentence like 'Here is a red shoe' confirms 'All non-black things are non-ravens' since a red shoe is a non-black non-raven. It should therefore also confirm the equivalent sentence 'All ravens are black', which seems absurd. Various questions arise from this, e.g. is there any difference between satisfying a hypothesis (i.e. being compatible with it) and confirming it? How is confirming a hypothesis related to increasing our knowledge about it, and to testing it?

Goodman's paradox concerns similar problems from a different point of view. Let 'grue' mean 'green if and only if first examined before time t, and otherwise blue'. Assuming t is still future, the fact that all emeralds so far examined have been green (and therefore also grue) seems to confirm 'All emeralds are grue' as much as it confirms 'All emeralds are green'. Yet surely it would be absurd to infer the former. (There are variants of the paradox, and also of the definition of 'grue'.) Many who have discussed this have tried to distinguish normal predicates like 'green' from odd ones like 'grue'. They could then rule that only the normal ones could be 'projected', i.e. used in inferences as above. However, it is not obvious that the problem concerns only 'odd' predicates, and it seems to resemble the *curve-fitting problem*: When two independently measurable features, such as temperature and pressure of a gas, are plotted against each other on a graph the resulting set of points must be finite because we can only perform finitely many measurements. They may suggest a simple curve connecting them, but they are compatible with infinitely many curves. What, then, justifies us in choosing the suggested one?

These and similar problems have led to some scepticism about whether there is a logical relation of confirmation at all. (Goodman's paradox in particular also raises problems for INDUCTION.) Popper replaces confirmation by *corroboration*, which he defines in terms of falsifiability and the passing of tests. He insists that he is not claiming that the hypothesis corroborated is thereby more likely to be true. Others concentrate on *acceptability*, which differs from confirmation because to give rules for when it is rational to accept a hypothesis need not involve any reference to a logical relation and can take account of such things as what the accepter knows already, and what risks acceptance involves him in. (In fact Popper's rules for corroboration are acceptance rules.) Also it may be rational to accept a hypothesis with a low probability, if its rivals have even lower probabilities; if there were just three competing hypotheses, with probabilities respectively of 40 per cent,

Confirmation

30 per cent and 30 per cent, it would be rational to accept the first, even though its probability was less than a half.

See also PROBABILITY, INDUCTION, LIKELIHOOD.

P. Achinstein, 'On evidence: a reply to Bar-Hillel and Margalit', *Mind*, 1981. (Defends an earlier article on relations between evidence, probability and explanation.)

S. Blackburn, *Reason and Prediction*, Cambridge UP, 1973. (See chapter 4 for discussion of 'grue' paradox.)

R. Carnap, *Logical Foundations of Probability*, RKP, 1950, Chicago UP, 1962. (Full treatment of confirmation and two kinds of probability, with chapter summaries. See pp. 211ff. for total evidence requirement, and pp. 562 ff. for $c*$ and $c\dagger$).

L. J. Cohen, *The Implications of Induction*, Methuen, 1970. (Develops theory of confirmation not based on calculus of chances, though he prefers to call it 'support'. Also discusses acceptability.)

N. Goodman, *Fact, Fiction and Forecast*, Athlone Press, 1954, revised in later editions. (Introduction and discussion of 'grue' paradox.)

C. Glymour, *Theory and Evidence*, Princeton UP, 1980. (Develops a theory of confirmation, with extensive use of actual case-studies, and criticisms of various different theories.)

C. G. Hempel, 'Studies in the logic of confirmation', *Mind*, 1945, reprinted with addition in his *Aspects of Scientific Explanation*, Free Press, 1965. (Starts with discussion of his paradox, and then elaborates his own theory of confirmation. See index of *Aspects* for discussion of requirement of total evidence.)

J. Hullett and R. Schwartz, 'Grue: some remarks', *Journal of Philosophy*, 1967. (Survey of ways of treating Goodman's paradox. Several other relevant articles in same and preceding volume. Cf. also D. Stalker (ed.), *Grue! The New Riddle of Induction*, Open Court, 1984. (Fifteen essays, about half specially written, with introduction and 176–page bibliography summarizing, often in great detail, 316 items.)

W. Kneale, *Probability and Induction*, Oxford UP, 1949. (Introduction to these subjects, though getting more technical towards end. § 23 discusses confirmation and elimination.)

K. Popper, *The Logic of Scientific Discovery*, Hutchinson, 1959 (German original 1934). (Chapter 10 introduces corroboration.)

I. Scheffler, *The Anatomy of Inquiry*, Knopf, 1963, RKP, 1964. (Contains discussion of Hempel and Goodman paradoxes.)

R. Swinburne, *An Introduction to Confirmation Theory*, Methuen, 1973. (See first chapter for confirmation and probability.)

Connectionism

Conjunction and disjunction. A compound sentence is a *conjunction* if its component sentences are joined by 'and'. It is a *disjunction* if they are joined by 'or'. The component sentences are, respectively, *conjuncts*, which are *conjoined*, and *disjuncts*, which are *disjoined*. 'Conjunction' and 'disjunction' can also mean the logical operations of forming such expressions. 'And' and 'or' here have only their joining force, without signifying, e.g. temporal order (as in 'He came and went'). 'Or' is usually *inclusive* ('either and perhaps both'), but can be *exclusive* ('either but not both'). Sometimes *alternation* replaces 'disjunction', with *alternant* and *alternate* for 'disjunct' and 'disjoin'. Occasionally 'disjunction' and 'alternation' are distinguished, 'disjunction' being kept for the exclusive sense. Conjunctions in the ordinary sense ('and', 'or', etc.) are in logic called *connectives*, and are among constants (see VARIABLE) and OPERATORS. See also AGGLOMERATION.

P. F. Strawson, *An Introduction to Logical Theory*, Methuen, 1952, pp. 77–92. (Connectives in logic and ordinary language. Cf. R. E. Gahringer, 'Intensional conjunction', *Mind*, 1970 (brief note on senses of 'and').)

Connected. A relation is connected or connective if it holds, one way or the other, between any two among those objects which can, without absurdity, have the relation to something. It is *connected in a domain* (i.e. sphere, class) if it is connected when only the objects in that domain are considered, e.g. *earlier than* is connected in the domain of years (of any two years one is earlier than the other), but not in that of events (two different events can be simultaneous).

Connectionism. Any group of theories of the mind which model it on information processing systems known as 'neural networks', using the idea of 'parallel processing', whereby several different sets of interactions between nodes in a computer network occur simultaneously, or in parallel. In this way, separate elements to carry separate pieces of information are not needed, in contrast to theories like the trace theory of MEMORY or the LANGUAGE OF THOUGHT hypothesis. How far this represents a fundamentally new approach is disputed.

B. Beakley and P. Ludlow (eds), *The Philosophy of Mind: Classical Problems/Contemporary Issues*, MIT Press, 1992. (Part IV includes relevant items.)

W. Bechtel and A. Abrahamsen, *Connectionism and the Mind*, Blackwell, 1991; *An Introduction to Parallel Processing in Networks*, Blackwell, 1991. (General introduction.)

Connective

*P. N. Johnson-Laird, *The Computer and the Mind: an Introduction to Cognitive Science*, Fontana, 1988, chapter 10. (Elementary introduction. Cf. also T. Crane, *The Mechanical Mind: a Philosophical Introduction to Minds, Machines and Representation*, Penguin, 1995, pp. 154–62.

Connective. See CONJUNCTION, CONNECTED.

Connotation. See MEANING.

Consciousness. The word 'conscious' seems to have more than one sense, a fact which may have led to confusion on some of the topics mentioned below. In particular, two senses need distinguishing. In a strong sense to be conscious involves reflective awareness and perhaps a conception of oneself as opposed to other things. In this sense consciousness involves some intellectual or rational capacity and may be limited to the human level. But in a weaker sense anything that can have sensory experiences, especially that of feeling pain, can be called conscious. Problems will then also arise about the relations between these senses, and perhaps others: where, for instance, do being conscious *of* something and being conscious *that* something fit in, and what sort of things can one be conscious of?

In the early and mid-twentieth century the influence of verificationism led to a decaying of introspective psychology and encouraging of behaviourism and materialism, at least in their methodological versions; consciousness therefore, while seldom denied outright, received little attention, in either of its senses. Recently, however, it has returned to favour. How far can any description be given of what seems ineffable, e.g. the colour red as it appears to our sight? Cf. QUALE and the problems mentioned there. Can consciousness, without necessarily being denied, be dispensed with in describing our mental life in physical or FUNCTIONALIST terms? Can consciousness be studied and defined in its own right, or can it only be regarded as a feature of various mental phenomena, such as feelings, thoughts or emotions? Are animals conscious, and could artefacts ever be so? What would count as their being so? Freud taught us that desires etc. can be unconscious, so what account should we give of these? See MIND.

P. Carruthers, 'Brute experience', *Journal of Philosophy*, 1989. (Claims non-human animals are not conscious.)

M. Davies and G. W. Humphries (eds), *Consciousness*, Blackwell, 1993. (Essays, both new and reprinted, covering psychological and philosophical issues, and with a long introduction.)

Consequentialism

D. C. Dennett, *Consciousness Explained*, Little, Brown, 1991. (Offers to explain how consciousness arises.)

F. Dretske, 'Conscious experience,' *Mind*, 1992. (Consciousness of and consciousness that, etc.)

O. Flanagan, *Consciousness Reconsidered*, MIT Press, 1992. (Claims that consciousness, though real, is 'neither miraculous nor terminally mysterious' (p. xi), and can be explained in terms of the science of the brain.)

R. Kirk, *Raw Feeling*, Clarendon, 1994. (Claims to bridge the gap between physical phenomena in the brain and conscious phenomena like sensations by showing that there are essential links between them.)

W. G. Lycan, *Consciousness*, MIT Press, 1987. (Defends a version of functionalism.)

T. Nagel, 'What is it like to be a bat?', *Philosophical Review*, 1974, often reprinted. (Influential in rehabilitation of interest in consciousness.)

K. V. Wilkes, 'Is consciousness important?', *British Journal for the Philosophy of Science*, 1984. (No.)

Consequences. See CAUSATION.

Consequential characteristics. See SUPERVENIENCE.

Consequentialism. Doctrine that the rightness of an act is to be judged solely in terms of its consequences, either actual or expected. A weaker form holds that there are no moral principles which cannot at least sometimes be legitimately overridden because of the consequences of applying them. UTILITARIANISM is one form of consequentialism. On the difficulty of distinguishing acts from their consequences cf. ACTION. Consequentialism is much the same as teleology in ETHICS, though perhaps slightly wider in allowing aims like increasing one's own virtue.

J. Cargile, 'On consequentialism', *Analysis*, vol. 29, 1969.

P. Foot, 'Utiltarianism and the virtues', *Mind*, 1985. (Attacks consequentialism. Discussed by S. Scheffler, ibid.)

D. Parfit, *Reasons and Persons*, Oxford UP, 1986. (Part 1 discusses consequentialism.)

P. Pettit (ed.), *Consequentialism*, Dartmouth Publishing Company, 1993. (Wide-ranging collection of relevant essays. Fuller and more advanced then Scheffler (ed.).)

S. Scheffler, *The Rejection of Consequentialism*, Clarendon, 1982. (Tentatively defends compromise between consequentialism and deontology.)

Consistent

*S. Scheffler (ed.), *Consequentialism and its Critics*, Oxford UP, 1988. (Anthology.)

M. Slote, *Common Sense Morality and Consequentialism*, RKP, 1985. (Balances these two against each other. Cf. also H. Sidgwick, *The Methods of Ethics*, Macmillan, 1874, final version, 1907, part 3.)

Consistent. One or more propositions form a consistent set if no contradiction can be deduced from the set. An AXIOM SYSTEM is consistent if no contradiction can be derived within it, i.e. by the rules it specifies. For some purposes, e.g. for systems without negation, other definitions are given, such as that a system is consistent if not every well-formed formula (see AXIOM SYSTEM) of the relevant kind can be derived in it. But the equivalence of different definitions cannot be taken for granted. Usually it is held that a logically false proposition or a contradiction is inconsistent with every proposition since every set it belongs to will imply a contradiction. But some have rejected this and insisted that whether two propositions are consistent with *each other* cannot be determined on the basis of either alone (Nelson); they would say, e.g., that 'Twice two is five' is consistent with 'Twice three is seven', but not with 'Twice two is seven'. See also VALID (for 'sound').

W. A. Hodges, *Logic*, Penguin, 1977. (See its index.)

E. J. Lemmon, *Beginning Logic*, Nelson, 1965. (See its index.)

E. J. Nelson, 'Intensional relations', *Mind*, 1930. (Consistency as involving both of two propositions.)

Constant. See VARIABLE.

Constatives. See SPEECH ACTS.

Content. A term whose use has altered between its appearance in the nineteenth century and its present-day uses. Propositional attitudes (attitudes which involve propositions, like belief, desire, fear, doubt, thought, imagination, surmise) have something which they are or consist in and something (real or unreal) which they are of or directed towards. Meinong called the former the idea and the latter the object; he then distinguished within the idea the act itself and the content, being among the first to insist on this distinction between content and object. Later writers, however, use 'content' rather differently, and more in the sense in which Meinong used 'object'. The content of a belief is the proposition or state of affairs towards which it is directed, while the object is the thing (real or unreal) which the belief is about; both of these seem nearer to what Meinong meant by 'object', and the content is no longer part of the propositional attitude (or 'idea') itself. If I believe that Napoleon won at Waterloo, you believe that Wellington won at Waterloo, and Smith believes that Don Quixote won at Waterloo, then the contents of our respective beliefs are the propositions that Napoleon won at Waterloo, that Wellington did so, and that Don Quixote did so, while the objects of the beliefs are respectively Napoleon, Wellington and Don Quixote.

Perception too has a content, though this may differ from the content of judgments based on it. I might see a statue as a man, or the sun as larger at sunset than at noon, without being deceived in either case. My perception has a content representing the world as containing a man before me, or as containing an enlarged sun, while my judgments have contents conflicting with these. A further question is whether perceptual content always involves the perceiver's having the relevant concepts. Could a child's perception represents something (rightly or wrongly) as being, say, octagonal, if the child lacked the concept of an octagon?

An important distinction in the philosophy of mind has recently been made between broad (or wide) and narrow content in analysing a mental state. This corresponds to the distinction explained in the first paragraph of INTERNALISM AND EXTERNALISM. The broad content of a mental state is that content which it would have on an externalist analysis, while the narrow content is that which it would have on an internalist analysis. There is then a question about whether some or all of those mental states that have a content in the sense we are discussing can have both types of content. The terms 'broad' (or 'wide') and 'narrow' are applied similarly to various related notions.

See also INDIVIDUALISM.

P. A. Boghossian, 'The status of content', *Philosophical Review*, 1990. (Argues against irrealism (see REALISM) concerning content.)

*T. Crane, *The Mechanical Mind: a Philosophical Introduction to Minds, Machines and Mental Representation*, Penguin, 1995, chapter 1. (Elementary introduction.)

F. Jackson and P. Pettit, 'Functionalism and broad content', *Mind*, 1988. (Claims that functionalism as a theory of mind can cope with the broad/narrow distinction. Cf. also discussion by M. Rowlands in *Mind*, 1989.)

A. Meinong, *On Emotional Presentation*, Northwestern UP, 1972 (German original, 1917). (See chapter 7.)

J. A. Passmore, *A Hundred Years of Philosophy*, Duckworth, 1957, 2nd edn, 1966. (See pp. 179–83; pp. 178–81 in Penguin edn, 1968.)

Constructivism

C. Peacocke, *Sense and Content*, Oxford UP, 1983, chapters 1 and
2. (Distinguishes sensational properties and representational content in the case of perception, followed by applications of the
distinction. Cf. also his 'Analogue content' in *Proceedings of
the Aristotelian Society*, supplementary vol., 1986, for a (difficult)
discussion of non-conceptual content in the case of perception,
going beyond his former position: see p. 16, and for further references p. 14, n. 11. See also T. Crane (ed.), *The Contents of Experience*, Cambridge UP, 1992, chapters 5 and 6, and J. McDowell,
Mind and World, Harvard UP, 1993, Lecture III, claiming content
that is to be available for rational thought must itself involve
concepts (difficult).)

S. Sajama and M. Kamppinen, *A Historical Introduction to Phenomenology*, Croom Helm, 1987. (Historical discussion of earlier
treatments of content.)

A. Woodfield (ed.), *Thought and Content: Essays on Intentionality*,
Clarendon, 1982. (General essays on the nature, types, structure
and roles of content.)

Constructivism. See INTUITIONISM.

Contextualism. In general, any view emphasizing the importance
of appeal to a context in answering a given question. In aesthetics,
the doctrine that a work of art can only be appreciated in terms of
its context. In philosophy of science, the doctrine that theoretical
terms like 'electron' have meaning (*contextual meaning*) only by
appearing as terms in deductive systems containing theorems which
are empirically testable. In ethics, the doctrine that all values are
instrumental (see GOOD), or else that moral problems both arise
and can be solved only when we already accept some moral principles. These principles can be questioned only in the light of further
principles.

Contingent. Normally, neither necessary nor impossible. See
MODALITIES.

Contradiction. A proposition false on logical grounds, or (though
less commonly in philosophy) the propounding of something inconsistent, either in itself or with something already propounded. The
law or *principle of contradiction* (also called that of non-
contradiction) says that nothing can simultaneously have and lack
the same property, or that a proposition and its negation cannot
both be true. Two propositions are *contradictories* if one is the
negation of the other, or if they cannot both be true nor both false
('X is black', X is not black'). They are *contraries* if they cannot

both be true but can both be false ('*X* is black', '*X* is white'), and
sub-contraries if they cannot both be false but can both be true ('*X*
is not black', '*X* is not white'). These terms can also be applied to
predicates. 'Black' and 'white' are contrary predicates because '*X*
is black' and '*X* is white' are contrary propositions. But contraries
need not be opposites, i.e. at opposite ends of a scale which does
not stretch further in either direction. 'Black' and 'grey' are contraries but not opposites, and so are red and yellow if regarded as on
a scale stretching towards purple at one end or green at the other
or both. Of two contradictory terms one and only one must apply
to anything in their range of significance, but neither need apply to
things outside that range. 'Black' and 'not black' are contradictory
predicates even if neither is true (or false) of, say, numbers. But if
we say both are false of numbers they become contraries. In a loose
sense a proposition contradicts its contraries, since it entails (see
IMPLICATION) their contradictories. '*X* is black' contradicts '*X* is
white', if it entails '*X* is not white'.

Contraposition. In a categorical proposition of traditional formal
logic, replacement of a proposition by another (its *contrapositive*)
which follows logically from it and is got by negating the subject
and predicate and interchanging them. The contrapositive of 'All
cats are animals' is 'All non-animals are non-cats'. Contraposition
can be validly carried out on only some of the traditional types of
proposition. Contraposition of a conditional or hypothetical proposition negates its antecedent and its consequent and interchanges
them. 'If grass is green, snow is white' has as contrapositive 'If
snow is not white, grass is not green'. This latter process is occasionally called *transposition*.

Contraries. See CONTRADICTION.

Contravalid. See VALID.

Conventionalism. In logic and mathematics, any doctrine according
to which A PRIORI truths or necessary truths are thought to be true
by linguistic convention. Applied to science, conventionalist views
emphasize that the laws and hypotheses we accept or postulate
depend on convention (though we may have good reason for adopting one convention rather than another): we *can* explain the data
of astronomy by Ptolemaic epicycles, it is claimed, though at the
price of extreme complexity. For a conventionalist, a law found to
be successful for predicting, etc., becomes analytic, i.e. nothing is
any longer allowed to count as falsifying it. On some views it is only

Convention T

at this stage that it becomes a law. The real issue is perhaps *how far* convention enters in.

Conventionalism is close to INSTRUMENTALISM and PRAGMATISM. See also MODALITIES, and cf. the views of Quine as discussed under ANALYTIC and TRANSLATION.

K. Britton, J. O. Urmson, W. C. Kneale, 'Are necessary truths true by convention?', *Proceedings of the Aristotelian Society*, supplementary vol., 1947.

H. Poincaré, *Science and Hypothesis*, 1902, transl. 1905. (Supports a conventionalist view of science.)

K. R. Popper, *The Logic of Scientific Discovery*, Hutchinson, 1959 (German original, 1934). (Critical of some aspects (only?) of conventionalism in science.)

W. V. O. Quine, 'Truth by convention' in his *The Ways of Paradox and Other Essays*, Random House, 1966 (originally published 1936 and variously reprinted). (Quine's early view, developed in his later writings.)

A. Sidelle, *Necessity, Essence, and Individuation: a Defense of Conventionalism*, Cornell UP, 1989.

Convention T. See MEANING.

Conversion. In traditional formal logic, replacement of a proposition by a logically equivalent one (its *converse*) having as subject the original predicate (*simple conversion*). 'No dogs are cats' is the converse of 'No cats are dogs'. In *conversion per accidens* the converse is implied by, but does not imply, the original. 'Some pets are dogs' is the converse per accidens of 'All dogs are pets'. Conversion of either type can be validly carried out only on some of the traditional types of proposition.

Corroboration. See CONFIRMATION.

Cosmological argument. An argument for God's existence, originating with Aristotle but taking various forms. Some versions of it are called the *first cause argument*. This is that everything requires a cause and God must exist to be the first cause – usually not first in time (Aristotle thought the universe was eternal) but as a sustaining cause. Aristotle gives the example of a stick moving a stone but itself simultaneously moved by a man. Another version of the cosmological argument, which is due to Aquinas, is that the universe exists only CONTINGENTLY (see MODALITIES), and therefore must depend on something which exists necessarily, namely God. Kant claimed that this version shared the main defect of the ONTOLOGICAL

ARGUMENT. The argument is called cosmological because it argues from the nature of the cosmos or universe, which the ontological argument, and that from religious experience, do not. However, the argument from DESIGN, which also argues from the nature of the universe, is usually treated as distinct from the cosmological argument.

W. L. Craig and D. Smith, *Theism, Atheism, and Big Bang Cosmology*. Clarendon, 1993. (Debate between theist and atheist in alternate chapters. Sometimes technical. For historical account, distinguishing three importantly different versions, see W. L. Craig, *The Cosmological Argument from Plato to Leibniz*, Macmillan, 1980.)

A. Flew, *An Introduction to Western Philosophy*, Thames and Hudson, 1971, revised edn, 1989, chapter 6.

A. Kenny, *The Five Ways*, RKP, 1969. (Aquinas's arguments for God's existence. First three are relevant.)

J. L. Mackie, *The Miracle of Theism*, Clarendon, 1982, chapter 5. (This and Flew are critical of the argument.)

Counterfactuals. See CONDITIONALS.

Counterpart. See POSSIBLE WORLDS.

Count noun. Roughly, *count nouns* have plurals and can take numerical adjectives (e.g. 'cat'), while *mass nouns (mass words, mass terms)* do neither of these things (e.g. 'snow', in its main sense). Many words are both, in different senses (e.g. 'wood'). Count nouns, if defined in this grammatical way, need not provide a principle of counting (see SORTAL); 'thing' is grammatically a count noun, but one cannot unambiguously count the things in a room: what constitutes one thing? Mass nouns may or may not include some abstract nouns. See also SORTAL.

N. Griffin, *Relative Identity*, Oxford UP, 1977, chapter 2. (Count terms and mass terms. See also review by H. W. Noonan, *Mind*, 1979, p. 300.)

F. J. Pelletier (ed.), *Mass Terms: Some Philosophical Problems*, Reidel, 1979. (Includes bibliography.)

R. Smith, 'Mass terms, generic expressions, and Plato's theory of Forms', *Journal for the History of Philosophy*, 1978. (Mainly on Plato, but includes discussion of relevant issues.)

Covering law model. See EXPLANATION.

Criterion. Something providing a conclusive way of knowing

Criterion

whether something exists, or whether a word is used correctly. Criteria must be logically, and not merely inductively, evidence for what they are criteria of. Philosophical interest in criteria stems mainly from Wittgenstein, though what precisely he meant by the term is disputed. If some disease is defined as the presence of a certain bacillus, then finding that someone has the bacillus gives us a criterion for saying he has that disease, while finding simply that he has an inflammation gives us only a symptom. A symptom is something that we know from experience always accompanies the thing in question, but it does not have to do so by definition. Symptoms are therefore one kind of evidence of the thing's presence. Another kind is what only sometimes accompanies the thing. Wittgenstein emphasizes that criteria and symptoms fluctuate as circumstances differ or alter.

But a criterion, though linked by definition with what it is a criterion of, need not be present in every case. Horses are by definition quadrupeds, so that being a quadruped is part of a criterion for being a horse, but occasional freaks may have five legs. More importantly, we only have a concept of pain, Wittgenstein thinks, because there are publicly accessible criteria for telling when someone is in pain – but pain or its absence can be simulated. This suggests that criteria are important for applying a concept in general rather than in particular cases (see Hamlyn). Cf. also Wittgenstein's 'family resemblance' view of UNIVERSALS. A concept may have more than one criterion.

A feature is often loosely called a criterion of something if it is one of a set of features which jointly constitute a criterion of it in the strict sense. If being maned, neighing and a quadruped is a criterion of being a horse, being maned is loosely a criterion of it, though not all maned things are horses. See GOOD for meaning and criteria, which some writers (e.g. Hare) relate differently in the case of value terms like 'good' than in the case of other terms.

Sometimes epistemological and metaphysical senses of 'criterion' are distinguished (MacDonald), though these may be aspects of the same thing.

For *Criterion T* see MEANING.

R. Albritton, 'On Wittgenstein's use of the term "criterion" ', *Journal of Philosophy*, 1959, reprinted with afterthoughts in Pitcher (below). (Thinks Wittgenstein had two views on criteria. Many detailed references to text.)

J. W. Cook, 'Human beings', in P. Winch (ed.), *Studies in the Philosophy of Wittgenstein*, RKP, 1969. (Both these discuss criteria and their use in philosophy of mind.)

Cybernetics

D. W. Hamlyn, *The Theory of Knowledge*, Macmillan, 1970, pp. 68–75. (Concepts and criteria.)

R. M. Hare, *The Language of Morals*, Oxford UP, 1952, chapter 6. (Meaning and criteria, with reference to 'good'.)

S. MacDonald, 'Aristotle on the homonymy of the good', *Archiv für Geschichte der Philosophie*, 1989. (See p. 159 n. 26.)

J. McDowell, 'Criteria, defeasibility, and knowledge' in J. Dancy (ed.), *Perceptual Knowledge*, Oxford UP, 1988. (Offers interpretation of 'criterion' in context of how we know of someone else's feelings or thoughts, and more generally of a world independent of ourselves.)

L. Wittgenstein, *The Blue and Brown Books*, Blackwell, 1958, written much earlier, pp. 24–5. (Nearest Wittgenstein comes to defining 'criteria'. Cf. section on criteria in N. Malcolm's review of Wittgenstein in *Philosophical Review*, 1954, revised and reprinted in Malcolm's *Knowledge and Certainty*, 1963, and in G. Pitcher (ed.), *Wittgenstein*, Macmillan, 1966, and cf. for further references N. Griffin, *Relative Identity*, Oxford UP, 1977, p. 49 n. 3).

C. Wright, *Realism, Meaning, and Truth*, 2nd edn, Blackwell, 1993. (Chapters 12 and 13 (7 and 8 in 1st edn, 1987) discuss role and usefulness of criteria in theory of meaning, tending to sceptical conclusion.)

Croce, Benedetto, 1866–1952. Born in Abbruzzi, he worked mainly in Naples. Though he wrote also on economics, ethics, politics and history, he is now best known for his work in aesthetics and literary criticism, in which he influenced COLLINGWOOD. His system was idealist in flavour, influenced by HEGEL and VICO, and centred on art as the expression of 'intuition', which is a certain kind of knowledge. Croce claims that aesthetics ends up as the general study of language. *Estetica come scienza dell'espressione e linguistica generale (Aesthetic)*, 1902. *Breviario di Estetica (The Essence of Aesthetic)*, 1913 (shorter work, originally published in translation in America (Houston), 1912).

Curve-fitting problem. See CONFIRMATION.

Cybernetics. From a Greek word for 'steer', cognate with 'govern'. The science of self-steering or self-adjusting machines, raising questions for philosophy like 'Can machines think?'.

M. A. Arbib, *The Metaphorical Mind: an Introduction to Cybernetics as Artificial Intelligence and Brain Theory*, Wiley, 1972, 2nd edn, 1988.

N. Wiener, *Cybernetics, or Control and Communication in the*

Cybernetics

Animal and the Machine, MIT Press, 1948, corrected and expanded, 1961. (Introduction by a pioneer in it. See also J. F. Young, *Cybernetics*, Iliffe Books/Elsevier, 1969, who accuses Wiener of unnecessary mathematics.)

D

Dasein. See EXISTENTIALISM.

Davidson, Donald. 1917–. Born in Springfield, Mass., he has worked mainly in Stanford, Chicago and Berkeley. He is notable equally for his contributions to the philosophies of language and of mind. In particular, he has used an idea of TARSKI'S to analyse meaning in terms of TRUTH CONDITIONS, given an important role to EVENTS, and made causation respectable in explanations of action with his 'anomalous MONISM'. His publications include *Essays on Actions and Events*, 1980; *Inquiries into Truth and Interpretation*, 1984; both these reprint important earlier articles.

Decidable. Theories, in the sense in which arithmetic is a theory, are decidable if formalizations exist for them which are COMPLETE. In systems without CONTINGENT propositions, such as formalizations of arithmetic, a well-formed formula (see AXIOM SYSTEM) is decidable if and only if it or its negation is a theorem. Where contingent propositions enter, as in formalizations of the propositional CALCULUS, a well-formed formula is decidable if and only if one can prove whether it is logically true, logically false, or neither. A *decision procedure* (one kind of ALGORITHM) lets one decide this mechanically by simply following a rule in finitely many steps. Decision procedures exist for the propositional and monadic predicate CALCULI, but not, in general, for more complex systems. Proof that such a procedure exists, or does not exist, for a given sphere is called a *positive* or *negative solution*, respectively, to the *decision problem*. The negative solution for the predicate calculus (beyond the monadic) is *Church's theorem* (1936).

Decision problem

See also RECURSIVE.

Decision problem. See DECIDABLE.

Decision procedure. See DECIDABLE.

Decision theory. The mathematical theory of how it is rational to act when confronted with alternatives which have various utilities and various probabilities. Where one is playing against rational opponents, not against nature or 'blind chance' (e.g. in taking account of the weather), we have *game theory* or *theory of games*. But game theory is sometimes treated as a part of decision theory. See also PRISONER'S DILEMMA.

M. Bacharach and S. Hurley (eds), *Foundations of Decision Theory: Issues and Advances*, Blackwell, 1991. (Set of essays treating the issues from various angles.)
*M. D. Davis, *Game Theory*, Basic Books, 1970. (Elementary.)

Deduction. An argument is deductive if it draws a conclusion from certain premises on the grounds that to deny the conclusion while keeping the premises would lead to a contradiction. Given 'All men are mortal and Socrates is a man' we can deduce 'Socrates is mortal', because it would be contradictory to deny it. But 'deduction' is used more loosely by early philosophers and outside philosophy. See also NATURAL DEDUCTION.

Defeasible. Concepts, and claims about where they apply, are called defeasible when they are always open to objection, and the objections are irredeemably heterogeneous; e.g. it is sometimes held that no definite criteria can be given for when concepts like freewill and responsibility apply. Compare the notions of *imperfect* and *prima facie duties* (see OUGHT).

H. L. A. Hart, 'The ascription of responsibility and rights', *Proceedings of the Aristotelian Society*, 1948–9, reprinted in A. Flew (ed.), *Logic and Language*, 1st series, Blackwell, 1951. (Hart has since withdrawn this paper, for reasons not affecting this reference.)

Definist fallacy. See NATURALISM.

Definition. A definition gives a *definiens* or defining expression for a *definiendum* or what is to be defined. 'Definition' itself can stand for the sentence doing the defining, for the process of doing it, or for the definiens. Various rules for definitions have traditionally

Definition

been given, but these are now widely regarded as unduly restrictive, or as mere practical guides.

In a *real* or *essentialist definition* the definiendum is an essence or concept. A real definition is therefore an analysis of a concept (but see Mill). In a *nominal definition* the definiendum is a term or word. 'Real' here means applying to the thing to concept, as against the word. 'Nominal' means 'applying to the word, as against the thing or concept'. The phrase 'real definition' is little used now. However, even a nominalist (i.e. here, one who accepts only nominal definitions) may reserve a word for a certain concept and then use a definition of the word to analyse the concept.

A definition may aim to clarify the meaning of an already existing term (*lexical* or *dictionary definitions*, e.g., ' "Puppy" in English means "young dog" '.) Or it may introduce an abbreviation or stipulate how a term is going to be used (*stipulative definitions*, e.g. 'By "puppy" I shall mean any dog shorter than twelve inches'.) Stipulative definitions are *prescriptive* in that they prescribe how a word is to be used, as are lexical definitions in so far as they do not merely report usage but prescribe standards of 'good' usage. Normally it is not the case that just any explanation of a term counts as a definition. A definition must have a certain adequacy, completeness, and universality. A definition should normally state NECESSARY AND SUFFICIENT CONDITIONS for applying the definiendum. 'A puppy is a dog' is true, but not a definition for not all dogs are puppies.

Contextual definitions or *definitions in use* define a term indirectly by giving an equivalent for a whole context in which it occurs. One might define 'average' by explaining how it is used in sentences like 'The average man has two and a half children'. Two rather technical notions may be briefly mentioned. In a *recursive definition* the term defined occurs in the definiens, but in a way that avoids circularity. The term 'ancestor of' might be recursively defined as 'parent of, or ancestor of a parent of'. Cf. RECURSIVE. An *inductive definition* or *definition by induction* defines what it is for a term x in a series to have a certain property; it does this by defining what it is for the first term in the series to have the property, and then defining what it is for any term to have it, given that its predecessor has it. Taking the above example we define x as being an ancestor of y by saying that a parent of y is an ancestor of y, and any parent of an ancestor of y is an ancestor of y. Recursive and inductive definitions thus come to the same thing.

In an *ostensive definition* (not properly a definition at all) an instance of what the term applies to is physically pointed to ('Red is that colour there', or just 'Red!', said while pointing to a tomato). For *impredicative definitions* see theory of TYPES. In *persuasive defi-*

77

Democracy (paradox of)

nitions an emotionally charged term is given a revised factual significance, to which the emotional charge than attaches. If one dislikes those who live on rent, one might redefine 'fascist' to include them. For *extensional* and *intensional definitions*, see UNIVERSALS.

What kinds of words can be defined will largely depend on the kind of definition, and on how rigorously we interpret 'definition'. A common problem is whether a given term can be defined without going outside a specified set of terms, e.g. can 'life' be defined in chemical terms?

J. S. Mill, *A System of Logic*, Longmans, Green and Co., 1843, book 1 chapter 8. (See § 5 for real definitions.)

K. R. Popper, *The Open Society and its Enemies*, RKP, 1945. (Vol. 2 includes famous attack on use of definitions outside technical contexts.)

R. Robinson, *Definition*, Clarendon, 1950. (Full-scale study, taking very liberal view of what counts as definition.)

C. L. Stevenson, *Ethics and Language*, Yale UP, 1945, chapter 9. (Persuasive definitions.)

A. Tarski (see bibliography to TRUTH AND FALSITY. *Inter alia*, distinguishes formal correctness and material adequacy of definitions.)

Democracy (paradox of). See VOTING PARADOX.

Denial. See NEGATION.

Denial of antecedent. Fallacy of arguing that if the antecedent of a conditional statement is false, so is the consequent, e.g. 'If all cats are black, Tiddles is black; but not all cats are black; so Tiddles is not black.'

Denotation. See MEANING, INTENSIONALITY, DESCRIPTIONS.

Denoting phrases. See DESCRIPTIONS.

Deontic. See ETHICS.

Deontological. See ETHICS.

Descartes, René. 1596–1650. Born at La Haye in France and educated by the Jesuits, he travelled in his youth and then lived mostly in Holland, but finally at the Swedish court. Usually known as the first of the 'continental RATIONALISTS', he contributed to mathematics, as well as philosophy, inventing 'Cartesian co-ordinates' and

Descriptions (theory of)

analytical geometry. In philosophy he aimed to establish a basis for certainty by pursuing SCEPTICISM as far as possible, using a 'method of doubt' until he reached something he could not doubt, his principle 'Cogito ergo sum' ('I think therefore I am'), on which he built up a systematic philosophy. He is particularly noted for his body/mind dualism. *Discours de la méthode pour bien conduire sa raison et chercher les vérités dans les sciences (Discourse on Method)*, 1637. *Meditationes de Prima Philosophia (Meditations on the First Philosophy)*, 1641. *Principia Philosophiae (Principles of Philosophy)*, 1644. See also ANALYTIC, CARTESIAN, FOUNDATIONALISM, HOBBES, INCORRIGIBLE, MALEBRANCHE, RYLE, SPACE, SPINOZA, SUBSTANCE, THINKING.

J. Cottingham *et al.* (eds), *The Philosophical Writings of Descartes*, 3 vols, Cambridge UP, 1985, 1984, 1991.

Descriptions (theory of). Theory devised by Russell to analyse sentences containing 'denoting phrases'. Russell originally recognized two ways of picking something out in discourse. One could name it. Or one could *denote* it, pick it out by using terms with a general meaning. 'Socrates' names Socrates. 'That man' does not name Socrates, or anyone, but might serve to pick Socrates out because of general rules for the use of 'that' and 'man'. Russell therefore recognized what he called *denoting phrases*. These were of two kinds. *Definite descriptions* begin with the definite article or its equivalent ('That man' equals 'The man over there'). *Indefinite descriptions* begin with the indefinite article. But because definite and indefinite descriptions can occur in meaningful sentences where there is nothing for them to denote, as in 'The present king of France is bald', he concluded that they cannot really function by denoting after all, and that the grammatical form of sentences containing them is misleading as to their logical form. In fact he abandoned denoting, though he temporarily kept the term 'denoting phrase'. The theory of descriptions says that the logical form of the above example is: 'There is exactly one present king of France, and there is no present king of France who is not bald.' Variant alternative formulations exist. Since what a sentence means should not depend on what happens to exist, Russell applied this analysis to all denoting phrases, including 'the present queen of England' as well as 'the present king of France'. These phrases are then called *incomplete symbols* (see LOGICAL CONSTRUCTIONS).

Contrasted with denoting phrases are *logically proper names*, whose meaning is what they name. Ordinary proper names which do not name anything (and ultimately, for various reasons, all ordinary proper names) he regarded as disguised descriptions, and so as

Descriptivism

incomplete symbols, e.g. 'Apollo' stands for 'The Greek sun-god'. Cf. MEANING.

K. Donnellan, 'Reference and definite descriptions', *Philosophical Review*, 1966. (Often reprinted. Distinguishes attributive and referential ways of interpreting definite descriptions.)

L. Linsky, *Referring*, RKP, 1967. (Mediates between Russell and Strawson.)

S. Neale, *Descriptions*, MIT Press, 1990. (Develops and defends Russell's theory, in particular treating pronouns at length.)

B. Russell, 'On denoting', *Mind*, 1905, reprinted in his *Logic and Knowledge*, Allen and Unwin, 1956, and elsewhere. (Original version of theory of descriptions.)

R. M. Sainsbury, *Russell*, RKP, 1979. (Chapter 4 discusses the theory.)

P. F. Strawson, 'On referring', *Mind*, 1950, often reprinted. (Attacks the theory. Cf. also Strawson's 'Identifying reference and truth-values', *Theoria*, 1964, reprinted (with 'On referring') in his *Logico-Linguistic Papers*, Methuen, 1971. Russell replies in 'Mr Strawson on referring', *Mind*, 1957, reprinted in his *My Philosophical Development*, Allen and Unwin, 1959.)

Descriptivism. See NATURALISM.

Design (argument from). Argument, with many versions, for God's existence, relying on apparent pattern, design or purpose in the universe. Also called the teleological argument, and, by Kant, the *physico-theological argument*. See also COSMOLOGICAL ARGUMENT.

A. Flew, *An Introduction to Western Philosophy*, Thames and Hudson, 1971, revised edn, 1989, chapter 6.

J. L. Mackie, *The Miracle of Theism*, Clarendon, 1982, chapter 8.

Designate. A name designates its bearer, and so only designates at all if it has a real bearer, though it may be quite intelligible without one ('Pickwick'). Occasionally 'designates' means 'connotes' (see MEANING). A *rigid designator* is a term which, if it designates an object at all, would designate it in any situation provided only that the object still exists and that language remains the same. 'Square of three' is a rigid designator of nine. 'Victor of Waterloo' is a non-rigid designator of Wellington, since he could have lost the battle. The proviso about existence distinguishes the weak (and usual) from the strong sense of 'rigid designator'.

S. Kripke, 'Identity and necessity', in M. K. Munitz (ed.), *Identity*

Dialectic

and Individualism, New York UP, 1971, and in T. Honderich and
M. F. Burnyeat (eds), *Philosophy As It Is*, Penguin, 1979. (See
pp. 144–9 of original version for rigid designator.)

Designated values. See TRUTH-VALUE.

Determinates and determinables. Red is a determinate of the determinable colour, while oak is a species of the genus tree. To be an
oak is to be arboreal and deciduous, etc., but to be red is not to be
coloured and something else; red is simple in a way oak is not.

W. E. Johnson, *Logic*, Dover, 1964, vol. 1, chapter 11. (Origin of
the distinction.)
A. Prior, 'Determination, determinates and determinants', *Mind*,
1949 (in 2 parts.)
J. R. Searle. 'On determinables and resemblance', *Proceedings of
the Aristotelian Society*, supplementary vol. 1959.

Determinism. See FREEWILL.

Dewey, John. 1859–1952. Educationalist and philosopher who was
born in Vermont and worked in various American universities, the
last being Columbia. His philosophical views are usually classed as
PRAGMATIST and INSTRUMENTALIST. In particular, he is noted for his
use of *warranted assertibility* in connexion with the notion of truth.
Much of his work was concerned with applying his pragmatist views
to the study of educational theory and reform. *How We Think*,
1910. *Democracy and Education*, 1916. *Reconstruction in Philosophy*, 1920. *Human Nature and Conduct*, 1922. *The Quest for
Certainty*, 1929. *Logic: The Theory of Inquiry*, 1938.

Diagonal procedure. See RICHARD'S PARADOX

Dialectic. Literally, 'a method of conversation or debate'
(etymologically akin to 'dialogue'). 'Dialectic' originally referred to
debating tournaments, but Socrates and, at first, Plato thought that
the cultivation of philosophy, and discovery of philosophical truths,
could best be achieved by the interplay of opinions in co-operative
enquiry by question and answer. Plato therefore used 'dialectic' for
philosophical method in general, and came to apply it to whatever
method of enquiry he favoured at the time, or to the highest stage
thereof. Aristotle kept the sense of conversational interplay; but
though he confined dialectic to serious enquiry rather than *eristic*
or argumentativeness, he thought it an inferior, though sometimes
indispensable, method of enquiry because it had to start from prem-

Dialetheism

ises which were agreed to by the interlocutors rather than those which could be demonstrated to be true.

The use of 'dialectic' for debates where one reduced an opponent to contradiction helped to make 'dialectic' largely synonymous with 'logic' for the Stoics and the Middle Ages. The Aristotelian feature whereby dialectic relies on inadequate premises is seen again in Kant. In many later writers, notably Hegel and Marx, the sense of 'interplay' is transferred from the development of thought to that of the world itself. The world develops dialectically by the interplay of opposites. See also MATERIALISM.

R. Norman and S. Sayers, *Hegel, Marx and Dialectic: a Debate*, Harvester/Humanities, 1980. (Has partly annotated bibliography. Conflicting interpretations by two British philosophers who agree a dialectical philosophy cannot be the mere dogmatism Marxism is often said to be.)

G. E. L. Owen (ed.), *Aristotle on Dialectic*, Clarendon, 1968. (Essays on dialectic up to Aristotle. Varying in difficulty. Most accessible are items by Ryle (controversial), Moreau and Moraux (both in French).)

H. H. Williams, *Hegel, Heraclitus, Marx's Dialectic*, Harvester Wheatsheaf, 1989. (Shows how Hegel and Marx have different approaches to notion originated by Heraclitus.)

Dialetheism. The view that some contradictions are true, or that some things are both true and false. See also PARACONSISTENCY.

G. Priest, 'Contradiction, belief and rationality', *Proceedings of the Aristotelian Society*, 1985–6.

R. M. Sainsbury, *Paradoxes*, Cambridge UP, 1988 (revised 1995), chapter 6. (Balanced discussion.)

Dichotomy paradox. See ZENO'S PARADOXES.

Differentia. What distinguishes a species from other species of the same genus. For Aristotle there was a problem about which CATEGORY the differentia of a substance-species (man, horse, etc.) belonged to.

Disciplinary matrix. See PARADIGM.

Disjunction. See CONJUNCTION.

Disposition. Sometimes a disposition to behave in a certain way may be ascribed to something simply because it does so behave often, or, because it does so always when certain conditions are fulfilled, no matter why. But usually it is assumed that something underlies the disposition and causes its manifestations when the relevant conditions are fulfilled; then something may have a disposition without ever manifesting it, as a lump of sugar may be disposed to dissolve in water even if in fact it is never immersed. In principle, dispositions of either type can be acquired or lost; something may acquire a disposition of the first kind if it simply starts behaving in a certain way upon occasion, not having previously done so. 'Brittle', 'labile', 'greedy', 'intelligent' are typical terms for which a dispositional analysis may be offered. The usual contrast term to 'dispositional' is *occurrent*, used for what is actually in the process of happening. Sometimes 'dispositional' is contrasted with 'categorical'.

C. B. Martin, 'Dispositions and conditionals', *Philosophical Quarterly*, 1994. (Argues against conditional analysis of dispositions).

D. H. Mellor, 'In defense of dispositions', *Philosophical Review*, 1974, reprinted in his *Matters of Metaphysics*, Cambridge UP, 1991. (He asserts that dispositions are real; they must be connected to other properties, but need not have a non-dispositional base.)

E. W. Prior, R. Pargetter and F. Jackson, 'Three theses about dispositions', *American Philosophy Quarterly*, 1982. (Claims that dispositions must have causal bases, but are different from them, and are themselves causally inert. For further development see Prior's *Dispositions*, Aberdeen UP, 1985.)

Distribution. In traditional SYLLOGISTIC logic the subject of a universal proposition (see QUANTIFIER WORDS for 'universal' and 'particular') and the predicate of a negative proposition are said to be distributed. This has been taken to mean that a universal proposition and a negative proposition say something about every member of the classes which their subject and predicate, respectively, denote. The *laws* or *rules of distribution* then say that in a valid SYLLOGISM the middle term must be distributed at least once, and any term distributed in the conclusion must be distributed in its premise.

The rationale, and indeed the need and effectivenes, of the doctrine have been much disputed. Perhaps the best interpretation is this (due to Fogelin and Sinnott-Armstrong): Let S stand for the subject, and P for the predicate, in the proposition concerned. Then universal affirmative propositions say that any S is identical to some P (e.g. 'All cats are black' says that any cat is identical to some black thing); universal negative propositions say that any S is distinct from any P; particular affirmative propositions say that some S is

Division

identical to some *P*; and particular negative propositions say that some *S* is distinct from any *P*.

This notion is unconnected with the *distributive laws* or *rules* of modern logical and mathematical algebras, which govern the interchange of 'and' and 'or' (or analogous notions).

*R. Fogelin, *Understanding Arguments: an Introduction to Informal Logic*, Harcourt, Brace, Jovanovich, 1978; 4th, revised, edn (with W. Sinnott-Armstrong), 1991. (Chapter 8 gives elementary introduction.)

P. T. Geach, *Reference and Generality*, Cornell UP, 1962, chapter 1. (Attacks distribution. Cf. also his *Logic Matters*, Blackwell, 1972, chapter 2 § 1, chapter 3 §2.)

D. Makinson, 'Distribution in traditional logic', *Nous*, 1969. (Defends and generalizes distribution. Moderately technical.)

W. C. Wilcox, 'Another look at distribution', *Mind*, 1971. (Another criticism. Moderately technical.)

Division. See COMPOSITION.

Double aspect theory. Theory that mind and matter as a whole (Spinoza), or that individual minds and their corresponding bodies, are two aspects of a single substance. See also IDENTITY THEORY OF MIND.

K. Campbell, *Body and Mind*, Macmillan, 1970. (See pp. 113–16 for brief account of the theory. For Spinoza see, e.g., his *Ethics*, part 2, p. 21 n.)

Double effect. See ETHICS.

Doxastic. Concerning or involving belief or judgment. *Sub-doxastic* has been used for implicit knowledge in the second sense (see TACIT, and the Smith and Davies references there, p. 131 n. 31), i.e. for a mental state which has CONTENT but in some sense does not amount to belief, though it contributes to the formation in the mind in question of states which do. *Doxastic voluntarism* is the view that one can choose, at least to some extent, what to believe. See also INCONTINENCE.

Dualism. Any view which claims to see in the universe as a whole or in some area of concern just two fundamental entities or kinds of entity or properties, e.g. the views that a person's mind and body are irreducibly different entities, or that physical and mental properties are of irreducibly different kinds, or that all propositions can be sharply and exhaustively distinguished into the ANALYTIC and the synthetic. Antidualists may claim the alleged distinction does not exist, or is not sharp, or is not exhaustive. See also MONISM.

Duhem, Pierre, M. M. 1861–1916. Born in Paris, he worked in various French universities. He did important scientific work, notably in thermodynamics, and also engaged in the history of science. In philosophy his chief contribution was to philosophy of science. His position was akin to positivism and to conventionalism, but while he insisted on the separation of science from metaphysics, he gave metaphysics the role of providing explanations and, it might be relevant to add, he remained a Catholic. Science itself, he thought, should elaborate theories, whose purpose was not to explain but simply to systematize phenomena in ways which science found convenient. *La Théorie physique, son objet et sa structure. (The Aim and Structure of Physical Theory)*, 1906.

Dummett, Michael A. E. 1925–. Born in London, he has worked in Oxford, and is the leading exponent of antirealism (see REALISM), which he develops on the basis of mathematical INTUITIONISM. He is a leading interpreter of the philosophy of FREGE (and has also devoted much time to promoting racial harmony in the UK). His publications include *Frege: Philosophy of Language*, 1973; *Elements of Intuitionism*, 1977; *Truth and Other Enigmas*, 1978 (collected essays, probably the best introduction to his work); *The Interpretation of Frege's Philosophy*, 1981; *Frege and Other Philosophers*, 1991; *The Logical Basis of Metaphysics*, 1991; *Frege: Philosophy of Mathematics*, 1991; *Origins of Analytical Philosophy*, 1993 (German version, 1988); *The Seas of Language*, 1993 (mainly collected essays, supplementing *Truth and Other Enigmas*).

Duration. See SPACE.

Duty. See OUGHT.

Dyadic. See MONAD.

E _____

Education (philosophy of). The study of general theoretical problems of an A PRIORI kind, about the possibility, nature, aims and methods of education.

The ancient *paradox of learning* (you can't learn what you don't know, because you won't know what to seek, and won't recognize it when found) is now dead as a paradox, but not before stimulating our thought on topics such as INNATE ideas, A PRIORI knowledge, and referring; and one can still ask what *is* involved in learning.

How does education differ from indoctrination, training and programming and must indoctrination etc. be totally, or only partially, excluded? What is presupposed in the learner, e.g. what degree of rationality? Is a teacher needed, or can one educate oneself, deliberately or accidentally? Can one be educated to be rational, in any sense, and what is involved in acquiring one's first language (cf. PRIVATE LANGUAGE)?

These questions about the nature of education affect questions about its aims and methods. Is the primary aim to instil knowledge, or to instil the ability to acquire knowledge, or neither? How far is education concerned with FACTS, and of what kinds? What is involved in education in morality and (aesthetic or other) taste? Does education aiming at knowledge differ from education aiming at action?

Questions of method largely belong to the theory and practice of education rather than to its philosophy, but answers to the above questions are relevant both here and to traditional questions on the roles of nature, training, practice, play, example.

86

S. C. Brown (ed.), *Philosophers Discuss Education*, Macmillan, 1975. (Five symposia from British conference).

W. Jaeger, *Paideia*, Blackwell, 1934 and after, transl. 1939–45. (Extended treatment of education and related topics in and before the age of Plato.)

J. Kleinig, *Philosophical Issues in Education*, St Martin's Press and Croom Helm, 1982. (Philosophical discussion of wide range of issues with full bibliographies.)

A. O'Hear, *Education, Society and Human Nature*, RKP, 1981. (General introduction.)

R. S. Peters (ed.), *The Philosophy of Education*, Oxford UP, 1973. (Readings, with annotated bibliography.)

Plato, *Meno*. (Can 'virtue' (or excellence) be taught? (For paradox of learning see §§ 80–1). Cf. also *Protagoras, Republic*, books 2, 3, *Laws*, books, 1, 2, 7.)

B. Spiecker and R. Straughan (eds), *Philosophical Issues in Moral Education and Development*, Open UP, 1988. (Six papers from an international conference.)

R. Straughan and J. Wilson (eds), *Philosophers on Education*, Macmillan, 1987. (Views of some philosophers on education.)

R. Straughan and J. Wilson, *Philosophising about Education*, Holt, Rinehart and Winston, 1983. (Tries to induce critical thinking in the area.)

Effects. See CAUSATION

Egocentric particulars. See TOKEN-REFLEXIVES.

Egocentric predicament. Predicament that EMPIRICISTS tend to find themselves in because of their view that our knowledge must start from what is directly accessible to us, namely our own sensations, images, ideas, etc. This makes it hard to see how we can ever know anything else, and so leads to solipsism (see SCEPTICISM). The term was invented by R. B. Perry (1876–1957).

Eidos. See FORM.

Eleatics. Parmenides and his disciple Zeno (not Zeno the STOIC) started a philosophy of extreme monism in Elea in south Italy in the early fifth century BC. As usually interpreted, Parmenides held that reality must consist of a single, undifferentiated and unchanging object, and Zeno defended him by revealing paradoxes in rival views. With Melissus of Samos (mid fifth century), who developed Parmenides, they influenced PLATO among others. See also PARADOX, SPACE, SUBSTANCE, ZENO'S PARADOXES.

Elenchus

Elenchus. Usually, especially in Socratic context, an attempted refutation by questioning. In Aristotle it means refutation, sometimes limited to refutations in SYLLOGISTIC form. *Ignoratio elenchi*: ignoring the issue.

Emergence. Roughly, a property or phenomenon is emergent if it appears in a system without appearing in the component parts of the system. But the relations between emergence and REDUCTIONISM are somewhat complex.

T. Nagel, 'Panpsychism', in his *Mortal Questions*, Cambridge UP, 1979. (Discusses emergence in context of how conscious experiences can exist in organisms that seem to be purely physical. For two senses of 'panpsychism' itself see first and last paragraphs.) See also bibliography to REDUCTIONISM.

Emotivism. See NATURALISM.

Empirical. See A PRIORI.

Empiricism. Any of a variety of views to the effect that either our concepts or our knowledge are, wholly or partly, based on experience through the senses and introspection. The 'basing' may refer to psychological origin or, more usually, philosophical justification. For some of the complexities see A PRIORI. Extreme empiricists may confine our knowledge to statements about SENSE DATA, plus perhaps ANALYTIC statements. Less extreme empiricists say that such statements must form the basis on which all our other knowledge is erected (cf. FOUNDATIONALISM). Other empiricists, however, may simply deny that there are any a priori propositions, or any synthetic or non-analytic a priori ones. Or they may say that if there are any a priori propositions, there are still no innate concepts. A weak form of empiricism may say only that we can acquire some knowledge through the senses. An empiricist view of some given concept or proposition bases it somehow on experience.

Sometimes empiricism has taken the form of a doctrine of meaning, saying that a word or sentence has meaning only if rules involving sense experience can be given for applying or verifying it. Analytic sentences are excepted. Such rules may further *constitute* the meaning. This is often called *logical empiricism*. For this and *consistent empiricism* see POSITIVISM.

Radical empiricism is a name for the philosophy of W. James; cf. PRAGMATISM.

Constructive empiricism is B. Van Fraassen's view that a scientific theory should imply all the truths that can be found by observation

Epicureans

in the relevant sphere, even though the theory itself may postulate unobservable entities, 'Constructive' refers to its constructing models rather than seeking a logic of discovery.

'British empiricists' is a traditional label for Locke, Berkeley and Hume, in particular, and for sundry lesser or later figures regarded as sharing their general outlook. See also RATIONALISM.

H. Moritz (ed.), *Challenges to Empiricism*, Methuen, 1980. (Selections from leading philosophers, with partly annotated bibliography.)
D. Odegard, 'Locke as an empiricist', *Philosophy*, 1965. (Discusses senses of 'empiricist', in connection with Locke's philosophy).
B. Van Fraassen, *The Scientific Image*, Clarendon, 1980. (Constructive empiricism. See its index.)
R. S. Woolhouse, *The Empiricists*, Oxford UP, 1988. (Discusses Bacon, Gassendi and Hobbes, as well as Locke, Berkeley and Hume, and without prejudging how far they all *are* empiricists.)

Empiriocriticism. See POSITIVISM.

Enantiomorphs. See INCONGRUENT COUNTERPARTS.

En soi. See BAD FAITH.

Entailment. See IMPLICATION.

Entelechy. In Aristotle, actuality as against potentiality. He defines soul as the first entelechy of an organic body, meaning, roughly, the set of things the organism can do when active. The second entelechy is the actual doing of these things, though Aristotle does not use the phrase. It is unclear how far entelechy is general or particular, i.e. whether each individual animal, etc. has its own entelechy, or only has that of its species. In Leibniz 'entelechy' is another term for 'MONAD'. The term also occurs elsewhere.

Aristotle, *De Anima (On the Soul)*, book 2, chapter 1.
G. W. Leibniz, *Monadology*, 1714, esp. §§ 18–19, 63, 70.

Enthymene. Argument in which one or more premises, or interim conclusions, are silently assumed.

Epicureans. Epicurus of Samos (342–271 BC) founded a school (sometimes called the Garden, from its meeting-place in Athens) which rivalled the STOICS till Roman times, though producing few famous names. Like the Stoics, the Epicureans were materialists, but they added the concept of empty space and were atomists

Epiphenomenalism

(following Leucippus and Democritus of the fifth century). They also rejected determinism by allowing an uncaused 'swerve' to their atoms, though its exact nature and its role in their system are obscure. Like the Stoics they were interested in epistemology, but they were less interested in logic. In ethics, as well as rejecting determinism they advocated HEDONISM, but of a very restrained kind: their hedonism was largely a matter of emphasizing the role of feeling, but their stress on the pains that followed excess led to their recommendations differing little in practice from those of Stoicism. A version of the system is eloquently expounded in Lucretius' (c.99–c.55BC) poem *De Rerum Natura (On the Nature of Things)*. See also PHILOSOPHY, SUBSTANCE.

A. A. Long, *Hellenistic Philosophy*, 1974.
A. A. Long and D. N. Sedley, *The Hellenistic Philosophers*, Cambridge UP, 1987. (Vol. 1 contains translated texts and vol. 2 Greek texts with commentary.

Epiphenomenalism. Doctrine that mental phenomena are entirely caused by physical phenomena in the brain or central nervous system, and themselves have no effects, mental or physical. An *epiphenomenon* is a by-product, itself without (significant or relevant) effects, of some process.

Epistemic. Concerning or involving knowledge.

Epistemology. Also called *theory of knowledge*, occasionally *gnoseology*. Enquiry into the nature and grounds of knowledge. 'What can we know, and how do we know it?' are questions central to philosophy, and knowledge forms the main topic of epistemology, along with its relation to other cognitive notions like BELIEF, understanding, REASON, JUDGEMENT, SENSATION, PERCEPTION, INTUITION, guessing, learning, forgetting. See philosophy of MIND (last paragraph) for philosophy of mind and epistemology.

Questions about knowledge can be divided into four main, though overlapping, groups, concerning its nature, its types, what is known, and its origin. Knowledge clearly differs in its nature from purely psychological states like feeling sure, for in straightforward contexts the word 'know', like 'realize', 'REFUTE', and many other words, can only be used by a speaker who himself has certain beliefs on the matter in question. If I say 'Smith knows (or, Smith does not know) that fairies exist' I commit myself to their existence, which I do not if I say 'Smith believes (feels sure, is sure) . . .' Verbs like 'know' are sometimes called *factive* to express this feature. Knowing is usually thought to involve believing, though some say that it *replaces* belief, or that one can believe one thing while somehow knowing the opposite.

It is often thought that knowledge is justified true belief, but even if belief *is* involved there are objections to this view. No agreed account has yet been produced of what counts as justification, and sometimes no justification seems called for; do we have to justify claims to know our own intentions, or where our limbs are? Some say we have a special *knowledge without observation* of certain things, e.g. (in normal health) where our limbs are, which others can only know by observing us.

Justification may be internalist or externalist (see INTERNALISM AND EXTERNALISM). Internalist justification focuses on the knowers' state of mind and demands that he be aware of (have at least a true belief in), and preferably be able to produce some adequate reason for the truth of, the relevant belief, though what counts as adequate can be disputed: obviously if one is in error one has not knowledge, but must error be not only absent but impossible (cf. INCORRIGIBLE)? If so, knowledge will be rare. Externalist justification stresses the difference between knower and known and demands some real connection between them. This may take the form of a suitable causal link whereby what is known causes the knower's belief, or is perhaps jointly with the belief caused by some third thing; this would allow for knowledge of the future etc. The knower may be allowed to make inferences, but purely intellectual knowledge, e.g. of logic or mathematics, may be hard to cater for, since causation does not seem to apply there. Another difficulty is that causation was introduced to prevent the belief being merely accidentally true, but the causal chain itself may be of a deviant kind; e.g. suppose a volcano causes some lava to cover a field, which causes a farmer to remove it, which causes a conservationist fanatic to replace it, which causes a newcomer to perceive it and infer the volcano's existence: does the newcomer know the volcano existed?

Another externalist approach is *reliabilism* (sometimes used to include causal theories). This may be a criterion for knowledge, or simply for justification (whereby a belief is justified if it is produced by a method that normally produces true beliefs, even if it happens to be false this time; for knowledge of course it must be true). Reliabilism may, however, be partly internalist if it is insisted that the believer be aware of the method used and of its reliability. (Similarly a causal theory may become partly internalist if the knower must be aware of the relevant causal chain.) If a belief so produced is true it can be called knowledge, but an objection is that even a normally reliable method may sometimes produce a belief which is true but only by chance or for reasons unconnected with the method: would that still count as knowledge? Also has

Epistemology

one knowledge if one is regularly right but can give no reasons, though the subject-matter seems to demand them (e.g. successful soothsaying)?

Internalists and externalists agree that knowledge must in a certain sense be not accidental. Suppose that by chance I witness a traffic accident. The event was accidental (it could even be uncaused for all that concerns us here) and my knowing of it is accidental (I only saw it by chance); but it is not accidental that my belief that there was an accident is true.

Other accounts of knowledge introduce causation, or make 'know' a performative verb (see SPEECH ACTS) or say that to know is to be able to tell.

Does knowing involve knowing that one knows? How far do knowledge and the other cognitive notions involve consciousness and rationality: can humans have unconscious knowledge? Can animals and machines have knowledge at all?

The types of knowledge often occur in pairs. A PRIORI and empirical knowledge have long been contrasted (see also below on origins), and the ANALYTIC/synthetic distinction is relevant here. If a priori knowledge is analytic it risks having no content, since analytic propositions seem merely to repeat (part of) the subject in the predicate, inplicitly or implicitly, or to do something analogous to that. Kant postulated synthetic a priori propositions, known by TRANSCENDENTAL ARGUMENTS, but their existence is controversial.

Knowing propositions or facts (propositional knowledge, e.g. knowing that Paris is the capital of France) is contrasted with knowing objects (i.e. knowing Paris). 'OBJECTS' must presumably be wide enough to include things like someone's character, and knowing objects may anyway involve knowing facts about them.

Russell distinguished *knowledge by acquaintance* from *knowledge by description*, a distinction only intelligible in the light of his theory of DESCRIPTIONS. If I am acquainted with an object it can be a constituent of a proposition I understand, and its logically proper name will be the subject of that proposition. If I know such a proposition to be true I have knowledge by acquaintance of the object. If on the other hand I know the proposition *that the last French king was beheaded*, whose subject is a description, I have knowledge by description of that king, whether or not I am also acquainted with him. By acquaintance Russell apparently means a form of immediate knowledge which is not propositional but consists in confrontation. 'Immediate knowledge' might cover some propositional knowledge like knowledge without observation, some perceptual knowledge, telepathy and intuition, but there are difficulties over just what acquaintance, in Russell's sense, consists in.

Epistemology

Ryle contrasts *knowing how* and *knowing that*, and this distinction has been widely used in, for example, ethics and philosophy of mind, e.g. moral knowledge might consist in knowing how to behave.

Some types of knowledge are partly defined in terms of what is known, including memory, of the past, and precognition, of the future.

The objects we have knowledge of are legion, and apart from the general problems of SCEPTICISM some of these objects raise special problems about how, rather than whether, we know them. One such sphere is knowledge about ourselves, especially about our existence, our feelings and their locations (when they have them; see SENSATIONS), our mental states and characteristics, and the position of our limbs (see above). A controversial notion relevant here is private or privileged ACCESS. Some philosophers, notably Wittgenstein, claim that we cannot have knowledge unless the idea of our being mistaken makes sense, e.g. we cannot know, nor not know, that we are in pain. Other such spheres include the past (including dreams), the future, general facts and scientific laws, logical and mathematical facts, philosophical, religious, moral and aesthetic facts. In many of these cases it is disputed whether, strictly, there are any such facts to be known.

RATIONALISTS and EMPIRICISTS have traditionally battled over the origin of knowledge. Can the mind to any degree actively originate its contents, or are those contents entirely built up from what it passively receives through the senses or introspection, as the *tabula rasa* or blank tablet theory suggests? The strong empiricist and sceptical trend in English-language philosophy earlier in this century has now largely broken down as the issue has become less clearcut. Here too belong questions about conceptual schemes, or basic ways of looking at the world. How fundamental can differences between them be? e.g. must we view the world in terms of substances and attributes, etc., or could we substitute an alternative scheme? Cf. CATEGORIES.

Epistemology includes further questions somehow related to knowledge. Rigour and provability concern the acquisition of knowledge. TRUTH and PROBABILITY concern the assessment of it. MEANING and other notions relating to language concern the vehicle of it. METAPHYSICS, LOGIC, and philosophies of MATHEMATICS, SCIENCE and LANGUAGE are all relevant here.

Genetic epistemology, associated largely with J. Piaget (1896–1980) and his followers, studies empirically the acquisition of concepts and mental abilities by children, and belongs to psychology rather than philosophy. For *moral epistemology* see ETHICS.

Naturalized epistemology, a notion mainly associated nowadays

Epistemology

with Quine though having its roots in Hume, is what results when instead of trying to justify in the traditional manner our claims to knowledge we offer a causal account, particularly in terms of evolution, of how we come, and inevitably come, to have the kinds of belief we have (cf. NATURALISM).

J. L. Austin, 'Other minds', in his *Philosophical Papers*, 1961. ('Know' as performative verb.)

A. J. Ayer, *Problem of Knowledge*, Macmillan, 1956, Penguin, 1990. (Empiricist approach.)

E. Craig, *Knowledge and the State of Nature*, Clarendon, 1990. (Aims not to define knowledge but to account for it in terms of why we have the concept.)

*J. Dancy, *Introduction to Contemporary Epistemology*, Blackwell, 1985.

J. Dancy (ed.), *Perceptual Knowledge*, Oxford UP, 1988. (Reprinted essays on knowledge as connected with perception.)

D. Davidson, 'On the very idea of a conceptual scheme' in his *Inquiries into Truth and Interpretation*, Clarendon, 1984. (Attacks idea that knowledge is relative to conceptual schemes.)

A. I. Goldman, 'A causal theory of knowing', *Journal of Philosophy*, 1967. (Cf. also B. Skyrms, 'The explication of "X knows that p"', ibid. Goldman is reprinted with discussions in Pappas and Swain. For his later views see his *Epistemology and Cognition*, Harvard UP, 1986, which also discusses reliabilist criterion for knowledge (chapter 3) and for justification (chapter 5).)

A. P. Griffiths (ed.), *Knowledge and Belief*, Oxford UP, 1967. (Articles and bibliography, with introduction. Note E. Gettier's objections to the 'justified true belief' definition of 'knowledge'.)

D. W. Hamlyn, *Theory of Knowledge*, Macmillan, 1970. (More advanced introduction.)

N. Malcolm, 'The privacy of experience', in A. Stroll (ed.), *Epistemology*, Harper and Row, 1967. (Wittgensteinian view of knowledge and error. Compare (and contrast) his article in Griffiths, above.)

Midwest Studies in Philosophy, vol. 5, 1980. (Single topic journal issue entitled *Studies in Epistemology*.)

G. S. Pappas and M. Swain (eds), *Essays on Knowledge and Justification*, Cornell UP, 1978. (General readings.)

B. Russell, 'Knowledge by acquaintance and knowledge by description', in his *Mysticism and Logic*, Penguin, 1918. (Cf. INTUITION.)

G. Ryle, *The Concept of Mind*, Hutchinson, 1949, chapter 2. (Knowing how and that. For criticism see D. G. Brown, 'Knowing how and knowing that, what', in G. Pitcher and O. Wood (eds),

Ryle, Macmillan, 1970, and for use in ethics J. Gould, *The Development of Plato's Ethics*, 1955.)

G. Ryle, 'Epistemology', in J. O. Urmson (ed.), *The Concise Encyclopaedia of Western Philosophy and Philosophers*, 1960. (Brings out breakdown of rationalist/empiricist contrast.)

W. V. O. Quine, 'Epistemology naturalized', in his *Ontological Relativity and Other Essays*, Columbia UP, 1969. (Cf. also M. J. Woods, 'Scepticism and natural knowledge', *Proceedings of the Aristotelian Society*, 1979–80, D. Papineau, 'Is epistemology dead?', *Proceedings of the Aristotelian Society*, 1981–2.)

C. Sartwell, 'Knowledge is merely true belief', *American Philosophical Quarterly*, 1991, 'Why knowledge is merely true belief', *Journal of Philosophy*, 1992. (Defends this claim, first article answering objections and second giving positive account.)

G. N. A. Vesey, *The Embodied Mind*, Allen and Unwin, 1965, Chapter 7, § 5. (Discussion of knowledge without observation.)

D. Wilson, *Presuppositions and Non-Truth-Conditional Semantics*, Academic Press, 1971, Gregg Revivals, 1991. (See index for factives.)

*A. D. Woozley, *Theory of Knowledge*, Hutchinson, 1949. (Elementary introduction.)

Epoche. See PHENOMENOLOGY.

Equivalence. Reciprocal implication, in any sense of 'IMPLICATION'.

Equivalence class. See NUMBERS.

Equivalence relation. Any SYMMETRIC AND TRANSITIVE relation, e.g. *equal in size to*. Its terms are equivalent in the sense that there is some determinable property, like size, which they all have to the same degree or in the same determinate form, and whatever any of them has the relation to, so do the others. If *a* is equal in size to *b*, then if *a* is equal to *c, b* also is equal to *c*.

Equivocal. See AMBIGUITY.

Eristic. See DIALECTIC.

Erotetic. Concerning questions.

Essence. A *nominal essence* is a group of terms used to define a concept. For example, if I define a horse as 'anything with a mane and four legs that neighs', then this phrase or group of terms forms the nominal essence of *horse*. A *real essence* may be a group of

Essentialism

concepts or UNIVERSALS objectively given in nature independently of our definitions (e.g. Socrates' question 'What is courage, really and truly and irrespective of mere human opinions?' presupposes that courage has a real essence); 'essence' by itself usually means this, which derives from Aristotle and normally applies to species, though sometimes to individuals (see FORM, HAECCEITY). Alternatively (with Locke) a real essence is an underlying structure of an object, e.g. an atomic structure. See also FORM.

J. Locke, *An Essay concerning Human Understanding*, 1690, book 3, chapters 3–6.

Essentialism. See MODALITIES.

Eternal recurrence. See METAPHYSICS.

Ethics. Perhaps on the dominant view an enquiry into how men ought to act in general, not as means to a given end. Etymology supports this: see MORAL. The primary concepts are then ought, obligation, duty, right, wrong, though not in all their uses. For the other main view the primary topic is value and the primary concepts are the valuable, the desirable, the good in itself. All these notions are normally included under ethics, though the second group can also be excluded as belonging rather to *axiology*, the study of value in general (in aesthetics, economics, etc., as well as ethics). An ethics based primarily on value can be called an *axiological ethics*.

These two views *of* ethics correspond closely to two outlooks *in* it. For *deontologists* (notably Kant, W. D. Ross, H. A. Prichard) duty is prior to value, and at least some of our duties, such as promise-keeping, are independent of values. *Deontological* properly means connected with, or favouring, this outlook. *Deontic* means, simply, connected with duty and related notions, as in 'deontic LOGIC'. For *teleologists*, notably UTILITARIANS, our only duties have reference to ends and are to produce value, or perhaps to distribute it in certain ways; cf. CONSEQUENTIALISM. These views may not be sharply distinguishable, since deliberate action must always aim at some end; and even Kant emphasized moral worth. Also the slogan 'Do right, whatever the consequences' faces difficulties over distinguishing acts from their consequences (cf. ACTION).

However, though this distinction still holds, it has recently been supplemented with other approaches less easy to classify, notably rights-based ethics, where rights are prior to duties in the sense that duties are defined in terms of them, and VIRTUE-based ethics,

Ethics

where the promotion of the virtues and of actions based on them
is taken as the proper aim.

The distinction between views *of* ethics and views *in* ethics is
reflected in two groups into which ethical questions are often
divided. These are usually contrasted as *ethics/morals, metaethics/
ethics, philosophical ethics/normative ethics*, or *metaethics/norma-
tive ethics*, the subject as a whole being called *ethics, moral philosophy*, or sometimes *morals*.

In the first group are conceptual questions, which introduce other
branches of philosophy, notably logic, philosophy of language, and
epistemology. During this century questions about the meaning
of ethical terms and the CRITERIA for applying them have been
emphasized. How do the terms relate to each other, including the
'bad' terms, like 'bad', 'evil', 'wrong', etc., though in practice
these 'bad' terms receive much less attention? How do moral uses
of all these terms relate to non-moral uses, and in general what
distinguishes the MORAL as such? Other questions concern how we
should analyse sentences containing these terms. Cf. NATURALISM,
on the prescriptivist/descriptivist issue and the fact/value distinction.
A connected question is whether there are any objective moral
truths (as moral realism holds), and whether moral conclusions can
be objective even if not strictly describable as 'true'. Questions
about how such conclusions might be known, and, in general about
how moral arguments can be justified, what part is played in them
by reason, feeling and intuition, and about the nature and role of
conscience, belong to *moral epistemology*. An important notion in
this area is that of UNIVERSALIZABILITY, and the MORAL sphere can
often be compared with others, e.g. the aesthetic or that of rational
action in general. Cf. also GOOD, OUGHT.

Questions of the second main group mentioned above concern
actual moral issues, like: What things are good, right, etc.? What
are our duties? Are there any natural rights? Do animals have
rights? When if ever is abortion, or genetic engineering and exper-
imentation, permissible? When and how far can war be justified,
especially when mass destruction is involved?

These two groups were sharply distinguished (and the first
preferred) both by logical POSITIVISM because of its restrictions on
what could be true or false, and by the succeeding linguistic
PHILOSOPHY because in rejecting the restrictive dogmatism of the
positivists it also thought the philosopher should avoid dogmatizing
on substantial issues. However, this all implies that every position on
questions of the first group is compatible with every position
on those of the second. This compatibility results from the particular
answers positivism and linguistic philosophy gave to questions of
the first group. These answers, and therefore the sharpness of the

Ethics

distinction, have been attacked because of doubts on the fact/value distinction and more willingness to allow reason a role in moral arguments, not just in factual or logical preliminaries. The second group has therefore received much more attention recently, and subjects such as business ethics, legal ethics, medical ethics, environmental ethics (the last two overlapping with *bioethics* or the ethics of life), are flourishing parts of what is often called *applied philosophy*.

Many questions seem not to belong to either group alone, such as analyses of particular virtues and vices, and questions about merit and responsibility and about moral ideals. Questions belonging to philosophy of mind rather than ethics, but clearly relevant here, concern FREEWILL, psychological HEDONISM and INCONTINENCE. Such borderline questions are often classified as *moral psychology*, along with analyses of notions like motive, intention, desire, voluntary, deliberation, pain, pleasure, happiness; ethics proper examines their moral relevance. Interest is a more specifically ethical notion, and the distinction between one's own and others' interests leads to questions about egoism and altruism.

One question involving both moral psychology and ethics concerns the Catholic *double effect* doctrine: we may not intentionally produce evils, but we may sometimes rightly do what we foresee will produce evils, provides we do not intend these, but regard them as unwanted side-effects, not as indispensable steps. Does this make sense? If so, is it psychologically possible? And is it morally acceptable?

Metaphysical and religious justifications for ethical positions are uncommon now, but one concept deserving mention is that of the FUNCTION of man, appealed to especially by Aristotle.

A distinction is sometimes made between *agent ethics* and *spectator ethics* because things like motives, and the difference between what is right and what the agent thinks is right, may play one role when one is deciding what to do, and another role when one is judging what someone else does or should do.

Casuistry is the application of moral principles to particular cases or types of case. Here it contrasts with *situational ethics*, or *moral particularism*, which insists on considering each moral situation as it arises, in isolation from others, and rejecting general principles. Casuistry has fallen into disrepute largely from the possibility of using ever more subtle features of a situation to reach a desired moral conclusion in the face of allegedly inadequate moral principles – 'inadequate' can be stretched to cover 'inconvenient'.

Descriptive ethics examines what moral views are actually held by various people or societies, and whether any are universally held. Though such questions might seem scientific rather than philosophical, they often involve analysis and interpretation as well as mere fact-finding, and indeed illustrate the blurring of the philosophy-science distinction.

*B. Almond and D. Hill (eds), *Applied Philosophy: Morals and Metaphysics in Contemporary Debate*, Routledge, 1991. (Selections from *Journal of Applied Philosophy* on environment, personal relations, war etc., justice and equality, and medical ethics. Cf. also B. Almond (ed.), *Introducing Applied Ethics*, Blackwell, 1995, and for a more theoretical and methodologically based collection, E. R. Winkler and J. R. Coombs (eds), *Applied Ethics: A Reader*, Blackwell, 1993, mainly new or revised essays with summaries linking them.)

Aristotle, *Nicomachean Ethics*. (Very influential, for methods rather than conclusions, on post-war British ethics; cf. R. Sorabji, 'Aristotle and Oxford Philosophy', in *American Philosophical Quarterly*, 1969. See book 1 for functions, books 2–5 for virtues and responsibility, book 7 for incontinence.)

J. Dancy, *Moral Reasons*, Blackwell, 1993. (Defends moral particularism, among other things.)

S. Darwall, A. Gibbard, P. Railton, 'Towards *fin de siècle* ethics: some trends', *Philosophical Review*, 1992. (Survey of developments from 1950 to 1990 with many references.)

J. N. Findlay, *Axiological Ethics*, Macmillan, 1970. (Discusses some less fashionable writers.)

P. Foot, *Virtues and Vices*, Blackwell, 1978. (Collection of articles by her on title topic and many others in ethics.)

*W. Frankena, *Ethics*, Prentice-Hall, 1963. (Short introduction, from modified Utilitarian standpoint.)

A. Gewirth, 'Metaethics and moral neutrality', R. C. Solomon, 'Sumner on metaethics', *Ethics*, 1968, G. H. von Wright, *The Varieties of Goodness*, RKP, Humanities Press, 1963, esp. chapter 1, G. J. Warnock, *The Object of Morality*, Methuen, 1971. (All these illustrate the breakdown of the sharp metaethics normative ethics distinction.)

R. M. Hare, *Freedom and Reason*, Oxford UP, 1963. (Includes discussion of moral ideals. Cf. J. O. Urmson, 'Saints and heroes', in A. I. Melden (ed.), *Essays in Moral Philosophy*, 1958, reprinted in J. Feinberg (ed.), *Moral Concepts*, Oxford UP, 1969.)

*G. Harman, *The Nature of Morality*, Oxford UP, 1977. (Elementary introduction.)

*A. C. MacIntyre, *A Short History of Ethics*, RKP, 1966.

J. L. Mackie, *Ethics: Inventing Right and Wrong*, Penguin, 1977. (Antirealist approach, i.e. opposing moral realism. Cf. also S. Blackburn, *Spreading the Word*, Clarendon, 1984.)

Event

J. T. Morgan, 'An historical analysis of the principle of double effect', *Theological Studies*, 1949.

H. A. Prichard, *Moral Obligation*, Clarendon, 1949, Oxford UP, 1968. (Early twentieth-century intuitionism. For examples of more recent revival of intuitionism see A. T. Kolnai, *Ethics, Value and Reality*, Athlone Press, 1977, D. Wiggins, *Needs, Values, Truth*, Blackwell, 1987, both collections of essays.)

J. Rawls, *A Theory of Justice*, Oxford UP, 1972. (Influential attempt to base morality on a hypothetical contract.)

*P. Singer (ed.), *Applied Ethics*, Oxford UP, 1986. (Selected readings on various moral issues).

M. Slote, *From Morality to Virtue*, Oxford UP, 1986. (Virtue ethics. See pp. xvi, xix, for ethics treated as wider than 'morality proper'.)

P. Thompson (ed.), *Issues in Evolutionary Ethics*, State University of New York Press, 1995. (Selections from Darwin onwards.)

*J. Waldron (ed.), *Theories of Rights*, Oxford UP, 1984. (Anthology.)

*B. A. O. Williams, *Morality*, Penguin, 1972. (Elementary introduction. His *Ethics and the Limits of Philosophy*, Fontana, 1985, is fuller but rather harder.)

Event. Generally regarded as either a change, usually of short duration, in the qualities or relations such as spatial relations of a thing, or as the possession of a property or relation by something at or for a time. Many of the problems about events concern how they are related to other things, e.g. OBJECTS, particulars (see UNIVERSALS), INDIVIDUALS, UNIVERSALS, FACTS, states of affairs, propositions (see SENTENCES), changes, ACTIONS. Can events be classed under any of these? Indeed are events needed as a separate ontological category at all? Also are events of radically different kinds? Are some events recurrent (e.g. 'annual events' perhaps?) and some unique, some instantaneous and some enduring, some mental and some physical? An important ambiguity is that sometimes 'event' means 'kind of event'. How should we individuate events (i.e. tell when we have one and when another)? Are events always datable? A murder is presumably an event, but if I murder someone by slow poison, does the murder occur when I administer the poison or when the victim dies, perhaps years later (cf. ACTION)? And can events move or change?

J. Bennett, *Events and Their Names*, Oxford UP, 1988. (Full treatment. Cf. discussions of it, with reply, in *Philosophy and Phenomenological Research*, 1991, pp. 625–62.)

R. Chisholm, 'States of affairs again', D. Davidson, 'Eternal versus

Excluded middle (Law or principle of)

ephemeral events', *Nous*, 1970. (Events, propositions, particulars. Further references in Davidson).

D. Davidson, *Essays on Actions and Events*, Clarendon, 1980. (Reprinted essays. See also criticisms, with Davidson's replies, in B. Vermazen and M. B. Hintikka (eds), *Essays on Davidson: Actions and Events*, Clarendon, 1985 and S. Evnine, *Donald Davidson*, Blackwell, 1991, esp. pp. 25–33.)

T. Horgan, 'The case against events', *Philosophical Review*, 1978. (One example of this view. For criticism see I. Thalberg, 'A world without events?' in B. Vermazen and M. B. Hintikka (eds), *Essays on Davidson: Actions and Events*, Clarendon, 1985, itself criticized by R. H. Feldman and E. Wieringa, 'Thalberg on the irreducibility of events', *Analysis*, vol. 39, 1979.)

L. B. Lombard, *Events*, RKP, 1986. (Full treatment.)

Z. Vendler, 'Causal relations', *Journal of Philosophy*, 1967, pp. 707–8. (Events and facts.)

Evidence (paradox of ideal). Suppose we assume that the a priori PROBABILITY of a certain penny falling heads on the next toss is ½, and that therefore it is rational to half-expect heads. Suppose we then find that in the past it has fallen heads and tails equally often. This evidence seems ideal justification for the rationality of this half-expecting. Yet the half-expecting was already the perfectly rational state of mind to adopt. Therefore the evidence seems superfluous. Offered by Popper as objection to (what he calls) subjective theory of PROBABILITY.

K. R. Popper, *The Logic of Scientific Discovery*, Hutchinson, 1959 (German original 1934), pp. 407–10.

R. H. Vincent, 'The paradox of ideal evidence', *Philosophical Review*, 1962. (Criticizes Popper.)

Examination paradox. See PREDICTION.

Excluded middle (Law or principle of). Often abbreviated as LEM. Traditionally, '*A* is *B* or *A* is not *B*' (any given thing either has or lacks any given property), or in the propositional calculus (where '*p*' stands for a proposition) '*p* or not *p*'. Under the influence of INTUITIONISM and antirealism (see REALISM) it has become standard to distinguish LEM from the principle or law of *bivalence*, that every proposition is true or false, a semantic rather than logical principle since it is *about* propositions and mentions truth. Intuitionism rejects LEM and bivalence, but replaces bivalence by a weaker principle, *tertium non datur* (there is no third truth-value), that no proposition is neither true nor false; for classical (i.e. non-

Existential import

intuitionist) logic this entails bivalence, but for intuitionism, which denies one half of the double NEGATION principle, it does not.

Many-valued logics (see TRUTH-VALUE) reject all three of these principles, a line taken (in effect) by Aristotle, followed by Lukasiewicz, in trying to avoid logical determinism (see FREEWILL, including its bibliography (Aristotle item)).

A traditional problem for LEM has lain in vague predicates like 'bald' (see HEAP). A vague predicate may be made precise ('precisified') in various ways; 'bald' may be precisified as 'having fewer than 100 hairs', or as 'having fewer than 10 hairs', and so on. One approach, that of SUPERVALUATION, treats a vague proposition as true if it is true however the vague term is precisified. This view keeps LEM but rejects bivalence. This is because 'p or not p' may hold for every precisification ('Smith is bald or not bald' may be true whether we let 'bald' mean 'having fewer than 100 hairs', or 'having fewer than 101 hairs' or whatever), while p does not hold for every precisification, and neither does 'not p' (it need not be the case that 'Smith is bald' is true for all precisifications of 'bald', and the same applies to 'Smith is not bald': if Smith has exactly 100 hairs he will be bald, if 'bald' means 'having less than 101 hairs', but not bald if it means 'having less than 100 hairs' (though in either case, 'Smith is bald or not bald' will be true, and so LEM is saved)).

P. T. Geach and W. F. Bednarowski, 'The law of excluded middle', *Proceedings of the Aristotelian Society*, supplementary vol., 1956. (Pre-Dummett discussions of vague predicates.)

G. Rosen, 'The shoals of language' (a 'critical notice' of M. Dummett, *The Seas of Language*), *Mind*, 1995. (Useful on bivalence and realism.)

*R. M. Sainsbury (see bibliography to HEAP.)

See also bibliography to INTUITIONISM, especially pages xix, xxx and index of Dummett's *Truth and other Enigmas*, Duckworth, 1978.

Existential import. See QUANTIFIER WORDS.

Existentialism. A movement primarily associated with Kierkegaard, Jaspers, Heidegger, Sartre, Marcel, though many others are often included. Its exponents have widely differing outlooks, in religion and politics as well as in philosophy, but share certain general themes.

The most important of these themes is an interest in humanity as such and its relations to the world, and in the notion of BEING. Existentialists normally contrast the sort of being that applies to humans, what Heidegger calls *Dasein*, with that which applies

Existentialism

to things, and to humans only in so far as they are things. Existentialists tend to regard the being which applies to humans as something which they only attain sometimes, and ought to struggle for. Sartre contrasts the *être-pour-soi* which partly does, and partly should, belong to humans, with the *être-en-soi* which belongs to things but which humans fail to escape from when they live in BAD FAITH. There seems therefore to be a certain tension in existentialism about whether what is described is the inevitable human condition, or an ideal, perhaps never fully attainable. The two poles of this tension give existentialism its two philosophical footholds, in metaphysics and ethics.

A feature of human existence, for existentialists, is that humans are active and creative while things are not. Things are simply what they are, but humans might be other than they are. Humans must choose, and (at least on some versions) must choose the principles on which they choose. They are not, like things, already determined. 'Existence precedes essence' for humans: they make their essences as they go along, and do not live out a predetermined essence or blue-print (but see also Cooper, chapter 4). Humans are free, and the reality and nature of freedom is a major concern for existentialists. Furthermore, humans are conscious of the contrast between themselves and things, of their relations with other humans, of their eventual deaths, and of their power to choose and become what they are not. All this leads to a notion of not-being, or 'Nothing', which, to the despair of logicians, existentialists often appear to treat as a thing or condition in its own right. Sometimes this 'Nothing', and sometimes the contingency of things in general, provokes an emotion or condition of dread (despair, anguish, Angst, angoisse).

In elaborating what being is for humans, and how they are related to the world, recent existentialists have been strongly influenced by Husserl's PHENOMENOLOGY, though rejecting some aspects of it.

J. Collins, *The Existentialists*, Regnery, Chicago, 1952, Greenwood Press, 1977.

*D. E. Cooper, *The Existentialists: A Reconstruction*, Clarendon, 1990. (Sympathetic general introduction, stressing what is common to the different thinkers.)

A. C. Danto, *Sartre*, Fontana, 1975. (Introduction.)

M. Heidegger, *Sein und Zeit*, 1927, transl. as *Being and Time*, Blackwell, 1962. (His main work.)

N. Langiulli (ed.), *The Existentialist Tradition*, Doubleday Anchor, 1971. (Selections from many writers, with brief biographies and full bibliographies of them. Very difficult. Items by Abbagnano, Buber, Marcel, Sartre perhaps easiest.)

Explanation

J. Macquarie, *Existentialism*, Hutchinson, 1972. (General introduction from theological point of view.)

A. R. Manser, A. T. Kolnai, 'Existentialism', *Proceedings of the Aristotelian Society*, supplementary vol., 1963. (Critical discussions of existentialist ethics.)

J.-P. Sartre, *L'Etre et le néant*, 1943, transl. as *Being and Nothingness*, Methuen, 1957. (His main work. Cf. also his. *Essays on Existentialism* (ed. W. Baskin), Citadel Press, Secaucus NJ, 1965, translated selections on leading topics in his work, including famous examples of young man and the Resistance (pp. 42 ff.) and waiter (pp. 167 ff.).)

D. M. Tulloch, 'Sartrian existentialism', *Philosophical Quarterly*, 1952.

*M. Warnock, *Existentialism*, Oxford UP, 1970. (Elementary introduction, though limited in coverage.)

Explanation. The process of making something intelligible, or saying why certain things are as they are, or the account used to do these things. The account is sometimes called the *explanans*, and the thing to be explained is called the *explanandum*. An explanation may do things like reducing the unfamiliar to the familiar, thus enlightening people. Things it does in this way are called its pragmatic features and they are relevant to the question of whether an explanation should be relative to the receiver. A child, a lay adult, and an expert seem to require different explanations of the same thing, since what is already familiar to them will differ. Yet a scientific explanation may be in terms hitherto unfamiliar even to the scientist, the lay person may study science to find 'the' explanation of something, and the familiar itself may need explaining, as Newton explained the falling of an apple by associating it with other, apparently quite unrelated, phenomena. Many writers have therefore regarded the pragmatic features as subjective and incidental, and have concentrated rather on various views of the logical form an explanation should take.

On one view, the *covering law model*, an explanation should state general laws and initial conditions which together logically entail the explanandum. 'All water heated at normal pressure to 100°C boils' and 'This water was so heated' together explain why this water boiled. The model can be adapted to explain laws themselves, and may have more complex applications, where covering laws are distinguished from supporting laws. However, not just any covering law will do. 'Whenever water is about to turn to steam it boils' and 'This water was about to turn to steam' do not explain the boiling. This suggests that an explanation must present what is 'more knowable absolutely' even though perhaps not 'more knowable to us' (Aristotle), and that pragmatic features are relevant, though they need not be subjective (cf. Dray, p. 74). An explanation therefore might present a cause, or something logically prior to the explanandum in the relevant system, as when the explanandum is a mathematical fact.

Often, however, scientific laws say that not all As are Bs, but that a certain proportion are. When the covering law model is extended to use laws of this type, explanations are called *statistical* or *probabilistic*. The previous kind, all As are Bs, are called *nomological*. Nomological explanations are DEDUCTIVE. The explanandum is deduced from the premises. Statistical explanations are usually (not always: see Hempel) INDUCTIVE. For reasons given under CONFIRMATION statistical explanations must be supplemented by Carnaps' *requirement of total evidence* (or Hempel's weaker form, the *requirement of maximal specificity*).

It is disputed whether any but deductive explanations are properly called explanations at all, and also how many kinds of explanation there are. In particular can the covering law model apply to subjects like history and psychology, and can teleological explanations, i.e. those in terms of purposes or final causes, be reduced to causal explanations? Also do questions beginning with Why?, How? etc. call for the same type of explanation? Is there a basic difference between explaining why-necessarily and how-possibly (Dray)? Can the covering law model account for explaining what something is, or what people are doing?

Further, how is explaining something related to describing it, and also to predicting it? Darwinism explains the variety of species, but does not seem fitted for predicting new species. Thales allegedly predicted the eclipse of 585 BC by consulting records but he could almost certainly not explain it. Do explanation and predictability nevertheless ultimately go together?

So far we have left the explananda vague. When not themselves laws, are they events, states, processes, situations, actions, forbearances, or are they statements describing these? To explain a statement one needs to explain one or more features of the relevant event, while to explain the event itself in its infinite richness would seem a hopeless task. Explaining meanings raises special problems.

After asking what an explanation is, we can ask when one is adequate, and whether the same explanandum can be given more than one explanation.

Explication, when not simply a synonym for 'explanation', is the process whereby a hitherto imprecise notion is given a formal definition, and so made suitable for use in formal work. The definition does not claim to be synonymous with the original notion,

Explanation

since it is avowedly making it more precise. (This is a form of logical analysis: see PHILOSOPHY.)

Aristotle, *Posterior Analytics*, 7lb33–2a6. ('More knowable absolutely' and 'to us'. See also early chapters for when scientific argument is explanatory.)

R. Carnap, *Logical Foundations of Probability*, RKP 1950, Chicago UP, 1962, chapter 1. (Explication. Cf. W. V. Quine, *Word and Object*, Wiley, 1960, §§ 53–4.)

W. H. Dray, *Laws and Explanation in History*, 1957. (Opposes covering law model for history.)

C. G. Hempel, *Aspects of Scientific Explanation*, Free Press, 1965. (Chapter 12 has full account of covering law model, and defends its adequacy in all fields. Chapter 9 (also in *Journal of Philosophy*, 1942) defends it regarding history. Cf. also his 'Explanation in science and in history', in R. G. Colodny (ed.), *Frontiers of Science and Philosophy*, 1962, reprinted in P. H. Nidditch (ed.), *The Philosophy of Science*, Oxford UP, 1968, and in W. H. Dray (ed.), *Philosophical Analysis and History*, Harper and Row, 1966, Greenwood Press, 1979.

*J. Hospers, 'What is explanation?', *Journal of Philosophy*, 1946, reprinted in A. Flew (ed.), *Essays in Conceptual Analysis*, Macmillan, 1956, St Martin's Press, 1966, Greenwood Press, 1981. (Elementary defence of covering law model as adequate for explanations-why of events.)

P. Kitcher and W. C. Salmon (eds), *Scientific Explanation*, Minnesota UP, 1989. (Specially written papers, including long historical survey, with chronological bibliography. Cf. also Salmon's *Scientific Explanation and the Causal Structure of the World*, Princeton UP, 1984, defending appeal to causation rather than to deductive inference or necessitation.)

D.-H. Ruben, *Scientific Explanation*, Routledge, 1990. (Partly historical and partly constructive. Elaborates realist view, whereby explanation is not just relative to human knowledge or interests.)

D.-H. Ruben (ed.) *Explanation*, Oxford UP, 1993. (General anthology of reprinted items.)

C. Taylor, *The Explanation of Behaviour*, RKP, 1964. (Distinguishes and defends need for, teleological and purposive explanations. T. L. S. Sprigge, 'Final causes', *Proceedings of the Aristotelian Society*, supplementary vol., 1971, assimilates teleological to causal explanations. Cf. also L. Wright, *Teleological Explanations: an Etiological Analysis of Goals and Functions*, California, 1976, which defends them.)

G. H. von Wright, *Explanation and Understanding*, RKP, 1971.

Extensionality thesis

(Causal and teleological explanations regarding human actions, etc. Good bibliography.)

Explication. See EXPLANATION.

Extension. See INTENSIONALITY AND INTENTIONALITY.

Extensionality thesis. See LEIBNIZ'S LAW, INTENSIONALITY AND INTENTIONALITY.

F _____

Fact. Usually, that which corresponds to a statement or makes it true (cf. the correspondence theory of TRUTH). As such, a fact has seemed somehow to exist in the world, independent of thought and language. Since statements have a structure, consisting of subject and predicate, etc., it has been thought that facts must also have a structure, so that the elements in the statement can correspond to elements in the fact; facts may simply be sets of objects in the world related in certain ways. If so, a cake will be a fact, which it is surely not, though its existence may be. Nor are facts quite the same as situations or states of affairs, for one can be 'in' these, and it is natural to talk of a situation, but less natural to talk of a fact, as enduring or being altered. This may suggest that while situations etc. are indeed in the world, facts represent rather ways we choose to describe the world, though of course the world severely constrains how we can describe it; the ways will also be objective rather than evaluative (but see NATURALISM on the sharpness of this distinction).

The view that facts are things in the world corresponding to parts of thought and language has led to difficulties about whether there are any facts corresponding to statements involving words like 'not', 'or', 'all', 'some', 'if', since these statements seem to be less directly about the world than are simple statements (cf. LOGICAL ATOMISM).

If we abandon strict correspondence theories of truth, which need facts as entities in the world for statements to correspond to, we can tie facts more closely to thought and language. Are facts simple true propositions, or 'truths'? 'It's true that . . .' and 'It's a fact that . . .' mean much the same, and we can say 'What he says is a fact'. But expressions like 'His statement is borne out by

108

(corresponds to) the facts' raise some difficulty. Facts but surely not true propositions can be causes ('The fact that the match was struck caused it to light'). (On propositions see SENTENCES.) Perhaps one should no more ask what facts *are* than what cases are when something 'is the case'. Some writers (e.g. Mellor) accept both these 'thin' facts and substantive facts.

Brute facts are either facts in general considered as given independently of how we see the world (emphasizing the objectivity mentioned above); or facts not holding in virtue of any other facts holding (cf. SUPERVENIENCE); or facts about the world not involving values, rules, or institutions, e.g. 'Grass is green', 'I like beer', but not 'Beer is good for you'. 'Smith scored a goal' is an example of an *institutional fact*, depending on rules or institutions.

'Factual' is used in various ways and in each case false statements as well as true ones can be called factual. Contrasted with 'fictional' it refers to the real world. Contrasted with 'evaluative' it refers to what is objectively and decidably there and not merely contributed by human attitudes as evaluation may seem to be. Contrasted with 'theoretical', it refers to what is decidable, directly even if not conclusively, by observation. Contrasted with 'logical' or 'necessary', it refers either to what concerns the world rather than thought or discourse, or to what is merely contingently true or false. However, since statements in logic can normally be proved to be true or false, one can also talk of facts of logic or mathematics (cf. MODALITIES). Whether one can talk of moral etc. facts is disputed. See also SENTENCES, EVENTS.

G. E. M. Anscombe, 'On brute facts', *Analysis*, vol. 18, 1958.

D. Davidson, 'True to the facts', *Journal of Philosophy*, 1969, reprinted in his *Inquiries into Truth and Interpretation*, Clarendon, 1984. (Why facts cannot ground a correspondence theory of truth, and what should replace them.)

D. W. Hamlyn, 'The correspondence theory of truth', *Philosophical Quarterly*, 1962. (Defends a weak version.)

D. H. Mellor, *The Facts of Causation*, Routledge, 1995.

B. Rundle, *Facts*, Duckworth, 1993. (Discusses nature of facts, and their relations to theories and values. Short and non-technical, but best suited to those with some appreciation of the later philosophy of Wittgenstein.)

P. F. Strawson, 'Truth', *Proceedings of the Aristotelian Society*, supplementary vol, 1950, § 2, reprinted in G. Pitcher (ed.), *Truth*, Prentice-Hall, 1964, and in Strawson's *Logico-Linguistic Papers*, Methuen, 1971. (Rejects substantive facts.)

J. O. Urmson, *Philosophical Analysis*, Oxford UP, 1956, part 1, esp. § 5. (Facts and logical atomism.)

Factive

Factive. See EPISTEMOLOGY.

Fact/value distinction. See NATURALISM.

Fallibilism. Doctrine that nothing or nothing about the world can be known for certain, or alternatively that knowledge does not require that the evidence be logically conclusive or the possibility of error totally absent.

False. See TRUTH AND FALSITY.

Fatalism. See FREEWILL.

Feeling. Any one of indefinitely many ways of experiencing situations, real or imaginary, in the world or in oneself. Feelings are akin to SENSATIONS, and many of the philosophical problems that arise are best treated under that head. Both can be bodily, in which case they partly coincide, but feelings can also cover emotions and attitudes, and also opinions, especially when one wishes to disclaim any but obscure reasons for these.

One problem concerns how feelings are to be identified and described. How far can they be distinguished from each other intrinsically and without reference to causes or accompanying inclinations or dispositions? What is their role in the emotions, and how far can emotions and things like consciousness and PLEASURE be elucidated in terms of these? How do we use feelings in acquiring knowledge of the world and of other people? How do we know that they exist, if we do, in ourselves or others? Can we be deceived about our own feelings? Pain in particular has been a prime example in the PRIVATE LANGUAGE dispute.

S. R. Leighton, 'On feeling angry and elated', *Journal of Philosophy*, 1988. (Discusses feelings as they occur in emotions, with references.)

A. R. Mele, 'Akratic feelings', *Philosophy and Phenomenological Research*, vol. 50, 1989–90. (Can there be an analogue in feelings to INCONTINENT action?)

R. Moran, 'The expression of feeling in imagination', *Philosophical Review*, 1994. (The role of feeling in our aesthetic response to fiction.)

R. C. Roberts, 'What is an emotion? A sketch', *Philosophical Review*, 1988. (First main section discusses different kinds of feelings and relations between feelings and emotions.)

G. Ryle, 'Feelings', *Philosophical Quarterly*, 1951, reprinted in his *Collected Papers*, Hutchinson, 1971, vol. 2. (Various uses of 'feel' and relations between them. Cf. also his *The Concept of Mind*, Hutchinson, 1949.)

Figure. See SYLLOGISM.

Finitism. A mathematical method or system is finitist or finitary if it refuses to recognize any objects (numbers, etc.) which cannot be constructed (see INTUITIONISM) in a finite number of steps; but some variation exists about whether the construction must be possible in practice or only in principle. Finitism is thus, like intuitionism, a form of constructivism, but unlike intuitionism, appeals primarily to what can be done in a finite number of steps with a finite number of elements. It is therefore sometimes more rigorous than intuitionism, and is associated more with formalism (see INTUITIONISM). It is more of a method rather than, like intuitionism and formalism, a theory. Extreme forms of it, which allow only constructions which can be carried out in practice and in a feasible number of steps, or insist like Wittgenstein that a mathematical statement only gets sense from the way it is proved, are sometimes called *strict finitism*. One question which arises is whether there is a largest class. To say that there is goes beyond merely saying, with Aristotle, that the infinite is only potential and never actual (see METAPHYSICS).

P. Benacerraf and H. Putnam (eds), *Philosophy of Mathematics*, Blackwell, 1964, part 4. (Wittgenstein. Cf. esp. p. 505.)

S. Körner, *The Philosophy of Mathematics*, Hutchinson, 1960, esp, pp. 77–9.

G. Kreisel in *The British Journal for the Philosophy of Science*, vol. 9, 1958–9, pp. 147–9. (For fuller treatment see C. Wright, 'Strict finitism', *Synthèse*, vol. 51, 1982, esp. p. 204 and the note at pp. 269–70 (which wrongly refers to Kreisel as 'volume 8').

First cause argument. See COSMOLOGICAL.

Focal meaning. See AMBIGUITY.

Folk psychology. The supposed commonsense 'theory' by means of which we explain actions in terms of ordinary beliefs and desires etc. Folk psychology contrasts with more science-based theories, some of which even deny that there are such things as beliefs and desires. By analogy, 'folk' has come to be used more widely, e.g. 'folk physics'.

W. E. Lycan (ed.), *Mind and Cognition*, Blackwell, 1990. (Part VI has relevant articles, including Horgan and Woodward.).

Form

S. P. Stich, *From Folk Psychology to Cognitive Science: the Case Against Belief*, MIT Press, 1983. (Expresses scepticism about folk psychology. For a defence of it see J. A. Fodor, *Psychosemantics*, MIT Press, 1987, and T. Horgan and J. Woodward, 'Folk psychology is here to stay', in *Philosophical Review*, 1985.)

Form. In metaphysics a form is a general nature or ESSENCE belonging to a species, or else a particular nature or essence belonging to an individual (see HAECCEITY). For Plato's transcendent Forms (often distinguished by a capital F) see IDEA, UNIVERSALS. For Aristotle forms normally existed only in combination with matter (an exception may be God), though forms which did so could also exist in the mind *qua* known by the mind. A horse was a lump of flesh 'informed' by the form or essence of horse, i.e. made into something having the essential properties and powers of a horse. Basically therefore an Aristotelian form is that which makes an object what it is. It can also be called the *formal cause* of the object. In the Middle Ages this notion was called a *substantial form*. A substantial form classified an object as what it basically is, while an *accidental form* was any set of properties of an object, whether essential to it or not. It is not always clear whether there is a different substantial form for each individual object, or only for each type or species. The Aristotelian form is itself unclear in this respect.

In logic the form of a proposition is the kind or species to which it belongs; a proposition can be, e.g., universal or negative in form. The form is contrasted with the content or matter (cf. 'subject-matter'), what the proposition is individually about. Form is also relative: 'All cats are black' and 'No dogs are brown' are of the same form in that both are universal, but of different forms in that only one is negative.

The distinction between form and content is often hard to make. A proposition's form seems to be an abstract pattern it exemplifies, in virtue of which formal inferences can be drawn from it. 'Every *a* is a *b*, so every non-*b* is a non-*a*' is a valid inference pattern, because an inference exemplifying it is valid irrespective of the meanings of whatever terms replace '*a*' and '*b*'. 'Smith is a bachelor, so he's unmarried' is valid, but only because of what 'bachelor' means. It is a non-formal inference. Formal inference also depends on what words like 'every' mean, and it is hard to say when a pattern is abstract enough to be called formal. Is '*x* exceeds *y* and *y* exceeds *z*, so *x* exceeds *z*' an abstract pattern, i.e. can 'exceeds' count as a formal word?

Other questions include whether form really belongs to propositions. Does it belong to sentences instead? And how is logical form related to grammatical form? See also STRUCTURE.

112

Formal mode

G. E. M. Anscombe and P. T. Geach, *Three Philosophers: Aristotle, Aquinas, Frege*, Blackwell, 1962. (See pp. 75–88 for substantial forms.)

Aristotle, *Metaphysics*, book 7 (also called Z), esp. chapters 4–6, 10–17. (His main discussion. Very difficult. For Plato's Forms see esp. his *Phaedo, Republic*, books 5–7, *Parmenides*, §§ 126–37, *Timaeus*, and for Aristotle's criticism see his *Metaphysics*, book 1 (also called A), chapters 6 and 9.)

J. Bennett, *Kant's Analytic*, Oxford UP, 1966, pp. 79–81. (This and Whiteley raise difficulties about form.)

A Kenny, *Aquinas*, Oxford UP, 1980. (See its index for substantial forms.)

W. Leszl, *Logic and Metaphysics in Aristotle*, Editrice Antenore, Padua, 1972, part 6. (Includes discussion, largely intelligible by itself, of form and matter. Occasional Greek.)

D. Mitchell, *An Introduction to Logic*, Hutchinson, 1962, chapter 1. (Form and validity. Cf. also chapter 5 and pp. 151–3.)

R. M. Sainsbury, *Logical Form: an Introduction to Philosophical Logic*, Blackwell, 1991. (General treatment of philosophical logic, centring on notion of form.)

P. F. Strawson, *Introduction to Logical Theory*, Methuen, 1952, pp. 40–56. (Logical form, including its relations to patterns.)

*R. D. Sykes, 'Form in Aristotle: universal or particular?', *Philosophy*, 1975. (Fairly elementary discussion.)

C. H. Whiteley, 'The idea of logical form', *Mind*, 1951.

Formalism. Any doctrine somehow emphasizing FORM against matter or content (e.g. in aesthetics; but not metaphysical doctrines emphasizing form in the way Platonists or Aristotelians do). In ethics, the doctrine that an action's value or rightness depends on what kind of act it is (e.g. one of promise-keeping), not on its consequences; cf. deontology (ETHICS). For formalism in mathematics see INTUITIONISM.

Formal mode. Sentences about words, such as ' "Red" is a quality-word' or ' "Red" is an adjective', are said to be in the *formal mode*. Sentences about objects, qualities, etc., are said to be in the *material mode*. Thus 'Red is a quality' is in the material mode. Philosophers, especially some logical POSITIVISTS, have sometimes thought that 'metaphysical' notions like substance, quality, etc., could and should be dispensed with by translating sentences involving them into sentences about language, i.e. out of the material mode and into the formal mode, as illustrated above. Such translation has been called *semantic ascent*.

Formation rules

R. Carnap, *The Unity of Science*, Kegan Paul, Trench, Trubner, 1934, pp. 37–42.

W. V. O. Quine, *World and Object*, Wiley, 1960, § 56. (Semantic ascent.)

Formation rules. See AXIOM.

Foundationalism. The view that knowledge requires foundations, in the sense that unless we start from a set of things we know with absolute certainty, and from which we can derive in various ways the rest of our knowledge, we can never know anything at all. A notable example of a foundationalist is Descartes. See also INCORRIGIBLE. Epistemological and psychological versions of foundationalism are possible, as they are of the rival *coherentist* view that our knowledge is mutually supporting, none being basic to all the rest.

R. Audi, 'Psychological foundationalism', *Monist*, 1978. (Different versions of foundationalism and coherentism.)

Four-term fallacy. Arguing in a SYLLOGISM whose premises are true, if at all, only if the middle term has a different sense in each, e.g. 'All cats miaow; that woman is a cat; therefore that woman miaows.'

Freewill and determinism. Our natural feeling that, special circumstances apart, we always could do otherwise than we do is often thought to conflict with the view that every event is caused and that human actions cannot be excepted. Resolutions of this conflict have naturally been viewed mainly in the light of how they affect moral responsibility.

Fatalism holds that the future is fixed irrespective of our attempts to affect it. Seldom held as a philosophical doctrine this view often appears in literature (e.g. the Oedipus legend). A view often leading to the same effects, though for quite different reasons (without appealing to the 'will of fate' etc.), is *logical determinism*. This argues that a given future event must either occur or not occur. Whichever happens, the prediction that it would happen will turn out to be correct, and therefore was correct all along, whether or not we knew it. Therefore since one statement about the apparent future alternatives is already true, nothing we can do will alter matters. This puzzle affects the nature of TRUTH: can a statement (one about the future) be true at one time (when the future comes) and not at another (before the future comes), or is it senseless to talk of a statement as true 'at a time'? Or is logical determinism true but harmless, until we confusedly infer that the future is there-

Freewill and determinism

fore already causally fixed, which suggests that deliberation is pointless? Strictly, 'logical determinism' is a misnomer, since the doctrine is not about things being determined but about certain statements being true.

Causal determinism says that everything that happens is caused; it allows that our choices and actions are effective as links in the causal chain, so that deliberation has a point, but insists that they are themselves caused. Determinists are sometimes divided into hard and soft. *Hard determinists* say that our actions are caused in a way that makes us not as free as we might have thought, so that responsibility, if it implies freewill, is an illusion. The causes may be physical and physiological (events in the brain), or else mental (e.g. conscious or unconscious desires, and childhood experiences which cause such desires). *Soft determinists*, by far the largest class in recent times, say that our actions are indeed caused, but we are not therefore any less free than we might be, because the causation is not a constraint or compulsion on us. So long as our natures and choices are effective as items in the causal chain, the fact that they are themselves caused is irrelevant and does not stop them being what they are. *Indeterminists*, however, insist that determinists, of whatever complexion, can give no sense to the sentence 'He could have done otherwise', where this means something more than simply 'He *might* have done otherwise (had his nature or circumstances been different)'. Soft determinists often hold that what justifies praise and blame is solely that they can influence action. This, say indeterminists, misses the point of these concepts, which are essentially 'backward-looking'. Hard determinists are *incompatibilists*, i.e. think freewill and universal causation are incompatible. Soft determinists are *compatibilists*. Indeterminists may be either, but are usually incompatibilists.

One difficult with indeterminism is that mere absence of causation does not seem enough. If our actions are no more than random intrusions into the causal scheme of things how can we be any more responsible for them than if they were caused? Indeterminists may sometimes appeal to scientific doctrines like Heisenberg's uncertainty principle (see CAUSATION), or the unpredictability of the behaviour of individual particles in quantum theory. If, as physicists seem to believe, there are no hidden VARIABLES at work here, indeterminists may hope to use the idea that causation is only probabilistic or statistical, and not strictly deterministic (see CAUSATION again), to allow a point of entry for freewill to operate on our neural mechanisms (without of course our knowing just what we are doing, any more than we need know what muscles we are moving); but whether this idea can be coherently worked out is unclear. Indeterminists are sometimes called *libertarians*. But

Freewill and determinism

more strictly, libertarians are those who postulate a special entity, the 'self', which uses the body to intervene from outside, as it were, in the causal chain of events, but is itself immune to causal influence. Sometimes this self is said to be immune only where moral considerations arise, with obvious difficulties about which considerations are MORAL.

Such a self must at least be open to pressure from things in the world (or why would it ever make a wrong or weak-minded choice?), and to define its actual relations to the world seems difficult. More usually now indeterminists appeal not to a separate entity but to the very nature of those things (choosing, intending, deciding, acting, etc.) which characterize persons as such, whatever may be the relation between being a person and having (or being?) a body. It may not make sense for choices or actions to be caused. Reasons offered for this include the following: physical causes can only cause physical movements, like an upward movement of a leg, but not ACTIONS, like a kick, for actions always involve things like intentions and a context, which go beyond mere movement (Peters). On the other hand, alleged mental causes like desires, intentions, motives, etc., are not separate states or events: they are features of actions which provide ways of classifying them. (Ryle says one's greed is not something causing one to act but consists simply in one's acting in a greedy manner.) Another view (sometimes called the *logical connection argument*) is that a desire, etc. can only be specified as the desire to do a certain action, and so is not sufficiently independent of the action to be able to cause it, for a cause and its effect must be two *separate* things (Melden, though this oversimplifies Melden's view; cf. MODALITIES (para. beginning '*Non-contingent . . .*')).

Recently these views have been attacked, and causation has returned to favour. But there are still difficulties about reason. If our beliefs are caused physiologically, or by non-rational mental events, why should we assume they are reliable? Yet are rational considerations, as such, suitable for being causes? On the other hand we do not normally, if ever, choose our beliefs, but do not think our freedom diminished because we are 'compelled by the evidence' to believe something. Again reasoning, whether on theoretical or practical matters, and also choosing and deciding, seems to be possible only if we at least believe that their outcome is not yet determined. We cannot try, or even want (as against idly wishing), to do something we firmly think impossible.

A related problem concerns causation, prediction and explanation. To act freely is not to act unpredictably or inexplicably, as indeterminism in the sense of *mere* absence of causation seems to imply. On the other hand even a caused event cannot be predicted

116

without adequate information, and it seems that we could never know enough to predict our own actions strictly, since we cannot take into account the result of the prediction itself. (Cf. how opinion polls affect elections they predict.) Therefore it seems that an action may be unpredictable even though caused, or predictable even though uncaused. This raises questions about what grounds are in fact available to us for predictions, and what sorts of explanation can be given of actions.

All these problems clearly have bearings on the mind–body problem (philosophy of MIND). See also CAUSATION, REASON, EXPLANATION.

G. E. M. Anscombe (see bibliography to CAUSATION).

Aristotle, *De Interpretatione*, chapter 9, transl. with notes in J. L. Ackrill, *Aristotle's Categories*, Oxford UP, 1963. (Classic discussion of logical determinism. For modern development of Aristotle's view see also J. Lukasiewicz, 'On determinism' in S. McCall (ed.), *Polish Logic 1920–1939*, Clarendon, 1967, reprinted in Lukasiewicz's *Selected Works*, ed. L. Borkowski, North-Holland, 1970. For Aristotle on freewill generally cf. his *Nicomachean Ethics*, 3, 1–5, and on determinism and chance *Metaphysics*, book 6 (also called E), chapters 2–3 and *Physics*, book 2, chapters 4–6, with discussion by R. K. Sorabji in his *Necessity, Cause, and Blame*, Duckworth, 1980, chapters 1–2.

*B. Berofsky (ed.), *Free Will and Determinism*, Harper and Row, 1966. (Contains many classic discussions, including R. E. Hobart, 'Free will as involving determination and inconceivable without it', *Mind*, 1934, A. I. Melden, *Free Action*, RKP, 1961 (selection. See text above), D. Davidson, 'Actions, reasons, and causes', *Journal of Philosophy*, 1963 (often reprinted. Rehabilitation of role of causation), A. C. MacIntyre, 'Determinism', *Mind*, 1957 (the role of rationality), J. L. Austin's 'Ifs and Cans' (criticism of soft determinist analyses of 'could have . . .' in terms of 'would have . . . if . . .'; cf. also his 'A plea for excuses', *Proceedings of the Aristotelian Society*, 1956–7). For the rehabilitation cf. also D. W. Hamlyn, 'Causality and human behaviour', *Proceedings of the Aristotelian Society*, supplementary vol., 1964, reprinted in N. S. Care and C. Landesman (eds), *Readings in the Theory of Action*, Indiana UP, 1968, and G. Madell, 'Action and causal explanation', *Mind*, 1967.)

D. C. Dennett, *Elbow Room*, Oxford UP, 1984. (Defends version of compatibilism. Cf. also his 'I could not have done otherwise – so what?' *Journal of Philosophy*, 1984, with reply by van Inwagen.)

S. Evnine, *Donald Davidson*, Polity Press/Blackwell, 1991, pp. 47–9.

Frege, Gottlob

(Brief discussion of logical connection argument, with references.)

H. G. Frankfurt, 'Freedom of the will and the concept of a person', *Journal of Philosophy*, 1971, reprinted in Watson below. (Appeals to the notion of second-order volitions.)

J. Heil and A. Mele (eds), *Mental Causation*, Oxford UP, 1994. (Specially written essays by many notable writers. Cf. also W. Child, *Causality, Interpretation and the Mind*, Clarendon, 1994, for a partly, though only partly, related issue involving compatibilism.)

S. Morgenbesser and J. Walsh (eds), *Free Will*, 1962. (Includes medieval contributions.)

*D. F. Pears (ed.), *Freedom and the Will*, Macmillan, 1963. (Based on BBC series of popular talks. Two rather more advanced anthologies are T. Honderich (ed.), *Essays on Freedom of Action*, RKP, 1973 and K. Lehrer (ed.), *Freedom and Determinism*, Random House, 1966).

R. S. Peters, *The Concept of Motivation*, RKP, 1958.

K. R. Popper, 'Indeterminism in quantum physics and in classical physics', *British Journal for the Philosophy of Science*, 1950. (Prediction in people and machines.)

G. Ryle, *The Concept of Mind*, RKP, 1949. (Classic discussion of, *inter alia*, emotions, motives, the will, terms like 'voluntary' and 'involuntary'.)

P. van Inwagen, *An Essay on Free Will*, Oxford UP, 1983. (Defends incompatibilism. Cf. also his 'Ability and responsibility', *Philosophical Review*, 1978.)

*G. Watson (ed.), *Freewill*, Oxford UP, 1982. (Contains varied and important items.)

Frege, Gottlob. 1848–1925. German mathematical logician who was born in Wismar and worked in Jena. His work on the foundations of MATHEMATICS, which he hoped to derive from pure logic, was seriously interrupted when he was told of RUSSELL'S PARADOX by Russell. His greatest contributions to logic were his development of QUANTIFICATION and his elaboration of the distinction between sense and reference (see MEANING). Also influential were his distinction between CONCEPT and OBJECT, his use of the notion of FUNCTION, and his rejection of what was later called a 'speech act' analysis of NEGATION (which was later important for ethics: see NATURALISM). *Begriffsschrift*, 1879 (quantification), *Die Grundlagen der Arithmetik (The Foundations of Arithmetic)*, 1884. *Die Grundgesetze der Arithmetik*, 2 vols, 1893, 1903. P. T. Geach and M. Black (eds), *Translations from the Philosophical Writings of Gottlob Frege*, Blackwell, 1952 (contains 'Funktion und Begriff' ('Function and

Concept'), 1891, 'Über Begriff und Gegenstand' ('Concept and Object'), 1892, 'Über Sinn and Bedeutung' ('On Sense and Reference'), 1892, and 'Die Verneinung' ('Negation'), 1919, as well as chapter 1 of the *Begriffsschrift*). See also ASSERTION, FUNCTION, IDEA, IDENTITY, INTENSIONALITY AND INTENTIONALITY, NATURALISM, PSYCHOLOGISM, REFERRING, SENTENCES, UNIVERSALS.

Frege argument. Also known as the 'slingshot'. Argument based on alleged doctrines of Frege and claiming that if we allow intersubstitution of coextensive terms, and also of logically equivalent sentences, in certain areas where this seems plausible, then certain philosophical claims can be reduced to absurdity. For instance, it is argued, if we claim that causation holds between facts then it can be shown that any fact will be the cause of any other.

S. Evnine, *Donald Davidson*, Polity Press/Blackwell, 1991. (Appendix gives clear exposition of main argument.)

S. Kneale, 'The philosophical significance of Gödel's slingshot', *Mind*, 1995. (Examines at length two main versions of the argument, and their effects on topics like the analysis of definite DESCRIPTIONS, the existence of facts, and non-extensional logics.)

Function. (This entry is confined to logic and mathematics, except for its bibliography.) Some expressions have either numerical values or TRUTH VALUES which we can calculate once we give values to the VARIABLES in the expression. The rest of the expression is then called a function of the variables. Thus $3x + 7$ contains a variable, x, and a function $3(\ ) + 7$. But 'function' is often applied to the whole expression, including the variables. The function is then called a function of x. Its value in either case depends on he value given to x. Again if p and q are propositions, *p and q* (but not *p because q* is a *truth function* of p and of q. We can know the truth value of *p and q* (but not that of *p because q*) once we know the truth values of p and of q.

A value assigned to a variable in a function is called an *argument* of the function, and contributes to the value of the function. $x + 7$ has the value 19 for the argument 4.

Frege appealed to functions in analysing CONCEPTS and thereby predicates: . . . *is red* can be thought of as a function, because we can assign a truth value to *x is red* by assigning a value to x (i.e. replacing x by the name of something; *x is red* becomes true if we replace x by 'blood'), or alternatively by quantifying over x (see QUANTIFICATION).

x is red can be called a *propositional, statemental* (rare) or *sentential function*, according as *blood is red* is regarded as a proposition,

Functionalism

statement or sentence. Sentential functions are often called *open sentences*. The term *closed sentential function* is occasionally used of ordinary sentences.

J. Bigelow and R. Pargetter, 'Functions', *Journal of Philosophy*, 1987. (Discusses and defends one of four biological senses of the term.)

R. Carnap, *Introduction to Semantics*, Harvard UP, 1942, § 37. (Ambiguities, here ignored, of 'function' and 'propositional function'.)

R. Cummins, 'Functional analysis', *Journal of Philosophy*, 1975. (Criticizes two basic assumptions of previous analyses, and then offers his own. 'To ascribe a function to something is to ascribe a capacity to it which is singled out by its role in an analysis of some capacity of a containing system' (p. 765).)

P. T. Geach and M. Black, *Translations from the Philosophical Writings of Gottlob Frege*, Blackwell, 1952. (Contains Frege's 'Function and Concept' (cf. CONCEPT). Frege's symbolism is awkward and outdated. For sentences as referring to truth-values see his 'Sense and reference', ibid.)

P. Kitcher, 'Function and design', *Midwest Studies in Philosophy*, vol. 18, 1993. (Claims function implies design, but not intention or designer.)

R. Sorabji, 'Function', *Philosophical Quarterly*, 1964. (Non-logical senses.)

L. Wright, 'Functions', *Philosophical Review*, 1973. (Emphasizes their explanatory role, and offers an analysis which covers both conscious and natural functions, after discussing other views. For fuller development of appeal to natural selection which he makes see R. G. Millikan, *Language, Thought, and Other Biological Categories*, MIT Press, esp. chapter 1.)

Functionalism. Any view which analyses something in terms of how its functions, and especially in terms of its causes and effects. In particular, functionalism as an answer to the MIND/body problem defines mental states and properties in terms of what causes them, how they manifest themselves in behaviour, and how they interact with each other. Recently functionalism concerning the mind has developed from treating the mind as a kind of machine like a TURING MACHINE to treating it rather in terms of biological functions, on the grounds that this can better account for the mind's relation to the outer world (cf. INTENSIONALITY AND INTENTIONALITY). See also QUALE.

N. Block (ed.), *Readings in the Philosophy of Psychology*, vol. 1,

Functionalism

Harvard UP and Methuen, 1980. (Includes section on functionalism.)

T. Burge, 'Philosophy of language and mind: 1950–90', *Philosophical Review*, 1992. (See pp. 40–1 for a distinction between analytic and scientific functionalism.)

J. A. Foster, *The Immaterial Self*, Routledge, 1991, chapter 3. (Attacks functionalism.)

F. Jackson and P. Pettit, 'Functionalism and broad content', *Mind*, 1988. (Claims that the existence of broad (or wide) CONTENT is no objection to functionalism. Cf. also R. A. Wilson, 'Wide functionalism', *Mind*, 1994, which has further references as well.

W. G. Lycan (ed.), *Mind and Cognition*, Blackwell, 1990. (See item by Sober, which defends functionalism by distinguishing two kinds, Turing machine functionalism and teleological functionalism, through ending with some reservations. See also part VII for discussions of functionalism and qualia.)

N. Malcolm, ' "Functionalism" in philosophy of psychology', *Proceedings of the Aristotelian Society*, 1979–80. (Distinguishes and discusses four senses of the term.)

S. Shoemaker, *Identity, Cause, and Mind*, Cambridge UP, 1984, esp. chapters, 5, 8, 9, 12, 14, 15. (Defends functionalism. For definitions of it see pp. 111, 337.)

*P. Smith and O. R. Jones, *The Philosophy of Mind: an Introduction*, Cambridge UP, 1986. (See esp. chapters XI-XII, XV, XVI for sympathetic discussion.)

G

Gambler's fallacy. Assumption that if, for example, a coin has come down heads many times in succession, it is more likely to come down tails next time to 'restore the balance'. If the coin and its throwing are unbiased the tosses will be independent of each other and the coin is equally likely to come down heads next time. No finite run of heads, however long, violates the 'laws of chance'. (A long run of heads might suggest the coin is biased, so that the laws of chance do not apply, or not in the same way, and further heads should be expected. The 'gambler' assumes that the laws of chance do apply, and that therefore tails are to be expected. His mistake lies in the 'therefore'.) Cf. von Mises's 'principle of the impossibility of a gambling system', and the frequency theory of PROBABILITY.

R. von Mises, *Probability, Statistics and Truth*, Hodge, London, 1939 (German original, 1928), chapter 1.

Game theory. See DECISION THEORY.

General. See SENTENCES.

Generality constraint. Condition introduced by Evans in analysing what it is for someone to entertain (without necessarily believing) the thought that a certain object has a certain property. The person must be able to entertain the thought, concerning the same object, that it has any of the properties he has a conception of and also to entertain the thought, involving the same property, that any of the objects he can think about has it. To entertain the thought that Tom is tall one must be able to entertain the thoughts that Tom is

Gödel's theorems

short, clever, etc., and that Bill, George, etc., are tall. Thoughts which would be meaningless, e.g. that the person Tom is a prime number, are excluded, but other attitudes as well as belief are relevant: the thinker must be able to doubt, suppose, wish, etc. that Tom is tall.

G. Evans, *The Varieties of Reference*, Oxford UP, 1982, esp. pp. 100–5, 148. (Cf. also the occurrences of this term in the book's index, most of which are concerned with the application of the constraint to thoughts about oneself.)

Generative Grammar. See PSYCHOLINGUISTICS.

Genetic fallacy. Assumption that because the origins of something can be traced, the thing in question is somehow illegitimate or only apparent; e.g. that conscience is illusory if it develops from childhood fears. (How far can one compare: 'An oak is nothing but an acorn'?)

Genidentity. Sometimes things are said to have temporal parts or stages as well as spatial ones, the thing itself being regarded as a four-dimensional whole or 'space-time worm'. Two such parts of a single whole are then called genidentical (they are not of course identical since they are different parts). There are problems about when such stages do belong to the same whole, and whether things do have such temporal parts or stages is controversial. The term 'time-slice' is also used for 'temporal part'. I as I exist on Monday and I as I exist on Tuesday can be called time-slices of myself, but what is controversial is whether such time-slices are really parts of something, i.e. of a whole only part of which exists at any given time.

R. M. Chisholm, *Person and Object*, Allen and Unwin, 1976. (See esp. chapter 7 and Appendix A on identity through time and temporal parts.)

D. Lewis, *On the Plurality of Worlds*, Blackwell, 1986. (Doesn't use the term 'genidentity', but see its index under 'Persistence through time'.)

H. Reichenbach, *The Philosophy of Space and Time*, Dover Publications, 1957 (German original 1928), pp. 270–1.

Given. See PERCEPTION. Cf. also J. J. Ross, *The Appeal to the Given*, 1970.

Gnoseology. See EPISTEMOLOGY.

Gödel's theorems. In 1931 K. Gödel showed that for any AXIOM

123

Goldbach's conjecture

SYSTEM adequate to axiomatize arithmetic, starting from DECIDABLE axioms, there will always exist at least one well-formed formula (see AXIOM SYSTEM) not decidable in the system, even though we can see on other grounds that it is true. He also showed that a system's CONSISTENCY cannot be proved within the system itself. These are respectively his *first* and *second incompleteness theorems*: either or both are called *Gödel's theorem*. *Gödel's completeness theorem* (1930) says the first-order predicate CALCULUS is weakly COMPLETE.

J. R. Lucas, *The Freedom of the Will*, Oxford UP, 1970. (Makes controversial use of Gödel to distinguish men from machines.)
E. Nagel and J. R. Newman, *Gödel's Proof*, RKP, 1959. (Remarkably clear exposition for layman.)

Goldbach's conjecture. That every number greater than two is the sum of two primes. Common example of proposition necessarily true or necessarily false, but unproved and unrefuted, so that both its truth and its falsity are epistemically possible (see MODALITIES) though only one is logically possible.

Good. Very roughly, the property or characterization of a thing giving rise to commendation. Ever since Aristotle and his medieval followers failed to include 'good' in the scheme of CATEGORIES except by making it apply in all of them (see BEING on transcendentals), 'good' has caused bewilderment by its many uses. Indefinitely many things seem desirable as good, and for indefinitely many reasons. So what is the goodness which they all share, for surely some sort of unity must underlie all these various uses?

A famous claim made in 1903 by G. E. Moore was that goodness, in its primary sense, is a simple, unique, intrinsic and indefinable property, rather like yellow, only 'non-natural' – a term he never properly explained but which involves at least that goodness is not detectable by the senses or by scientific means, nor even by reason, but only by a sort of intuition; attempts to define it committed the 'naturalistic fallacy' (see NATURALISM).

Other writers, however, distrusting the apparent 'mysteriousness' of this, have defied Moore's strictures and offered a 'naturalistic' definition of goodness as a relational property, such as that of causing pleasure, or satisfying certain desires or interests. Such definitions have the merit of explaining why goodness appeals to us, but another approach has been common among empiricists such as logical POSITIVISTS and linguistic PHILOSOPHERS, though having its roots in the eighteenth century. This stresses the role in our life of words like 'good', which are mainly used in connection with

124

Good

commendation. 'That's a good car' might mean 'I hereby commend that car'. Originally such analyses were open to objections about cases where no commending seems to be in the offing, such as, 'If it's a good car, it'll be expensive'. 'If I hereby commend that car . . .', even if this makes sense, is clearly inadequate (cf. Searle). However, more sophisticated analyses might be tried, along such lines as, 'If I commend that car, then I shall be committed to expecting it to be expensive.'

One source of problems is that goodness, so far as it is a characteristic at all, is usually a consequential characteristic (see SUPERVENIENCE; in terms of the examples discussed there *good* is analogous to *right* rather than to *red*. *Good* is also sometimes said to be logically ATTRIBUTIVE. A good thief need not be a good man, and a knife good for cutting butter need not be good for cutting leather. But is *good* attributive in 'Pleasure, friendship and loyalty are all good'? All this suggests we should distinguish between the meaning of 'good' (or the nature of goodness) and the CRITERIA (loose sense) for applying it, i.e. the features which make a thing good. A good car and a good apple are not, or not obviously, good in different senses, but they are good for quite different reasons, and what may be *good-making properties* for one type of object may be bad-making ones for another (much as being red, round and luscious may make for beauty in a tomato, but not in a woman). Good-making properties may perhaps be logically or causally good-making. They are causally so if they cause their possessor to be good, as being an eater of certain foods may help to ensure that the eater is a good athlete. Logically, good-making properties, so far as they exist at all, may be expected mainly in artefacts or things with a function. Being sharp will cause a razor to be a good razor, but being able to remove beards in a short time while leaving the underlying skin intact may perhaps *constitute* being a good razor. Would it be contradictory to say a razor had this property but was not a good one, or perhaps was not a better one than an otherwise similar razor which did not have it? But here we return to the problems of SUPERVENIENCE.

As some of the above examples have implicitly shown, not all good things are intrinsically good. Things can be *instrumentally good*, i.e. good as means to an end, be the end itself good or not; or they can be *contributory goods*, serving as parts, perhaps valueless in themselves, of a good whole, as an otherwise neutral patch of paint may contribute to the value of a picture. The highest good, *summum bonum*, may be either that thing or feature which taken by itself is better than anything else, or that total situation which contains more good than any other. (Kant used '*supremum bonum*' for the former and '*summum bonum*' for the latter.) Both of these are

Good

distinct from what is merely *good on the whole*, where other things may be better. A further kind of goodness is *moral goodness*, which is limited mainly to people, actions and intentions, and perhaps emotions, desires and institutions, and facts or situations involving these (cf. MORAL). People sometimes say things like, 'Pain is not really evil; only sin is evil'. Do they mean the substantive judgment that only moral good and evil are really good and evil at all, or the triviality that pain in itself is not a moral evil? (Cf. on the Stoics, especially, below.)

The substantive question, 'What things are good?' was rather soft-pedalled by the logical positivists and the linguistic philosophers, who, though for different reasons in each case, thought it their business to analyse, not to preach. But earlier and later philosophers have been less hesitant. Moore picked on certain aesthetic experiences and personal relationships (and heavily influenced the 'Bloomsbury set' of the first quarter of the twentieth century.) Aristotle chose a life in accordance with (the highest) virtue as the main good, and the Stoics chose virtue as the only good, while Kant called the good will the only unconditional good. More recently an extremely influential view, especially among UTILITARIANS, has been that ultimately only states of mind can be good (Sidgwick); but this has been criticized on the grounds that the goodness of many states of mind presupposes that of other things desired for their own sakes (Wiggins). See also BETTER.

Aristotle, *Nicomachean Ethics*, book 1. (The good for man.)
P. T. Geach, 'Good and evil', *Analysis*, vol. 17, 1956, reprinted in P. Foot (ed.), *Theories of Ethics*, Oxford UP, 1967. (Claims that 'good' is attributive and descriptive (see NATURALISM.) See short bibliography added in reprint for examinations of linguistic behaviour of 'good'.)
R. M. Hare, *The Language of Morals*, Oxford UP, 1952. (Speech act analysis. Meaning and criteria. Can just anything be good? On this last cf. P. Foot, 'Moral beliefs', *Proceedings of the Aristotelian Society*, 1958–9, reprinted in P. Foot (ed.), *Theories of Ethics*, Oxford UP, 1967.)
N. M. Lemos, 'Higher goods and the myth of Tithonus', *Journal of Philosophy*, 1993. (Defends view that some goods are incommensurably higher than others.)
G. E. Moore, *Principia Ethica*, Cambridge UP, 1903. (Good as a simple indefinable quality. Last chapter discusses what things are good.)
R. Nozick, *The Examined Life*, Simon and Schuster, 1989, chapter 10. (Criticizes Sidgwick's outlook, though without mentioning him.)

J. R. Searle, 'Meaning and speech acts', *Philosophical Review*, 1962, reprinted with discussions and additions in C. D. Rollins (ed.), *Knowledge and Experience*, Pittsburgh UP, 1962. (Attacks speech act analyses of 'good'.)

H. Sidgwick, *The Methods of Ethics*, Macmillan, final version, 1907 (1st edn 1874), book IV, chapter XIV.

G. H. von Wright, *The Varieties of Goodness*, RKP, Humanities Press, 1963. (Full discussion of the different uses of 'good'.)

D. Wiggins, *Truth, Invention and the Meaning of Life* (pamphlet), *Proceedings of the British Academy*, 1976, reprinted in his *Needs, Values, Truth*, Blackwell, 1987; see esp. §§ 1–6, 10–15. (Discusses, *inter alia*, whether the ultimate good can consist in states of feeling or the satisfaction of desires. Difficult.)

Grammar (depth, surface). See STRUCTURE (DEEP AND SURFACE).

Grammars (generative etc.). A generative grammar is a set of elements and rules which will generate the grammatically acceptable sentences of a language in a way that reveals their grammatical structure. (Cf. the way the rules of chess generate possible situations on a chessboard.) N. Chomsky in his early work distinguishes three types of generative grammar, in order of increasing adequacy: *finite state grammars, phrase-structure grammars, transformational grammars*. To generate something rules are given for replacing one set of symbols by another. Sometimes the rules of a phrase-structure grammar specify that the relevant symbols are replaceable only if they precede or follow certain other symbols. Such more powerful rules, and grammars containing at least one of them, are *context-dependent (context-sensitive)*. The remaining replacement rules, and grammars limited to them, are *context-free*. See also STRUCTURE.

G. Harman (ed.), *On Noam Chomsky: Critical Essays*, Doubleday Anchor, 1974. (See especially Searle's article, 'Chomsky's revolution in linguistics', for general introduction.)

J. Lyons, *Chomsky*, Fontana, 1970, expanded 1977. (Elementary. For more elaborate treatment see J. Lyons, *Introduction to Theoretical Linguistics*, 1968.)

Greatest happiness principle. See UTILITARIANISM.

Grelling's paradox. See HETEROLOGICAL.

Grue. See CONFIRMATION.

H

Haecceity. Anglicized form of haecceitas (literally 'thisness'), introduced by SCOTUS for an individual essence, i.e. an essence peculiar to and distinguishing an individual, not an essence of a species. *Haecceitism* is the belief in haecceities, and *anti-haecceitism* their rejection, or else the rejection of primitive transworld identity (see POSSIBLE WORLDS).

R. M. Adams, 'Primitive thisness and primitive identity', *Journal of Philosophy*, 1979. (Discusses Leibniz's position, identity of indiscernibles, and defends primitive thisness and primitive transworld identities, though insisting they are different and independent notions.)

D. Kaplan, 'How to Russell a Frege-Church', *Journal of Philosophy*, 1975, pp. 722–3, reprinted in M. Loux (ed.), *The Possible and the Actual: Readings in the Metaphysics of Modality*, Cornell UP, 1979, pp. 216–17. (Haecceitism and anti-haecceitism.)

G. S. Rosenkrantz, *Haecceity: an Ontological Essay*, Kluwer, Dordrecht, 1993.

Hare, Richard M. 1919–. British philosopher, born at Backwell near Bristol and working in Oxford, then USA, whose main contribution has been to ETHICS, where his approach is inspired by 'linguistic philosophy'. He opposes NATURALISM, advocates a 'prescriptivist' analysis of moral judgements, and treats moral judgements and philosophical analyses as distinct and independent of each other. He combines all this with an emphasis, derived from KANT, on UNIVERSALIZABILITY as what distinguishes moral from other evaluative judgments. *The Language of Morals*, 1952. *Freedom and*

Reason, 1963 (develops his earlier book). *Moral Thinking: Its Levels, Methods and Print*, Oxford UP, 1981. See also CRITERION, GOOD, IMPERATIVE, OUGHT, PHRASTIC.

Heap (paradox of). Also called '*sorites*' (Greek for 'heaped') or (less often) 'bald man'. It seems that for any number *n*, if *n* grains form a heap so do *n*-1 grains; a heap cannot stop being a heap by losing just one grain. But if follows that *any* number of grains will form a heap, including one or even zero. The paradox affects all vague predicates, i.e. (it is usually claimed) most ordinary ones, and is important for the law of EXCLUDED MIDDLE; cf. also TRUTH, SUPERVALUATION. A special 'fuzzy logic' has been developed in connexion with this. See also VAGUENESS.

J. A Goguen, 'The logic of inexact concepts', *Synthese*, 1968–9. (Introduction to fuzzy logic, used to solve paradox.)

D. Raffman, 'Vagueness without paradox', *Philosophical Review*, 1994. (Appeals to psychological considerations to help solve paradox.)

*R. M. Sainsbury, *Paradoxes*, Cambridge UP, 1988 (revised, 1995) chapter 2. (Cf. also his 'Degrees of belief and degrees of truth', *Philosophical Papers*, 1986, which uses paradox to defend degrees of truth. Asterisk applies to first item.)

C. Travis, 'Vagueness, observation, and sorites', *Mind*, 1985. (Appeals to context of utterance rather than vagueness of predicates to solve paradox.)

Hedonism. *Psychological hedonism* has three main forms: That everyone desires only his own PLEASURE or happiness. That everyone necessarily aims only to maximize his own pleasure. That everyone always acts on his strongest desire. The term also sometimes applies to the theory that only pleasant thoughts can motivate actions. The three main senses can also (and the third properly speaking should) be called *psychological egoism*.

Ethical hedonism has two main forms: That only pleasure is ultimately good. That every action should aim to maximize pleasure (not necessarily the agent's).

For *qualitative hedonism* see PLEASURE.

The *paradox of hedonism* says that pleasure is often best attained by not seeking it. See also UTILITARIANISM.

Hegel, George W. F. 1770–1831. Born in Stuttgart, he worked at a various German universities, especially Berlin, where he died. He is usually classified as an objective IDEALIST. His system is characterized by the use of a DIALECTIC of thesis, antithesis and synthesis

Heidegger, Martin

(though some scholars warn against reading too much of this into Hegel), and could perhaps be described as an attempt to trace the development or emergence of 'spirit' or 'Geist', both systematically in a logical doctrine of categories and historically in the process of world history. He influenced such widely diverse thinkers as MARX, BRADLEY and CROCE, and stimulated vigorous hostility in KIERKEGAARD and SCHOPENHAUER. *Phänomenologie des Geistes*, 1807. *Wissenschaft der Logik*, 3 vols, 1812, 1813, 1816. *Die Encyclopädie der philosophischen Wissenshaften im Grundrisse*, 1817 (first part is often known as the 'Lesser Logic', second part concerns philosophy of nature, third part covers same ground as the *Phänomenologie*). *Grundlinien der Philosophie des Rechts*, 1820 (or 1821). See also DIALECTIC, IDEA, METAPHYSICS.

F. C. Beiser (ed.), *The Cambridge Companion to Hegel*, Cambridge UP, 1993. (See pp. 488–90 for list of translations.)

Heidegger, Martin. 1889–1976. Born in Baden, he lived and taught in Germany, especially in Freiburg. He was a leading EXISTENTIALIST and his work centred round an investigation of 'being', both that which is proper to human beings, '*Dasein*', and that which belongs to things in general. In his early days he was much influenced by HUSSERL. *Sein und Zeit (Being and Time)*, 1927. *Kant und das Problem der Metaphysik (Kant and the Problem of Metaphysics)*, 1929. *Holzwege (Woodpaths)*, 1950. *Einführung in die Metaphysik (Introduction to Metaphysics)*, 1953. *Die Frage nach dem Ding; zu Kants Lehre von den transzendentalen Grundsätzen*, 1962. See also JASPERS, MARCEL.

Hereditary property. If an object a stands in relation R to an object b, any property of a which must *ipso facto* belong to b is R-hereditary. If R is the relation *greater by two than*, then the property of being even is R-hereditary among numbers, since if a given number is even then any number it is greater by (exactly) two than must also be even. Sometimes a property of numbers is called hereditary if it must belong to the successor of any number to which it belongs. Here R is being implicitly specified as 'has as its successor'.

Hermeneutic. Concerning interpretation. *Hermeneutics*, originating in Biblical studies, has developed, through F. Schleiermacher (1768–1834) and W. Dilthey (1833–1911) in particular, to an approach now associated especially with H.-G. Gadamer (1900–) which in interpreting history and thought denies both that there is a single objective true interpretation transcending all viewpoints and that we are for ever confined within our own viewpoint. Interpretation is rather something to be arrived at by a gradual interplay between the subject-matter and the interpreter's initial position.

H.-G. Gadamer, *Philosophical Hermeneutics*, California UP, 1976. (Selected essays in translation. See editor's introduction, which links Gadamer with Wittgenstein and other Continental writers. Cf. R. Rorty, *Philosophy and the Mirror of Nature*, Blackwell, 1979 (see index), which also links hermeneutics with W. Sellars and Quine. For further connexion with Anglo-Saxon philosophy see B. Harrison, *An Introduction to the Philosophy of Language*, Macmillan, 1979, pp. 166–7.

Heterological. Not applying to itself. 'German' (which is not a German word) and 'monosyllabic' (which is not a monosyllabic word) are heterological adjectives. *Homological* (or *autological*) means 'applying to itself'. 'English' (which is an English word) and 'polysyllabic' (which is a polysyllabic word) are homological adjectives.

The heterological paradox, attributed to K. Grelling (1886–1942, died in Auschwitz) and H. Weyl (1885–1955), asks whether 'heterological' is itself a heterological adjective. If it is, it does not apply to itself, and so is not heterological. If it is not, it does apply to itself, and so is heterological. A related, but different, paradox asks whether the attribute (not adjective) *not-possessing-itself* possesses itself. Both paradoxes are of the kind sometimes called semantic (see PARADOX, and also RUSSELL'S PARADOX, TYPES).

G. Ryle, 'Heterologicality', *Analysis*, vol. 11, 1951, reprinted in M. Macdonald (ed.), *Philosophy and Analysis*, Blackwell, 1954, and in Ryle's *Collected Papers*, Hutchinson, vol. 2, 1971.

Heuristic. Concerning discovery, as against proof. *Heuristics* is the study of methods and discovery. A *heuristic* is a procedure for achieving a result which does not consist simply in applying certain general rules which are *guaranteed* to lead to the result in question. Contrast ALGORITHM.

G. Polya, *How to Solve It*, Princeton UP, 1945, 1957, 1971, Doubleday, 1957.

Historicism. Originally, any of several views of emphasizing the importance of history, especially the view that things should always be seen in terms of their historical development. But for Popper, who uses *historism* for the above, historicism is the view that historical events are determined by inevitable laws, which history aims to

Historism

predict, and that corporate wholes cannot be reduced to the individuals composing them.

D. E. Lee and R. N. Beck, 'The meaning of "historicism" ', *American Historical Review*, 1953–4. (Cf. also G. D. Mitchell (ed.), *A Dictionary of Sociology*, RKP, 1968.)

K. R. Popper, *The Poverty of Historicism*, 1957, written earlier. (Cf. his *The Open Society*, RKP, 1945.)

Historism. See HISTORICISM.

History (philosophy of). History proper seems limited to the sphere of human action, natural events being included only so far as they affect or are affected by human action; things like the 'history of the universe' seem rather secondary. Problems in the philosophy of mind, about action, freewill, causation, rationality, are therefore especially relevant to the philosophy of history, and are connected to the question what is the aim of history: is this to describe the course of events or to explain it, and what sorts of EXPLANATION can be given? Are general laws to be sought, and if so, of what kinds? Is history a science?

Another set of problems concerns how history is possible and how historical claims can be justified. The reality of the past and the justifiability of using memory are subjects for metaphysics and epistemology, but the philosopher of history asks how statements about the past can be verified, both in general and taking account of the various kinds of statement and kinds of evidence, and what is their meaning. Are they really, as some logical positivists held, about the extant evidence? On what principles are facts and topics to be selected, and how far can or should the historian be objective and neutral? Should he 'stick to the facts'? What counts as doing this?

The purpose *of* history must be distinguished from purpose *in* history. Can purposes or patterns be discerned in history either as a whole or in parts? Is history in any way cyclic? What can we learn from it? *Critical philosophy of history*, as well as covering the questions mentioned previously, asks what kind of answers these latter questions can have and what count as answers. The answers themselves are the province of *speculative philosophy of history*. Some questions, e.g. the elucidating of concepts like *progress, historical event, historical period*, may fall between these provinces.

Metahistory properly means philosophy of history, but is often limited to the speculative branch. See also HISTORICISM, EXPLANATION.

R. F. Atkinson, *Knowledge and Explanation in History: An Intro-*

duction to the Philosophy of History, Macmillan, 1978. (Covers relations between philosophy and history, how we can know of the past, objectivity, explanation, causation, values.)

A. Bullock, 'The historian's purpose', C. Dawson, 'The problem of meta-history', *History Today*, 1951 (February, June). (Both on metahistory.)

W. H. Dray, *Philosophy of History*, Prentice-Hall, 1964. (This and Walsh are two introductions to both critical and speculative sides.)

*P. Gardiner (ed.), *The Philosophy of History*, Oxford UP, 1974. (Anthology on relevant issues.)

S. Hook (ed.), *Philosophy and History*, New York UP, 1963. (Discussions between philosophers and historians.)

E. Loone, *Soviet Marxism and Analytical Philosophies of History*, Verso, 1992, trans. by B. Pearce from 1980 Russian original. (Discussion by Estonian analytical philosopher with Marxist background. Foreword by E. Gellner.)

W. H. Walsh, *An Introduction to Philosophy of History*, Hutchinson, 1951.

Hobbes, Thomas. 1588–1679, Born at Malmesbury he lived in England and France. He is now best known for his political philosophy, defending an absolute sovereignty as the only way to ensure social security and prevent life from being 'solitary, poor, nasty, brutish and short', as it would be in the 'state of nature'. This sovereignty he based on a social contract among men, but the sovereign had duties only to God. As usually interpreted, he based the duty of political obedience on self-interest. (Cf. also ROUSSEAU.) He also developed a nominalist view of UNIVERSALS, and a philosophy of nature which analysed everything, including man, in terms of matter and motion. He was also much influenced by his study of geometry. At one point he engaged in controversy with Descartes. *De Cive*. 1642 (political). *Leviathan*, 1651 (main political work, including also treatment of man). *De Corpore*, 1655, transl. 1656 as *Elements of Philosophy, The First Section, Concerning Body* (metaphysics and treatment of inanimate nature). See also COLLINGWOOD, MODALITIES.

Holism. Any theory which approaches its subject-matter as a whole rather than bit by bit. An example would be Quine's view that 'our statements about the external world face the tribunal of sense experience not individually but as a body', because we can always avoid accepting, or avoid rejecting, any given scientific view by making sufficient adjustments elsewhere in our system. Elsewhere holism may insist that the properties of a whole cannot be predicted

Homological

or explained in terms of those of its parts, or (especially in political philosophy) that the whole is more important than the parts. *Holistic explanation* claims that certain things, especially in psychology, must be explained not in terms of individual beliefs or desires (say) but only of complete systems of them.

J. Foder and E. Le Pore, *Holism: a Shopper's Guide*, Blackwell, 1992. (Discussions of some notable modern views.)

C Peacocke, *Holistic Explanation*, Oxford UP, 1979. (Discusses issues arising because explaining action requires appealing to both belief and desire, and explaining perception requires appealing to both one's location and what the world is like there. Difficult.)

W. V. O. Quine, 'Two dogmas of empiricism', *Philosophical Review*, 1951, revised and reprinted in his *From a logical Point of View*, Harvard UP, 1953. (For quotation see p. 38 of original, p. 41 of reprint. The second 'dogma' is the view that 'each meaningful statement is equivalent to some logical construct upon terms which refer to immediate experience' (opening paragraph).)

Homological. See HETEROLOGICAL.

Homophonic. See MEANING.

Humanity (principle of). See CHARITY.

Hume, David. 1711–76. Scottish, born in Edinburgh, and generally regarded as the greatest of 'British empiricists', Hume was an historian and a man of letters as well as a philosopher. His religious opinions stood in the way of his having an academic post but he was for a short time Chargé d'Affaires in Paris where he was much celebrated and he later came to hold the post of Under-Secretary of State in England from which he resigned in 1769. He examined meticulously our modes of thinking, both deductive and inductive, and claimed that they were far less powerful than we assumed. This led him to generally sceptical conclusions about such notions as REASON, CAUSATION and necessity (see MODALITIES), and about how far we are justified in postulating a world outside ourselves, or indeed a self for it to be outside (as against a mere set of experiences). (Cf. also NATURALISM.) He developed a philosophy based on 'impressions', and making substantial use of the then relatively new doctrine of the *association of ideas*; he drew out the implications of this philosophy also for psychology and ethics. KANT claimed that it was Hume who 'aroused him from his dogmatic slumbers'. *A Treatise of Human Nature*, 1739–40. *An Enquiry con-*

cerning Human Understanding, 1748. *An Enquiry concerning the Principles of Morals*, 1751. (The two *Enquiries* are shorter and later versions of parts of the *Treatise*.) *Dialogues concerning Natural Religion*, 1779. L. Selby-Bigge (ed.), *Hume's Treatise of Human Nature*, Clarendon, 1888, and *Enquiries concerning Human Understanding and concerning the Principles of Morals*, Clarendon, 2 vol. edn, 1902. (These are the standard modern editions and contain full analytical indexes.) See also ANALYTIC, HUTCHESON, IDENTITY, MORAL SENSE (bibliography), NATURALISM, PERCEPTION, POSITIVISM, REID, ROUSSEAU, RUSSELL, SCEPTICISM.

Husserl, Edmund. 1859–1938. Born in Moravia, he spent his life teaching in German universities. He is usually regarded as the leading figure in PHENOMENOLOGY, which took two successive forms in his own work, descriptive and transcendental. His early work (1891) was still under the influence of PSYCHOLOGISM, which in his mature and phenomenological stages he vigorously rejected. His early phenomenology (1900–1) has some affinities with linguistic philosophy. He was influenced especially by BRENTANO and in turn influenced EXISTENTIALSIM. *Philosophie der Arithmetik*, 1891. *Logische Untersuchungen*, 1900–1. *Ideen zu einer reinen Phänomenologie und phänomenologischen Philosophie*, 1913. *Meditations Cartésiennes*, 1931. *Die Krisis der europäischen Wissenschaften und die transzendentale Phänomenologie*, 1936 (in part; full edition 1954). See also CATEGORIES, HEIDEGGER, MERLEAU-PONTY, NATURALISM.

Hutcheson, Francis. 1694–1746 (or 1747). Born in Ulster, he worked in Dublin and at Glasgow university. Though he also wrote on metaphysics and logic, he is important mainly as a theorist of the MORAL SENSE school who also anticipated some features of utilitarianism. He developed and systematized the work of SHAFTESBURY, and influenced HUME, *Inquiry into the Original of Our Ideas of Beauty and Virtue*, 1725. *An Essay on the Nature and Conduct of the Passions and Affections with Illustrations on the Moral Sense*, 1728. See also PRICE, SMITH.

Hypothesis. See LAWS.

Hypothetical. See CONDITIONALS.

Hypothetical constructs. See LOGICAL CONSTRUCTIONS.

Hypothetico-deductive method. See INDUCTION.

I

Icons. See SIGN.

Idea. The Greek words *idea* and *eidos*, virtually synonymous, and etymologically linked with 'vision', may originally have meant 'visible form' but by Plato's time could mean 'nature', 'essence' or 'kind'. Plato's Ideas were non-material objects outside the mind, though the mind could know them. The translation 'Form' is therefore often preferred as less misleading. (Cf. FORM, UNIVERSALS.) Plato considered but rejected the view that 'ideas' were something in our minds. Some Stoics adopted it, but in later Greek and medieval writings ideas tended to be in the mind of God.

For many modern philosophers 'idea' has been a technical term important for their systems, used in many senses, often in the same philosopher (notably Locke), but almost always for something in or having reference to the mind.

Its meanings include: what is immediately present to the mind in an experience (SENSE DATUM, feeling); what is before the mind when it reflects, remembers, introspects, imagines (images, etc.); what the mind preserves from its experiences, or finds within itself, or constructs in various ways out of simpler ideas (one's idea of red, colour, gratitude, number); things like these latter but common to different people ('the' idea of red); a quality in an object which causes experiences (Locke, but rarely even there); the meaning of a word; the subjective associations of a word, contrasted with its meaning (Frege); a representation of something that cannot be experienced (Kant, based on Plato). For Hegel 'idea' means something like the overall pattern or purpose in the universe or is a term whose use centres on this. In aesthetics 'idea' is sometimes used in a Platonic sense, for what a work of art aims to embody or copy.

Because it is so ambiguous, particularly between uses for datable existents (sense datum, image, etc) and logical uses (meaning of a word, 'the' idea of . . . , etc.), 'idea' has largely been replaced for technical purposes by more specific terms like 'sense datum', 'image', 'CONCEPT'.

See also INNATE.

F. H. Bradley, *Principles of Logic*, 1883, 2nd (revised) edition 1922. (Opening chapter, based on idealist standpoint, criticizes confusion due to ambiguity of 'idea').

I. Hacking, *Why Does Language Matter to Philosophy?*, Cambridge UP, 1975. (Discusses seventeenth-century usage of 'idea'.)

Ideal. Entity or attribute of a kind suggested by 'IDEA'. 'Ideal' suggests freedom from the imperfections of the material world, together with unattainability (cf. Platonic 'Ideas'), but also the unreality of what depends simply on the mind. There is also the neutral sense, 'connected with ideas, or the mind'. The 'unreality' and 'neutral' strands are rather commoner in philosophy, especially before the twentieth century, than in popular usage.

Idealism. A doctrine, or set of doctrines, to the effect that reality is in some way mental. Idealism is concerned with 'IDEA' more closely than with 'IDEAL'. It is not primarily concerned with ethics or conduct, though certain ethical views have sometimes been associated with it. Idealism is contrasted primarily with REALISM, though also with MATERIALISM. Rarely, it means simply that the universe is spiritual in the sense of depending on God. Sometimes, however, views are called idealist which hold that reality is outside the mind, but can only be described from some point of view – there are different ways of looking at reality, none of which is more correct that the others, rather as whether Oxford is to the right of Cambridge depends on where one is looking from. In this wide sense, such outlooks as PRAGMATISM and CONVENTIONALISM are idealist. Kant, similarly, held that reality existed independently, but that how it appeared to us was determined by the structure of the human mind. Public empirical knowledge was therefore possible, but only of appearances ('phenomena'). He called himself an empirical realist but a transcendental idealist, meaning by this that what we perceive is in general not illusory, but as real as perceptible things could be, but that nevertheless philosophy forces us to assume that they are appearances of things which in themselves are quite unknowable by us.

Identically true, false

Full-blooded idealism holds that reality is mental. 'To be is to be perceived', as Berkeley said. Matter does not exist except in the form of ideas in the mind, or as a manifestation of mental activity. The 'mind' in question may be one's own mind (solipsism: see SCEPTICISM), minds in general, or the mind of God (Berkeley).

Absolute idealism developed after Kant, notably with Hegel, and was popular in Britain from about 1865 to 1925. It takes many forms, but its central point is that there is only one ultimately real thing, the Absolute, which is spiritual in nature. Other things are partial aspects of this, or illusory appearances generated by it. Here idealism becomes a form of MONISM. The Absolute is so called because it alone does not depend on or presuppose anything and does not have its properties relative to something else.

A distinction is sometimes made between *subjective* and *objective idealism*. 'Subjective idealism' is used mainly of views that the only reality is ideas in the mind, especially the human mind. The term is often, however, applied to Berkeley, though he himself used *immaterialism*. 'Objective idealism', like absolute idealism, applies mainly to forms of idealism which place reality outside the human mind. It is used especially when the arguments in favour of idealism say that appearances are contradictory, and therefore are *mere* appearances of a reality lying behind them; subjective idealism, by contrast, says that appearances and minds are the only reality (cf. also PHENOMENALISM).

Plato's theory of IDEAS, or FORMS, is not usually called idealism now, since these Ideas, though not material, are not mental or mind-dependent. See also BEING.

A. C. Ewing, *Idealism: a Critical Survey*, 1934. (Sympathetic, though not himself an idealist.)

A. C. Ewing (ed.), *The Idealist Tradition*, Free Press, 1957. (Selections from leading idealists.)

J. Foster, *The Case for Idealism*, RKP, 1982. (Defence of a moderate version)

J. Hospers, *Introduction to Philosophical Analysis*, RKP, 1956, chapter 8. (Discusses subjective idealism in relation to other theories.)

R. Le Poidevin, 'Fables and models', *Proceedings of the Aristotelian Society*, supplementary vol., 1991. (See p. 73 for a distinction between idealism and phenomenalism.)

A. Quinton, *Absolute Idealism*, 1972. (Dawes Hicks lecture at British Academy, 1971).

Identically true, false. See IDENTITY.

Identity. Attribute of being a single thing or single kind. In ordinary speech two things may be called numerically identical (or one in number: 'Persia and Iran are identical'), or identical (or one) in type or species (exactly similar, as with 'identical twins'). Philosophers keep 'identical' for the first sense, using 'indiscernible' for the second (see LEIBNIZ'S LAW). But what is identity, in this first sense? Is it a relation between a thing and itself? If so, every true statement of identity should be trivial, or else senseless. Hume used time to solve the problem, saying that identity statements state that an object existing at one time is the same as itself existing at another, e.g. 'This chair is the same as the one here yesterday.' This could suggest that GENIDENTITY is in question, but anyway this covers only some cases. Suppose Smith is mayor of a certain town. Then 'Smith is Smith' is trivial but 'Smith is the mayor' is not, even though the words 'the mayor' refer to Smith. It was this that made Frege distinguish between sense and reference (see MEANING), saying that what gave content to an identity statement was the different ways in which the object was described.

A distinction exists between two approaches to identity statements. On a *conceptualist* approach one can only say '*a* is the same so-and-so as *b*' where 'so-and-so' is a SORTAL term. On a *realist* approach 'so-and-so' can be replaced by a non-sortal term like 'thing' or 'object'. The identity is here given, as it were, in the world itself and does not depend on the concepts we apply. It is a further question, however, whether identity is relative, in the sense that *a* might be the same so-and-so, but not the same such-and-such, as *b*, e.g. was Nixon the same official (namely the American president), though not the same man, as Eisenhower?

This distinction between two approaches may be relevant to various problems which arise because things persist in time, for they may persist for different periods if described in different ways. Suppose a gold coin melts. Then it seems that the coin is destroyed but the piece of gold is not. If the coin *is* the piece of gold, then the same thing seems to be destroyed and not destroyed. If the coin is not the piece of gold, then we seem to have two things in the same place at the same time (though not *throughout* the same time). Perhaps the gold is not identical with, but 'constitutes', the coin (Wiggins; cf. BEING).

Furthermore, a coin which melts is presumably destroyed, but a baby which grows up is not destroyed, though it stops being a baby. But *what* stops being a baby and lives to be eighty? And how long does the baby last? Eighty years? (Terms like 'baby' are called *phase terms* or *phase universals.*)

Also can 'identity statements be contingent? 'Smith is the mayor' seems contingent. Yet 'Smith is Smith' seems necessary. See MODALITIES.

Identity

Sometimes *a* is called *strictly identical* with *b* if whatever can be said of one can be said of the other (INTENSIONALITY apart). Some would say that an adult is identical, but not strictly identical, with the baby he once was, on the grounds that the adult but not the baby could be called, for example, married: one can say, 'The baby you knew is now married.' But there are no married babies. 'Strict' or 'perfect identity' is also sometimes used for identity that cannot be reduced to GENIDENTITY.

Further problems concern the criteria of identity, both for objects and for events, properties, propositions, etc. Is the property red identical with that of reflecting or emitting light of certain wavelengths? Spatiotemporal continuity is an obvious criterion to use for objects, but a suit need not possess it (if trousers and coat are separated), and a sound or toothache can be intermittent. We must also ask, continuity of what? Not of matter, since a body, and still more a flame, are constantly changing their matter; and perhaps they change their shape and other properties too. Furthermore we must be able to individuate places and times themselves, i.e. tell when we have one and when another, if we are to use them to individuate objects. Particular attention has been given to the question of *personal identity*. What is a PERSON? How are persons, minds and bodies related? What role do things like memory and traits of character play?

Questions of identity are also important in aesthetics. How is Olivier related to Hamlet when it is true to say both that Olivier is now alone on the stage and that Hamlet is now alone on the stage?

On whether identity is intrinsic or extrinsic, and for the 'ship of Theseus' problem, see INTRINSIC AND EXTRINSIC.

To identify *a* with *b* is simply to claim, or assume, that *a* and *b* are identical. To identify *a* as *b* (or as a *b*) is to pick out *a* by either taking it to be identical with *b* or attributing *b*-type characteristics to it. I can identify Smith *with* a spy only if I already have some spy in mind, but I can identify him *as* a spy without this.

The *law of identity*, one of the traditional 'laws of thought', says that everything is what it is, or that if something is true, it is true. A proposition that is an instance of this law (e.g. 'A cat is a cat'), or one that can be transformed into such an instance by applying to it the rules of logic (e.g. 'If Tiddles is a cat, Tiddles does not fail to be a cat'), can be called *identically true*, and its negation identically false. See also LEIBNIZ'S LAW, IDENTITY THEORY OF MIND, GENIDENTITY.

D. Hume, *Treatise*, 1739, book 1, part 4, § 2 (pp. 200–1 in L. A. Selby-Bigge's edition, Clarendon, 1888 (1946 reprint)).

Identity of indiscernibles

S. Kripke, *Naming and Necessity*, Blackwell, 1980, original version 1972. (Discusses, *inter alia*, both identity across POSSIBLE WORLDS and the nature of identity.)

J. Locke, *Essay concerning Human Understanding*, 1690, part 2, chapter 27. (Pioneering discussion of personal identity. See discussions by A. Flew, 'Locke and the problem of personal identity', *Philosophy*, 1951, and (more difficult) D. Wiggins, 'Locke, Butler, and the stream of consciousness: and men as a natural kind', *Philosophy*, 1976, both reprinted in Perry, and for elaboration and defence of Locke's view see C. Rovane, 'Self-reference: the radicalization of Locke', *Journal of Philosophy*, 1993.

M. K. Munitz (ed.), *Identity and Individuation*, New York UP, 1971. (Essays, including S. Kripke's 'Identity and necessity', which is also in S. P. Schwartz (ed.), *Naming, Necessity, and Natural Kinds*, Cornell UP, 1977, and (with editorial introduction) in T. Honderich and M. F. Burnyeat (eds), *Philosophy As It Is*, Penguin, 1979.)

H. Noonan (ed.), *Identity* and *Personal Identity*, Dartmouth Publishing Co., 1993. (Two wide-ranging volumes of essays. See also his own *Personal Identity*, Routledge, 1989, which discusses historical and modern views while developing his own.)

J. Perry (ed.), *Personal Identity*, California UP, 1975. (Important discussions, historical and modern, though less full than Noonan.)

A. O. Rorty (ed.), *The Identity of Persons*, Cornell UP, 1976. (Readings.)

M. Schechtman, 'Personhood and personal identity', *Journal of Philosophy*, 1990. (Traits of character, memory, etc., are inadequate as criteria for grounding personal identity.)

S. Shoemaker, *Self-Knowledge and Self-Identity*, Cornell UP, 1963. (Extended discussion of personal identity. See pp. 36–8 for 'strict' or 'perfect' identity as not reducible to genidentity (though not so called).)

D. Wiggins, *Sameness and Substance*, Blackwell, 1980. (Discussion of identity, substance, and personal identity. Conceptualist but claims identity never relative. Cf. his 'On being in the same place at the same time', *Philosophical Review*, 1968 (rather easier), and symposium with M. J. Woods, 'The individuation of things and places', *Proceedings of the Aristotelian Society*, supplementary vol., 1963. On identity and constitution see also H. W. Noonan, 'Constitution is identity', *Mind*, 1993.)

B. A. O. Williams, 'Personal identity and individuation', *Proceedings of the Aristotelian Society*, 1956–7. (Bases personal identity on bodily continuity.)

Identity of indiscernibles. See LEIBNIZ'S LAW.

Identity theory of mind

Identity theory of mind. Theory that various conscious phenomena are identical with states or processes in the brain or central nervous system. *Brain process theory, physicalism, central state materialism,* or just *materialism*, are alternative names for the theory (the third for the version using the central nervous system). The conscious phenomena concerned may be limited to sensations and pains, or may include also thoughts, beliefs, desires, emotions. In the former case a BEHAVIOURIST explanation of emotions, etc., may be given.

The theory may take two main forms, called TYPE and TOKEN IDENTITY THEORY. The former identifies types of sensations etc. with types of brain-states etc., so that whenever a certain sensation (e.g. a certain kind of headache) occurs a brain-state of that type will be present and identical with it. The token theory claims merely that each occurrence of the headache will be identical with some brain-state. Early versions of the theory, in either form, insisted that the identity was contingent (see MODALITIES), like (it was claimed) that of a lightning flash with an electrical discharge. But since Kripke separated the necessary/contingent and a priori/empirical distinctions (see A PRIORI) contingent identity has fallen into disfavour, and the claim is rather that the identity is empirical though still necessary. Criticisms of the theory include asking how it could be verified, and whether the IDENTITY could be strict. The theory stems largely from Australia in the mid-1950s, though akin to the DOUBLE ASPECT THEORY and to neutral MONISM.

D. M. Armstrong, *A Materialist Theory of the Mind*, Routledge, 1968, revised 1993.

G. Bealer, 'Mental properties', *Journal of Philosophy*, 1994. (Defends theory against four common objections, but then attacks it.)

C. V. Borst (ed.), *The Mind/Brain Identity Theory*, Macmillan, 1970. (Expository and critical essays, including several main original sources.)

T. Burge, 'Philosophy of language and mind: 1950–90', *Philosophical Review*, 1992. (Survey article with many references. See pp. 32–9.)

*K. Campbell, *Body and Mind*, Macmillan, 1970, chapters 5, 6. (Elementary discussion.)

C. S. Hill, *Sensations: a Defense of Type Materialism*, Cambridge UP, 1991.

J. O'Connor (ed.), *Modern Materialism: Readings on Mind–Body Identity*, Harcourt, Brace, and World, 1969. (Further essays, overlapping with Borst.)

J. Ross, 'Immaterial aspects of thought', *Journal of Philosophy*,

Imagery

1992. (Claims thinking cannot be any physical process or any function of one.)

See also bibliography for MIND (PHILOSOPHY OF).

Identity theory of predication. Theory that apparent subject/predicate statements, like '*X* is red,' are properly to be analysed as identity statements of the form '*X* is identical with some red thing'.

Idiolect. A language considered as spoken or written by a given individual.

If. See CONDITIONALS.

Iff. If and only if.

Illocutions. See SPEECH ACTS.

Illusion (argument from). See PERCEPTION.

Imagery. Mental imagery fell into disrepute in the mid-twentieth century in both philosophy and psychology. Statements about one's images were not publicly assessable, and so fell foul of Wittgenstein's PRIVATE LANGUAGE argument, while psychology had no means of studying them or using them in scientific accounts of human beings. They also suffered from being apparently indeterminate in nature. Recently, however, scientists have found ways of studying them, and integrating their study with that of vision, and following this their study has become respectable again in philosophy too. (Cf. at least in part the similar revival of SENSE DATA.)

Interest has centred mainly on visual images, and two main theories are current about what these are, pictorialism and descriptionalism.

Pictorialists argue first that images do indeed exist and are used in solving various imaginative problems, and that they do so by representing the relevant material in a spatial manner. Pictorialists use experimental data, such as that when subjects are asked to say whether two diagrams are congruent, where this could be found by rotating one of them, the time needed to answer is proportional to the size of the angular rotation required; this, pictorialists claim, suggests that subjects do indeed mentally rotate one of them.

Descriptionalists emphasize such things as the indeterminacy of images, and claim that they represent things more as linguistic items do. A verbal description of a scene, for instance, will inevitably ignore many features of it altogether – which is different from representing them as blurred or hidden, as a picture might. An

Imitation game

image of a red tomato represents something *as* a red tomato, but does not itself contain something red, as a picture normally would. Pylyshyn, a leading descriptionalist, insists that we must distinguish whether 'image' refers to 'what I experience when I imagine a scene, . . . surely *that* exists in the same sense that any other sensation or conscious content does (e.g. pains, tickles, etc.)' or to 'a certain theoretical construct that is claimed to have certain properties (e.g. to be spatially extended) and to play a specified role in certain cognitive processes'. He gives a large role to '*tacit knowledge*' (see TACIT AND IMPLICIT KNOWLEDGE), and also insists that in 'image of object *X* with property *P*', *P* belongs to the object, not the image; ignoring this, he thinks, is 'probably the most ubiquitous and damaging conceptual confusion in the whole imagery literature'.

However, pictorialists agree that there is no actual picture in the brain – it would involve an inner eye to see it, and how would that work? Imaging a red tomato does not involve a circular bit of the brain being red. Rather, as with the descriptionalists, we represent something *as* a red tomato, only the representing is spatial rather than linguistic. Also the indeterminacy objection does not hold, they claim: an ordinary stick-picture of a person may leave it indeterminate, and not merely blurred or hidden, whether it is male or female, clothed or unclothed, etc.

But now the issue itself is becoming blurred (see Block's 'Introduction' to *Imagery*), and others, such as Tye, present an alternative or compromise view.

B. Beakley and P. Ludlow (eds), *The Philosophy of Mind: Classical Problems/Contemporary Issues*, MIT Press, 1992. (Part III has relevant items.)

N. Block (ed.), *Imagery*, MIT Press, 1981. (Includes important articles on both sides; see pp. 152, 153 for quotations from Pylyshyn. See also Block (ed.), *Readings in the Philosophy of Psychology*, vol. 2, Harvard UP and Methuen, 1981.)

S. Kosslyn, *Image and Brain: the Resolution of the Imagery Debate*, MIT Press, 1994. (Full discussion of images, defending their existence and importance with very extensive bibliography.)

W. G. Lycan (ed.), *Mind and Cognition*, Blackwell, 1990.

M. Tye, *The Imagery Debate*, MIT Press, 1991. (Discusses the two main views both philosophically and scientifically, offering his own alternative.)

Imitation game. See TURING TEST.

Immaterialism. See IDEALISM.

Implication and entailment

Imperative. Kant divided imperatives into *categorical* (or *apodictic*) and *hypothetical*. The former were unconditional ('Do X') and the latter conditional on some end ('If (or since) you want Y do X'). Since he was concerned only with imperatives, of each kind, valid for all rational agents he recognized only one categorical imperative, which formed the basis of morality. He formulated it variously, but the general point was, roughly, that one should act only in ways that are UNIVERSALIZABLE. The problems of the categorical imperative are largely those of universalizability. But is the hypothetical imperative really an imperative at all, and not just a statement that fully willing the end involves willing the means? Recently imperatives have been important in prescriptivist views of ethics (see NATURALISM), and there has also been discussion of what logical relations they can stand in.

R. M. Hare, *The Language of Morals*, Oxford UP, 1952, part 1. (Logic of imperatives. Also prescriptivism.)

J. H. McDowell, 'Are moral requirements hypothetical imperatives?', *Proceedings of the Aristotelian Society*, supplementary vol., 1978. (No.)

H. J. Paton, *The Moral Law*, Hutchinson, 1948. (Best translation of Kant's *Grundlegung*. Cf. also Paton's commentary, *The Categorical Imperative*, 1947.)

B. A. O. Williams and P. T. Geach, 'Imperative inference', *Analysis*, 1963 (supplement). (Can one infer one imperative from another?)

Implication and entailment 'Implication' is the most general name for those relations between propositions or statements in virtue of which we can infer the truth of a proposition or statement from something else. A minimum condition for such a relation to hold (except contextual implication: see below) is that if one proposition, p, implies another, q, it is not the case that p is true and q is false. Whenever this condition is fulfilled, and provided p and q are each either true or false, we say that p *materially implies* q. Hence a false proposition materially implies any proposition (for if p is false it is not the case that p is true and q false), and any proposition materially implies a true proposition; these facts are called the 'paradoxes' of material implication, though they are only paradoxical in the sense of sounding odd because 'implies' in ordinary speech suggests a stronger relation. Material implication is usually symbolized by '⊃', which is specific to it, or '→', which can also stand for other relations, including entailment.

Strict implication (C. I. Lewis; usually symbolized by '∍') holds from p to q when it is logically impossible (see MODALITIES) for p

145

Implication and entailment

to be true and q false. Hence it too has 'paradoxes', that an impossible (i.e. necessarily false) proposition strictly implies any proposition, and any proposition strictly implies a necessary proposition.
Occasionally the impossibility and necessity involved may be not
confined to the logical.

Entailment is a special relation introduced by Moore, who said it
held from p to q when and only when q can be logically deduced
from p. Entailment in this sense, as against the looser popular sense,
can be called *logical entailment* (whether or not it is purely a logical
relation: see below). Entailment is often thought to differ from
strict implication, by requiring that the propositions that it links
have some relevance to each other, or connexion of meaning, so
that the paradoxes of strict implication do not apply to it. On this
view entailment is not always purely a logical relation. Many writers
have tried to formalize this relevance requirement and show that
it avoids the paradoxes, but these attempts, sometimes called *relevance logics*, remain controversial.

Logical implication is implication that holds as a matter of logic,
or is logically necessary. Though often equated with strict implication, logical implication is more general. It need not be limited
to a relation whereby a contradiction implies any proposition and
any proposition implies a necessary proposition. If entailment is a
logical relation different from strict implication (so not purely
a logical relation), 'logical implication' can cover both. 'Logical
implication' is also used as a general contrast to 'contextual implication' (see below).

Presuppositions are carried by certain statements, questions etc.
'Have you stopped beating your wife?' presupposes that you have
one and have beaten her. Strawson and others distinguish presuppositions from entailments because when p entails q, if q is false p is
false, but when p presupposes q, so does not-p, and if q is false p
is neither true nor false (if you have no wife it is neither true nor
false that you have stopped beating her). It is disputed, however,
whether presupposition and entailment in fact exclude each other
(Linsky). *Absolute presuppositions* is Collingwood's term for statements which are not (as most statements are, he thought) answers
to questions. They are neither true nor false, but underlie the
thought of persons or epochs.

Contextual or *pragmatic implication* is related to, and not always
easily distinguishable from, presupposition. '*Implicature*' (Grice) is
also used for much the same notion. Perhaps the main difference
is that presupposition affects the truth of what is said, while contextual implication affects the rationality or correctness of saying it.
Normally if one says something one contextually implies that one
believes it. If I say 'It's raining' I contextually imply that I believe

146

Implication and entailment

it is; but it could be raining even if I do not believe it is. 'A speaker in making a statement contextually implies whatever one is entitled to infer on the basis of the presumption that his act of stating is normal' (Hungerland). Gricean implicature has become important recently in connexion with entailment, CONDITIONALS, and other contexts involving the relations between formal logics and ordinary language. For both presupposition and contextual implication it is disputable what does the presupposing, etc. Is it what is said, the saying of it, or the sayer? Saying (which here includes asking, etc.) may even be replaced by something non-linguistic: 'By (deliberately) frowning he implied he was angry.' A non-deliberate frown could only 'imply' anger causally, rather as rainbows imply rain. Contextual implication lies between such a causal sense and logical implication. See also CONDITIONALS, INFERENCE.

A. R. Anderson and N. Belnap, 'Tautological entailments', *Philosophical Studies*, 1962 (Relevance logics. For fuller development see their *Entailment: the Logic of Relevance and Necessity*, vol. 1, 1975 (see index). See also G. Iseminger, 'Is relevance necessary for validity?', *Mind*, 1980.)

R. G. Collingwood, *An Essay on Metaphysics*, Oxford UP, 1940, esp. part 1. (Absolute presuppositions.)

H. P. Grice, 'Logic and conversation' in D. Davidson and G. Harman (eds), *The Logic of Grammar*, 1975, reprinted in revised form with other relevant material in Grice's *Studies in the Way of Words*, Harvard UP, 1989. See also his 'The causal theory of perception', § 3, *Proceedings of the Aristotelian Society*, supplementary vol., 1961, reprinted in G. J. Warnock (ed.), *The Philosophy of Perception*, Oxford UP, 1967, esp. § 3. (Some kinds of implication.)

I. Hungerland, 'Contextual implication', *Inquiry*, 1960. (Contextual implication and presupposition. For quotation see p. 255.)

C. I. Lewis and C. H. Langford, *Symbolic Logic*, Century, 1932, chapter 8. (Equates entailment with strict implication. Cf. also J. Bennett, 'Entailment', *Philosophical Review*, 1969, a general survey defending Lewis.)

B. Mates, *Stoic Logic*, California UP, 1961, chapter 4. (Philonian, Diodorean and Chrysippean implication, i.e. various Greek anticipations of modern discussions.)

G. E. Moore, *Philosophical Studies*, RKP, 1923, p. 291. (Entailment introduced.)

E. J. Nelson, 'Intensional relations', *Mind*, 1930. C. Lewy, J. L. Watling. P. T. Geach, 'Entailment', *Proceedings of the Aristotelian Society*, supplementary vol., 1958. T. J. Smiley, 'Entailment and deducibility', *Proceedings of the Aristotelian Society*, 1958–9. (All

Implicature

these try to separate entailment from strict implication. See also Anderson and Belnap (above).)

W. Sellars, 'Presupposing', P. F. Strawson, 'A reply to Mr Sellars', *Philosophical Review*, 1954. (These discuss Strawson's earlier views on presupposition, and its relation to entailment. Cf. also L. Linsky, *Referring*, 1967, chapter 6.)

G. H. von Wright, 'A note on entailment', *Philosophical Quarterly*, 1959. (Comments on Geach above.)

D. Wilson, *Presuppositions and Non-Truth-Conditional Semantics*, Academic Press, 1975. (Rejects logical and pragmatic presuppositions, preferring a non-logical but semantic 'suggestion'.)

Implicature. See IMPLICATION.

Incomplete symbol. See LOGICAL CONSTRUCTIONS.

Incongruent or **incongruous counterparts.** Also called *enantiomorphs*. Pairs of things differing only as an object and its mirror-image do, or a pair of hands, or opposite spirals. The precise characterization of this difference (probably first attempted by Kant) is difficult, and may be important for studying the nature of space.

J. Bennett, 'The difference between right and left', *American Philosophical Quarterly*, 1970.

Inconsistent triad. See ANTILOGISM.

Incontinence. Also called *acrasia (akrasia), weakness of will*. The 'Socratic paradox' that no one errs willingly (for a willing error is not an error) raises the problem whether one can act against one's better judgment, be the judgment moral or prudential, etc. Similarly, can one assent to something against the evidence, or deceive oneself (*doxastic incontinence*; cf. BAD FAITH)?

*W. Charlton, *Weakness of Will*, Blackwell, 1988. (General introduction to topic, using ancient and modern discussions.)

J. Gosling, *The Weakness of the Will*, Routledge, 1990. (1st half historical, 2nd half positive.)

A. R. Mele, *Irrationality: an Essay on Akrasia, Self-deception, and Self-control*, Oxford UP, 1987. (Treats both action and belief. See Preface to paperback edition (1992) for references to his more recent work, and see bibliography to FEELINGS.)

G. W. Mortimore (ed.), *Weakness of Will*, Macmillan, 1971. (Selections ancient and modern.)

D. Wiggins, 'Weakness of will, commensurability, and the objects of deliberation and desire', *Proceedings of the Aristotelian Society*,

Indifference (principle of)

1978–9, reprinted with revisions in his *Needs, Values, Truth*, Blackwell, 1987, and in A. O. Rorty (ed.), *Essays on Aristotle's Ethics*, UCLA Press, 1981. (Fairly difficult.)

Incorrigible. A statement is incorrigible for someone if he cannot be in error in believing or disbelieving it. Whether such statements exist is disputed, but typical candidates are reports of immediate experience like, 'I now seem to see something red.' Incorrible statements are not the same as necessarily true or false statements. The above example, if true, is only contingently true, and we can make mistakes about necessary statements (e.g. in mathematics). In a weaker (though etymologically more correct) sense a statement is incorrigible if we can be mistaken about it but there is no way of correcting us, e.g. perhaps statements reporting our dreams.

A statement is *indubitable* for someone if he cannot rationally doubt or reject it. I can reject the statement that I seem to see something red, but not, according to Descartes, the statement that I exist. 'Incorrigible' and 'indubitable' are often used more loosely, and even interchangeably. See also FOUNDATIONALISM.

J. L. Mackie, 'Are there any incorrigible empirical statements?', *Australasian Journal of Philosophy*, 1963. (No. Uses 'incorrigible' in weak sense, and 'indubitable' for strong sense.)

R. W. Miller, 'Absolute certainty', *Mind*, 1978. (Defends an analysis of it which, he claims, avoids danger of leading to scepticism.)

R. Warner, 'Incorrigibility', in H. Robinson (ed.), *Objections to Physicalism*, Clarendon, 1993. (Defends modified version of it.)

Independent. See AXIOM.

Indeterminism. See FREEWILL.

Indexicals. See TOKEN-REFLEXIVES.

Indicator terms. See TOKEN-REFLEXIVES.

Indifference (principle of). Also called *principle of insufficient reason* (different from Leibniz's principle of SUFFICIENT REASON). Principle that if we have no reason to expect one rather than another of *n* mutually exclusive and collectively exhaustive possibilities to be realized, we should assign a probability of $1/n$ to each of them. The principle's validity is disputed. See also PROBABILITY.

W. C. Kneale, *Probability and Induction*, Oxford UP, 1949, §§ 31, 34. (Criticizes principle, but defends variant of it. Cf. S. Black-

Indiscernibility of identicals

burn, *Reason and Prediction*, Cambridge UP, 1973, chapter 6 for another defence.)

Indiscernibility of identicals. See LEIBNIZ'S LAW.

Individualism. In recent philosophy of mind and psychology, this has come to denote a view very similar to INTERNALISM in its main sense, holding that the content of an individual's thought or experience depends simply on that individual, and does not logically (though of course it may causally) depend on things in the individual's environment. Sometimes, however, a distinction is made between individualism as a doctrine about mental states and internalism as a doctrine about the contents of those states, and it is claimed that individualism does not entail internalism (Egan, 1992).

Methodological individualism covers various views to the effect that facts about societies are explainable in terms of facts about individuals, while *methodological holism* denies this.

T. Burge, 'Individualism and the mental', *Midwest Studies in Philosophy*, vol. IV, Minnesota UP, 1979. (Cf. also his 'Individualism and psychology', *Philosophical Review*, 1986. Burge introduces individualism in this sense, arguing against it. M. Davies, 'Individualism and perceptual content' and G. Segal, 'Defence of a reasonable individualism', both in *Mind*, 1971, respectively defend and attack Burge's position.)

F. Egan, 'Must psychology be individualistic?', *Philosophical Review*, 1991. (Attacks both Burge and Fodor, and claims the answer depends on the goal of the theorizing.)

F. Egan, 'Individualism, computation, and perceptual content', *Mind*, 1992.

J. A. Fodor, *Psychosemantics*, MIT Press, 1987, chapter 2. (Defends individualism in psychology. See also his 'A modal argument for narrow content', *Journal of Philosophy*, 1991, for a distinction between individualism and internalism.)

D.-H. Ruben, *The Metaphysics of the Social World*, RKP, 1985. (See especially pp. 150ff. for methodological individualism. See also K. R. Popper, *The Open Society and its Enemies*, RKP, 1945, chapter 14.)

Individuals. There seem to be four main senses: (i) whatever can be counted, one by one ('individuated'), or can be talked of or referred to (logical subjects: see MEANING). In this sense all particulars (see UNIVERSALS) are individuals, but not vice-versa. Beauty is an individual. We can talk about it and distinguish it from other things, but it is a universal and not a particular (it seems not to

Induction

exist 'all at once' like an object in space and time). Tennis is an individual, though not a particular, nor perhaps a universal ('tennis' does not seem to behave like words in ' –ity', ' –ness', ' –hood', etc.). 'Individual' in this first main sense resembles 'OBJECT' when the 'existence' strand of that word is dominant.

(ii) In logic individuals are contrasted with predicates or functions (i.e. universals). They are what 'individual VARIABLES' range over, and so they are whatever the subject of a logical expression can refer to – but the expression must belong to the first-order (or 'restricted') predicate CALCULUS, and must not appear only in the 'extended' predicate calculus (where predicates can be referred to).

(iii) Same as 'particular'.

(iv) What cannot be further divided. On this view absolutely specific properties will be individuals, e.g. if red can be divided into crimson and scarlet but scarlet cannot be further divided then scarlet will be an individual.

(ii) has affinities with both (i) and (iii), and the senses are not sharply distinguished. (iii) is the oldest sense.

R. Jackson, 'Locke's distinction between primary and secondary qualities', *Mind*, 1929, reprinted in C. B. Martin and D. M. Amstrong (eds), *Locke and Berkeley*, Macmillan, n.d. (Another individuals/particulars distinction.)

F. Sommers, 'Predicability', in M. Black (ed.), *Philosophy in America*, Allen and Unwin, 1965, esp. pp. 277 ff. (Defines individuals, in sense perhaps nearest to (iii), in terms of what can be predicated of them.)

P. F. Strawson, *Individuals*, Methuen, 1959. (See esp. pp. 226–7, and his 'Categories' in O. P. Wood and G. Pitcher (eds.), *Ryle.* Macmillan, 1970, pp. 196, 199. Cf. also Strawson's *Introduction to Logical Theory*, Methuen, 1952, p. 144.)

J. Valberg, 'Improper singular terms', *Proceedings of the Aristotelian Society*, 1970–1, esp. pp. 136–41. (Some difficulties in defining 'individual'.)

Indubitable. See INCORRIGIBLE.

Induction. In its widest sense, any rational process where from premises about some things of a certain kind a conclusion is drawn about some or all of the remaining things of that kind. An argument is inductive in a narrow or strict sense (to which the rest of this article is confined) if it claims to draw such a conclusion from such premises directly in a single step (as opposed, e.g., to Popper's method: see below). If this step consists in arguing that because some (or all observed) As are Bs therefore further (or all) As are

Induction

Bs, we have *simple* or *enumerative induction*. Those who accept that induction is, given certain conditions, a rational process are often called *inductivists*.

The traditional form of simple induction, 'All observed As are Bs, so all As are Bs, can be regarded as a special case (where $n = 100$) of the general form (where n ranges from 0 to 100) 'n per cent of observed As are Bs so n per cent of all As are Bs. Of course it will often be impossible for arithmetical reasons for the total population of As to have exactly the same ratio of Bs as the sample, but this does not affect the general idea. Some writers, notably J. S. Mill, think that inductive inference goes from particulars to particulars, i.e. to further instances, not to a generalization. Others think a conclusion about particulars can be reached only through a generalization, i.e. that one can only argue from 'All (or, for some value of n, n per cent of) observed ravens have been black' to 'The next raven will be black' by using the intermediate conclusion 'All (or n per cent of all) ravens are black'. Of course the smaller n is, the weaker the argument will be.

Anti-inductivists say that induction is not a rational process, and that inductive arguments in fact work in other ways. They may claim that inductive arguments are really DEDUCTIVE arguments some of whose premises have been suppressed; if these premises were made explicit the deductive nature of the argument would become clear. Alternatively they may claim that inductive arguments really work by the *hypothetico-deductive method*, whereby a hypothesis is set up and conclusions are deduced from it and tested against experience: if the conclusions turn out false the hypothesis is rejected. Inductivists can also use this method, but anti-inductivists, notably Popper, believe that the hypothesis cannot be directly supported: all we can do is try to falsify it.

Inductivists and anti-inductivists agree nowadays that no formal rules can be given for reaching (as opposed to confirming) the right hypothesis (cf. PSYCHOLOGISM), which does not imply that ways of reaching it cannot be assessed as rational. What distinguishes inductivists is that they think the hypothesis, however acquired, may be supported directly by evidence (not merely indirectly, by its surviving attempts to falsify it). Anti-inductivists tend to think that an INFERENCE, or a step in argument, is 'deductive or defective' (A. C. MacIntyre).

Hypotheses about objects not directly observable such as electrons or magnetic fields are sometimes called *transcendent hypotheses*. They cannot be reached or directly confirmed by simple induction. The process by which they are reached or confirmed has sometimes been called *secondary induction* (Kneale), especially when it is regarded as rationally assessable and not merely a matter of psychology. 'Secondary induction' can also refer to any induction whose premises themselves result from induction. We might conclude inductively that all ravens have feathers, and that all swans do, and then conclude by a further induction from ravens and swans that all birds do.

Much of inductive logic, i.e. the general study of induction, consists in asking whether induction has any place in scientific enquiry, and, if so, what rules can be elaborated to govern its use as a method of CONFIRMATION. *The problem of induction* has traditionally been the problem of justifying not so much particular rules as induction in general, and especially simple induction (sometimes by the back-handed method of reducing it to disguised deduction; cf. the first type of anti-inductivist above, and (ii) below). However, a major problem for inductivists has also been provided by Goodman's 'grue' paradox (see CONFIRMATION); this raises the question what counts as induction, i.e. *what* conclusion is the relevant inductive conclusion with respect to some given evidence. The main attempts to justify simple induction are as follows.

(i) Mathematical facts about the relations between samples and their parent populations are used.

(ii) Some grand overall premise is sought which can turn inductive arguments into deductive ones: that the future resembles the past, that nature is uniform, that every event has a cause, and that the variety in the universe is finite in amount, have been favourite candidates. The difficulties have concerned formulating these premises (how closely must the future resemble the past? What counts as a cause?) and then justifying them. (ii) is now unpopular.

(iii) Perhaps induction can be used to justify itself. This seems circular, but is the circularity only apparent?

(iv) The *pragmatic* or *practicalist* approach has it that induction cannot indeed be validated, in the sense of being shown to be likely to work, but it can be rationally justified as a practical policy because every alternative is less rational; the claim is here that induction is likely to work *if any method is*. 'Vindicated' is sometimes used here. We do not know what the actual universe is like. In some possible universes induction would work better than other methods, while in some (notably, chaotic ones) no method would work. But in no possible universe, it is claimed, would any method work better than induction. Infinitely many methods are possible, but we must distinguish alternatives which deliberately predict results conflicting with inductive predictions (*negative induction* or *counter-induction*) from those which are merely indifferent to induction (e.g. appeal to soothsayers). The former are easier to deal with. The 'long-term' problem of whether a certain method is rational if given an indefinitely long time to work in differs from

Induction

the 'short-term', and more interesting, problem of whether it is rational when we are only interested in a finite time ahead.

(v) Induction may not need justification because it is a going concern. There are generally acknowledged criteria of inductive soundness. We may well study in detail what they are, but it is senseless to reject them because they are our touchstone for rejecting any inductive arguments, and so we should be appealing to them even in rejecting them (cf. PARADIGM CASE ARGUMENT).

(vi) (A strengthened form of (v).) Induction not only is a going concern but is inevitably so, since it is necessarily involved in one way or another in all rational thinking and behaviour; but we cannot abandon it, whether we want to or not. This is a form of TRANSCENDENTAL ARGUMENT.

Various processes called 'induction' must be distinguished from induction proper. *Intuitive induction* is a process where particular cases serve as psychological causes rather than rational justifications for generalizations whose justification is a priori. If we notice that something coloured is extended, this may make us *realize* rather than infer that all coloured things are extended. Proof by *mathematical, recursive* or *course-of-values induction* is the process whereby we prove that something holds for every term in a series (e.g. for every natural number) by proving that it holds for the first term, and that it holds for the successor of any term for which it holds. Cf. also DEFINITION by induction. 'Mathematical induction' is different from the use of simple induction as a preliminary move in mathematics. A mathematician might argue, 'All examined even numbers are the sum of two primes, so (perhaps) all even numbers are', and then try to prove this conclusion. *Perfect induction* or *induction by complete enumeration* (not by simple enumeration, which is simple induction) consists in asserting, e.g. 'All the chairs in this room are wooden' after checking them one by one. The 'inductive leap' consists simply in assuming that the chairs checked are all there are in the room. See also CONFIRMATION, PROBABILITY, CAUSATION.

S. F. Barker, 'Must every inference be either deductive or inductive?', in M. Black (ed.), *Philosophy in America*, Allen and Unwin, 1965.

M. Black, 'Self-supporting inductive arguments', *Journal of Philosophy*, 1958. P. Achinstein, 'The circularity of a self-supporting inductive argument', *Analysis*, vol. 22, 1962. (Both reprinted in P. H. Nidditch (ed.), *The Philosophy of Science*, Oxford UP, 1968. Cf. further debate between Black and Achinstein in *Analysis*, vol. 23, 1962–3, and see R. B. Braithwaite, *Scientific Explanation*,

Harper 1953, chapter 8. All these are in Swinburne (below). Cf. also Mellor (below).

S. Blackburn, *Reason and Prediction*, Cambridge UP, 1973. (Attempts justification by version of principle of indifference, and offers solution to 'grue' paradox.

P. Edwards, 'Bertrand Russell's doubts about induction', *Mind*, 1949, reprinted in A. Flew (ed.), *Logic and Language*, vol. 1, Blackwell 1951 and in Swinburne below. (Claims induction needs no defence.)

N. Goodman, 'Seven strictures on similarity', in L. Foster and J. W. Swanson (eds), *Experience and Theory*, Duckworth, 1970. (Induction and resemblance.)

W. Kneale, *Probability and Induction*, Oxford UP, 1949. (Part 2 discusses various kinds of induction and pseudo-induction (intuitive etc.).)

A. C. MacIntyre, 'Hume on "is" and "ought" ', *Philosophical Review*, 1959. (See p. 453 for 'deductive or defective', a disjunction which MacIntyre rejects.)

D. H. Mellor, 'The warrant of induction' in his *Matters of Metaphysics*, Cambridge UP, 1991. (Inaugural lecture defending the existence of such a warrant.)

K. Popper, *The Logic of Scientific Discovery*, Hutchinson, 1959 (German original 1934). (Advocates hypothetico-deductive method, but based solely on falsification, without confirmation. Cf. Popper's 'personal report' in C. A. Mace (ed.), *British Philosophy in the Mid-Century*, 1957, reprinted in Popper's *Conjectures and Refutations*, RKP, 1963, chapter 1; and cf. his *Objective Knowledge*, Oxford UP, 1972, chapter 1.)

H. Reichenbach, *The Theory of Probability*, California UP, 1949 (German original 1935), final section. (Vindication of induction from point of view of frequency theory of PROBABILITY; cf. also his *Experience and Prediction*, Chicago UP, 1938, §§ 38–40, and also H. Feigl, 'De principiis non disputandum . . .?', in M. Black (ed.), *Philosophical Analysis*, Cornell UP, 1950, esp. pp. 129–39.)

B. Russell, *Problems of Philosophy*, Howe University Library, 1912, chapter 6. (Classic statement of problem of induction.)

R. Swinburne (ed.), *The Justification of Induction*, Oxford UP, 1974. (Includes several of above items, and also discussions of pragmatic approach by W. C. Salmon and J. W. Lenz.)

J. O. Wisdom, *Foundations of Inference in Natural Science*, Methuen, 1952. (Follows Popper in general. Chapter 24 offers vindication. Chapter 23 criticizes mathematical justification of simple induction.)

Inference. Assertion on the basis of something else. 'All cats are

Infinity

black, so this cat is black' represents an inference, though 'inference' can refer to the conclusion, 'This cat is black', as well as to the process. 'If all cats are black then this cat is black', where neither antecedent nor consequent is actually asserted, represents an IMPLICATION. Inferences need not necessarily be DEDUCTIVE (for J. S. Mill they cannot be, since deduction does not represent a substantial enough transition of thought).

In *immediate inference* a conclusion is drawn from a single premise, especially by OBVERSION, CONVERSION, CONTRAPOSITION and INVERSION. In *mediate inference* two or more independent premises are involved, as in a syllogism. This distinction, however, is not exact. See also INDUCTION.

M. Deutscher, 'A causal account of inferring', in R. Brown and C. D. Rollins (eds), *Contemporary Philosophy in Australia*, Allen and Unwin/Humanities, 1969.

J. S. Mill, *A System of Logic*, Longmans, Green, 1843, book 2, chapter 1. (Nature of inference.)

G. Ryle, ' "If", "so", and "because" ', in M. Black (ed.), *Philosophical Analysis*, Cornell UP, 1950. (Inference and implication.)

Infinity. See METAPHYSICS.

Innate. Cf. A PRIORI throughout, and especially for the relations between it and 'innate'. 'Innate' means 'inborn' but what being innate amounts to is complex and disputed. Basically the innate is what is prior to experience, where the priority is the chronological or psychological one of acquisition rather than the epistemological one of justification. But an innate idea or concept may be any of the following: (i) an idea we can acquire without our being presented with an instance in experience, and without having to construct it from ideas so presented (as perhaps we construct *unicorn* from *horse* and *horn*), (ii) an idea we must so acquire, if we acquire it at all, since experience could not supply us with it, e.g. the ideas of *validity* or *negation*, (iii) an idea we can acquire without any experience at all, or never acquire but have always had; *substance* and *cause* may be examples, (iv) an idea we can apply without using experience; we do not use the senses to find whether an argument is *valid* – but perhaps this sort of idea might be better called *a priori*.

Similarly a belief or proposition may be innate in any of several senses: (i) a proposition we believe from birth, (ii) one we believe, or may come to believe as soon as we acquire the relevant ideas or concepts – for instance, once we acquire the ideas of *red* and *green* we may believe that nothing can be simultaneously red and green all

Innate

over (cf. the *relatively a priori* under A PRIORI), (iii) one we assent to as soon as we are presented with it, (iv) one we cannot understand without believing it, (v) one we cannot learn from experience but nevertheless do believe. Any of these may be called *a priori* to the extent that 'know' may properly be substituted for 'believe' or 'assent to'. But this cannot always be done. An innate belief may be false, and even when it is true we may require the support of observation before we can properly be said to know it. However, Leibniz thought that our innate beliefs must amount to knowledge, or God would be deceiving us, and sometimes an evolutionist justification is offered for claiming that at least most of our innate beliefs must be true, or we would not have survived the course of evolution, so that such beliefs do in general amount to knowledge, and are a priori to the extent that we do not need to appeal to current experience to justify them – though evolution could indeed produce a false belief (Quinton, pp. 133–4).

In the mid- to late twentieth century the appeal to innateness has taken a different turn with Chomsky's claim that we have an innate tendency to learn and use certain grammatical structures more easily than others, and could not otherwise learn our native language as quickly as we do.

Nativism is the view that some ideas are innate.

B. Beakley and P. Ludlow (eds), *The Philosophy of Mind: Classical Problems/Contemporary Issues*, MIT Press, 1992. (Part v has relevant items.)

N. Block (ed.), *Readings in the Philosophy of Psychology*, vol. 2, Harvard UP and Methuen, 1981. (Contains discussions, some with replies, mainly on Chomsky etc.)

*N. Chomsky, *Reflections on Language*, Maurice Temple Smith and Fontana, 1976. (Fairly elementary exposition of his ideas.)

J. Locke, *Essay Concerning Human Understanding*, 1689, Book 1. (Attacks some versions of innate ideas. Criticized by G. W. Leibniz, *New Essays Concerning Human Understanding*, 1763, written earlier. See chapter 2 of Stich.)

*J. Lyons, *Chomsky*, Fontana, 1970, expanded 1977. (Elementary introduction to his ideas.)

R. Nozick, *The Nature of Rationality*, Princeton UP, 1993. See especially chapter iv. (Offers partial evolutionist justification for treating innate beliefs as true.)

*A. Quinton, *The Nature of Things*, RKP, 1973, pp. 132–4. (The innate, the a priori, and the instinctive.)

S. P. Stich (ed.), *Innate Ideas*, California UP, 1975. (Discussions both of older material and of Chomsky.)

Inscription

Inscription. A written token (see UNIVERSALS). *Inscriptivism (inscriptionism)* is any view making significant use of inscriptions, e.g. the *inscriptional theory of intentionality* explains intentionality (see INTENSIONALITY) in terms of relations between utterers and token sentences (considered as written, for convenience).

W. V. O. Quine, *Word and Object*, Wiley, 1960, pp. 214–15.

Instrumentalism. Theory that scientific laws and theories are instruments for predicting observable phenomena, and are therefore to be judged by their usefulness and not classified as propositions which can be true or false. Somewhat similar to CONVENTIONALISM. 'Instrumentalism' is also used for a development of PRAGMATISM by Dewey, and for the view that values (generally, or in some sphere, e.g. aesthetics) are instrumental (e.g. in promoting satisfaction); see GOOD.

I. Hacking, *Representing and Intervening; Introducing Topics in the Philosophy of Natural Science*, Cambridge UP, 1983. (Discusses scientific objectivity ('representing') and experimental method ('intervening').)

K. R. Popper, *The Logic of Scientific Discovery*, Hutchinson, 1959 (German original, 1934), p. 423 (Critical, with references.)

S. E. Toulmin, *The Philosophy of Science*, Hutchinson, 1953. (Example of instrumentalist outlook.)

Insufficient reason (principle of). See INDIFFERENCE.

Intensionality and intentionality. Historically these terms have different origins, but whether there is really one notion or two underlying modern uses of them is disputed, and if two, how they are related. 'Non-extensional' is often used for 'intensional', perhaps to avoid this question. 'Extension' and its derivatives are always spelt with 's'. So far as they are different notions 'intensional' primarily concerns the sphere of logic and 'intentional' that of philosophy of mind. This entry will treat them in order.

Intuitively extensions can be thought of as the extents which certain kinds of terms range over and intensions as that in virtue of which they do so. Extensions correspond roughly to classes, and intensions to properties. A property like that of being a man determines at most one class. There is only one class of men, though it may have sub-classes. But one and the same class may correspond to more than one property. The class of ruminants, for example, is the same as the class of cloven-hoofed animals. A class itself can be defined in extension or in intension; see UNIVERSALS.

So long as we are interested only in a group of objects and not

Intensionality and intentionality

in the properties in terms of which they are viewed, we can substitute for our first description of them any other description that picks out the same class (e.g. 'cloven-hoofed things' for 'ruminants'), and what we say will remain true, if it was true with the first description. If all ruminants are mammals, then all cloven-hoofed things are mammals. This is expressed by saying we can substitute the second description *salva veritate* (lit.: 'preserving truth'). Similarly if we study propositions only in respect of their TRUTH-VALUES (as logicians often do. Cf. truth-FUNCTIONS), then for any proposition another with the same truth-value can be substituted salva veritate. Therefore truth-values count among extensions. Propositions themselves, which cannot be substituted like this when our interests are less restricted, count among intensions which are sometimes called *intensional objects* (but 'extensional objects' is not used).

Extensions are simpler than intensions, in that, to speak loosely and roughly, they concern things as they are in themselves rather than as picked out in terms of the various properties they have. Many logicians therefore prefer extensions, and would like to dispense with intensions, by translating statements containing intensional notions into statements free from them. The view that this can be done is called the *extensionality thesis* (cf. LEIBNIZ'S LAW) and defended by LOGICAL ATOMISTS, logical POSITIVISTS, nominalists, and in general those who prefer a sparse and austere universe. It is attacked by those who accept the richness and complexity of the universe at its face value and as indispensable. Its defenders, notably Quine, also argue that if it is not accepted no coherent system of logic can be elaborated, i.e. they claim that there is no intensional logic. This view can itself be called a version of the extensionality thesis.

If in a certain context a referring phrase cannot, salva veritate, be replaced by another phrase referring to the same thing, the context is called *opaque*. Otherwise it is *transparent*. (Cf. MODALITIES on the de dicto/de re distinction). For example, if they are just nine planets we can say 'The number of the planets is the number of the planets' and 'The number of the planets is nine', but, it is claimed, while we can prefix 'necessarily', to the first statement we cannot prefix it to the second – there might have been some other number of planets. 'Necessarily' generates an opaqe context. So far opacity is in effect the same as intensionality, though applied more narrowly. Contexts can be opaque. Properties, etc. can be called intensional, but not opaque. Perhaps opacity should be called an effect of intensionality.

Intentional situations may be thought of as those where a relation appears to exist but does not really, as 'want' in 'I want a unicorn' seems to relate me to a unicorn, though there are no unicorns for

Intensionality and intentionality

me to relate to (but there are difficulties: see next paragraph). This happens primarily in certain psychological contexts, and the basic problem concerning intentionality has been to define it so that it picks out and explains the peculiarities of just these psychological contexts. Sometimes, as we have seen with the 'number of planets' example, the truth of statements about an object depends on how the object is described. This is especially so with psychological notions like believing, thinking, wanting. Cicero and Tully are one man, but Smith may believe that Cicero is an orator without believing that Tully is one (though he believes *of* Tully that he is one, since his belief concerns that man (Cicero) who in fact is also Tully); cf. BELIEF on this use of the de re/de dicto distinction. Similarly he may believe that Hitler was hanged without believing that Hitler suffered the same fate as Goebbels, even if Goebbels was hanged, since he may not know this. Also the object may not exist. Smith may believe that Apollo is an orator, or that unicorns live in Africa. This gives an alternative criterion for opacity to the above substitutional one. Roughly, a context is opaque if it carries no implications about the existence of the thing it mentions. 'He saw Apollo' is transparent, but 'He worships Apollo' is opaque, since Apollo need not exist for him to do so. But on the former criterion 'He worships Apollo' is transparent, since, if Apollo is a beast, 'He worships a beast' must follow. But the substitutional criterion itself has its complexities. If Oedipus brought it about that Laius died he brought it about that his father died, so 'brought it about that' generates a transparent context; but it generates an opaque one in that one cannot substitute just any truth for 'Laius died', as one could after 'It is true that'. Since Brentano, who brought these issues to light and revived some medieval terminology, objects like Cicero, Apollo and unicorns, in these contexts, are called *intentional objects*, and are sometimes said to have *intentional inexistence* (existence in the mind, or as an object of the mind's activity). One can perhaps think of them as what the mind is intent upon, though this may be historically inaccurate (Kneale). Sometimes, as with Cicero but not Apollo, the intentional object corresponds to a real object. The relations between the two are then not clear. If they are identical, the intentional object of Smith's belief should also be Tully. If they are not identical, the intentional object seems to be merely in the mind, but this is unsatisfactory, since the belief, in both the Apollo and Cicero cases, claims to be about something outside the mind. The whole notion of intentional objects is thus difficult (cf. THINKING), and various theories exist about their nature and reality.

It is tempting to pick out the psychological contexts as those in which no assumptions are made about the existence or non-exist-

Intensionality and intentionality

ence of the things mentioned, i.e. which are opaque by the second criterion above. Two sorts of difficulty arise here. First it is not clear how far the 'psychological' extends. 'John is shooting at unicorns' mentions a physical activity, though with a psychological aspect. Since, on one interpretation, it does not imply that there are any unicorns it is on that interpretation presumably intentional. On the other hand 'John knows (realizes, admits) there are unicorns' is presumably psychological and yet does imply there are unicorns. ('Know' is a 'factive' verb: see EPISTEMOLOGY). Moreover, perception and feeling pain are surely psychological but do not seem always to involve ways of looking at things, or assumptions about existence, i.e. they do not seem to be psychological in the way required.

The second difficulty is that whatever features are picked out to mark off the psychological contexts as intentional seem to apply also to many clearly non-psychological contexts, e.g. modal ones (see MODALITIES): 'Possibly unicorns are vegetarian' need not imply that there are unicorns or that there are not, and so seems to be intentional. It is this that raises doubts about the distinction between intentionality and intensionality (since modal contexts are agreed to be intensional).

However intentionality is to be defined questions involving it have been central in recent philosophy of mind with its emphasis on analysing the CONTENT of mental states and its discussions of INTERNALISM AND EXTERNALISM.

Intentions in the ordinary sense form just one kind of intentional context, and have no special privilege in their connexion with the intentionality here at issue. See also MEANING, THINKING, MIND.

*T. Crane, *The Mechanical Mind: a Philsophical Introduction to Minds, Machines and Mental Representations*, Penguin, 1995, chapter 1, esp. pp. 31 ff. (Elementary introduction to intentionality and to its distinction from intensionality.)

P. T. Geach, 'Teleological explanation', in S. Körner (ed.), *Explanation*, 1975, esp. pp. 83–4. ('Brought it about that', etc.)

A. Kenny, *Action, Emotion and Will*, RKP, 1963. (Chapters 9 ff. discuss 'objects' of emotions, etc., referring to Chisholm, etc. Spells with 's'.)

Proceedings of the Aristotelian Society, supplementary vol., 1968. (Includes two relevant symposia: J. O. Urmson (easiest) and L. J. Cohen, 'Criteria of intensionality', equate intentionality with intensionality and discuss criteria stemming from R. Chisholm. W. C. Kneale and A. N. Prior, 'Intentionality and intensionality', distinguishing these notions and discuss various problems, including the relations of these notions to nominalism. Kneale includes

Intentionality

historical material, for more of which see M. Spencer, 'why the 's' in intension?', *Mind*, 1971.)

W. V. O. Quine, 'Reference and modality' in *From a Logical Point of View*, 2nd (revised) edn, Harvard UP/Harper and Row, 1961, reprinted with some (difficult) discussions following from it in L. Linsky (ed.), *Reference and Modality*, Oxford UP, 1971. (Opacity and its effects on model logic and intensional logic in general.)

R. Scruton, 'Intensional and intentional objects', *Proceedings of the Aristotelian Society*, 1970–1. (Separates them and makes further distinctions within intentionality.)

J. R. Searle, *Intentionality: an Essay in the Philosophy of Mind*, Cambridge UP, 1983. (General discussion, distinguishing sharply between 's' and 't' versions; see its index.)

L. S. Stebbing, *A Modern Elementary Logic*, Methuen, 1943. (Chapter 6 discusses relevant terminology in traditional logic.)

Intentionality. See INTENSIONALITY AND INTENTIONALITY.

Internalism and externalism. A set of related dichotomies applying in various spheres, notably philosophy of mind and epistemology. In general, internalism about something analyses it in terms confined to a certain relevant sphere, while externalism insists that the analysis must involve terms outside that sphere. In philosophy of mind, the debate concerns the contents of various mental states. Internalism treats them as confined within the person who has them and as independent of anything outside, so that to find whether a person has a given mental state we need only examine that person, while externalism insists that for at least some cases this may not be so, notably for thinking, believing, etc., where it may quote Putnam's slogan, ' "Meanings" just ain't in the *head*!'. Putnam imagines a world called Twin Earth. This is exactly like Earth (and is inhabited by counterparts or *doppelgängers* of ourselves) except that the liquid in its seas and lakes etc. is not H_2O but has a different chemical composition, XYZ, but this can only be detected by scientists, since the liquid in ordinary situations behaves just like water. For Putnam, the liquid cannot then be water, but we could call it 'twater'. Twin Earthians, however, *call* it 'water', i.e. they use the same sound 'water' for it, since all the physical facts about them, including the sounds they utter, are the same as those true of us in the corresponding circumstances; 'water' is *our* word for *their* liquid, and they would only utter 'twater' if they envisaged some further Twin Twin Earth. Now suppose that Smith, on Earth, thinks, 'Water is wet'. His *doppelgänger* on Twin Earth will also have a thought he will express as 'Water is wet', but he will be thinking not of water but of twater, the only liquid he has met.

Intersubjective

Similarly, externalism claims, if I have never heard of, say, Vesuvius, and have had no kind of contact with it, then I cannot be thinking of Vesuvius, even if I have a mental picture that happens to resemble Vesuvius closely and I use the sound 'Vesuvius' to name it. In each case, for externalism, what one is thinking of depends essentially on something outside the thinker. Externalism grounds an apparent objection to the IDENTITY THEORY OF MIND, for if thoughts or sensations depend essentially on things outside the thinker, how can they be identical with states of the brain, which do not in the relevant sense depend on anything external?

For internal and external realism see REALISM.

For the epistemological sense of internalism and externalism see EPISTEMOLOGY.

In ethics, 'internalism' has been used of the view that reasons for acting, and especially moral requirements, must be capable of providing motivations for action if they are to be such; and of the view that they do provide such motivations. Externalism denies this need. Various versions of the distinction exist.

See also CONTENT, INTENSIONALITY AND INTENTIONALITY, INDIVIDUALISM, MIND.

T. Burge, 'Individualism and the mental', *Midwest Studies in Philosophy*, vol. IV, Minnesota UP, 1979. (Cf. also his 'Individualism and psychology', *Philosophical Review*, 1986. Burge is a pioneer in advocating externalism in philosophy of mind.)

S. Darwall, *Impartial Reason*, Cornell UP, 1983, esp. chapter 5. (Internalism and externalism in ethics. See also D. Brink, *Moral Realism and the Foundations of Ethics*, Cambridge UP, 1989, esp. chapter 3.)

R. Jay Wallace, 'How to argue about practical reason', *Mind*, 1990. (See p. 356 for ethical sense of 'internalism'.)

C. Macdonald, 'Weak externalism and mind-body identity', *Mind*, 1990. (Uses one version of strong/weak distinction to claim externalism is compatible with one version of identity theory of mind.)

C. McGinn, *Mental Content*, Blackwell, 1989. (Defends one kind of weak externalism and draws some implications. Cf. also review by D. Owens in *Mind*, 1990.)

H. Putnam, 'The meaning of "meaning" ', in his *Mind, Language and Reality*, vol. II, Cambridge UP, 1975. (Putnam and Burge are pioneers of the main philosophy of mind debate in its modern form, though it has earlier roots. For slogan, see p. 227.)

Intersubjective. Something is intersubjective if there are ways of reaching agreement about it, even though it may not be independent of the human mind (and hence not objective), e.g. the hypo-

Intervening variables

thesis that a certain chemical tastes like pineapple might be intersubjectively testable. Intersubjectivity is usually contrasted with subjectivity rather than with objectivity, which it may include. See also SUBJECTIVISM.

Intervening variables. See LOGICAL CONSTRUCTIONS.

Intrinsic and extrinsic. In metaphysics, an 'extrinsic' view of identity holds that whether two apparently different things are in fact identical may depend on the existence or not of some further thing, while an 'intrinsic' view denies any such dependence. Hobbes' 'ship of Theseus' problem arises here: Theseus' ship was preserved, but gradually repaired plank by plank until all the planks had been replaced. The old planks were then gathered together and reconstituted into a ship. Which ship was the original? A related problem arises in philosophy of mind. For instance, suppose that after you die someone with all your memories and characteristics etc. appears on Mars: will it be you? It may be tempting to say yes – but then what if two or more such people appear? As they are not identical with each other they cannot all be identical with you (assuming identity is TRANSITIVE), and then it may seem arbitrary to say that any of them is.

P. Mackie, 'Essence, origin and bare identity', *Mind*, 1987. (Defends what is in effect an 'intrinsic' view of identity, drawing some implications of doing so. Cf. discussion by B. Garrett in *Mind*, 1988, and Mackie's reply in *Mind*, 1989.)

H. Noonan, 'The closest continuer theory of identity', *Inquiry*, 1985. (Attacks this 'extrinsic' view of identity – for which see R. Nozick, *Philosophical Explanations*, Harvard UP, Oxford UP, 1981, chapter 1 – defending a rival 'intrinsic' one.)

Intuition. Generally a direct relation between the mind and some object, analogous to what common sense thinks is the relation between us and something we see unambiguously in a clear light.

Bergson contrasts intuition as a means of knowing reality as it is in itself with intellect as a means by which we manipulate reality for purposes of action.

What we are said to intuit may be objects not accessible to the senses (numbers, universals, God, etc.), or truths, and intuitions have been divided into 'intuitions of' in the former case and 'intuitions that' in the latter. The emphasis is on the directness of the relation, free from any influence of the environment or interpretation. Hence Kant used 'intuition' for our relation to sensible objects too, so far as this was considered as abstracted from anything contributed by the mind. Intuition thus considered has something in common with Russell's 'acquaintance' (cf. EPISTEMOLOGY). Locke claimed that we have intuitive knowledge of our own existence, Husserl that we have it of essences, and Spinoza that we have it of elementary mathematics.

Intuition of truths may take the form of knowledge which we cannot account for, simply because we are unconscious of the reasons which led us to it. In the case of such 'hunches' investigation will often uncover the reasons. More philosophically important are cases where, allegedly, there are no reasons to be uncovered, and no means of checking the truth of apparent intuitions, except perhaps by their coherence with further intuitions.

Intuitions of this kind have been important especially in philosophy of mathematics (see INTUITIONISM) and ethics, and also in logic and metaphysics. Whether such intuitions can be accepted, and whether ultimately they are unavoidable, are disputed questions. Cf. also RATIONALISM.

In ethics especially, and concerning topics like personal IDENTITY, philosophers often appeal also to the 'pre-reflective' intuitions of common sense to act as a check on the acceptability of the conclusions they come to on theoretical grounds.

H. L. Bergson, 'Introduction to metaphysics', 1903 (translated 1912 and in his *The Creative Mind*, Philosophical Library, New York, 1946), *Creative Evolution*, 1907 (trans., Macmillan 1911).

D. Føllesdal, D. Bell, 'Objects and concepts', *Proceedings of the Aristotelian Society*, supplementary vol., 1994. (Includes discussion of Husserl on intuitions.)

H. L. A. Hart, G. E. Hughes, J. N. Findlay, 'Is there knowledge by acquaintance?', *Proceedings of the Aristotelian Society*, supplementary vol., 1949.

W. Hudson, *Ethical Intuitionism*, Macmillan, 1967. (Brief introduction.)

J. Locke, *Essay concerning Human Understanding*, 1690, book 4, chapter 9. (Intuition of the self.)

D. Pole, *Conditions of Rational Inquiry*, Athlone, 1961, chapter 1. (General discussion of intuition.)

H. Sidgwick, *Methods of Ethics*, Macmillan, 1874, (7th edn and final version, 1907), esp. book 1, chapter 8. (Types of ethical intuitionism.)

B. Spinoza, *Ethics*, book 2, § 40 n. 2, *Treatise on the Improvement of the Understanding*, §§ 19, 22–4. ('Scientia intuitiva' introduced.)

Intuitionism. Any doctrine emphasizing the role of INTUITION. Mathematical intuitionism, associated especially with L. E. J. Brouwer

Intuitionism

(1881–1966) and A. Heyting (1898–1980), confines the subject-matter of mathematics to what is given in intuition. In particular it refuses to assume that infinite sets actually exist, though it allows rules which generate ever larger finite sets. It is a form of *constructivism*, which insists that we should postulate entities (numbers, etc.) only if we know how to construct them, i.e. how to specify them systematically in terms of things we already accept. But intuitionism insists further that in mathematics we should call something true or false only if we either know it intuitively or know how to prove or disprove it, using steps known by intuition. (Hence an acceptable proof of something's existence involves constructing it.) Intuitionism therefore introduces a special kind of negation for use in mathematics, which has the consequence that we can deny a (non-counter-intuitive) proposition only if we can disprove it. Since intuitionists think that some (non-intuitive) mathematical propositions cannot be proved or disproved, they insist that the law of EXCLUDED MIDDLE does not apply to this kind of negation. On negation outside mathematics they have no united view, though discussions of them usually refer to the above version.

Formalists too limit mathematics to what is in a sense within our control. Some of them (e.g. H. B. Curry) make mathematics consist of formal systems whose elements are mere symbols or meaningless marks, to be operated on by fixed rules. Mathematics is not about abstract objects like numbers or classes that these marks might be thought to stand for. D. Hilbert (1862–1943), the most famous formalist, thought the logical paradoxes showed that non-finitary mathematics (see FINITISM) needed justifying. He therefore interpreted it as a formal system and used finitary means to prove the consistency of this system (cf. METAMATHEMATICS). See also INTUITION (for bibliography on ethical intuitionism).

P. Benacerraf and H. Putnam (eds), *Philosophy of Mathematics*, Blackwell, 1964, esp. pp. 66–77 (Brouwer), 134–51 (Hilbert).

M. A. E. Dummett, *Truth and Other Enigmas*, Duckworth, 1978. (Collected essays including many relevant and influential items. See esp. Preface, pp. xxiv-xxix, chapter 14. For revision of some of his views see his later *The Seas of Language*, Oxford, 1993, with its Preface.)

K. G. Hossack, 'A problem about the meaning of intuitionist negation', *Mind*, 1990. (Distinguishes strong and weak intuitionism and attacks former.)

W. and M. Kneale, *The Development of Logic*, Oxford UP, 1962. (See its index.)

G. T. Kneebone, *Mathematical Logic and the Foundations of Math-*

Isomorphic

ematics, Van Nostrand, 1963. (Pp. 243–50 gives elementary account of intuitionism, showing link with Kant.)

S. Körner, *The Philosophy of Mathematics*, Hutchinson, 1960. (Includes full treatment of intuitionism and formalism.)

W. V. Quine, *Philosophy of Logic*, Prentice-Hall, 1970, pp. 87–8. (Intuitionism and constructivism.)

Inversion. In traditional formal logic, replacement of a proposition by another (its *inverse*), which follows logically from it (assuming, as the traditional logic did, that all the relevant classes have members) and has as subject the negation of the original subject, e.g. 'Some non-cats are non-black' is the inverse of 'All cats are black'. Inversion can be carried out on only some of the traditional types of proposition.

Isomorphic. Sharing the same structure. Two or more sentences are *intensionally isomorphic* (Carnap) if they are logically equivalent, and have the same number of component sentences, and any component sentence in one is logically equivalent to the correspondingly placed component sentence in each of the others. The definition can be extended to certain other expressions. *Isomorphism* is the property or state of being isomorphic.

R. Carnap, *Meaning and Necessity*, Chicago UP, 1947, pp. 56–9.

J

James–Lange theory. Sometimes called the *peripheric theory*. Theory that emotions are consequences, not causes, of bodily disturbances, that 'the bodily changes follow directly the perception of the exciting fact, and that our feeling of the same changes as they occur *is* the emotion'. 'A purely disembodied human emotion is a nonentity' (though not a contradiction).

W. James, *The Principles of Psychology*, 1901, vol. 2, chapter 25. (Quotations on pp. 449, 452.)

James, William. 1842–1910. Psychologist and philosopher, and brother of novelist Henry James, he was born in New York and spent his life partly travelling and partly working at Harvard. Philosophically he is best known as a leading PRAGMATIST, though also in connexion with the JAMES–LANGE THEORY of the emotions and with neutral MONISM. *The Principles of Psychology*, 1890 (includes much philosophy too). *The Varieties of Religious Experience*, 1902. *Pragmatism*, 1907. *The Nature of Truth*, 1909 (supplement to *Pragmatism*). *Essays in Radical Empiricism*, 1912 (neutral monism). See also EMPIRCISM, SANTAYANA.

Jaspers, Karl. 1883–1969. Born in Oldenburg in Germany, he worked mainly at Heidelberg and Basel. He was a leading EXISTENTIALIST philosopher, whose work was much influenced by his early training in medicine and psychiatry, and has greater connexions with contemporary social and political problems than does that of HEIDEGGER. He treats human existence in terms of various notions, including *Dasein*, which he uses in a sense different from

168

Judgment

Heidegger's sense. *Philosophie*, 1932. *Vernunft und Existenz*, 1935 (5 lectures). *Existenzphilosophie*, 1938 (3 lectures). *Die Schuldfrage*, 1946 (on German war guilt). *Von der Wahrheit*, 1947. *Vernunft und Widervernunft in unserer Zeit*, 1950 (3 lectures). See also MARCEL.

Judgment. Act of judging, or, less commonly, proposition, or content of an act of judging. Acts of judging by different people or at different times, but with the same content, may, however, count as a single judgment (e.g. if you and I both judge that grass is green). Whether it is acts or contents that logic is primarily concerned with has been disputed. Idealists and pragmatists have tended to prefer acts, and formal logicians contents. Judgment is often equated with BELIEF, or with the formation of belief, though belief is a state or disposition rather than an act; 'judgment' itself, however, has a dispositional sense in phrases like 'in my judgment . . .', 'a person of judgment'.

Judgments are sometimes limited, in both 'act' and 'content' senses, to cases where an element of assessment or evaluation is concerned, e.g. moral *judgments* may be contrasted with *statements* of fact. See also SENTENCES, THINKING.

P. T. Geach, *Mental Acts*, RKP, 1957. (One view of judgments. Fairly difficult.)

K _____

Kant, Immanuel. 1724–1804. German philosopher who spent all his life in Königsberg (now Kaliningrad). He is often regarded as synthesizing the 'British EMPIRICIST' and 'Continental RATIONALIST' schools by standing back from the questions they asked ('What is the nature of the world?', 'How do we know about the world?') and saying we must first give a critique of our faculties; he asks what it is *possible* for any mind like the human mind to know. Hence his philosophy after 1781 is often called the 'critical' philosophy. Much of his philosophy centres round his defence of synthetic a priori propositions, see ANALYTIC. He also tried to derive morality from reason alone, and to elaborate a notion of the self compatible with our possession of freewill. *Kritik der reinen Vernunft (Critique of Pure Reason)*, 1781 (2nd edn 1787). *Grundlegung der Metaphysik der Sitten (Fundamental Principles (or Groundwork) of the Metaphysic of Morals)*, 1785. *Kritik der praktischen Vernunft (Critique of Practical Reason)*, 1788. *Kritik der Urteilskraft (Critique of Judgment)*, 1790. See also APPERCEPTION, A PRIORI, BEING, CATEGORIES, COSMOLOGICAL, DESIGN, EPISTEMOLOGY, ETHICS, FORM (bibliography), GOOD, HARE, HEIDEGGER, HUME, IDEA, IDEALISM, IMPERATIVE, INCONGRUENT, INTUITION, MANIFOLD, MODALITIES, NOUMENON, OUGHT, PHENOMENOLOGY, REASON, REID, SCHOPENHAUER, SPACE, STRAWSON, TRANSCENDENTAL ARGUMENTS, UNIVERSALIZABILITY.

N. Kemp Smith (trans.), *Immanuel Kant's Critique of Pure Reason*, Macmillan, 1929. (Standard translation.)

H. J. Paton (trans.) *The Moral Law: Kant's Groundwork of the Metaphysic of Morals*, Hutchinson, 1948. (Kant's most important ethical work.)

Kierkegaard, Søren A. 1813–55. Danish philosopher who spent his life as a pastor in Copenhagan and is normally considered the first EXISTENTIALIST. His principal interest was in ethics, where he emphasized the importance of pure choice, but, more than many later existentialists, developed his philosophy in a Christian framework. He also, like SCHOPENHAUER, reacted against the then prevalent philosophy of HEGEL. *Either/Or*, 1843. *Philosophical Fragments*, 1844. *The Concept of Dread*, 1844. *Concluding Unscientific Postscript to the Philosophical Fragments*, 1846.

Knowledge. See EPISTEMOLOGY.

Kripke, Saul A. 1940–. Born in Bay Shore, NY, he has worked mainly at Princeton. Coming to philosophy from mathematics he has worked mainly in logic and metaphysics, and more recently in the interpretation of Wittgenstein. He has developed a causal theory of the MEANING of names and 'natural kind words' (such as 'horse' and 'iron') and pioneered (with PUTNAM) a revival of essentialism, insisting also that the a priori/empirical and necessary/contingent distinctions do not, as usually then thought, coincide (see also PUTNAM). His publications include 'Naming and necessity' in D. Davidson and G. Harman (eds), *Semantics of Natural Language*, 1972 (republished as separate book, 1980); *Wittgenstein on Rules and Private Language*, 1972.

L

Language (philosophy of). Not the same as linguistic PHILOSOPHY, nor as *linguistics*, which studies the general features of natural languages structurally (*synchronic*) or historically (*diachronic*, also called *philology*).

As a separate study, philosophy of language is a recent offshoot of logic, connected also to epistemology, metaphysics and philosophy of mind. It asks general questions about language as such, not (like linguistics) about particular languages. The latter, of course, provide examples.

The primary end of language is communication. Other ends, like getting people to do things, depend on this. Many things can be communicated – information, requests, commands, ideas, innuendoes, etc. (cf. SPEECH ACTS). Whether the primary function of language is to inform (or assert) may be disputed, but this function in fact receives most attention. Two concepts which are therefore of central importance are TRUTH and FACTS. The question of how communication is possible, or how language works, involves us in studying the notion of MEANING CONCEPTS, propositions and statements (see SENTENCES) have been thought necessary to account for meaning, and they raise problems about what they are and what properties they have (e.g. the ANALYTIC/synthetic distinction).

A study of language in general will naturally ask whether there are any features every language must share. Such features might be ones without which a language could not exist. It might be claimed, for example, that every language must include ways of referring to particular objects, or ways of negating; or the features might be needed because human nature is what it is. (N. Chomsky claims that certain features of language are universal and throw

Language (philosophy of)

light on how the mind works. Cf. CATEGORIES.) It is also claimed (Davidson) that to be learnable a language must be compositional, i.e. the meanings of sentences must depend systematically on the meanings of words.

Further general questions about language include how far animals can have language, whether there can be a PRIVATE LANGUAGE, and whether ideal languages are possible, of which natural languages are defective versions (as, for example, Russell and perhaps Plato thought). Artificial languages, whether used in science or computing or constructed for theoretical interest, can also be studied.

After the Second World War, naming and verificationist theories of MEANING were rejected, and there followed the piecemeal approach of linguistic PHILOSOPHY, dominated by Wittgenstein and Austin. METAPHYSICS has also used philosophy of language on topics like SUBSTANCE. Recently there has been some return to large-scale theorizing stemming from Chomsky, whose contribution involves applying mathematical techniques to problems connected with the attempt to specify all the sentences constructable in a given language. There have also been substantial developments in the theory of meaning, pioneered by writers like Davidson and Putnam; see REALISM.

*W. Alston, *Philosophy of Language*, Prentice-Hall, 1964. (General introduction.)

J. L. Austin, *How to Do Things with Words*, Oxford UP, 1962. (Functions of language, by major exponent of speech act analyses).

J. F. Bennett, *Rationality*, RKP, 1964. (Can animals have language?)

S. Blackburn, *Spreading the Word*, Clarendon, 1984. (General introduction to philosophy of language, combined with positive philosophizing and developing his 'quasi-realism'.)

T. Burge, 'Philosophy of language and mind: 1950–90', *Philosophical Review*, 1992. (Survey article with many references. See esp. 1st half for philosophy of language.)

D. Davidson, *Inquiries into Truth and Interpretation*, Oxford UP, 1984. (Collected essays of major contributor to recent developments.)

*J. Lyons, *Chomsky*, Fontana, 1970, expanded 1977. (Elementary introduction. cf. also Chomsky's lecture series *Languages and the Problems of Knowledge*, MIT Press, 1988.)

H. Putnam, *Philosophical Papers, Volume 2: Mind, Language and Reality*, Cambridge UP, 1975.

P. F. Strawson, *Individuals*, Methuen, 1959. (Part 2 discusses role of referring.)

Language game

L. Wittgenstein, *Philosophical Investigations*, Blackwell, 1953. (Probably most important of his many books. Cf. his *Tractatus* (see bibliography to LOGICAL ATOMISM) for earlier stage in his thought.)

Language game. Wittgenstein discussed the way language works by inventing small-scale languages for special spheres, such as house-building, and asking how they might work and what they must be like. Comparing them to certain children's games he called them language games. He then compared them to the complexities of actual language, and used them to emphasize the role of words in certain human practices like doing science and play-acting. He originally thought of them as primitive or autonomous, i.e. as not presupposing the rest of language. But 'language game' came to be applied also to certain parts or spheres of already existing languages, e.g. religious language, or language as used in connexion with promising, can be called language games, though they could hardly exist except as parts of a language used more generally.

R. Rhees, *Discussions of Wittgenstein*, RKP, 1970, chapter 6. (Discussion of some difficulties by sympathizer.)
L. Wittgenstein, *Philosophical Investigations*, Blackwell, 1953, esp. part 1, §§ 7, 23.

Language of thought. Fodor's name for his view (also called the *representational theory of mind*) that mental states have a syntactic (see SEMIOTIC) structure corresponding to the semantical structure of the propositions which form their objects, i.e. that mental states represent their objects by having parts which represent parts of the objects in a systematic way. The language is also called 'Mentalese'.

*T. Crane, *The Mechanical Mind: A Philosophical Introduction to Minds, Mechanics and Mental Representation*, Penguin, 1995, chapter 4. (Elementary introduction; see pp. 154–62 for comparison of language of thought with CONNECTIONISM.)
J. A. Fodor, *The Language of Thought*, T. Y. Crowell, 1975, Harvester, 1976. (See also his *Psychosemantics*, MIT Press, 1987, esp. its Appendix, for briefer version and see bibliography to PSYCHOSEMANTICS and also W. G. Lycan (ed.), *Mind and Cognition*, Blackwell, 1990, part v.)

Law (philosophy of). The study of problems concerning prescriptive laws (as against laws of nature, often called descriptive, which are studied by philosophy of science. On 'natural law', see LAWS).)

There are widely different views about what a law is. Is it a command of the sovereign? Or a prediction of what judges will decide? Or a prediction that certain actions will be followed by sanctions? Or a statement of an intention to impose sanctions? Or something else? Are there formal conditions (as against conditions affecting its content) that a law must satisfy to count as a law at all, like being initiated in certain ways by a body with special authority, or not being inconsistent with itself or with other laws in the same system? Are there restrictions on content, e.g. is an alleged law not a law at all if it prescribes what is impossible, or violates divine, natural, or moral law? And are these kinds of law, if they exist, all law in the same sense? Also is a law still a law if there is either no prescribed sanction or no power of enforcement?

Some of these questions raise issues of justification. To justify a law or to justify a legal system may be either to show that it really is one, or to show that it is good, fair, proper, impartial, etc. How closely these tasks are related is disputable. Other things that need justifying are judgments within a legal system, e.g. those of lawyers or of judges, and the duty of obedience. Closely related are questions about the justification of punishment, be it of punishment in general, of particular penalties for particular types of case, or of individual cases. The notions of intention and strict liability (i.e. liability irrespective of intention) are relevant here.

Certain problems concern the different branches of law (constitutional, civil, commercial, criminal) and how they relate to each other and to equity. Constitutional law in particular raises questions about how it can change. In other branches the role of judges in making law is relevant. Questions of sovereignty and sanctions lead to problems about the possibility and nature of international law.

H. L. A. Hart, *The Concept of Law*, Oxford UP, 1961. (Full discussion of many problems.)

H. L. A. Hart, *The Morality of the Criminal Law*, Oxford UP, 1965. (Hart's side in famous debate with Lord Devlin, Cf. P. Devlin, *The Enforcement of Morals*, 1959, reprinted with other relevant items in book of same title,1965.)

T. Honderich, *Punishment: the Supposed Justifications*, Hutchinson, 1969.

R. S. Summers (ed.), *Essays in Legal Philosophy*, Blackwell, 1968, *More Essays in Legal Philosophy*, Blackwell, 1971. (First volume covers questions of analysis and justification. Second discusses historical figures. See Summers's introductions for survey of issues.)

Laws. The traditional distinction between 'prescriptive' laws (legal, moral, divine) and 'descriptive' laws (scientific) is convenient, but

Laws

not necessarily accurate. 'Prescriptive' laws (see philosophy of LAW) may not be prescriptions, and 'descriptive' laws may not describe the world. The laws of logic and mathematics are simply accepted statements, usually important, in those subjects. The *laws of thought* are the logical laws of identity, contradiction and EXCLUDED MIDDLE. Whether they are more important than other logical laws is disputed. The rest of this entry mainly concerns scientific laws.

Generalizations may be closed (limited in space and time: 'All the coins now in my pocket are silver') or open ('All ravens, at all times and places, are black'). But on another interpretation open generalizations have the form, 'Anything whatever, if it is so-and-so, is such-and-such', where 'so-and-so' may or may not contain spatiotemporal restrictions like 'now in my pocket'. On this interpretation both the first two examples would be closed, because they each have a limited subject-matter (coins and ravens), and any generalization could be formulated as an open generalization of the second kind.

In so far as scientific laws are generalizations, they are usually regarded as open on the first interpretation (though this excludes those of Kepler (see below) and Galileo). They also are usually taken to imply counterfactuals (see CONDITIONALS): 'All ravens are black', if a law, implies 'If there were ravens on Mars (though there aren't) they would be black'. For both these reasons laws cannot be conclusively verified. Also many laws seem to have no direct application: 'All bodies unacted on by forces move with constant velocity in a straight line' – but there are no such bodies. For these and other reasons scientific laws are sometimes thought to be rules governing the scientist's expectations, and so prescriptive, or else idealized descriptions to which the world approximates, as triangles on a blackboard approximate to Euclidean triangles. On this last view the point of Newton's first law of motion (quoted above) is that any deviation of an object from uniform rectilinear motion must be attributed to its being acted on by forces. Some writers refuse to call laws 'true' on the grounds that they are not straightforwardly descriptive.

Normally a *hypothesis* is a statement not yet accepted as true, or as a law, while a law is only called a law if it is accepted, whether or not we call it 'true'. But occasionally laws, though accepted, are still called hypotheses, e.g. 'Avogadro's hypothesis'. A *lawlike statement* is sometimes a statement resembling a law except that it is not accepted and is perhaps rejected, and sometimes a statement not general enough to be a law because it refers to individual objects (e.g. Kepler's 'laws' about how 'the' planets go round 'the' sun, which do not mention suns and planets in general). Occasionally it is a statement attributing dispositional characteristics, e.g. 'Glass is brittle'.

Theory has various meanings: (i) One or more hypotheses or lawlike statements (either of first two senses), regarded as speculative. (ii) A law about unobservables like electrons or evolution, sometimes called a theory because evidence about unobservables is felt to be inevitably inconclusive. (iii) A unified system of laws or hypotheses, with explanatory force (not merely like a railway timetable). (iv) A field of study (e.g. in philosophy: theory of knowledge, logical theory). These senses sometimes shade into each other.

A *principle* may be a high-grade law, on which a lot depends, or it may be something like a rule. To call all scientific laws principles suggests they hover between being rules and being idealized descriptions. Legal, moral, aesthetic, etc., principles may resemble scientific laws in being descriptions of ideal worlds, set up to govern actions as scientific laws are to govern expectations. However, they differ from them by not being idealized descriptions of the real world, to be rejected unless the real world approximates to them in the relevant ways. (Other uses of 'law' and 'principle' exist.)

Scientific laws are often called *laws of nature* or *natural laws*. *Natural law* (generic singular) is the moral law (i.e. set of laws) regarded as derivable from the general nature of the universe by reason alone, without appeal to revelation, feelings, interests, etc. See also EXPLANATION, MODALITIES, CONVENTIONALISM, INSTRUMENTALISM.

D. M. Armstrong, *What is a Law of Nature?*, Cambridge UP, 1983. (A connection between universals.)

R. B. Braithwaite, *Scientific Explanation*, Harper, 1953. (Pp. 300–3 analyse scientific laws in terms of their explanatory function.)

J. W. Carroll, *Laws of Nature*, Cambridge UP, 1994. (Defends realist view of them, connecting with causation.)

A. P. D'Entreves, *Natural Law*, Hutchinson, 1951, 2nd edn republished with new introduction by C. J. Nederman, Transaction Publishers 1994. (Sympathetic discussion, more historical and less analytical than Finnis.)

J. Finnis, *Natural Law and Natural Rights*, Clarendon, 1980. (Full discussion from mainly philosophical rather than historical point of view. Cf. also, for an anthology, J. Finnis (ed.), *Natural Law*, 2 vols, Dartmouth Publishing Company, 1991.)

W. Kneale, *Probability and Induction*, Oxford UP, 1949. (Part 2 discusses various kinds of scientific law, and claims that they express objective necessities.)

M. Singer, *Generalization in Ethics*, Eyre and Spottiswoode, 1963, chapter 5. (Moral rules and principles).

Learning paradox

S. E. Toulmin, *Philosophy of Science*, Hutchinson, 1953. (Advocates 'idealized description' view, though without so calling it, and discusses other views.)

Learning paradox. See EDUCATION.

Leibniz, Gottfried W. 1646–1716. German mathematician and philosopher who was born in Leipzig and, after holding various court posts, worked as a librarian and historian in Hanover. He and Newton, independently, invented the differential calculus. He is usually included among the 'Continental RATIONALISTS', and in METAPHYSICS he claimed that all true propositions are really ANALYTIC, and that reality consists of independent MONADS, which mirror but do not influence each other, and contain within themselves a sort of blue-print of their entire life-histories, which they work through according to a 'pre-established harmony' arranged by God. Leibniz is also noted for LEIBNIZ'S LAW, and although he denied the reality of relations, he defended a relational view of SPACE and time (in letters to S. Clarke, who represented Newton). Discours de Metaphysique, written 1685–6, published 1846. *Principes de la nature et de la grace, fondés en raison*, written 1714, published 1718. *La Monadologie*, written 1714, first published in German 1720. *Nouveaux Essaies sur l'entendement humain*, written 1704, published 1765 (critique of LOCKE's *Essay*). He also wrote important letters to A. Arnauld. See also APPERCEPTION, CONCEPT (bibliography), ENTELECHY, INNATE, INTENSIONALITY, OCCASIONALISM, PSYCHOPHYSICAL, SUBSTANCE, SUFFICIENT REASON.

G. W. Leibniz, *New Essays concerning Human Understanding* (trans. A. G. Langley), Macmillan, 1986. (Originally published, 1916. Includes also shorter relevant pieces by Leibniz and indexes. For more recent translation, with notes see G. W. Leibniz, *News Essays on Human Understanding* (trans. P. Remmant and J. Bennett), Cambridge UP, 1981.)

L. Loemker (ed.), *Gottfried Wilhelm Leibniz: Philosophical Papers and Letters*, Chicago UP, 1956. (Translated selections (c. 650 pp.), with long introduction. For a similar but shorter selection see R. Ariew and D. Garber (eds), *G. W. Leibniz: Philosophical Essays*, Hackett, 1989. Both volumes include some of the shorter substantive works.)

Leibniz's law. There are two principles which together form what is now called Leibniz's law, though Leibniz himself seems only to have held the first of them. The *identity of indiscernibles* is the principle that if a group of things have all their properties in common, or belong to exactly the same classes, they are identical in the sense of being really only one thing. The *indiscernibililty of identicals* (Quine) is the principle that if a group of things are identical (i.e. are really one thing, though perhaps described in different ways), they have all their properties in common. Sometimes the term, 'Leibniz's law' is limited to the second principle.

The identity of indiscernibles can be held in various forms, which differ in strength according to what sort of properties are considered relevant. In a weak, and thereby more plausible, form spatiotemporal properties are included. The principle then says only that things sharing all their properties, including their positions in space and time, are identical. But a stronger form says that things will be identical if they have all their non-relational properties in common (i.e. properties which do not, like spatiotemporal ones, involve a relation to something else). This would mean there cannot be two or more things exactly similar. In the weaker form, but not in stronger ones, the identity of indiscernibles is the converse of the indiscernibility of identicals.

Leibniz himself often said that things are identical when they can be substituted for each other without making a true proposition false. This leads to apparent limitations of the law because of problems connected with intentionality (see INTENSIONALITY AND INTENTIONALITY and the Cicero example there). However, it is really words or descriptions, not things, that can be substituted for each other. The law therefore (since, as viewed so far, it concerns things, not words) does not apply to the Cicero case, and so need not be limited. But the law might be regarded as giving rise to a principle of substitutivity, whose two halves will say that if whatever can be said of *a*, so described, can be said of *b*, so described, then *a* and *b* are identical (weak form of identity of indiscernibles), and vice versa (indiscernibility of identicals); co-referring terms can therefore be intersubstituted preserving truth. It then seems necessary to allow exceptions to this principle. The view that these exceptions can, however, be ultimately dispensed with (or alternatively that only in so far as they can is formal logic possible) is called the *extensionality thesis, principle*, or (especially in formal contexts) *axiom*. See also IDENTITY, SPACE, INTENSIONALITY, SUFFICIENT REASON.

H. G. Alexander (ed.), *The Leibniz–Clarke Correspondence*, Manchester UP, 1956. (See Introduction, p. xxiii, for references to text.)

F. Feldman, 'Leibniz and "Leibniz' Law",' *Philosophical Review*, 1970. (What Leibniz himself held.)

L. Linsky, *Referring*, RKP, 1967. (Substitutivity distinguished from Leibniz's law on p. 79.)

Lewis, David K.

M. J. Loux (ed.), *Universals and Particulars*, Anchor Books, 1970. (Includes items on identity of indiscernibles.)

P. F. Strawson, *Individuals*, Methuen, 1959. (Chapter 4 discusses a strong form of the identity of indiscernibles, partly in terms of Leibniz.)

D. Wiggins, *Sameness and Substance*, Blackwell, 1980. (Discusses significance for the nature of identity of various formulations of each of the principles, though keeping title 'Leibniz's law' for indiscernibility of identicals. See its index. Difficult.)

Lewis, David K. 1941–. Born in Oberlin, Oh., he has worked mainly at Princeton. He has developed an influential analysis of counterfactuals (see CONDITIONALS) in terms of POSSIBLE WORLDS, and then gone on to develop this latter notion, holding an extreme realist view of them whereby, though not actual, they are as real as the actual world but spatiotemporally disconnected from it. More recently he has turned to aspects of MEREOLOGY. His publications include *Convention*, 1969; *Counterfactuals*, 1973; *Philosophical Papers*, vol. 1, 1983; vol. 2, 1986; *On the Plurality of Worlds*, 1986; *Parts of Classes*, 1991.

Liar paradox. 'This statement is false' seems to be false if true, and true if false. Traditionally attributed to Epimenides the Cretan in the (inadequate) form, 'All Cretans are liars', this paradox is often called a semantic PARADOX. It raises difficulties especially for the correspondence theory of TRUTH, for it is hard to find a fact for 'This statement is false' to correspond to, or fail to correspond to. This paradox was also mainly responsible for the semantic theory of TRUTH taking the form that Tarski gave it. See also RUSSELL'S PARADOX, TYPES.

J. Barwise and J. Etchemendy, *The Liar*, Oxford UP, 1987.

R. L. Martin (ed.), *The Paradox of the Liar*, Yale UP, 1970. (Brief history, followed by recent discussions. Extensive bibliography.)

R. L. Martin (ed.), *Recent Essays on Truth and the Liar Paradox*, Oxford UP, 1984. (Specially written essays, with discussions.)

G. Ryle (see bibliography to HETEROLOGICAL).

R. M. Sainsbury, *Paradoxes*, Cambridge UP, 1988 (revised 1995), chapter 5. (Compares the Liar with Russell's paradox.)

Libertarianism. See FREEWILL.

Likelihood. If we know how a property is distributed in a population (e.g. how many of all the swans in the world are white) we can infer the probability of any given distribution of the property in any random sample. But the converse inference from sample to population involves a simple inversion, which (unlike the inversion involved in BAYES'S THEOREM) will not work for probabilities. R. A. Fisher (1890–1962) therefore introduced *likelihood* as a notion for which this simple inversion is valid. (But outside technical contexts 'likelihood' is usually synonymous with 'probability'.)

To see how Fisher's likelihood relates to probability, consider the probability that a ball is white when randomly chosen from a bag of three balls, each white or black. Let h_n be the hypothesis that the bag contains exactly n white balls and $3-n$ black balls. Let w/h_n and b/h_n signify the probabilities that the chosen ball is white or black, respectively, given h_n. The $w/h_n + b/h_n = 1$, i.e. the probabilities on a given hypothesis add up to one. Now consider the four probabilities w/h_0, w/h_1, w/h_2, w/h_3. These, though exhaustive and non-overlapping, do not add up to one (but to two, in this case). They are therefore called likelihoods, but is obscure what likelihoods are, unless we merely say they are probabilities grouped in a way that stops them obeying the laws of PROBABILITY theory. They can indeed usually be mathematically manipulated to add up to one. But this does not lessen the difficulty.

A. W. F. Edwards, *Likelihood*, Cambridge UP, 1972; expanded edn, Baltimore, 1992. (Full technical treatment.)

I. Hacking, *Logic of Statistical Inference*, Cambridge UP, 1965. (See index.)

M. G. Kendall and A. Stuart, *The Advanced Theory of Statistics*, vol. 1, Griffin, 1958, chapter 8.

Locke, John. 1632–1704. Born in Somerset, he worked mostly in Oxford and London when not in exile because of his political activities against the Stuarts before 1688. His central work was in epistemology, where his 'new way of IDEAS' has led to his being regarded as the first main 'British EMPIRICIST'. He insisted that ideas could only come from experience, though connexions between them could be known A PRIORI, and he elaborated the primary/secondary QUALITY distinction. He also wrote on political theory from a liberal point of view. *Letters concerning Toleration*, 1689 and after. *Two Treatises of Government*, 1690. *An Essay concerning Human Understanding*, 1690. See also BERKELEY, BUTLER, ESSENCE, IDENTITY (bibliography), INNATE (bibliography), MEANING, PERCEPTION, SHAFTESBURY, SORTAL, SPACE, SUBSTANCE.

Locutions. See SPEECH ACTS.

Logic. The central topic of logic is valid reasoning, its systematiz-

Logic

ation and the study of notions relevant to it. This gives it two systematically related areas of concern, *formal logic* and *philosophical logic* (also called *logical theory*, though usage varies and *philosophy of logic* is sometimes confined to the study of logical systems and their applications).

The main task of *formal logic* is to axiomatize (see AXIOM SYSTEM) various subject-matters, constructing in particular the propositional and predicate CALCULI. Theorems are then proved in and about the resulting systems to bring out their properties. The important properties include CONSISTENCY, COMPLETENESS and the possession of DECISION PROCEDURES. The study of such properties is often called *metalogic*.

Systems complex enough to axiomatize mathematics on the basis of DECIDABLE axioms turn out to have these properties only to a severely limited extent (see GÖDEL'S THEOREMS). Also the logical PARADOXES make it harder to construct these systems. Much of modern formal logic consists in trying to avoid or minimize these limitations and difficulties. How relevant they are in the sphere of philosophical logic, or even outside it, is disputed. The main issues are the nature of truth, especially in view of the LIAR PARADOX, and the relations between formal systems and ordinary language. Some, especially adherents to linguistic PHILOSOPHY, have argued from these or other considerations that ordinary language has no exact logic (cf. also OPEN TEXTURE). The study of ordinary language from this point of view is sometimes called informal logic, though this can also refer to the study of those inferences which depend on the content rather than form of the sentences concerned. We infer 'Smith is unmarried' from 'Smith is a bachelor' because of the meaning of 'bachelor' not because 'Smith is a bachelor' has a certain form. A formal inference from 'Smith is a bachelor' might yield 'Bachelors include Smith' (see FORM); this raises some of the problems concerning the ANALYTIC.

Formal logic also studies NATURAL DEDUCTION, and formal parts of modal and deontic logic (see below).

A topic related to formal logic is *set theory* (see CALCULUS). This and *proof theory* (see METAMATHEMATICS) are normally together called *mathematical logic*, and lead towards the philosophy of MATHEMATICS. Modern formal logic and mathematical logic are each, or together, often called *symbolic logic*, to mark the more intensive use of symbols, or *logistic*.

Deontic logic studies logical relations between propositions containing terms like 'obliged', 'commanded', 'permitted', 'forbidden', though the term tends to be confined to the construction of formal systems using deontic terms, and the problems these systems raise. A rather similar subject is the *logic of preference*, which asks, for

182

Logic

example, what sets of preferences can consistently be held together (e.g. can one prefer *a* to *b*, and *b* to *c*, but *c* to *a*?) Cf. VOTING PARADOX.

Philosophical logic examines the concepts involved in formal logic and uses its results, but is not concerned with the mechanics of the various systems; however, the boundaries between these areas of logic are not sharp. It also studies the nature of logical systems as such, and whether there can be alternative logics (see below).

As a study devoted to valid reasoning, it naturally asks about reasoning in general and how many kinds of it there are. Is all reasoning, properly speaking, deductive, or is there also inductive reasoning (see INDUCTION, philosophy of SCIENCE), and perhaps other kinds, e.g. in morals, history, aesthetics? Are there several kinds of validity? Validity is closely connected to logical necessity, and thence to necessity in general and other modal concepts such as possibility and impossibility (see MODALITIES). Modal concepts are studied by *modal logic*, though in practice this term, like 'deontic logic', tends to be confined to the study of formal systems using modal terms. General analyses of necessity, etc. belong to philosophical logic, which also asks how these modal notions are related to the A PRIORI and the ANALYTIC.

Reasoning involves passing from premises to conclusions, and so involves a relation and the things which it relates. Both of these are subjects for philosophical logic. The relation in its most general form is IMPLICATION, which raises problems about its different kinds and its relation to INFERENCE. The things it relates are SENTENCES, propositions or statements, which again raise problems about what they are.

Attempts to relate logic to epistemology may be said to lie behind the development of INTUITIONIST logic, perhaps the main alternative to two-valued *classical logic* (recognizing only the two TRUTH-VALUES truth and falsity). But other '*deviant logics*' have also been developed for various purposes, such as the alleged needs of quantum mechanics.

Logic also studies meaning in general, of ordinary words as well as of formal words like 'all', 'and', etc., and of both words and sentences. This broadens into the study of language in general: how it does what it does and how it relates to the world (cf. above on relating ordinary language to formal systems). How are the various roles that words fulfil, such as meaning, referring, describing, predicating, to be distinguished and related? These problems now form a subject of their own, philosophy of LANGUAGE, but they still fall broadly under logic. Two further notions important in this area are DEFINITIONS and TRUTH (see above; truth also belongs to

Logic

epistemology). Logic borders on metaphysics when we ask how far various logical views commit us to asserting that certain kinds of things, like propositions, exist, and how we should analyse existential QUANTIFICATION (cf. BEING).

Formal logic effectively began with Aristotle, who systematized immediate INFERENCE and the SYLLOGISM, which remained the basis of *traditional logic* until about a century ago. Vigorous developments in both formal and philosophical logic were made by the Stoics, and in philosophical logic in the Middle Ages, but these were forgotten and have only recently been revived. The syllogism is now seen to form a small part of the predicate calculus.

A key feature in the history of modern logic since about the middle of the nineteenth century has been the development of a *logic of relations*. This comes from realizing, and taking seriously, that not all propositions consist of a subject and predicate linked by the copula, 'is' ('are'). Traditional logic had unduly restricted itself by assuming that they do, and could not formalize so simple an argument as 'Ten exceeds nine and nine exceeds eight, so ten exceeds eight', where the main verb stands for a relation. See also TOPIC-NEUTRAL, QUANTIFIER WORDS.

*I. Copi, *Introduction to Logic*, Macmillan 6th edn, 1982. (Covers formal, informal, and inductive logic and has many examples, some with answers. See also W. A. Hodges, *Logic*, Penguin, 1977 (has exercises with answers).)

J. N. Crossley *et al.*, *What is Mathematical Logic?*, Oxford UP, 1972. (Brief. Fairly elementary.)

*A. Grayling, *An Introduction to Philosophical Logic*, Harvester, 1982; 2nd edn, Duckworth, 1990. (Mainly elementary with two rather harder chapters at end.)

G. E. Hughes and M. J. Cresswell, *An Introduction to Modal Logic*, Methuen, 1968. (Comprehensive.)

J. N. Keynes, *Formal Logic*, 1884, 4th (revised) edn 1906. Standard and full treatment of traditional logic.)

W. and M. Kneale, *The Development of Logic*, Oxford UP, 1962. (Very full treatment of historical development of the subject.)

*E. J. Lemmon, *Beginning Logic*, Nelson, 1965. (Adopts NATURAL DEDUCTION approach.)

B. Mates, *Stoic Logic*, California UP, 1953.

*W. V. O. Quine, *Philosophy of Logic*, Prentice-Hall, 1970. (General introduction from Quine's own point of view.)

*R. M. Sainsbury, *Logical Forms: An Introduction to Philosophical Logic*, Blackwell, 1991. (Claims to bridge gap between elementary formal logic and more advanced philosophical logic.)

P. F. Strawson, *Introduction to Logical Theory*, Methuen, 1952.

Logical atomism

(Represents 'linguistic philosophy' outlook, that there is no exact logic of ordinary language.)

G. H. von Wright, *The Logic of Preference*, Edinburgh UP, 1963. (Introduction.)

G. H. von Wright, *An Essay in Deontic Logic*, North-Holland, 1968. (Introduction, with bibliography.)

F. Waismann, 'Are there alternative logics?', *Proceedings of the Aristotelian Society*, 1945–6, reprinted in his *How I See Philosophy*, Macmillan, 1968. Cf. S. Haack, *Deviant Logic*, Cambridge UP, 1974, and *Philosophy of Logics*, Cambridge UP, 1978 (which includes glossary).

Logical atomism. Theory associated mainly with Russell (middle period) and Wittgenstein (early period) which seeks to analyse thought and discourse in terms of indivisible components. *Atomic propositions* consist of a subject term and a predicate term ('John is clever'), or a set of terms linked by a relation term ('John hates Tom'), and they are true if they correspond directly to FACTS, which are all (for this theory, at least in its purest form) atomic. *Molecular propositions* are truth FUNCTIONS of atomic ones and correspond in complex ways to those same facts. This shows, it is claimed, that the logical connectives (see CONJUNCTION) do not name or correspond to elements of facts, or anything else. They simply connect propositions. However, it was not clear on this view how atomic propositions could be false, and various kinds of propositions supposed to be molecular in the above sense created difficulties when treated as such. e.g. general (see UNIVERSAL) and negative propositions; it was difficult to make them correspond, even in complex ways, to atomic facts.

As for the constituents of atomic facts, Wittgenstein left them unspecified, calling them simply 'objects'. Russell regarded 'John is clever' etc. as only apparently atomic, because only simple things we are acquainted with could be constituents of atomic propositions and named by logically proper names (see DESCRIPTIONS, MEANING), and such simples were confined to our own SENSE DATA, which made it hard for him to give any genuine examples of atomic propositions and therefore of atomic facts. See also INTENSIONALITY AND INTENTIONALITY (for the 'extensionality principle').

D. F. Pears, *Bertrand Russell and the British Tradition in Philosophy*, Fontana, 1967. (Fuller and harder than, and sometimes critical of, Urmson.)

B. Russell, 'The philosophy of logical atomism', *The Monist*, 1918, reprinted in his *Logic and Knowledge*, Allen and Unwin, 1956, and D. Pears (ed.), *Russell's Logical Atomism*, Fontana/Collins,

Logical constructions

1972. (A popular account. The essay 'Logical atomism', in both these volumes is harder.)

R. M. Sainsbury, *Russell*, RKP, 1979, chapter II.

J. O. Urmson, *Philosophical Analysis*, Oxford UP, 1956. (Fairly elementary.)

L. Wittgenstein, *Tractatus Logico-Philosophicus*, 1921, transl. D. F. Pears and B. F. McGuinness, RKP, 1961. (Very difficult.)

Logical constructions. When we say 'The average man has 2.4 children' we are really saying something about Smith, Jones, etc. The sentence is analysable into a set of sentences in which the phrase 'the average man' does not appear. The average man is therefore a *logical construction*, and 'the average man' is an *incomplete symbol*. These notions were introduced by Russell.

Later writers, especially Wisdom, distinguished weak and strong senses of 'incomplete symbol'. A symbol was incomplete in a weak sense if (i) it purported to refer to something, (ii) the sentence containing it would be replaced, in a proper logical language, by sentences not containing it, but (iii) these new sentences would only be true, in simple affirmative cases, if the thing apparently referred to did indeed exist. If 'The present king of France is bald' is analysed by the theory of DESCRIPTIONS, 'the present king of France' is an incomplete symbol in a weak sense. A symbol was incomplete in a strong sense if (i), like 'the average man', it disappeared when the sentence containing it was properly reformulated, but (ii) the reformulated version could be true, in simple affirmative cases, even though what the symbol apparently referred to did not exist (no man with 2.4 children exists). 'Logical construction' (or 'construct') was thereafter kept for what incomplete symbols in a strong sense purported to refer to, i.e. the average man, but not the present King of France, would be a logical construction. There is, however, a complication: Moore held that if 'the average man' is an incomplete symbol, then so is 'has 2.4 children'; but this latter does not seem, straightforwardly, to involve a logical construction.

Logical constructions, therefore, lost the role they had in the theory of descriptions, but they remained a powerful tool for reductive analysis (see PHILOSOPHY, PHENOMENALISM). Although Russell sometimes used the phrase *logical fictions*, logical constructions are not hypothetical, inferred, fictitious or imaginary entities. The average man is none of these. They are often contrasted with inferred entities (i.e. entities we infer to exist, but cannot observe). In scientific contexts those logical constructions which purport to be properties (as the average man purports to be an object), e.g. density, which can vary in degree, are sometimes called *intervening variables*, while inferred entities are called *hypothetical constructs* (but usage varies).

L. W. Beck, 'Constructions and inferred entities', *Philosophy of Science*, 1950, reprinted in H. Feigl and M. Brodbeck (eds), *Readings in the Philosophy of Science*, Appleton-Century-Crofts, 1953. (Compares treatment of things like electrons as logical constructions and as inferred entities.)

N. MacCorquodale and P. E. Meehl, 'Hypothetical constructs and intervening variables', *Psychological Review*, 1948, reprinted in H. Feigl and M. Brodbeck (above). (Discussed in succeeding volumes of *Psychological Review*).

J. O. Urmson, *Philosophical Analysis*, Oxford UP, 1956, pp. 27–41. (Traces how strong sense incomplete symbols grew out of weak sense ones.)

J. Wisdom, 'Logical constructions', *Mind*, 1931–3. (Series of articles forming locus classicus for strong sense logical constructions. Cf. esp. 1931, pp. 188–95.)

Logical fictions. See LOGICAL CONSTRUCTIONS.

Logical geography. See SPACE.

Logically proper names. See MEANING, DESCRIPTIONS.

Logical subject. See MEANING.

Logicism. See MATHEMATICS.

Logics (many-valued). See TRUTH-VALUE.

Logistic. See LOGIC.

Logos. The Greek concept has two basic and interconnected strands: (i) the result of speaking, i.e. speech, discourse, theory (as against practice), sentence, story. (ii) The result of picking out or counting, i.e. account, formula, rationale, definition, proportion, reason (both as 'a reason' and as 'the power of reason'). For examples in English of how the two strands tend to merge cf. 'recount', 'all told'.

W. K. C. Guthrie, *A History of Greek Philosophy*, vol. 1, Cambridge UP, 1967, pp. 419ff.

Lottery paradox. In a fair lottery with 100 tickets the chance that any given ticket will lose is 99 per cent. It therefore seems reason-

Lottery paradox

able, for any given ticket, to believe, or *accept* as a basis for action, the statement, 'This ticket will lose'. Yet the conjunction of such statements for all the tickets must be false, since some ticket will win, so we can hardly accept the conjunction. We seem to have to accept each statement separately, but not the conjunction of them. The paradox raises difficulties especially for the notion of the *acceptance* of inductive conclusions (cf. CONFIRMATION).

H. E. Kyburg, *Probability and Inductive Logic*, Macmillan, 1970, pp. 176–7, 179.

M

Mach, Ernest W. J. W. 1838–1916. Born in Moravia, he worked mainly in Prague and Vienna; in 1901 he became a member of the Austrian house of peers. He contributed significantly to physics as well as to philosophy of science, and his name is applied to various phenomena connected with shock waves. In philosophy of science Mach developed a form of POSITIVISM. *Die Mechanik in ihrer Entwicklung historisch-kritisch dargestellt* (*The Science of Mechanics*), 1883. *Beiträge zur Analyse der Empfindungen*, 1886 (5th edn enlarged as *Die Analyse der Empfindungen und das Verhältnis des Physischen zum Psychischen*, 1906). *Populärwissenschaftliche Vorlesungen* (*Popular Scientific Lectures*), 1894 (or 1896). *Erkenntnis und Irrtum: Skizzen zur Psychologie der Forschung* (*Knowledge and Error: Sketches on the Psychology of Enquiry*), 1905.

Mach's Principle. The principle that a body's inertial mass depends on the mass of every other body in the universe. This can be used to defend a relational view of SPACE because the 'fixed' stars, which form the main repository of mass in the universe, provide a frame for deciding when a body is rotating without appealing, as Newton did, to absolute space. Variants of the principle exist, and it is not explicit in Mach himself. One question is whether the stars cause the inertial mass to be what it is, or whether they merely provide a frame of reference (so that the dependence is merely metrical rather than causal).

J. Bradley, *Mach's Philosophy of Science*, Athlone, 1971, chapter 6.

McTaggart, John McT. E.

McTaggart, John McT. E. 1866–1925. Cambridge metaphysician, born in London, who developed an idealist (and atheistic) system centring on the notions of substance and the part/whole relation (and also involving human reincarnation). He denied the reality of many things, such as material objects and space, but is now best known for his argument against the reality of time (see SPACE). *The Nature of Existence*, 1921 (vol. 1), 1927 (vol. 2).

C. D. Broad, *An Examination of McTaggart's Philosophy*, Cambridge UP, 1933 (vol. 1), 1938 (vol. 2). (Standard commentary.)

Magnitudes (extensive and intensive). A magnitude is extensive if (a) things can be ordered in accordance with it, and (b) there are units of it such that, for any number *n*, things with *n* such units can be constructed out of *n* things with one unit each. A magnitude is intensive if only the ordering is possible. Roughly, *M* is an intensive magnitude if 'more *M* than' makes sense but 'twice as *M* as' does not. It is extensive if both makes sense. *Long* is clearly extensive, and *beautiful* presumably intensive, but examples are often hard to classify.

H. L. Bergson, *Time and Free Will*, Allen and Unwin, 1910 (French original, 1889), chapter 1. (Criticizes notion of intensive magnitudes.)

B. Ellis, *Basic Concepts of Measurement*, Cambridge UP, 1966. (More extended and technical than smart. See p. 85.)

J. J. C. Smart, 'Measurement', *Australasian Journal of Philosophy*, 1959. (Measurement in general. Confines 'magnitude' to extensive magnitudes.)

Major premise, term. See SYLLOGISM.

Malebranche, Nicholas. 1638–1715. Born in Paris, he became a member of the religious society called the Oratoire de France. Starting largely under the influence of DESCARTES he elaborated a system which is now known chiefly for his OCCASIONALISM and his doctrine that we 'see all things in God', i.e. that the objects of almost all our knowledge are ideas, which exist independently of us and in God; we know external objects only as represented by ideas. Malebranche also wrote on science and morality. *De la Recherche de la vérité*, 1674–5. *Traité de la nature et de la grace*, 1680. *Traité de morale*, 1684. *Entretiens sur la métaphysique et sur la religion*, 1688.

Manifold. A variegated complex of elements considered as it is before being organized. For Kant especially, the sensory manifold is the as yet unstructured variety of material presented to the senses, which the mind then organizes through concepts, so that perception results.

Many-sorted logic. A logical system is *many-sorted* if different groups of individual VARIABLES in it are restricted to ranging over different kinds of things. Where all the individual variables have the same range the system is *one-sorted*.

Marcel, Gabriel. 1889–1973. French philosopher and dramatist born in Paris. He is usually classed as an EXISTENTIALIST, though of a theistic kind as opposed to SARTRE, HEIDEGGER or JASPERS (he joined the Catholic church in 1929), but the aptness of this classification has been disputed. *Journal métaphysique*, 1927. *Être et avoir*, 1935. *Présence et immortalité*, 1959. (These three volumes form a philosophical diary.) *The Philosophy of Existence*, 1949 (republished as Philosophy of Existentialism, 1961; translated essays). *The Mystery of Being (Le Mystère de l'être)*, 2 vols, 1950–1.

Maritain, Jacques. 1882–1973. French Catholic philosopher born in Paris, who worked mainly there and in North America. After being influenced by BERGSON in his youth he became interested in Thomism (see AQUINAS), developing a system which specially emphasized different kinds of knowledge (scientific, metaphysical, mystical). He also wrote on metaphysics, ethics, political philosophy and aesthetics. *Art et scholastique*, 1920. *Distinguer pour unir, ou les degrés du savoir*, 1932 (on the types of knowledge). *Humanisme intégral (True Humanism)*, 1936.

Marx, Karl H. 1818–83. Born in Trier, Germany, he worked in various cities of north-west Europe, and eventually in London. He was primarily a sociologist and economist, but his views have had considerable philosophical influence. He started from HEGEL's dialectic and, in collaboration with Engels, founded the doctrine of *dialectical* MATERIALISM, and developed a system of economic determinism which was supposed to govern human activities in every sphere. *Ökonomisch-philosophische Manuskripte aus dem Jahre 1844. Die deutsche Ideologie*, written 1845–6 (with Engels). *Misère de la philosophie (The Poverty of Philosophy*, 1847 (criticism of P.-J. Proudhon (1809–65)). *Manifest der kommunistischen Partei*, 1848 (with Engels). *Grundrisse der Kritik der politischen Ökonomie*, written 1857–8. *Zur Kritik der politischen Ökonomie*, 1859. *Das Kapital*, 3 vols, 1867, 1885, 1893 (this follows on from the two works last mentioned, and is itself followed by a historical fourth volume called *Theorien über den Mehrwert (Theories of Surplus Value)*, written 1862–3).

Mass noun

Mass noun. See COUNT.

Materialism. Usually the view that everything, or everything in a certain sphere, is made of matter: only matter exists, and mind, spirit, etc. are either illusory (*eliminative materialism*) or (a commoner view) can be somehow reduced to matter (*reductive materialism*). A non-reductive and non-eliminative materialism may also be based on SUPERVENIENCE. The IDENTITY THEORY OF MIND is often called simply materialism, and along with 'physicalism' the term may apply to any theory saying that the mental is nothing over and above the physical. (Materialists may or may not also deny the independent reality of abstract things like universals.) In another sense, uncommon as a sense of the word in philosophy, materialism says mind, etc. are real enough but causally dependent on matter: a weak version would say that if there had been no matter there would be no mind; a stronger version would add that if matter were destroyed mind would vanish too. Also uncommon in philosophy is 'materialist' in the sense of 'emphasizing material values (food and drink, etc.)'. *Dialetical materialism*, however, which applies Hegel's DIALECTICAL process to a material rather than spiritual reality, does emphasize material values in that it makes economic considerations both the cause and the proper end of human, and especially social, action. See also REDUCTIONISM.

D. M. Armstrong, *A Materialist Theory of Mind*, Routledge, 1968, revised 1993. (Cf. also his *Universals and Scientific Realism*, Cambridge UP, 1978, rejecting substantial universals but also extreme nominalism).

T. Horgan, 'From supervenience to superdupervenience', *Mind*, 1993. (See esp. §7 for kinds of materialism, with many references.)

A. Quinton, *The Nature of Things*, RKP, 1973. (Materialist standpoint.)

H. Robinson (ed.), *Objections to Physicalism*, Clarendon, 1993. (Specially written essays. See editor's 'Introduction', pp. 1–3, for uses of 'materialism' and 'physicalism'.)

D.-H. Ruben, *Marxism and Materialism: A Study in Marxist Theory of Knowledge*, Harvester, 1977, revised 1979. (Tries to mediate between Marxist and Anglo-Saxon philosophy. See Introduction for senses of 'materialism'.) See also bibliography to IDENTITY THEORY OF MIND.

Material mode. See FORMAL MODE.

Mathematics (philosophy of). The study of concepts and systems

Mathematics (philosophy of)

appearing in mathematics, of the nature of mathematical knowledge, and of the justification of mathematical statements.

The basic objects of mathematics are NUMBERS, of which there are various kinds (cardinal, ordinal, natural, real, etc.; see Russell). Whether numbers are real entities, and how we decide this, are questions shared with metaphysics (cf. BEING). *Platonists*, or *realists*, think that numbers are ABSTRACT entities in the sense of being outside space and time, and that mathematical truths, including those about infinite numbers, exist independently of our researches. *Constructivists* emphasize the dependence of mathematics on the activity of mathematicians (see INTUITIONISM, FINITISM). Numbers have been defined in terms of CLASSES or sets which are themselves studied by *set theory* (cf. CALCULUS). In fact the definition of 'equinumerous class' helped G. Cantor (1845–1918) to elaborate the study of infinite numbers. One class is equinumerous ('equivalent' and 'equipollent' are other terms used here) to another if for each member of one there can be found exactly one corresponding member of the other. These definitions enable the calculus of classes, and set theory, to be used to axiomatize mathematics (cf. AXIOM SYSTEM, LOGIC). One difficulty about classes stems from RUSSELL'S PARADOX. *Logicists*, however (notably Frege and Russell), who claim to reduce mathematics entirely to logic, have used classes for this purpose. They claim that mathematical objects can be defined in logical terms, via classes, and also that mathematical proofs can be reduced to logical proofs. But there are difficulties in proving the existence of classes in general from axioms which can be reasonably regarded as purely logical.

Geometry was originally regarded as fundamentally different from arithmetic, and as dealing with space. Kant's views on space provoked questions about how different geometries relate to each other and to real SPACE. Arithmetic suggests the question how different algebras relate to each other and to the world (cf. AXIOM SYSTEM). These questions are connected with the questions whether our knowledge of mathematical concepts and propositions is empirical as, in particular, J. S. Mill thought, or A PRIORI. Modern developments on all these questions have tended to unite arithmetic and geometry.

Other questions include: what is truth in mathematics, and how is it related to provability? Is every mathematical truth provable (cf. GÖDEL'S THEOREMS), and can we know mathematical truths by direct insight as well as by proof?

*S. F. Barker, *Philosophy of Mathematics*, Prentice-Hall, 1964. (Elementary.)

P. Benacerraf and H. Putnam (eds), *Philosophy of Mathematics*,

Meaning

Blackwell, 1964. (Important collection of readings, of varying difficulty.)

*G. Frege, *Foundations of Arithmetic*, Blackwell, 1884, trans. by J. L. Austin, 1950. (Fairly elementary discussion of numbers, etc. from Platonist and logicist viewpoint by a pioneer of modern logic. Includes more technical appendix on Russell's paradox.)

L. Goddard, ' "True" and "provable" ', *Mind*, 1958. (Cf. discussions in *Mind*, 1960, 1962.)

S. Körner, *Philosophy of Mathematics*, Hutchinson, 1960. (Rather more advanced.)

I. Lakatos, *Proofs and Refutations*, Cambridge UP, 1976, original version 1963–4. (Elaborate discussion, in dialogue form with historical notes, of genesis of some problems about proof.)

H. Lehman [see bibliography to A PRIORI.]

B. Russell, *Introduction to Mathematical Philosophy*, Allen and Unwin, 1919. (General.)

G. Ryle, C. Lewy, K. R. Popper, 'Why are the calculuses of logic and arithmetic applicable to reality?', *Proceedings of the Aristotelian Society*, supplementary vol., 1946.

*H. Wang, 'Process and existence in mathematics', in Y. Bar-Hillel, *et al.* (eds), *Essays on the Foundations of Mathematics*, Magnes Press, Hebrew University, Jerusalem, 1962. (Brings out some of the issues in mainly simple language.)

Meaning. Problems about meaning can be put into two main and interrelated groups: What is meaning, in the sense in which words and sentences have meaning? What different kinds of meaning are there, and how are they related to various other notions?

Discussions of what meanings are have mainly concerned words and sentences, which differ from each other: We *construct* sentences, and can understand ones we have not seen before. Sentences have meaning because of the words in them, while words only have meaning because they are fitted to play a role in sentences. Different words may have meaning in different ways, but whether all words have meaning is disputed. Do proper names (see below)? Does 'to' in 'I want to go'?

During the earlier part of the twentieth century notions like naming, referring to, or standing for have dominated such discussions. *Naming (denotative, referential) theories* of meaning say that a word's meaning is what it names or stands for, or else its relation to that. Cf. the slogan *unum nomen unum nominatum*: 'For every name there is exactly one thing named'. Proper names are taken as the primary case. Hence the nickname *'Fido'-Fido theory*. The word 'Fido' has as its meaning the dog Fido which it names. On this theory a general word like 'dog' could stand for the UNIVERSAL, doghood (Russell), or the class of dogs, or different dogs on different occasions (also Russell). 'Red' could stand for the colour red, 'runs' and 'running' for the action of running, even perhaps 'if' for the notion of doubt or conditionality.

Ideational theories make words stand for ideas or thoughts etc. (Aristotle, Locke). They provide a single kind of thing (ideas) for very different kinds of words to stand for, though usually without explaining the notion of *standing for*.

All these are *relational* or *correspondence theories*. They say that a word's meaning is or involves a thing (physical, mental or abstract) to which it is related. Largely through the influence of Wittgenstein they have been much attacked, though they have also experienced a certain revival recently.

This attack on relational theories implied that meanings are not 'things', and led to the slogan 'Don't ask for the meaning, ask for the use'. *Use theories* explain meaning in terms of use. They provoke questions about whether the connexion between meaning and use is the same for words and for sentences, whether meaning is as wide a notion as use (see below on speech acts), and whether what matters most is actual use or rules for use. This last distinction is one version of that between *de facto* and *de jure theories*. De facto theories explain meaning in terms of what happens or is the case, e.g. how people actually do use words. De jure theories explain it in terms of norms, rules, conventions, standards, or in general what ought to be the case, e.g. they might claim that 'I didn't do nothing' cannot properly mean 'I didn't do anything', despite Cockney usage.

Causal or *stimulus/response theories* explain the meaning of a word or sentence in terms of its effect on the hearer or the cause of the speaker's uttering it. They are examples of de facto theories, stemming from BEHAVIOURISM, and they claim the advantages of a scientific approach. They become naming theories too, if they say that the object named is the meaning while the object's effects are what make it the meaning. A causal theory of names and 'natural kind words' (like 'lion' 'water') has recently been advanced by S. Kripke and H. Putnam, in opposition to *description theories* like Russell's (see below). The same authors have advanced a causal theory of REFERENCE, whereby what if anything one refers to is partly determined by the things to which one stands in certain causal relations.

A theory of sentence-meaning also stimulated by science is the *verification theory*, whereby a sentence's meaning is the method of verifying it; cf. logical POSITIVISM for this, and for the operationalist theory of word meaning. *Picture theories* are analogues for sentences of naming theories for words and like naming theories they are correspondence theories. They are especially associated with

Meaning

LOGICAL ATOMISM, and with the correspondence theory of TRUTH. On picture theories sentences, whether true or false, have meaning because they picture possibilities; true sentences picture those possibilities which are facts. But can picture theories cater for the *stating* involved in stating facts?

A common modern theory says that to give the meaning of a standard indicative sentence is to give its TRUTH CONDITIONS. These, however, are not given for sentences individually but holistically, by constructing a 'theory of truth' for a whole language. This starts with axioms saying what the words mean and rules for combining them into sentences, in such a way that theorems can be derived, each of which says of some sentence that it is true if and only if so-and-so is the case, where 'so-and-so' represents what, intuitively, the sentence means. Such a theorem is called a *T-sentence*. An example would be, ' "Snow is white" is true if and only if snow is white'. When, as here, what follows 'if and only if' is the same, without the inverted commas, as what precedes it, the T-sentence is called *homophonic* (literally, 'same-sounding'). A theory of truth whose axioms yield the intuitively right T-sentences is said to satisfy *Convention* (or *Criterion*) *T*. See also TRANSLATION (for 'radical interpretation'). Discussion of all this has largely concerned whether truth conditions alone can provide adequate resources for a proper theory of meaning. See REALISM. In a more limited sphere a truth conditions account of meaning has been offered as a way of avoiding positing the existence of certain properties, such as that of being present: '1994 is present' will get its meaning by being true if and only if uttered during 1994, so that no property of 'presentness' is needed.

With the general question of what meaning is belongs also the question of *synonymy*, i.e. when words or sentences have the same meaning.

Turning to the second of the original questions, about kinds of meaning, and related notions, we can for suitable words distinguish between *intension* and *extension* (cf. INTENSIONALITY AND INTENTIONALITY), and between various allied notions. Thus Mill distinguishes *connotation* from *denotation*. A word denotes the things it applies to, and connotes the attributes it implies that those things have. 'Man' connotes, perhaps, the attribute *being a rational animal*, and denotes all men. 'Connotation' can refer to the relation or to what is connoted, and 'denotation' similarly. The comprehension of 'man' is the whole set of properties shared by all men, or else the set which (logically) must be shared by them.

Frege distinguishes *Sinn* and *Bedeutung*, standardly translated *sense* and *reference* respectively, though other translations exist, and 'meaning' has been used for each of them at different times. The phrases 'the evening star' and 'the morning star' have the same reference, Venus, but different senses. Frege uses this to explain why 'The evening star is the morning star' is not trivial, like 'Venus is Venus'.

The relations between these terms are complex. Roughly, a term denotes, independently of occasion, all those things we can refer to on a given occasion by using certain phrases containing the term. 'Cats' denotes cats in general, and we can use a phrase like 'that cat' to refer to, say, Tiddles on some occasion. Strictly it is we who refer to Tiddles by saying 'that cat', but the phrase 'that cat' can itself be said to refer to Tiddles on this occasion. ('Denote', especially, is often used loosely.)

A term has *divided reference* (Quine) if, like 'shoe' but unlike 'water' or 'red', it can be used, without additions like 'piece of', to refer to different objects.

The connotation/sense distinction is difficult, and controversial, but an example may illustrate one way of making the distinction. Is it contradictory to say, 'The queen of England is not queen at all but illegitimate'? Yes, if 'the queen of England' is interpreted as having connotation, since the statement then implies that the person referred to by the phrase has the property of reigning. But the sense of the phrase can be used to pick out the person, without committing the speaker to the truth of this implication, for a hearer, for example, who believes that Elizabeth II is legitimate. If the phrase is thus interpreted as still having sense, but not connotation, the statement is not contradictory. If Elizabeth II were not legitimate, the sentence could be used to say so without contradiction, and might be useful for ensuring that the supposed hearer knew who was being talked about. Sense and reference apply to subject expressions and sometimes to predicates and to sentences (Frege thought the reference of a predicate was a concept, and of a sentence was its TRUTH-VALUE). Connotation and denotation can apply to subject expressions and predicate expressions, but not to sentences. Sense is close to the non-technical notion of sense.

Proper names, which provide the model of meaning for naming theories, raise problems about whether they have connotation or sense or both. 'That man there' picks someone out as being a man and being in a certain place, but 'John' makes no obvious reference to any of its bearer's properties. In what sense are proper names words? Do they form part of a language? They are hardly meaningless, but they do not usually appear in dictionaries. Russell followed Mill in thinking they lack connotation. However, he thought this only of *logically proper names*, i.e. those names which were not abbreviated descriptions, as he thought ordinary proper names in fact were. He thought 'Socrates' was not really a name at all,

Meaning

but an abbreviation for, for example, 'the philosopher who drank hemlock'. (Cf. DESCRIPTIONS.) This is the view criticized by Kripke and Putnam (above). A *logical subject* is either the subject of a sentence in a logically ideal language, i.e. a language where a sentence's real and apparent subjects coincide, or it is what such a subject refers to.

Under the influence of logical positivism, cognitive, descriptive or factual meaning has been distinguished from other kinds, notably emotive, evaluative, and prescriptive: see NATURALISM. Arising out of these distinctions and generalizing from them is Austin's theory of SPEECH ACTS, which distinguishes between the meaning of what is said and what he calls the 'illocutionary force' of saying it. Attempts have been made to analyse the meanings of some words, including 'good', 'true', 'probable', in terms of speech acts they are used in making, and to ground meaning itself in illocutionary force (a kind of use theory). It is here that the different kinds of IMPLICATION (presupposition, implicature, etc.) and their roles become relevant.

It is also important to distinguish, especially concerning TOKEN-REFLEXIVES, between what meaning words and sentences have in general and what they mean, or what the speaker means by them, on a given occasion. This raises the question how meaning is related to intention, for people can 'mean something' both in the sense of referring to something ('I mean you') and as intending to do something ('I meant to come yesterday'). They may also 'mean' something in the sense of suggesting something beyond what they mean in the direct sense ('In saying "Time's getting on" he meant it was late, and he also meant it was time for you to go'. Cf. IMPLICATION again). An interesting question, discussed by Wittgenstein, concerns what it is to mean what one says.

In fact not only words, sentences, and people can be subjects of the verb 'mean' but also actions, works of art, and natural events, states and processes. 'Mean' can have natural objects or events as its subject when there are symptoms ('Those spots mean measles') or causes ('clouds mean rain') or things having value or importance ('That locket means a lot to me'). 'His life has no meaning' seems to come between this last sense and the sense of pattern, order, idea in which works of art have meaning. Actions have meaning either in these ways or in the way sentences have it. Grice distinguishes the various kinds of meaning into two main groups, *natural*, the group applying natural events etc., and *non-natural*, the group applying to people and symbols, words and sentences, etc.

A final question concerns meaninglessness; how many kinds of it are there, and how are they related to contradiction and falsity

Meaning

(cf. CATEGORIES)? See also REFERRING, AMBIGUOUS, DEFINITION, OPEN TEXTURE, REALISM, TRUTH CONDITIONS.

Aristotle, *De Interpretatione*, esp. chapters 1–4, trans. with commentary in J. L. Ackrill, *Aristotle's Categories and De Interpretatione*, Oxford UP, 1963. (Basis of Aristotle's theory of meaning, though only elementary.)

L. J. Cohen, *The Diversity of Meaning*, Methuen, 1962 (revised 1966). (Chapter 2 introduces de facto/de jure distinction.)

E. Daitz, 'The picture theory of meaning', *Mind*, 1953, reprinted in A. Flew (ed.), *Essays in Conceptual Analysis*, Macmillan, 1956.

D. Davidson, 'Truth and meaning', *Synthèse*, 1967, revised in 'Radical interpretation', *Dialectica*, 1973, both reprinted with other relevant material in his *Inquiries into Truth and Interpretation*, Clarendon, 1984. (Leading exponent of truth-conditions theory. See also for a contrasting view M. A. E. Dummett, 'What is a theory of meaning? II' in G. Evans and J. McDowell (eds), *Truth and Meaning*, Oxford UP, 1976, reprinted with other relevant material in his *The Seas of Language*, Clarendon 1993.)

G. Frege, 'Sinn und Bedeutung', 1892, trans. in P. Geach and M. Black, *Translations from the Philosophical Writings of Gottlob Frege*, Blackwell, 1952, and also in H. Feigl and W. Sellars (eds), *Readings in Philosophical Analysis*, Cornell UP, 1949.

N. Goodman, 'On likeness of meaning', *Analysis*, vol. 10, 1949, reprinted in M. Macdonald (ed.), *Philosophy and Analysis*, Blackwell, 1954. (Difficulties over synonymy.)

H. P. Grice, 'Meaning', *Philosophical Review*, 1957, reprinted in P. F. Strawson (ed.), *Philosophical Logic*, Oxford UP, 1967, and also, along with other relevant material, in Grice's *Studies in the Way of Words*, Harvard UP, 1989. (Criticizes causal theory and develops theory using intention (which might, however, itself be called a causal theory).)

J. N. Keynes, *Formal Logic*, 1884, 4th (revised) edn, 1906. (Full details of traditional terminology of intension and extension. For later terms cf. also R. Carnap, *Meaning and Necessity*, Chicago UP, 1947, chapter 3.)

S. Kripke, *Naming and Necessity*, 1980 Blackwell (original version, 1972). (Causal theory of names, natural kind words, and reference. Cf. also S. P. Schwartz (ed.), *Naming, Necessity and Natural Kinds*, Cornell UP, 1977, including *inter alia* articles by H. Putnam and G. Evans.)

J. Locke, *An Essay concerning Human Understanding*, 1689, book 3. (An intentional theory.)

J. S. Mill, *A System of Logic*, 1843, Longmans, Green, book 1,

Meaning postulates

chapter 2, esp. §5. (Connotation/denotation distinction. Classic discussion of names. Cf. final footnote on senses of 'connotation'.)

A. W. Moore (ed.), *Meaning and Reference*, Oxford UP, 1993. (Includes several classic items.)

Plato, *Cratylus*. (Earliest surviving connected discussion of meaning.)

W. V. O. Quine, *Word and Object*, Wiley, 1960, § 19. (Divided reference.)

B. Russell, *An Inquiry into Meaning and Truth*, Allen and Unwin, 1940, esp. chapters 1–7, 13–15. (Complex theory of meaning of words and significance (as he calls it) of sentences. Cf. his *My Philosophical Development*, Allen and Unwin, 1959, chapters 13, 14.)

J. R. Searle (see bibliography to GOOD.)

D. Wiggins, 'The sense and reference of predicates', *Philosophical Quarterly*, 1984, reprinted in C. Wright (eds), *Frege: Tradition and Influence*, Blackwell, 1984. (Relevant on sense and connotation, and on the interpretation (and correction) of Frege.)

L. Wittgenstein, *Philosophical Investigations*, Blackwell, 1953, esp. §§ 1–43. (Classic criticism of naming theories in favour of use theory.)

Meaning postulates. A device whereby implicitly ANALYTIC sentences, like 'Bachelors are male', are introduced into a formal language (one whose terms are rigorously defined) by postulates like 'Anything, if it is a bachelor, is (to count as) male'. More interestingly, 'Anything, if it is a raven, is (to count as) black' could be used as a meaning postulate to fix a sense of 'raven'. Anything we refuse to call black we will then refuse to call a raven.

R. Carnap, 'Meaning postulates', *Philosophical Studies*, 1952, reprinted in his *Meaning and Necessity*, 2nd edn, Chicago UP, 1956.

Meinong, Alexius. 1853–1920. Austrian, born in Lemberg (Lwow), he worked mainly in Graz. He developed BRENTANO's view by insisting on a distinction between the content and the object ('Gegenstand') of a thought, and his philosophy largely concerns the various kinds of such objects. These include chairs and tables, which exist, 'objectives' like the *being* of chairs, which are always positive or negative, higher-order objects like the *difference* between red and green, which merely subsist, dragons and the golden mountain and the round square, which neither exist nor subsist but still have 'Sosein' ('being so'). Objects which were not objectives he called 'Objekta'. He also supplemented Brentano's

Memory

distinction between ideas and judgments by introducing 'supposals' or 'assumptions' ('Annahmen'), and he elaborated a theory of value. 'Zur erkenntnistheoretischen Würdigung des Gedächtnisses', *Vierteljahrschrift für Wissenschaftliche Philosophie*, x, 1886. 'Über Bedeutung des Weber'schen Gesetzes', *Zeitschrift für Psychologie and Physiologie der Sinnesorgane*, xi, 1896. *Über Annahmen*, 1902 (importantly revised in 1910, and translated as *On Assumptions*, California UP, 1983). 'Über Gegenstandstheorie', in A. Meinong (ed.), *Untersuchungen zur Gegenstandstheorie und Psychologie*, 1904 (translated as 'On the theory of objects' in R. Chisholm (ed.), *Realism and the Background of Phenomenology*, Free Press, 1960). *Über Möglichkeit and Wahrscheinlichkeit*, 1915. *Über emotionale Präsentation*, 1917 (translated as *On Emotional Presentation*, Northwestern UP, 1972). *Zur Grundlegung der allgemeinen Werttheorie*, 1923. See also BEING, OBJECT, REFERRING.

Memory. In general a faculty of knowing, whose exercise can be called remembering, recollecting, recalling, being reminded, reminiscing; the relations between these form one of the problems involved, though 'remember' is the most general verb (it can also mean 'bear in mind'). 'Memory' can take the plural when it refers to experiences (or things experienced) which are remembered, or to rememberings of them.

We can remember people, places, objects, appearances, experiences, events, facts, as well as remembering to do things, how to do things, where to find things, etc. Memory involves some reference to the past, but what is remembered need not be the past; I can remember that five twelves are sixty, that tomorrow is Tuesday, as well as remembering to put the cat out. But I am not remembering something if the sole basis for what I am doing lies in the present. I can only *remember* to put the cat out if I have earlier had it in mind to put it out. Is remembering simply knowing because one has known? But there are difficulties with this (Martin and Deutscher, Munsat): not everything I know or knew (it is claimed) can be remembered; I can know, but can I remember, that if Hitler had won the war, British Jews would have perished? Perhaps only in the 'bear in mind' sense? Also if I tell someone a fact, forget it, and then learn it again from that person, I now know it only because I once knew it, but I am not remembering it; the causal theory of memory here faces an objection facing other causal theories too (e.g. of PERCEPTION), that of deviant causal chains: not just any old causal chain will do. It seems then that some 'trace' is needed, whether physical in the brain or mental, to be a causal link connecting my previous knowing with my present knowing. But the whole idea of 'traces' or causal theories of memory has been attacked on

Memory

the grounds that no coherent account can be given of what properties such a trace must have, or of how it could operate without a further trace to set it going, i.e. of how the brain could 'pick out' the right trace without a 'little man' ('*homunculus*') inside it to do so. Stimulus/response theories might seem to solve this 'picking out' problem, but how do the stimulus and response get associated, since there can be indefinitely many responses to any stimulus? (See BURSEN.)

Memory seems, at least in many cases, to give us knowledge of the past. Is this because we now have some mental item, e.g. an image, which represents the past (*representative theory*), or because we are now directly aware of the past, though distant in time, rather as we perceive things distant in space (*realist theory*)? Both theories raise problems. How can we know that such images do represent the past, and distinguish them from those which belong to imagination and don't? How could we be aware of a past no longer there to be known? How does this compare with seeing stars so distant they have already vanished? But must there anyway be some *object* we are aware of, be it past event or present image, any more than when we know a mathematical fact? Two further questions arise, a metaphysical one of whether the past must somehow be real if we are to know it or know about it, in whatever way, and an epistemological one: if, as the representative theory says, we are acquainted only with the present, how can we get a concept of pastness, and how can statements about the past have meaning if it is impossible in principle to verify them (cf. REALISM)? This leads on to the general question of scepticism about memory: how can we justify our reliance on memory, and how pervasive is that reliance? Can we know the world was not created five minutes ago with us and all our 'memories' ready made (Russell)?

Another question concerns how many different kinds of memory there are, and how they are related, for despite what was said above about memory not needing images and not always being of the past, sometimes we do suddenly remember something having a vivid image as we do so. How relevant is the image in these cases? Might we have a faculty similarly related to the future? How analogous are memory and precognition here? Do we discover facts about the past by inspecting the image, or must we, even in these cases, already know those facts in order to construct the image? What role is played by our intentions in constructing it? Is memory, even here, a source of knowledge, or only a kind of knowledge? It is these cases that make memory seem analogous to perception, and it is here that we talk of our 'memories' and say that we can only remember what we have witnessed: I remember *that* Caesar invaded Britain, but his doing so is not among my memories, and

Mereology

I cannot remember *it*. This suggests the question, in what sense can animals remember (see Munsat)? Also can we remember, or only seem to remember, what is false or did not happen?

Quasi-remembering, or *q-remembering*, is a notion developed recently in discussions of personal identity. A q-memory of an event must be preceded by an experience of that event, but that experience need not, as with ordinary memory, belong to the person doing the remembering. Ordinary memory, where the experience does belong to the rememberer, is then regarded as a special case of q-memory.

Finally how is remembering related to forgetting, and what is forgetting? Some help can be got for this and previous questions by studying the grammar of words like 'remember' and 'forget'. We can say 'He remembers (remembered) putting the cat out', but can we say 'He forgets (forgot) . . .', as opposed to 'He has forgotten (had forgotten, no longer remembers) . . .' or 'He forgot *that* he had put the cat out' (cf. Munsat)?

H. A. Bursen, *Dismantling the Memory Machine*, Reidel, 1978. (Attacks causal theories, especially 'trace' theories.)

R. F. Holland, 'The empiricist theory of memory', *Mind*, 1954, reprinted in S. Hampshire (ed.), *Philosophy of Mind*, Harper and Row, 1966. (Discusses *inter alia* relations between memory and imagination, and role of images.)

*D. Locke, *Memory*, Macmillan, 1971. S. Munsat, *The Concept of Memory*, Random House, 1966. (Two elementary introductions.)

C. B. Martin and M. Deutscher, 'Remembering', *Philosophical Review*, 1966. (Detailed discussion, advocating causal theory. Cf. also discussion in D. Owens, *Causes and Coincidences*, Cambridge UP, 1992, pp. 158–62.

D. Parfit, *Reasons and Persons*, Oxford UP, 1984. (See p. 220 for quasi-remembering, and cf. also S. Shoemaker, 'Persons and their pasts', *American Philosophical Quarterly*, 1970, reprinted in his *Identity, Cause, and Mind*, Cambridge UP, 1984, for that and related notions. For criticism of the notion of quasi-remembering see M. Schechtman, 'Personhood and personal identity, *Journal of Philosophy*, 1990, esp. § 3.)

B. Russell, *The Analysis of Mind*, Allen and Unwin, 1921. (See pp. 159–60 for world beginning five minutes ago.)

Mentalism. See PSYCHOLOGISM.

Mentioning. See REFERRING.

Mereology. Literally, 'theory of parts'. The relation between a whole

203

Merleau-Ponty, Maurice

and its parts, unlike that between a class and its members, is TRANSITIVE, and mereology names a theory of the Polish logician S. Lesniewski (1886–1939), which treated the structure of classes by using this transitive relation instead of the class-membership relation. He did this to avoid certain difficulties connected with the vicious circle principle and the theory of TYPES. (The term also has a technical use within the theory itself.)

Goodman also used the whole/part relation to deal with problems about stuffs, like water, or qualities, like red. He treated 'water' as a name for the whole quantity of water in the universe, so that the Pacific Ocean is a part of water. Similarly the colour red is treated as the totality of red things, a single large object split up over space.

Mereological essentialism is the theory that the parts of an object are essential to it, so that if any of its parts are lost or replaced it becomes a different object.

R. M. Chisholm, *Person and Object*, Allen and Unwin, 1976, Appendix B. (Mereological essentialism explained and defended.)

N. Goodman, *The Structure of Appearance*, Harvard UP, 1951 (3rd edn, Reidel, 1977).

C. Hughes, 'Is a thing just the sum of its parts?', *Proceedings of the Aristotelian Society*, 1985–6. (Defends mereological essentialism.)

P. Simons, *Parts*, Clarendon, 1987, chapter 1. (General treatment of the subject.)

Merleau-Ponty, Maurice. 1908–61. Born in Rochefort in France, he worked mainly in Lyon and Paris. He is best known for his work on the PHENOMENOLOGICAL description of the phenomena of consciousness, emphasizing particularly the role of the body. He disagrees in some respects with Husserl, and has affinities with existentialism. He also had ethical and political interests, and was a friend and associate of SARTRE, though differing in his attitude to Marxism. *La Structure du comportement*, 1942. *La Phénoménologie de la perception*, 1945. *Sens et nonsens* (*Sense and Nonsense*), 1948 (collected essays).

Meta-. See PHILOSOPHY, METAPHYSICS.

Metahistory. See HISTORY.

Metalanguage. A language rich enough for talking about some language (which may or may not be itself, or part of itself) is a *metalanguage* for the language talked about, which is an *object language* for it. 'Metalanguage' is thus a relative term, though a language rich enough for talking about a metalanguage for a given object language is sometimes called a metametalanguage relative to that object language; for example, a language L_2, could be a metalanguage for L_1 while being an object language for L_3, a situation likely to arise in systems where words like 'true' have 'typical' AMBIGUITY. 'Object language' means 'language which is the object of investigation'. A language lacking devices for talking about languages (i.e. lacking terms like 'word', 'true', 'say', or quotation marks) can only be an object language.

Metalogic. See LOGIC.

Metamathematics. Also called *proof theory*. Study of the concepts used in mathematics, especially of the properties of formal systems (see AXIOM). Often now confined to analyses springing from that of D. Hilbert (1862–1943), who insisted on FINITIST restrictions for metamathematics which he relaxed for mathematics itself. Cf. INTUITIONISM (for formalism).

D. Hilbert, 'On the infinite', in P. Benecerraf and H. Putman (eds), *Philosophy of Mathematics*, Blackwell, 1964.

Metaphysics. The original 'meta'-word, deriving from the title given to Aristotle's untitled treatise by his first-century BC editor Andronicus. It means that which comes after 'physics', the latter being the study of nature in general. Thus the questions of metaphysics arise out of, but go beyond, factual or scientific questions about the world.

A central part of metaphysics is *ontology*. This studies BEING, and in particular, nowadays, what there is, e.g. material objects, minds, PERSONS, UNIVERSALS, NUMBERS, FACTS, etc. There is the question of whether these all 'are' in the same sense and to the same degree, and how notions like BEING, existence, and subsistence are related together. One can also ask whether particular views on logic commit one to particular views on what exists (e.g. propositions, numbers). A particular theory about what exists, or a list of existents, can be called an ontology. Another question involving logic is whether or not existence is a predicate (or property). Ontology borders on philosophy of religion with questions like: Does anything exist necessarily (cf. ONTOLOGICAL and COSMOLOGICAL ARGUMENTS)? It is necessary that something, no matter what, should exist? Can any answer be given to the question, 'Why is there something rather than nothing?'? 'Ontology' is also a technical name for part of the system of S. Lesniewski (1886–1939).

Metaphysics is distinguished by its questions being general. As

Metaphysics

well as seeking an inventory of kinds of things that exist it asks what can be said about anything that exists, just in so far as it exists. Can we classify all that exists, or in some sense is, or has being, into different fundamental kinds, in one or more ways (see CATEGORIES)? Is there any hierarchy among kinds of things? Do some depend on others for their existence or being? These questions involve the relations between very general notions like thing, entity, OBJECT, INDIVIDUAL, UNIVERSAL, particular, SUBSTANCE, and also EVENT, process, state. Here three metaphysical outlooks, overlapping though not exhaustive, may be distinguished. One outlook (e.g. Plato, the rationalists), takes one or more substances as the basis of the universe. A second takes act and potency (e.g. Aquinas), and a third (PROCESS PHILOSOPHY) takes events and processes (e.g. Heraclitus, the Stoics, Hegel, Bergson, Whitehead). These outlooks, especially the first and third, are connected with attitudes towards change. Adherents of the first outlook have often held either that change is not fully real, or that the most basic things in the universe do not change except in secondary or unimportant ways. The third outlook puts change at the heart of things. It does not deny all unity and constancy, which would result in unintelligible chaos, but makes these depend essentially upon change.

The distinction of act from potency, or actuality from potentiality, derives from Aristotle, as does that of FORM from matter and 'privation' (i.e. the absence of form where it could be present). Both these distinctions, it is claimed, are needed when we examine the nature and kinds of change, and they lead us to examine matter itself and its relations to space and substance. SPACE AND TIME in fact provide a whole range of problems about their reality, nature, absoluteness and uniqueness. Change is also closely related to IDENTITY and CAUSATION, both of which also raise special problems in philosophy of mind, concerning personal IDENTITY and FREEWILL.

These notions of change, identity and causation lead to further questions about the general pattern of change in the universe. Is it, in the long run, random or does it lead in a certain direction? Or is it cyclic or repetitive, a view commoner among the Greeks than today though revived on some views in modern cosmology? Is there even, as was believed by some Pythagoreans and Stoics, followed by Nietzsche, an *eternal recurrence* of the same cycle, an endless repetition of exactly the same world-history? Here we must distinguish between repetitions of the same participants, including ourselves, and repetitions of the same pattern with different participants, our 'doubles'. The same problems arise over 'mirror universes' (cf. SPACE, LEIBNIZ'S LAW, SUFFICIENT REASON).

Questions about space and time suggest further questions about infinity. Is the universe finite or infinite? Here, as in the last paragraph, philosophy and science may overlap. And which is 'higher' or more real, the finite or the infinite? There is a distinction here between Christianity, emphasizing the limitations of finite things, and the Greeks, especially the Pythagoreans and Aristotle, who regarded the infinite as essentially incomplete; Aristotle believed that there could not be an actual infinite, and that the infinite is only potential, so that to say that (e.g.) numbers are infinite may be to say merely that you can can always take further numbers beyond those taken already.

All these enquiries about the overall nature of the universe lead to the question whether a necessary being, or God, must be postulated to explain the universe. What sort of EXPLANATIONS can be given? In particular, are teleological EXPLANATIONS needed or possible?

A further general question about the universe is whether in some relevant sense we should regard it as one (MONISM) or many (pluralism). Since monists must presumably admit that plurality is at least apparent, the real/apparent distinction becomes relevant, and with it questions about how far SCEPTICISM with regard to the reality of things can be consistently taken: How different can the world be from what it seems, and how far can we know things as they are? (Cf. EPISTEMOLOGY.) Another view which relies heavily on the real/apparent contrast, because it differs widely from common sense, is IDEALISM, which regards reality as basically mental or dependent on the mind. But idealism need not be sceptical.

An influential source of scepticism earlier in the twentieth century, however, has been interest in the influence of language. Some have thought, especially logical POSITIVISTS like Carnap, that the distinction between substance and attribute is simply a reflexion of the grammatical distinction between noun and adjective (without asking how that itself arose), so that instead of talking of things and qualities we should talk of *thing-words* and *quality-words*. We will then see, it is claimed, that we need not regard (say) beauty as a metaphysical entity merely because we have the thing-word 'beauty' (cf. FORMAL MODE). How far does 'ontology recapitulate philology'? Philosophers like the logical positivists, who emphasized language, often reacted against *speculative metaphysics* (the construction of all-embracing systems that cannot be tested by observation). Many empiricists, notably Hume, do so too, though the mantle of empiricism has at least partly fallen on antirealism (see REALISM). *Descriptive metaphysics* claims to avoid the vices of speculative metaphysics, without abandoning metaphysics altogether. It confines itself to analysing various concepts, like SUBSTANCE, which it claims to show are basic and unavoidable.

Metaphysics also borders on ethics and aesthetics. It asks whether

Metaphysics

values are grounded in the nature of things, or contribute to the cosmic process, and what kind of reality is possessed by works of art and the things that make them up (e.g. the figures in a painting).

Taken as the name of a subject 'metaphysics' is no longer a 'bad word', but the current mood, though far less restrictive than logical positivism, or linguistic philosophy, remains predominantly hostile to anti-common-sense speculations, including idealist or sceptical systems (though idealism has some following in the UK). At the same time it regards most forms of DUALISM as over-simplifying at best. The return of metaphysics is marked by a greater tolerance of large-scale systems, and also of such things as essentialism and substantive (not merely logical) necessity (see ESSENCE, MODALITIES). See also PROCESS PHILOSOPHY.

Aristotle, *Metaphysics*. (See esp. books 4 (or Γ) and 6 (or E), trans. with notes by C. Kirwan in Clarendon Aristotle series, 1971, 2nd edn, 1993, for Aristotle's conception of metaphysics. His *Physics* also contains much now regarded as metaphysics, including discussion of infinity in book 3.)

R. Carnap, *Meaning and Necessity*, 2nd edn, Chicago UP, 1956, supplement A, reprinted in C. Landesman (ed.), *The Problem of Universals*, Basic Books, 1971. (Holds that much metaphysics depends on language. See flyleaf to W. V. Quine, *Word and Object*, Wiley, 1960, for 'ontology recapitulates philology', attributed to J. G. Miller; cf. the biological slogan 'ontogeny recapitulates phylogeny'.)

*D. W. Hamlyn, *Metaphysics*, Cambridge UP, 1984. (General introduction from modern viewpoint, developing the speculative/descriptive contrast.)

S. Kripke, *Naming and Necessity*, Blackwell, 1980 (original version, 1972). (Influential in revival of essentialism. For an early example of this see also C. Kirwan, 'How strong are the objections to essence?', *Proceedings of the Aristotelian Society*, 1970–1.)

D. H. Mellor, *Matters of Metaphysics*, Cambridge UP, 1991. (Essays on various topics, amounting to a metaphysical position.)

Midwest Studies in Philosophy, vol. 4, 1979. (Single-topic journal issue entitled *Studies in Metaphysics*.)

W. V. O. Quine, *Word and Object*, Wiley, 1960, for 'ontology recapitulates philology', attributed to J. G. Miller; cf. the biological slogan 'ontogeny recapitulates phylogeny'.)

A. Quinton, *The Nature of Things*, RKP, 1973 (Discussions both of and in metaphysics.)

P. F. Strawson, *Individuals*, Methuen, 1959. (Defends descriptive metaphysics. Fairly difficult.)

P. van Inwagen, *Metaphysics*, Oxford UP, 1993. (Introduction by in-depth treatment of certain problems, though avowedly limited in scope.)

*W. H. Walsh, *Metaphysics*, Hutchinson, 1963. (General introduction from fairly traditional viewpoint.)

G. J. Warnock, 'Metaphysics in logic', in A. Flew (ed.), *Essays in Conceptual Analysis*, Macmillan, 1956. (Does logic commit one to metaphysical views?)

Methodological solipsism. In general, the view that one should adopt solipsism (see SCEPTICISM) as a device to help one investigate some sphere, without necessarily believing it. Usually, however, it appears as a term introduced into philosophy of mind by Putnam for 'the assumption that no psychological state, properly so called, presupposes the existence of any individual other than the subject to whom that state is ascribed', and used by Fodor as a consequence of his view that 'we should take it to be a condition upon specifications of mental operations that they apply to mental representations in virtue of their form'. Methodological, solipsism holds that a belief, say, is what it is independently of whether it is true, or succeeds in referring to anything. The view is thus an INTERNALIST one, but does not imply that one should ignore 'the relations between an organism's behaviour and the effects of its behaviour in the course of developing theories of the organism's mental states'. One point critics have made is that methodological solipsism seems to allow varying degrees, according to just how much the specification of the mental state is supposed to be independent of. See also INDIVIDUALISM.

J. A. Fodor, 'Methodological solipsism considered as a research strategy in cognitive psychology', *The Behavioral and Brain Sciences*, vol. 3, 1980, pp. 63–109. (Includes discussions and Fodor's reply. For quotations see p. 103 and for critical point see p. 98. The article, without the discussions, also appears in Fodor's *Representations*, Harvester Press, 1981.)

H. Putnam, *Mind, Language and Reality* (vol. 2 of his *Philosophical Papers*), Cambridge UP, 1975. (See p. 220 for quotation.)

Methodology. See SCIENCE.

Metric. A set of rules, with suitable units, for measuring extensive MAGNITUDES. As an adjective 'metric' or 'metrical' means 'measurable' ('metric SPACE') or 'involving measurement' ('metric geometry').

Middle term. See SYLLOGISM.

Mill, John Stuart

Mill, John Stuart. 1806–73. The son of James Mill (1773–1836), who was a philosopher of somewhat similar tendencies, Mill was born in London where he worked in the India office. He is noted as an EMPIRICIST and early PHENOMENALIST, and in ethics as a (somewhat wayward) UTILITARIAN and defender of liberty. He also wrote on political philosophy. His logic is largely remembered for his distinction between connotation and denotation (see MEANING), his criticism of the SYLLOGISM, his elaboration of a philosophy of science along the lines of Bacon's and his empiricist treatment of basic MATHEMATICAL propositions. His approach was of the general type now called extensionalist. *A System of Logic, Ratiocinative and Inductive*, 1843. *On Liberty*, 1859. *On Representative Government*, 1861. *Utilitarianism*, 1863. *An Examination of Sir William Hamilton's Philosophy*, 1865 (contains his phenomenalist views). See also BRADLEY, DEFINITION, INDUCTION, INFERENCE, MEANING, PLEASURE, RUSSELL, SELF-REGARDING, WHEWELL.

Millet paradox. See ZENO'S PARADOXES.

Mind (philosophy of). Sometimes called *philosophical psychology*. Psychology deals with questions that can be settled by observation, experiment and measurement, while philosophy of mind settles its different questions by reflection. Before the twentieth century the subjects were hardly distinguished, and the sharp divisions that have prevailed through much of that century are now becoming blurred again as philosophy of mind becomes ever more reliant on the findings of subjects like cognitive science (see COGNITIVE PSYCHOLOGY, CONNECTIONISM). The *philosophy of psychology* is a rather narrower subject concentrating on philosophical problems that arise from studying the nature of psychology as a science, such as the problem of the scientific status of Freudianism.

Recent philosophy of mind has been perhaps primarily, though far from exclusively, concerned with two main problems: first that of what mind is and how it relates to body, known as the *mind–body* or *body–mind problem*; this is a very ancient problem with soul or spirit, especially in older literature, sometimes replacing and sometimes being added to mind. The second main problem is that of how the mind relates to the external world in its dealings with that world in terms of thought, belief, perception, etc. (see INTENSIONALITY AND INTENTIONALITY). This too is a problem with ancient roots but owes its modern revival partly to the influence of BRENTANO and others, and partly to the developments of cognitive science mentioned above.

For the second problem see, as well as INTENSIONALITY, INTERNALISM AND EXTERNALISM, INDIVIDUALISM, CONTENT. Answers

Mind (philosophy of)

to the first problem range between idealist views that only the mind is real and materialist views that either the body alone is real (cf. BEHAVIOURISM) or mental phenomena are identical with certain physical ones (IDENTITY THEORY OF MIND). These views, along with the DOUBLE ASPECT THEORY, neutral MONISM, Strawson's view distinguishing bodies from PERSONS, and Aristotle's view that mind is to body as FORM to matter, are all MONIST views, in that they deny that mind or mental phenomena and body or bodily phenomena are distinct things. DUALIST views assert this distinctness and include interactionism, EPIPHENOMENALISM, PSYCHO-PHYSICAL PARALLELISM and OCCASIONALISM. A weaker dualism, however, applies to properties rather than substances (and would include, e.g., Strawson's view). FUNCTIONALISM is compatible with both monism and dualism.

Idealist and most dualist views are currently in a minority, though not unrepresented, while the identity theory is still being vigorously discussed. The related topic of personal IDENTITY is important for questions like: Can a mind animate several bodies, successively, as in reincarnation, or at once? Can several minds animate the same body (one view of 'multiple personality' cases), or one mind many bodies ('corporate personalities')? Can a mind exist without a body at all, whether or not originally joined to one? Clearly much depends on what counts as a mind. This is one of the few areas where philosophy may affect our predictions of the future. Discussion has been stimulated by the logical possibility of brain transplants. Early work in psychical research has been relevant here and in connexion with extrasensory perception, precognition, telepathy, etc. The question whether causal relations can link mental phenomena with each other and with physical phenomena, and if so, how, arises here.

A topic linking philosophy of mind closely to ethics is *philosophy of action*. The FREEWILL question again makes us ask whether actions can be caused, e.g. by reasons or intentions, and calls for a general analysis of concepts like motive, intention, volition, wanting, trying. Are they the sort of things that could be causes? Are they mental states? Can they be identified or described independently of actions? Are there limitations on our irrationality (cf. INCONTINENCE)? Ethics as well as philosophy of mind can ask whether there are logical limits to what we can approve of or feel obliged to do. Are there things such that nothing would *count* as our approving of them?

CONSCIOUSNESS is a topic which has seen a big revival of interest recently. Its study also raises questions about pleasure and pain (cf. psychological HEDONISM), and about FEELINGS and emotions. In what sense, for example, are feelings 'in' the body or mind, and how are emotions to be analysed and distinguished from feelings

Mind (philosophy of)

and from each other? Many such questions, like many on perceiving and imagining, border on aesthetics.

This brings us to the more centrally cognitive notions like perception, sensation, judgment, together with more specific ones like attending, noticing, observing, and the more purely intellectual ones like thinking, understanding, believing, doubting, feeling sure, reasoning, inferring. Epistemology concentrates primarily on questions of justification, while philosophy of mind analyses these concepts rather from the point of view of what logical conditions someone must satisfy if he is to be said to be perceiving, thinking etc. The second of the original main problems is relevant here. Knowledge is not in the above list, because knowing involves being correct or justified; its analysis therefore belongs to epistemology. Again, the question whether believing is being disposed to act in certain ways belongs primarily to philosophy of mind, but the question whether one can properly be said to believe something where one could not be wrong, such as believe one is in pain, belongs to epistemology. But the distinction is not rigid.

A. R. Anderson (ed.), *Minds and Machines*, Prentice-Hall, 1964. (Can machines think? and similar questions.)

D. M. Armstrong and N. Malcolm, *Consciousness and Causality: a Debate on the Nature of the Mind*, Blackwell, 1984. (Materialist and opponent debate issues concerning consciousness.)

P. Beakley and P. Ludlow (eds), *The Philosophy of Mind: Classical Problems/Contemporary Issues*, MIT Press, 1992. (Large anthology. Main headings: the mind–body problem, mental causation, mental imagery, associationism/connectionism, innate ideas.)

N. Block (ed.), *Readings in the Philosophy of Psychology*, 2 vols, Harvard UP/Methuen, 1980–1. (Mainly reprinted articles, in sections covering behaviourism, reductionism and physicalism, functionalism (vol. 1), mental representations, imagery, the subject matter of grammar, innate ideas (vol. 2).)

T. Burge, 'Philosophy of language and mind: 1950–90', *Philosophical Review*, 1992. (Survey article with many references, see esp. 2nd half, pp. 29ff., for philosophy of mind.)

*K. Campbell, *Body and Mind*, Macmillan, 1970. (Introductory.)

*T. Crane, *The Mechanical Mind: a Philosophical Introduction to Minds, Machines and Mental Representation*, Penguin, 1995. (Elementary introduction.)

D. Davidson, *Essays on Actions and Events*, Clarendon, 1980. (Influential articles on various topics, including his 'anomalous MONISM' (chapter 11). See also B. Vermazen and M. B. Hintikka (eds), *Essays on Davidson: Actions and Events*, Clarendon, 1985,

Modalities

and E. Le Pore and B. P. McLaughlin (eds), *Actions and Events: Perspectives on the Philosophy of Donald Davidson*, Blackwell, 1985.)

J. A. Foster, *The Immaterial Self*, Routledge, 1991. (Defends a dualist view.)

*J. Glover (ed.), *The Philosophy of Mind*, Oxford UP, 1976. (Readings.)

J. Heil and A. Mele (eds), *Mental Causation*, Oxford UP, 1994. (Specially written essays.)

W. James, 'Does "consciousness" exist?', in his *Essays in Radical Empiricism*, 1912 (written 1904). (Neutral monist approach.)

A. Kenny, *Action, Emotion and Will*, RKP, 1963. (Discussion of these concepts.)

*C. McGinn, *The Character of Mind*, Oxford UP, 1982. (Introduction to some issues.)

D. Rosenthal (ed.), *The Nature of Mind*, Oxford UP, 1991. (62 articles and extracts covering wide range of topics. Main headings: problems about mind, self and other, mind and body, the nature of mind, psychological explanation.)

C. Rovane, 'Self-reference: the radicalization of Locke', *Journal of Philosophy*, 1993. (Defends view of personal identity that takes seriously multiple and corporate personalities.)

G. Ryle, *The Concept of Mind*, Hutchinson, 1949. (Classic attack on some dualist ('ghost in the machine') mind-body views, with discussions of feelings, emotions, etc.)

*P. Smith and O. R. Jones, *The Philosophy of Mind: an Introduction*, Cambridge UP, 1986.

G. N. A. Vesey (ed.), *Body and Mind*, Allen and Unwin, 1964. (Selections from Descartes onwards.)

R. Warner and T. Szubka (eds), *The Mind–Body Problem: a Guide to the Current Debate*, Blackwell, 1994. (Mainly new essays, wide-ranging from physicalism to dualism.)

A. R. White, *The Philosophy of Mind*, Random House, 1967; Greenwood Press, 1978. (Combines general survey with detailed analyses.)

Minor premise, term. See SYLLOGISM.

Modalities. Ways in which something can exist or occur or be presented, or stand. *Sense modalities* are ways in which we perceive, namely seeing, hearing, etc. *Alethic modalities* are the necessity, contingency, possibility, or impossibility of something being true. 'Alethic' means 'concerned with truth'. *Deontic modalities* include being obligatory, being permitted and being forbidden. Among *epistemic modalities* are being known to be true, and being not

213

Modalities

known to be false. 'Epistemic modality' is potentially ambiguous as to whether it covers both being probable, certain, etc., and being believed, doubted, etc. Tenses are sometimes called modalities; cf. *moods* or a verb. 'Modality' is also used for the property of being or having a modality.

Unless otherwise specified, 'modal' and 'modality' normally refer to the alethic modalities, of which the most important are necessity, possibility and impossibility. Terms like 'necessary', 'possible', 'must', 'may' are called *modal terms*.

The relations between those modal terms are rather ambiguous. In particular the *possible* may include everything not impossible, including the necessary; or it may be limited to what is neither necessary nor impossible; or it may be further limited to the merely possible as against the actual. The *contingent* is normally what is neither necessary nor impossible. 'Factual', like 'actual' in one sense, may denote what is neither necessary nor impossible nor merely possible; but it can also be opposed to 'logical', and so apply to a kind of necessity (see below). 'Actual', in this sense, is not used of statements, but 'factual' in both senses, 'possible' in all the above senses and 'contingent' can apply to false statements as well as to true ones (cf. FACTS). The logical relations between modal terms, e.g. whether being necessary entails being possible, clearly depend on the senses in which the terms are taken.

A statement or proposition is necessary if it must be true. A statement which claims that something is necessary, one containing (in its main clause) modal terms like 'necessary' or 'must', is called *apodictic*. One containing modal terms like 'possible' or 'may' is called *problematic*. One containing no modal terms is called *assertoric*. A necessary statement need not be apodictic. 'Twice two is four' is necessary in standard arithmetic, but not apodictic: it contains no word like 'necessary'. Nor need an apodictic statement be necessary. 'Necessarily all cats are black' is apodictic, but not necessary nor even true. In fact whether a statement is apodictic, problematic or assertoric is independent of whether it is necessary or possible, etc. A statement containing 'impossible' or its equivalents counts as apodictic. 'Apodictic' can also mean 'connected with demonstration', as often in 'apodictic necessity', and is sometimes synonymous with 'necessary'. (Kant uses 'apodictic', etc. slightly differently, to indicate how judgments are thought, not expressed; cf. also IMPERATIVE). 'N', 'L', '□' are among symbols for 'necessarily' or 'it is necessary that' ('L' is limited to logical necessity (see below); in POLISH NOTATION 'N' means 'not'). 'M', '◇' are among symbols for 'possibly' or 'it is possible that'. Statements containing modal terms are the subject matter of *modal logic* (see LOGIC), which is not always limited to the alethic modalities.

Modalities

When a modal term is applied to a statement itself containing one, as in 'It is *possible* that that statement is *necessary*', we have *nested* or *iterated modalities*.

A difficult and controversial distinction, of medieval origin, is that between *de re* and *de dicto* modality. Roughly, cases where modal terms apply to the possession of an attribute by a subject are de re and cases where they apply to a statement or proposition are de dicto. 'De dicto' means 'concerning the proposition': 'de re' means 'concerning the thing'. Consider the sentence, 'The number of the gospels necessarily exceeds three.' On a de dicto reading this means that the statement that the number of the gospels exceeds three is necessary, which is false: the gospels do amount to more than three, but not necessarily. On a de re reading it means that the number of the gospels, i.e. the number four, necessarily exceeds three, which is true, if we allow (*pace* Quine) that things like numbers have their arithmetical properties necessarily. On the other hand consider the sentence, 'If I am sitting I am necessarily not standing.' On a de dicto reading this is true, since it is a necessary statement that if I am sitting I am not standing; I cannot be both. But on a de re reading it is false, since if I am sitting it is indeed a property of me that I am not standing, but not a necessary property; I could have been standing. But the notion of de re modality, and its relations to de dicto modality, are controversial. The difficulty concerns whether a thing's possession of its properties can be called necessary. On the de dicto interpretation only statements or propositions are said to be necessary. The view that de re modality is intelligible and that there are cases of it, even if ultimately they must be analysed in terms of de dicto modality, is the form usually taken in modern discussions by *essentialism*, when this means the doctrine that at least some objects have essences. Rejection of this is one form, or perhaps one aspect, of *nominalism* (cf. DEFINITION). Essentialism has enjoyed a revival recently. The de re/de dicto distinction is also important, and controversial, concerning propositional attitudes (see SENTENCES for these and BELIEF for the distinction here).

Properly speaking, necessity and possibility are *absolute*. But in a secondary sense they may be *relative* to (*conditional* on) some expressed or tacit condition or premise. In particular the conclusion of an argument may have *necessitas consequentis*, which is absolute, if it is necessary independently of the argument, or *necessitas consequentiae*, which is relative, if it merely follows necessarily from the premises: 'No spaniels have visited the moon' follows necessarily from 'All spaniels are dogs' and 'No dogs have visited the moon', but is not itself necessary, even though it and the premises are true. It therefore has only necessitas consequentiae. A conclusion in

Modalities

itself impossible may be possible relative to (i.e. may be consistent with) certain premises: 'Man lives without air' is possible relative to 'Man can do whatever fish can do'. If the impossibility is logical the situation is more complex: Is 'Twice two is five' consistent with 'Half five is two' (cf. IMPLICATION, CONSISTENT)? Similarly a conclusion possible in itself may be impossible relative to certain premises.

Epistemic possibility and *necessity* are relative to what we, or some given set of people, know, or to what we believe. Something possible given only what we know or believe may not be possible given everything that is the case, and something not possible given everything that is the case may be possible given only what we know or believe; similarly something necessary given everything that is the case may not be necessary given only what we know or believe, and something not necessary given everything that is the case may be necessary given only what we know or believe. In ancient times it was epistemically possible that Mars was inhabited, and epistemically necessary that the earth was flat. Its flatness *followed* from other beliefs then current.

Necessity and possibility may also be *logical*, or *physical* (*causal, scientific, natural, factual*), or of various other kinds such as moral, legal, aesthetic. Logical necessity and possibility may be *formal* or *non-formal* (see ANALYTIC. 'Logically necessary' normally amounts to the same as 'logically true'.)

The nature of physical necessity and possibility has been long disputed, especially since Hume. Are they independent of logical necessity and possibility, or ultimately reducible to them, or merely illusory? Are the logical/physical and absolute/relative distinctions related? Perhaps a physically necessary statement is simply one that follows logically from (i.e. is necessary relative to) the laws of an accepted scientific system. But are not the laws themselves necessary in some sense, and if so, in what sense?

It is hard to define modal terms without begging the question. The logically or physically necessary is sometimes defined as what happens in all logically or physically POSSIBLE WORLDS, but what are these? Perhaps all conceivable worlds, or all worlds compatible with certain laws; but 'conceivable' and 'compatible' have modal endings (' –ble'), and are not the laws themselves necessary? *Modal realism* is the view that such possible worlds are in some sense real; see POSSIBLE WORLDS again.

Is a logically necessary statement one which nothing would count as contradicting, so that 'All cats are animals' is necessary if nothing would count as a cat that was not an animal? But how do we know that nothing would so count? Is it because 'cat' and 'animal' mean what they do, so that 'All cats are animals' says nothing about cats but exhibits a rule of language, and language depends on us? This is the CONVENTIONALIST or *linguistic theory* of logical necessity. But to apply a convention (in this case, the convention to use words in certain ways) involves following a rule, and if the rule is itself a convention we shall be led into an infinite regress. It seems that we cannot avoid logical necessity as a constraining force, and at most may hope to decide where it shall constrain us. We may alter our language but we shall always be committed to something. We can make. 'Twice two is five' true by redefining 'five', but then we must accept 'Five is half eight' – unless we redefine 'eight', but we must stop somewhere.

Conceptually necessary is often loosely and used as synonymous with 'logically necessary'. But if 'logically necessary' is confined to that whose denial is contradictory, 'conceptually necessary' can cover also that whose denial is unintelligible but not strictly contradictory. 'Nothing can be red or green all over' is perhaps an example (cf. ANALYTIC). But there is a problem about when something is contradictory.

Non-contingent is often used for 'logically necessary', but properly it denotes a looser relation: one might say that intention was non-contingently related to action. Any given intention need not be followed by the relevant action, and so the relation is not strictly a necessary one, but the concept of intention could hardly have arisen unless intentions were usually followed by the relevant actions.

Sometimes one can arrange different kinds of necessity in order of degree of stringency, and treat formally the resulting relations between them.

Further questions concern absolute possibility and actuality. Can there be possibilities which remain so throughout all time but are never actualized? Aristotle and Hobbes, among others, said no. Cf. PLENTITUDE.

A logical possibility is anything not self-contradictory, but a *real possibility* may be either simply a physical possibility or something having at least some probability (or perhaps not too low a probability) that it will occur. See also ANALYTIC, CAUSATION).

Aristotle, *De Caelo* (*On the Heavens*), book 1, chapter 12. T. Hobbes, *Elements of Philosophy: Concerning Body*, 1655, chapter 10, § 4. (Aristotle and Hobbes reject eternal unrealized possibilities.)

R. Cartwright, 'Some remarks on essentialism', *Journal of Philosophy*, 1968. (Defends intelligibility of de re modality, while doubting if it is analysable in terms of de dicto modality.)

Mode

I. Kant, *Critique of Pure Reason*, 1781 (revised 1787), B.101. (His use of 'apodictic', etc.)

S. Kripke, *Naming and Necessity*, Blackwell, 1980 (original version, 1972). (Leading reviver of essentialism. Cf. S. P. Schwartz (ed.), *Naming, Necessity and Natural Kinds*, Cornell UP, 1977, for discussions, including items by fellow essentialist H. Putnam (who incidentally envisages a case where 'All cats are animals' is not even true: see p. 107). Cf. also C. Kirwan, 'How strong are the objections to essence?', *Proceedings of the Aristotelian Society*, 1970–1).

N. Malcolm, 'Are necessary propositions really verbal?', *Mind*,1940, pp. 189ff. (Defends linguistic view of logical necessity.)

Midwest Studies in Philosophy, vol. 6, 1986. (Issue devoted to essentialism.)

A. Plantinga, 'De re et de dicto', *Nous*, 1969. (Explains de re in terms of de dicto modality, criticizing W. C. Kneale in E. Nagel, P. Suppes, A. Tarski (eds), *Logic, Methodology and Philosophy of Science*, Stanford UP, 1962, who rejects the distinction. Cf. also Plantinga's *The Nature of Necessity*, Oxford UP, 1974, for defence of essentialism and de re modality.)

K. R. Popper, *The Open Society and Its Enemies*, RKP, 1945. (Contains famous attack on one version of essentialism.)

W. V. O. Quine, 'Truth by convention', in H. Feigl and W. Sellars (eds), *Readings in Philosophical Analysis*, Appleton-Century-Crofts, 1949. (Stresses limitations of conventionalist theory of logical necessity. His 'Reference and modality' in his *From a Logical Point of View*, Harper and Row, revised edn, 1961, represents one approach to the de re/de dicto distinction (though not so called), claiming that modal contexts are always opaque (see INTENSIONALITY AND INTENTIONALITY), and prefiguring but not accepting the revival of essentialism.)

Mode. See SUBSTANCE.

Models. A logical or mathematical model of an AXIOM SYSTEM, or of a sentence in an axiom system, is a set of entities, which may be numbers or classes and hence abstract, whose relations can be represented by that system or sentence. A structure of such entities is a model of a sentence S if S is true in the structure. The natural numbers, taken as related in the way they are by the relation *successor of*, are a model of Peano's axioms, since these are true of the natural numbers, so taken. ('So taken', because the axioms would not necessarily be true of the natural numbers if, e.g., these were taken in a different order.) Important problems concern what is true of *all* models of a given system. In some earlier literature a

Monad

theory can be called a model of another theory, or can contain an interpretation of it, if the sets of objects they study are models of the same axiom system, when they are taken in the way in which they are studied (see previous parenthesis). A scientific model is normally a theory intended to explain a given realm of phenomena, or a sort of picture intended to explain a theory by replacing its terms with more perspicuous ones (Braithwaite).

Model theory concerns logical and mathematical models. It studies relations between formal languages and interpretations of them, i.e. problems connected with saying that a sentence of a formal language (e.g. the restricted predicate CALCULUS) is true in an interpretation. This interpretation may be an abstract structure or a world, e.g. the real world as it was in 1970. The starting-point for all forms of model theory is A. Tarski's semantic definition of TRUTH.

M. Brodbeck, 'Models, meaning and theories', in L. Gross (ed.), *Symposium on Sociological Theory*, Harper and Row, 1959. (Discusses many different uses of 'model'. On scientific models see also R. B. Braithwaite, *Scientific Explanation*, Harper, 1953, chapter 4.)

*J. N. Crossley *et al.*, *What is Mathematical Logic?*, Oxford UP, 1972, chapter 3. (Brief fairly elementary account of model theory. For technical introduction, presupposing some mathematical logic, see J. E. Bell and A. B. Slomson, *Models and Ultraproducts: an Introduction*, North Holland, 1969, revised, 1971. Asterisk applies to Crossley.)

A. Tarski, *Introduction to Logic*, Oxford UP, 1941, § 37. (Models in logic.)

Modus ponens (lit.: method which asserts). Argument that if a conditional statement and its antecedent are true, so is its consequent, e.g. 'If this, then that. This. Therefore that.' (Some refinements are omitted.)

Modus tollens (lit.: method which denies). Argument that if a conditional statement is true but its consequent is false, then its antecedent is false, e.g. 'If this, then that. But not that. Therefore not this.' (Some refinements are omitted.)

Monad. Literally, group of one. Either a numerical unit or an object which is essentially unitary and indivisible. For Leibniz, simple substances, which are what is ultimately real. *Monadic* means either 'concerning monads' or 'having only one term'. Predicates like '(is) red' are monadic (occasionally called monadic relations), since only

Monism

one term needs adding to make a sentence. Relations proper are *dyadic* or *two-term* or *two-place* relations, or dyadic predicates, if two terms are needed (as with *bigger than*: '*a* is bigger than *b*'). They are *polyadic* or *many-term* or *many-place* if more than two are needed (*between* needs three: '*b* is between *a* and *c*').

G. W. Leibniz, *Principles of Nature and of Grace*, 1714, *Monadology*, 1914.

Monism. Any view which claims that where there appear to be many things or kinds of things there is really only one or only one kind. Weaker forms of monism may claim simply that the things in question are related together, or unified, in some significant way. What is said to be one in any of these ways may be the whole universe, or some lesser subject-matter. The most famous extreme monist, holding (as most commonly interpreted) that there is only one object, is Parmenides, writing about 500 BC. *Neutral monism* is a particular doctrine claiming that physical and mental phenomena can both be analysed in terms of a common underlying reality, sometimes called *neutral stuff*. Among major philosophers it is associated with James and Russell. *Anomalous monism* says that every mental event is identical with some physical event (the token IDENTITY THEORY OF MIND) but that there are no laws for explaining or predicting mental events as such.
See also SUPERVENIENCE, DUALISM.

D. Davidson, 'Mental events', in L. Foster and J. W. Swanson (eds), *Experience and Theory*, Duckworth, 1970, reprinted in Davidson's *Essays on Actions and Events*, Oxford UP, 1980. (Anomalous monism.)
W. James, *Essays in Radical Empiricism*, 1912, chapters 1 and 2, B. Russell, *The Analysis of Mind*, Allen and Unwin/Macmillan, 1921. (Two versions of neutral monism, which also appears, in effect though not in name, in H.-L. Bergson, *Matter and Memory*, Macmillan, 1910 (French original, 1896).)

Mood. See SYLLOGISM.

Moore, George E. 1873–1958. Born in Upper Norwood, he worked in Cambridge. He led the revolt against IDEALISM at the start of this century, and was one of the fathers of analytical PHILOSOPHY. He criticized the extravagances, as he saw them, of philosophers who flouted common sense with such doctrines as that time is unreal and that all RELATIONS are internal. He held influential, if somewhat idiosyncratic, views in ETHICS, and was particularly noted for his criticism of the 'naturalistic fallacy' (see NATURALISM). 'The Refu-

Moral

tation of idealism', *Mind*, 1903. *Principia Ethica*, 1903. *Some Main Problems in Philosophy*, 1953 (lectures given in 1910). 'External and internal relations', *Proceedings of the Aristotelian Society*, 1919–20. See also BEING, BRADLEY, GOOD, IMPLICATION, PHENOMENALISM, SCEPTICISM, SENTENCES, TRUTH, UTILITARIANISM.

Moral. Concerning habits, customs, ways of life, especially when these are assessed as good or bad, right or wrong. Etymologically the Latin 'moral' corresponds to the Greek 'ethical'. They both mean 'concerning habits, etc.'. 'Ethical' and 'unethical' tend often to be used of undesirable behaviour directed at interests other than those of the agent, at any rate where the agent is an individual person. Among things we call moral are theories, arguments, outlooks, rules, reasons, virtues, people, books, actions, intentions, and perhaps desires and feelings. There is an important ambiguity between 'moral' as against 'immoral' and 'moral' as against 'nonmoral'. People are normally called moral only in the first sense; problems can be moral only in the second. An immoral principle is still a moral principle in the second sense, as against, say, a legal or aesthetic principle. 'Morality' is similarly ambiguous. *'Amoral'* (which properly means 'non-moral', not 'immoral') is seldom used in philosophy.

Various ways of distinguishing the moral from the non-moral have been tried. A moral principle might be defined as one concerning things in our power and for which we can be held responsible. This would contrast moral principles with, for example, intellectual and aesthetic ones, which it might not be in our power to apply. Or a moral principle might concern the ultimate ends of human action, e.g. human welfare. Other views have it that a moral principle is one which people in fact prefer over competing principles, or else one which they should prefer. Others again make principles moral if a certain kind of sanction is applied when they are violated. UNIVERSALIZABILITY has also been used to define moral principles.

A view may offer a necessary condition of morality, or a sufficient condition, or both (see NECESSARY AND SUFFICIENT CONDITIONS). A further distinction is that in defining morality one may be saying what counts as moral for a given person or society, or giving one's own view of what counts as moral.

G. Harman, *The Nature of Morality*, Oxford UP, 1977. (General introduction to various issues concerning morality, though less concerned with defining the moral as such.)

G. H. von Wright, *The Varieties of Goodness*, RKP, 1963, esp. chapter 1 (last paragraph), chapter 6, §§ 5ff. (Moral goodness

Morals

and goodness generally. Acts and intentions. Assumes UTILITARIANISM).

*G. Wallace and A. D. M. Walker (eds), *The Definition of Morality*, Methuen, 1970. (Selected essays.)

*B. Williams, *Morality*, Penguin, 1972, esp. penultimate chapter. (Brief elementary introduction.)

Morals. See ETHICS.

Moral sense. An alleged sixth sense, whose existence was hotly disputed in the eighteenth century. Its proponents, who included SHAFTESBURY and HUTCHESON, held that our own and others' actions arouse agreeable or disagreeable 'sentiments', or feelings, in us according as the actions are, in conventional terms, virtuous or vicious. It is not always clear, however, what is the role of the sense, on this view, i.e. whether we perceive qualities by it, and if so, of what sort, or whether it simply arouses sentiments in us, or gives us a desire to act, when we perceive certain qualities in the ordinary way.

S. Darwall, A. Gibbard and P. Railton, 'Toward *fin de siècle* ethics: some trends', *Philosophical Review*, 1992. (A survey article. See pp. 152–65, on 'sensibility theories', for a modern outlook with some analogy to moral sense theories.)

D. D. Raphael, *The Moral Sense*, Oxford UP 1947. (Discussion, mainly historical.)

L. A. Selby-Bigge (ed.), *British Moralists*, 1897. (Vol. 1 contains selections from moral sense theorists, vol. 2 selections from their opponents. Cf. also the ethical writings of D. Hume (1711–76).)

Moving rows paradox. See ZENO'S PARADOXES.

N

Naturism. See INNATE.

Natural deduction. A system which systematizes those DEDUCTIONS which involve contingent propositions (see MODALITIES), not merely TAUTOLOGIES. It systematizes the 'natural' arguments of everyday life. Associated especially with G. Gentzen (1909–45) and S. Jaśkowski (1906–1965).

E. Lemmon, *Beginning Logic*, Nelson, 1965. (Uses it to introduce formal logic.)

Naturalism. There are two main applications of the term 'naturalism' in modern philosophy, one in metaphysics, epistemology and philosophy of mind and the other in ethics. What they have in common is the belief that the universe is all one, in the sense that all objects in it and all aspects of it are equally accessible to study by scientific method.

The empiricist tradition of Locke, Hume and J. S. Mill and others made no sharp distinction between what would now be called philosophy of mind and psychology. Questions about the justification of mental states such as beliefs tended to be assimilated to questions about their psychological origins. Towards the end of the nineteenth century and beginning of the twentieth, this tendency was fiercely attacked, in particular by Bradley, Frege and (eventually but not at first) by Husserl, usually under the name of PSYCHOLOGISM. The empiricist revival that dominated the first half of the twentieth century accepted and indeed insisted on this distinction between epistemology and psychology, and the difficulty

223

Naturalism

of finding epistemological justifications for various beliefs once psychological substitutes were discounted led to scepticism.

More recently, mainly under the influence of Quine, there has been a revival of naturalism but in a more self-conscious form, called *naturalized* EPISTEMOLOGY, in that epistemological questions are not just tacitly treated in a psychological manner but the change is avowed and deliberate. Among other writers this is also true of Hume, but Hume abandoned the search for justification, and tried to explain rather than justify our beliefs in such things as real causal connections and the existence of a world outside our own minds. (How far he either accepted those beliefs in fact or thought they could be disproved is disputed, but he claimed that scepticism, however irrefutable in theory, was impossible to accept in practice outside the philosophical study.) The recent revival is more inclined to claim that the psychological account itself constitutes a kind of justification. Cf. here *reliabilism* (see EPISTEMOLOGY).

The ethical version of naturalism claims that there is no unbridgeable gulf between ethics and other studies. It takes two main forms, that ethical terms can be analysed into non-ethical terms, and that ethical conclusions can be logically derived from non-ethical premises.

Modern discussions start from two famous attacks on these two forms respectively, by Moore and Hume. Moore insisted that 'good' is indefinable, and that the questions what 'good' means and what things are good must be sharply distinguished, e.g. pleasure may be good, and even possibly the only good thing, but 'good' does not *mean* 'pleasant' or 'producing pleasure', etc. He called the neglect of this distinction the *naturalistic fallacy*, and said goodness is a nonnatural quality. (He never successfully explained 'nonnatural', which is now not used of qualities. For 'nonnatural' see MEANING.) One of Moore's arguments was the *open question argument*: whatever definition of 'good' was offered, it would always be an open question whether what satisfies the definition *is* good. It is not clear, however, whether the naturalistic fallacy lies in defining 'good', defining 'good' in non-ethical terms, defining any ethical notion in non-ethical terms, defining any notion in terms of notions in a different sphere, or indeed simply confusing one notion with another (cf. Prior). In this last form the fallacy is sometimes called the *definist fallacy*. It is difficult, however, to mark off different spheres or notions, and the errors, if any, are not strictly fallacies – no fallacious inference is involved.

Hume, as usually interpreted, attacked naturalism by denying that conclusions whose main verb is an 'ought', or an equivalent, can be logically derived from premises not containing such a notion; he maintains what is now called the *is/ought distinction*. Hume was primarily concerned with the moral OUGHT, but the question also arises of whether his view applies to other 'oughts' (e.g. 'doctor's orders').

The alleged distinction underlying both these attacks is often if loosely, called the *fact/value distinction*, though 'ought' is not strictly a value term (and the fact/value and is/ought distinctions are sometimes separated: Wiggins, who accepts the former but rejects the latter).

Moore made his distinction between different qualities, all of which objectively belonged to their possessors: whether a thing is good no more depends on the observer than whether it is, say, spherical. Various later writers, however, have tried to make the same distinction in other ways, asking how words have meaning, and what the speaker's own attitudes contribute. Thus a distinction grew up between straightforward descriptions which claim to state facts and impart knowledge, and utterances whose purpose is to express or evince emotions or attitudes, to issue prescriptions or recommendations, or to evaluate. Utterances of the former kind, and the words used in them, had *descriptive, factual* or *cognitive meaning*; those of the latter kind had *emotive, evaluative, prescriptive* or in general *non-cognitive meaning*, and were subject to a SPEECH ACT analysis. The terms in the former list in general coincide (but for ambiguities in 'factual' see FACTS). Those in the latter list do not all coincide – to express emotion is not the same as to prescribe action or attitudes – but they share the property of being contrasted with the former list. Many utterances, however, especially ethical ones, had both kinds of meaning. 'He is courageous' might mean 'He knowingly takes great risks' (factual), 'and I hereby express approval of his doing so' (emotive), or 'I hereby recommend you to follow suit' (prescriptive). 'He is rash' might have the same factual meaning but the opposite non-cognitive meaning, i.e., as above, but with 'disapproval' for 'approval' and 'forbid' for 'recommend'. *Emotivists* and *prescriptivists* analyse ethical utterances in this way, emphasizing emotive and prescriptive meaning respectively, but *descriptivists* think that ethical utterances have meaning in the same way as factual ones do, i.e. they state facts, even if of an ethical kind. Descriptivism and naturalism are in practice closely similar, but Moore was a descriptivist but not a naturalist.

Understandably, the naturalist controversy is associated with another, concerning whether there are objective and agreed procedures for arriving at conclusions in matters of value or duty. Descriptivists and most naturalists claim that there are, even if they are hard to elaborate. They take the utterances in question to say something true or false about objective reality, and so to state facts.

Naturalism

Their opponents may deny that there are such procedures. Hence the attempt common among POSITIVISTS and linguistic PHILOSOPHERS to confine ethics to certain questions only: see ETHICS. Alternatively they allow that there are such procedures, but have special difficulty in elaborating them, since special kinds of reasoning seem needed to support conclusions claiming to do something other than state facts.

Recently the fact/value distinction has come under fire. There seems to be little unity on the value side, which has to cover expressions of emotion, commendations, prescriptions, etc., in each case sometimes moral and sometimes non-moral. Where a similar distinction seems viable it may still be relative (Anscombe). Emotivists and prescriptivists face objections connected with UNIVERSALIZABILITY. The theory that words like 'good' or 'ought' get their meaning by commending or prescribing, i.e. by their use in SPEECH ACTS, also faces difficulties (see GOOD).

The view that moral conclusions cannot be logically derived from non-moral premises may be called a weak non-naturalism or weak anti-naturalism if it admits that there are limits to the possible contents of ethical statements, i.e. to what we can *intelligibly* be said to commend or prescribe as a duty. Would we, for example, understand anyone who seriously thought it his duty to blink every five seconds, regardless of circumstances? It is a strong non-naturalism if it denies that there are such limits. (Cf. the question whether just anything can be GOOD). The phrase *autonomy of morals* or *of ethics* can apply to both these versions of non-naturalism, and also to the view that practical moral questions can be separated from theoretical ethical analysis because any position on the former can be combined with any position on the latter. This last view too has been attacked because of universalizability, among other things.

Perhaps the most central question is whether there is any way of *establishing* ethical or other valuational conclusions. If there is, there may seem to be little objection to using terms like 'true' and 'fact' in connexion with such conclusions, i.e. to adopting descriptivism; but this view has recently been disputed.

'Naturalism' is also used in other ways, notably in art, where it might be most obviously described as the attempt to represent nature (including human nature) as it is rather than in various stylized, symbolic, or romantic guises; cf. REALISM.

See also OUGHT, GOOD, MEANING, FACTS, ETHICS, SUPERVENIENCE.

G. E. M. Anscombe, 'On brute facts', *Analysis*, vol. 18, 1958. (Argues that distinction between 'brute' and 'institutional' facts is relative.)
R. F. Atkinson, 'The autonomy of morals', *Analysis*, vol. 18, 1958.

(Defends fact/value distinction against some attacks of a logical nature.)

C. Beck, 'Utterances which incorporate a value statement', *American Philosophical Quarterly*, 1967. R. W. Newell, 'Ethics and description', *Philosophy*, 1968. (Two attacks on fact/value distinction.)

*P. Foot (ed.), *Theories of Ethics*, Oxford UP, 1967. (Includes several notable discussions of naturalism.)

D. P. Gauthier, 'Moore's naturalistic fallacy', *American Philosophical Quarterly*, 1967. (Discusses Moore and Prior and offers own view on naturalistic fallacy.)

A. Gewirth, 'Positive "ethics" and normative "science" ', *Philosophical Review*, 1960. (Compares ethics and science as fields of enquiry.)

J. Griffin, 'Values: reduction, supervenience, and explanation by ascent' in D. Charles and K. Lennon (eds), *Reduction, Explanations, and Realism*, Clarendon, 1992. (Throws doubt on the natural/nonnatural distinction, and thereby on supervenience accounts of value: what exactly supervenes on what?)

*W. D. Hudson (ed.), *The Is/Ought Question*, Macmillan, 1969. (Discussions of Hume's attack on naturalism, plus some essays on evaluation.)

W. D. Hudson, *Modern Moral Philosophy*, Macmillan, 1970. (General introduction. Includes Hare's later views in discussing prescriptivism, etc. Cf. also p. 171 on terminology.)

F. Jackson, G. Oddy and M. Smith, 'Minimalism and truth aptness', *Mind*, 1994. (Argues against a too ready acceptance of terms like 'true' and 'fact' in connection with ethical statements.)

P. Kitcher, 'The naturalists return', *Philosophical Review*, 1992. (Extended survey of the revival of naturalism in metaphysics and epistemology.)

Midwest Studies in Philosophy, vol. 19, 1995. (Journal issue devoted to philosophical naturalism.)

G. E. Moore, *Principia Ethica*, Cambridge UP, 1903, chapter 1, esp. § B. (Locus classicus for naturalistic fallacy.)

L. Nochlin, *Realism*, Penguin, 1971. (Naturalism in art.)

D. Papineau, *Philosophical Naturalism*, Blackwell, 1993. (General discussion, relating naturalism to physicalism and applying it to problems in philosophy of mind and epistemology.)

A. N. Prior, *Logic and the Basis of Ethics*, Oxford UP, 1949. (Naturalistic fallacy in its historical setting.)

W. V. O. Quine, 'Epistemology naturalised' in his *Ontological Relativity and Other Essays*, Columbia, 1969. (Major influence in revival of naturalism.)

Naturalistic fallacy

A. K. Sen, 'Hume's law and Hare's rule', *Philosophy*, 1966. (Uses universalizability to defend naturalism.)

S. J. Wagner and R. Warner (eds), *Naturalism: A Critical Appraisal*, Notre Dame UP, 1993. (Specially written essays mainly critical of naturalism from wide variety of viewpoints, with introduction and summaries.)

D. Wiggins, 'Truth, invention, and the meaning of life' (pamphlet), *Proceedings of the British Academy*, 1976, reprinted in his *Needs, Values, Truth*, Blackwell, 1987. (See esp. p. 96 (of reprint) for separation of fact/value and is/ought distinctions. Difficult.)

Naturalistic fallacy. See NATURALISM.

Necessary. See MODALITIES.

Necessary and sufficient conditions. A necessary condition for something is one without which the thing does not exist or occur. The presence of oxygen is a necessary condition for human life. A sufficient condition for something is one given which the thing does exist or occur. Prolonged absence of oxygen is a sufficient condition for human death. Necessary or sufficient conditions need not precede what they are conditions of. The existence of humans is a sufficient condition for the presence of oxygen. As this last example shows, a sufficient condition may be causally connected with what it is a condition of, without being a cause of it. But necessary or sufficient conditions do not have to be causal: fine weather is a necessary condition of my going out today – because I have so decided. They can also be logical (being an equilateral Euclidean triangle is both necessary and sufficient for being an equiangular Euclidean triangle), or just accidental: if *all* dodos were eaten, however accidentally, being eaten is a necessary (though not causally necessary) condition for being a dodo. But 'necessary' and 'sufficient' are often tacitly limited to the non-accidental. 'Sufficient conditions' (plural) may refer to conditions jointly sufficient for something, or to conditions each of which is itself sufficient.

Negation. A distinction is sometimes made between *external* and *internal negation*. In external negation a whole proposition is negated, in internal negation only part of one. 'It's not thought that he'll come' involves external negation if it means simply that people don't think he will come, but internal negation if it means they do think he won't. There is a similar distinction between negating a proposition and negating a predicate or term, e.g. between 'This isn't red' and 'This is non-red'. '*Denial*' is sometimes kept for the negation of a predicate or term. It is also sometimes used for

Neoplatonists

the rejection of a claim already made, as opposed to an assertion, which even if it includes a negative element still claims something about the world (Barwise and Etchemendy). 'Positive' and 'affirmative' are generally synonymous.

The *double negation* principle says that any proposition implies and is implied by the negation of its negation. INTUITIONIST logic rejects the second half of this.

Various problems arise: Can negative and affirmative propositions be separately identified? Or can one only say that two propositions are negations of each other, neither being 'the' negative one? Is negating something a special activity? Is affirming somehow prior to negating? Can language dispense with negation?

A. J. Ayer, 'Negation', *Journal of Philosophy* 1952, reprinted in his *Philosophical Essays*, Macmillan, 1954. (Definition, and dispensability, of negation.)

J. Barwise and J. Etchemendy, *The Liar*, Oxford UP, 1987. (See pp. 16–17 for treatment of 'denial'.)

G. Buchdahl, 'The problem of negation', *Philosophy and Phenomenological Research*, 1961–2. (Is affirmation prior to negation?)

G. Frege, 'Negation', in P. T. Geach and M. Black (eds), *Translations from the Philosophical Writings of Gottlob Frege*, Blackwell, 1952. (Is negating something a special activity?)

J. D. Mabbott, G. Ryle, H. H. Price, 'Negation', *Proceedings of the Aristotelian Society*, supplementary vol., 1929. (What does negation presuppose?)

B. H. Slater, 'Internal and external negations', *Mind*, 1979. (Uses the distinction to solve various problems.)

Neoplatonists. Various groups of philosophers influenced by Plotinus (AD 205–70) and claiming Platonic inspiration. Plotinus in his *Enneads* claimed to interpret and develop PLATO, basing himself especially on certain passages suggesting that reality is somehow derived from a single thing, called the One or the Good, which transcends existence (i.e. is on too high a plane to be said to 'exist') and is unknowable. Plotinus also developed an epistemology. The Neoplatonists also tried to unify Plato and ARISTOTLE. They are now often regarded as having misinterpreted Plato. Leading Neoplatonists after Plotinus include Porphyry (c. 232–c. 304), Iamblichus (c. 270–c. 330), Proclus (c. 409–c. 487), Philoponus (sixth century), Simplicius (sixth century), Boethius (c. 480–525).

E. K. Emilsson, *Platonism on Sense-Perception*, Cambridge UP, 1988. (Plotinus' epistemology. First chapter also contains good introduction to Plotinus' general philosophy.)

R. T. Wallis, *Neoplatonism*, 1972.

Neustic

Neustic. See PHRASTIC.

Newcomb's paradox. You are offered two boxes. The first contains a thousand pounds. The second contains either a million pounds or nothing. You can take either both boxes or the second alone. Many other people have made the choice. All or nearly all who chose both boxes found the second empty. All or nearly all who chose the second box found it full. Which should you choose? Induction suggests the second alone. Yet the boxes have already been arranged, so how can your now choosing both boxes affect the contents of the second? Surely then you should choose both?

J. L. Mackie, 'Newcomb's paradox and the direction of causation', *Canadian Journal of Philosophy*, 1977, reprinted in his *Logic and Knowledge*, 1985. (Non-technical discussion. See p. 200 for connexion with PRISONER'S DILEMMA.)

R. Nozick, 'Newcomb's problem and two principles of choice', in N. Rescher (ed.), *Essays in Honor of Carl G. Hempel*, 1969. (Original place of publication of the paradox. Clear exposition followed by sometimes rather technical discussion of it and variants.)

R. M. Sainsbury, *Paradoxes*, Cambridge UP, 1988, revised, 1995. (See pp. 51–63 (53–65 in revised ed.) for elementary introduction.)

Nietzsche, Friedrich. 1844–1900. Born in Prussia, he taught classes at Basel and then lived in Switzerland and Italy, and died after eleven years of insanity. He contrasted the Apolline and Dionysian elements in Greek tragedy, and in his view of ethics, where he contrasted 'master' and 'slave' morality and made pungent criticisms of utilitarianism and Christian ethics, and of notions, like equality, common in the Enlightenment. Linked with these latter views are his concepts of the 'will to power' and the 'superman'. How far his own ideal involves aggressive egoism is disputed. He also took a pragmatic attitude to truth, and revived the PYTHAGOREAN and STOIC notion of eternal recurrence (see METAPHYSICS). He is sometimes associated with EXISTENTIALISM. *The Birth of Tragedy*, 1872. *Beyond Good and Evil*, 1886. *Towards a Genealogy of Morals*, 1887. *Thus Spake Zarathustra*, 1883–5.

W. Kaufmann (ed. and tr.), *The Portable Nietzsche*, Viking Press, 1954, revised 1968, *Basic Writings of Nietzsche*, Modern Library, New York, 1968. (Between them these contain the above works and five other works complete, with extracts from further ones.)

Nomic. See NOMOLOGICAL.

Numbers

Nominalism. Normally any view which treats a given (apparently non-linguistic) subject-matter in terms of words or language rather than in terms of substantial realities. In fact, however, there are two versions: (i) the view that there are no abstract entities, and that abstraction depends on things being described in certain ways; (ii) the view that there are no universals (also called PARTICULARISM). Only (i) falls under the opening definition above. (ii) is followed by Armstrong in particular (see bibliography to UNIVERSALS). See UNIVERSALS, BEING, DEFINITION, MODALITIES, REALISM, SUBSTANCE.

Nomological. Concerning or involving laws. *Nomic* means this, or sometimes 'lawlike' (see first sense of this under LAWS).

No-ownership theory. Theory that states of consciousness are not owned by anything, mental or physical.

P. F. Strawson, *Individuals*, Methuen, 1959, chapter 3. (Critical, with references.)

Normative. A term or sentence, etc. is normative if its basic uses involve prescribing norms or standards, explicitly or implicitly, e.g. 'ought' is normative, and so is 'good' for anyone holding that, for example, 'Piety is good' either means or entails 'One ought to be pious'.

Noumenon. Plural: 'noumena'. Adjective: 'noumenal'. Literally, thing known by the mind as against the senses. Kant called *things-in-themselves* noumena because they would be intuitable by a suitable intellectual intuition; we, however, cannot intuit them, but must postulate them, though without knowing what they are like, to account for the appearances (*phenomena*) we are confronted with.

I. Kant, *Critique of Pure Reason*, 1781, 1787. (See index to N. Kemp Smith's translation, 1929.)

Numbers. The natural numbers (also called finite cardinal numbers or *cardinals*) are the non-negative integers: 0, 1, 2 .... They are nowadays often defined in terms of sets (see CLASSES). As Frege pointed out, two sets, whether finite or infinite, are equivalent if they can be paired off so that for each member of one there is exactly one corresponding member of the other. ('Equipollent' often replaces 'equivalent', which can then have a wider sense.) The *equivalence class* of a set is the class of all sets equivalent to it. If there are twelve apostles, twelve months of the year and twelve signs of the zodiac, these three sets are members of the same

Numbers (law of large)

equivalence class and share the same cardinality. For technical reasons, their cardinal (12) is regarded as a particular set selected from this equivalence class by, for example, the following general method, due to J. von Neumann: 0 is the (unique) empty set. 1 is the set whose only member is 0; 2 is the set whose only members are 0 and 1, and so on. 12 is therefore the set whose only members are 0, 1, 2, . . . 11, and in general each finite cardinal is the set of all smaller cardinals. This method can be extended to define infinite cardinals too.

Two equivalent sets, each ordered in a certain way, are *similar* or have equal *order-types* if they can be paired off so that each set preserves its own order; the apostles in any given order can be paired off with the months in any given order so that at each stage the next apostle goes with the next month. Finite equivalent ordered sets are always similar, but infinite ones (sometimes also called *transfinite* in mathematics) need not be; the set of positive integers in ascending order is not similar to the same set in the reverse or descending order (. . . , 2, 1, 0), because the latter has no first term to go with the first term (0) of the former. Ordered sets of which every non-empty subset has a first member are called *well-ordered*, and the order-type of a *well-ordered* set is an ordinal number or *ordinal*. The ordinal of one well-ordered set is greater than that of another if the second set as a whole is similar to an initial segment (only) of the first.

Philosophers are divided about whether numbers are real non-material entities, those who think they are, such as Plato or Frege, often being called Platonists. For other kinds of numbers (negative, rational, real, complex, transcendental, etc.) see dictionaries of mathematics.

See also MATHEMATICS (PHILOSOPHY OF).

A. A. Frankel, *Abstract Set Theory*, revised edn, North-Holland, 1961 (1st edn 1953). See its index.

A. W. Moore, *The Infinite*, Routledge, 1990. (General introduction, both historical and positive.)

Numbers (law of large). Various related theorems about possibilities for events, among them Bernoulli's theorem and Poisson's theorem. For a rough illustration of the general idea, suppose that a tossed coin is equally likely to fall heads or tails. Then, the law says, the longer the series of tosses, the greater the probability that the frequency of heads will be within some given distance of 50 per cent (e.g. between 49 per cent and 51 per cent; it cannot be exactly 50 per cent except after an even number of tosses). The law is not itself a prediction. If we *assume*, on whatever grounds, that the coin

Numbers (law of large)

will behave in certain ways, e.g. that it will not show any bias, then the law spells out what it is that we are assuming. To see what lies behind this illustration, consider all possible results, in terms of heads and tails, that a series of tosses of a fair coin could yield. Then the longer the series the greater the proportion, among the possible results for that series, of results containing between 49 per cent and 51 per cent heads. See also Bayes's Theorem.

I. Hacking, *The Taming of Chance*, Cambridge UP, 1990. (See chapter 12 for some historical material on Bernoulli, Poisson and Chebyshev, who developed the law.)

J. R. Lucas, *The Concept of Probability*, Clarendon, 1970, chapter 5. (Offers proof of Bernoulli's theorem. See also W. C. Kneale, *Probability and Induction*, Oxford UP, 1949, § 29, who is clearer on what the theorem actually says.)

J. O. Wisdom, *Foundations of Inference in Natural Science*, Methuen, 1952, chapter 20. (Brief statement of some relevant theorems, with proof of one.)

O

Object. Literally, what 'lies before' something. Anything which has independent existence (qualities, etc. have dependent existence); or, and perhaps more commonly in philosophy, what a change is instigated to produce, or a mental attitude is 'directed at' (see INTENSIONALITY AND INTENTIONALITY on 'intentional objects'). Cf. 'the object in my pocket', 'the object of my ambition'. These meanings are often intermingled. Kenny distinguishes what is perhaps a third sense: the object of an action is that which is changed by the action. (He spells 'intentional' with an 's'.) Meinong distinguished the object of an act like thinking from its content, but insisted that the object had something called 'BEING SO'. Frege treated objects as whatever can be named, and contrasted them with CONCEPTS. In this wide sense 'object' approximates to 'thing', though usually, when the 'independent existence' meaning is dominant, objects are limited to particulars (see UNIVERSALS). In the case of emotions, etc. the object may be hard to distinguish from the cause.

A. Kenny, *Action, Emotion and Will*, RKP, 1963. (See index.)

A. Meinong, 'The theory of objects' in R. Chisholm (ed.), *Realism and the Background of Phenomenology*, Free Press, 1960 (trans. from German original of 1904). (A famous and influential, though controversial, theory.)

J. A. Passmore, *A Hundred Years of Philosophy*, Duckworth, 1957, revised and expanded, 1966. (See index esp. pp. 176–87 (173–85 in Penguin edn) for Brentano and Meinong on objects.)

J. J. Valberg, 'The puzzle of experience' in T. Crane (ed.), *The Contents of Experience*, Cambridge UP, 1992, esp. §4 (reprinted from Valberg's *The Puzzle of Experience*, Oxford UP, 1992.

Ockham, William of

Objectivism. See SUBJECTIVISM

Object word. (i) Word standing for OBJECTS (in first sense) e.g. 'cat', but not 'red' or 'snow'. (ii) Word in an object language (see METALANGUAGE).

Obligation. See OUGHT.

Obversion. In traditional formal logic, obversion negates the predicate of a categorical proposition and negates the proposition itself. The result (the *obverse*) is logically equivalent to the original. 'All cats are black' and 'No cats are non-black' are obverses of each other.

Occam. See OCKHAM.

Occasionalism. Doctrine that things or events are caused only by God, never by other things or events. God uses apparent causes as occasions (hence called *occasional causes*) for creating their apparent effects. Associated especially with Malebranche and others of his time, where however, the main emphasis is on the apparent causal relations between mind and body. Leibniz's similar view is not occasionalism, because his God programmed the course of events from the creation, and did not interfere on each occasion. See also PSYCHOPHYSICAL PARALLELISM.

N. Malebranche, *Dialogues on Metaphysics and on Religion*, 1688, transl. 1923, 7th Dialogue.

Ockham, William of. c. 1285–1349. English Franciscan theologian, born at Ockham (Surrey), who worked mainly in Oxford, Avignon and Munich. He worked against the same general background as AQUINAS and Duns SCOTUS, but he separated philosophy further from theology by severely limiting the extent to which God's existence can be proved. He is commonly regarded as a nominalist (see UNIVERSALS), and is famous for OCKHAM'S RAZOR. He contributed substantially to logic and the theory of meaning, among other topics. His writings include the *Summa Logicae, Quodlibeta Septem* (seven miscellanies), and commentaries on the *Sentences* of Peter Lombard and on various works of ARISTOTLE.

P. Boehner (ed. and tr.), *William of Ockham: Philosophical Writings: A selection*. Nelson, 1957, updated, Hackett, 1990. (Has Latin text with English translation.)
M. Loux (ed. and tr.), *Ockham's Theory of Terms: Part I of the Summa Logicae*, Notre Dame, 1974.

Ockham's razor

Ockham's razor. Principle attributed to William of Ockham, that 'entities are not to be multiplied beyond necessity' (not his own words), i.e. it is arbitrary to postulate the existence of things, or kinds of things, unless one has to. More generally, one should choose the simplest hypothesis that will fit the facts. A stronger form claims that only what cannot be dispensed with is real and that to postulate other things is not only arbitrary but mistaken.

Omnipotence (paradox of). See RELIGION.

Omniscience (paradox of). See RELIGION.

One-many problem. See UNIVERSALS.

One-sorted. See MANY-SORTED.

Ontological argument. An argument of God's existence, stemming from Anselm. Very roughly: God is by definition the most perfect being; it is more perfect to exist than not to exist; therefore God exists. More generally, any argument can be called an ontological argument which infers that something really exists because certain concepts are related in certain ways. Discussion of the topic has been closely linked with the question whether existence is a predicate (or attribute).

J. Barnes, *The Ontological Argument*, 1972. (Detailed examination.)
J. Bennett, *Kant's Dialectic*, Cambridge UP, 1974, §§ 72–4. (Discusses existence as a predicate and necessary existence.)
J. L. Mackie, *The Miracle of Theism*, Clarendon, 1982, chapter 3. (Critical.)
A. Plantinga (ed.), *The Ontological Argument*, 1968. (Versions and discussions from Anselm to present day.)
A. Plantinga, *The Nature of Necessity*, Oxford UP, 1974, chapter 10. (Defends a version of the argument. See also, for criticism of him, M. Tooley, 'Plantinga's defence of the ontological argument', *Mind*, 1981, and Mackie.)

Ontology. See METAPHYSICS.

Opaque. See INTENSIONALITY.

Open question argument. See NATURALISM.

Open texture. Loosely, a term's indeterminacy of meaning. Waismann thought that with most empirical predicates (see A PRIORI) we

Original position

cannot guarantee to be able to apply or refuse to apply them in all cases. However precise we made their meaning a borderline case could always turn up in the future. He called this feature open texture, and distinguished it from VAGUENESS, which is a feature of already existing uses of predicates, not of possible future uses (see AMBIGUITY). Vagueness can be minimized by giving more accurate rules, but open texture cannot because we cannot predict future borderline cases .He compared open texture to possibility of vagueness. Open texture and vagueness are important in connexion with verifiability (see POSITIVISM) and the law of EXCLUDED MIDDLE. It is not clear that they are, as often thought, confined to empirical predicates.

F. Waismann, 'Verifiability', *Proceedings of the Aristotelian Society*, supplementary vol., 1945, reprinted in his *How I see Philosophy*, Macmillan, 1968, and in G. H. R. Parkinson (ed.), *The Theory of Meaning*, Oxford UP, 1968. (Open texture and verifiability.)

L. J. Cohen, *The Diversity of Meaning*, Methuen, 1962, chapter 9. (Significance of vagueness.)

I. Lakatos (see bibliography to MATHEMATICS). (Open texture of mathematical concepts.)

Operationalism. See POSITIVISM.

Operator. A logical operator is any expression whose function is to affect in a specific way the logical properties (e.g. the entailments) of an expression or expressions to which it is attached, e.g. 'and' operates on two propositions by joining them into a whole, which has entailments neither of them has separately. See also VARIABLE.

Or. See CONJUNCTION.

Order. See TYPES (THEORY OF).

Original position. A device used by Rawls in constructing his theory of justice. Rawls imagines a set of people about to be incarnated into a society, which will be run on political and moral principles which they are now to choose. They are rather idealized figures, supremely rational and intelligent but situated, in this 'original position', behind a *veil of ignorance*. They have general scientific and economic knowledge, but no knowledge of the detailed arrangements in the society except that resources will not be over-plentiful, nor of their own position in it, nor of their own individual interests, abilities, tastes or opinions, or even of their conception of the good. They are motivated solely by their own interests, which

Other minds problem

need not be selfish, and indeed are to take account of the interests of their own immediate descendants, but they ignore the interests of their fellow choosers, with whom they cannot make bargains. Once the basic principles have been chosen, the veil of ignorance is gradually lifted to enable more detailed principles to be reached. Basically justice is then defined in terms of the principles such choosers would unanimously choose. The result, however, is to be checked by comparison with our native intuitions, and the initial result and the intuitions are then to be allowed to modify each other in a process aimed at reaching a REFLECTIVE EQUILIBRIUM by modifying the conditions under which the original position is set up. Problems arise about how far such bloodless and abstract creatures as the choosers could come to any rational choice at all, and how far they can keep their present conceptions of the good when considering different conceptions that they may have later, and indeed how far they are allowed to differ from each other at all – why not just have one chooser, who will naturally be unanimous?

J. Rawls, *A Theory of Justice*, Oxford UP, 1972, esp. section 4 (for original position) and section 24 (for veil of ignorance).

Other minds problem. See SCEPTICISM.

Other-regarding. See SELF-REGARDING.

Ought, obligation, duty. Etymologically a corruption of 'owe it', *ought* suggests a gap which requires to be filled. But the gap may not always exist: to say the kettle ought to be boiling when it clearly is boiling is normally pointless, but 'It ought to be boiling by now' does not imply that is is not; when told that it is boiling we can say 'and so it ought to be'. (But *saying* that it ought may often 'contextually imply' that it is not: see IMPLICATION.) Presumably what requires that the kettle should be boiling is the laws of science, plus statements that the gas is lighted, etc.

A term related to the closing of a gap is obviously well suited for use when guiding action. In 'You ought to take quinine' what requires it is presumably your state of health, the laws of medicine, and your interest in recovering. It is harder to explain the moral 'ought'. There may be laws of morality corresponding to those of medicine, but what corresponds to the agent's interest in recovering, without which taking quinine would be pointless? This makes us ask how morality relates to self-interest. Does it presuppose it? In fact several questions concern 'ought' and motivation. Even if 'Smith ought to *X*' does not imply he already has a motive to *X*, must 'ought' carry a motive with it?, i.e. can he coherently say, 'I

Ought, obligation, duty

acknowledge that I ought to X, but that gives me no motive to X'? Would this count as genuine acknowledgment? And can it be true that one ought to X, if one thinks one ought but remains completely unmoved? Also is it the case that we ought to act from certain motives?

Furthermore, what is requirement, which presumably is a metaphorical notion? If it is said that God does the requiring, so that the requiring is not metaphorical, why should we obey Him? And can we deduce moral conclusions (either general laws or statements about specific cases or kinds of case) from purely non-moral premises? (Cf. NATURALISM.)

We also use 'ought' to express what we ought to do, *all* things considered (see MORAL). How does this so-called 'final ought' relate to the moral 'ought', and in general is there really only one sense of 'ought'? Some think even the moral 'ought' ambiguous, according as it does or does not imply that we *can* do the relevant act, i.e. that the slogan 'Ought implies can' does or does not apply: if we do the more urgent of two competing moral acts, is there a sense in which we still ought to do the other, or ought to *have* done it, even though we could never have done both? Cf. AGGLOMERATION.

A further place for moral conflict can arise between what we ought to do and what we think we ought to do, when these differ. Is there a sense which what we think we ought to do can supersede in these cases what we ought to do, and become what we really ought to do, just because we think this? Or is this really incoherent? How far ought we to follow our conscience, as it is sometimes put? On the moral 'ought' see also IMPERATIVE, MORAL.

Obligations are normally things we incur because of specific circumstances (e.g. a promise, or favours received). The basis of many obligations is a contract, which need be only implicit, if implicit contracts are possible. There may be many reasons why I *ought* to obey the law, but I only have an *obligation* to obey it if I have incurred that obligation, perhaps on some form of the social contract theory (see POLITICAL PHILOSOPHY). Obligations are primarily moral or legal. They are also *to* some moral agent (including corporations, God, etc.). If I buy a dog I no doubt ought to feed it, but any obligation I am under must be to the seller, or perhaps to society.

Being obliged is wider than being under an obligation. What matters now is the lack of alternatives, not the element of incurring. The alternatives excluded may be physically or prudentially rather than morally or legally impossible ('I was obliged, but not under an obligation, to hand over my purse'). Also one need not, though one may, be obliged *to* someone. But one cannot be obliged to do

Ought, obligation, duty

what is not morally at least excusable: a soldier is not *obliged* to flee the battle, however prudent that may be.

Obligatory belongs roughly with 'obligation'. It is not confined to the moral and legal (there can be obligatory moves in a game), but it presupposes rules and does not cover cases of being physically or prudentially obliged.

Duty is primarily connected with roles, whether or not these are voluntarily undertaken. One has duties *as* a secretary, father, son, etc. Duties tend to be of longer standing and less ad hoc than obligations: one *meets* one's obligations as one incurs them, but *does* one's duty or discharges one's duties in the normal course of things.

Duties and obligations are therefore special kinds of things we morally or legally ought to do, though it does not follow that we always ought to perform them, since they may be overridden, whether by other duties, etc., or even by something non-moral: see above on the 'final ought'.

Another question introduces rights. Must there be a correlative right wherever there is a duty or obligation, and vice versa? Do animals have rights, and do we have duties to them?

Since Kant, especially, 'duty' has often been used loosely for whatever we morally ought to do, and 'obligation' is often used with similar looseness. Kant, following others, distinguished *perfect duties*, which were absolute and could never be overridden, from *imperfect duties*, which could be overridden by other duties or even by inclinations (e.g. benevolence: we need not, perhaps could not, give to charity on every possible occasion, but must sometimes). This makes us ask whether the same act can be both dutiful and meritorious, and raises the question of *supererogation*, i.e. whether an act can be meritorious though not one that we ought to do. *Prima facie duties* (Ross) are general duties such as benevolence and promise-keeping, which may be overridden in a given situation. The term has been objected to because it implies that when overridden they cease to be duties at all. Cf. DEFEASIBLE, and the discussion above of competing moral claims.

Finally, could there be religious, as against moral, duties?

F. H. Bradley, *Ethical Studies*, Oxford UP, 1876, essay 5 ('My station and its duties'). (Famous idealist account of basis of moral 'ought'.)

H. N. Castañeda, 'Imperatives, oughts and moral oughts', *Australasian Journal of Philosophy*, 1966. (Meaning of 'ought'. Moral and overriding ('final') 'ought'.)

W. K. Frankena, 'Obligation and motivation in recent moral philosophy', in A. I. Melden (ed.), *Essays in Moral Philosophy*, Washington UP, 1958.

D. P. Gauthier, *Practical Reasoning*, Oxford UP, 1963. (Includes discussion of obligation and duty.)

*R. M. Hare, *The Language of Morals*, Oxford UP, 1952, part 3. (Influential analysis of 'ought' and its relation to imperatives and to 'right' and 'good'.)

H. L. A. Hart, 'Legal and moral obligation', in A. I. Melden (ed.), *Essays in Moral Philosophy*, 1958.

P. Helm (ed.), *Divine Commands and Morality*, Oxford UP, 1981. (Why should we obey God? and related questions.)

D. A. Lloyd Thomas, 'Why should I be moral?', *Philosophy*, 1970.

J. K. Mish'alani, ' "Duty", "obligation" and "ought" ', *Analysis*, vol. 30, 1969.

E. Page, 'On being obliged', *Mind*, 1973. (Senses of 'obliged'.)

P. L. Quinn, *Divine Commands and Moral Commandments*, Clarendon, 1978.

W. D. Ross, *The Right and the Good*, Clarendon, 1930. (See chapter 2 for prima facie duties. Cf. also his later book, *Foundations of Ethics*, Clarendon, 1939 (sometimes called called 'The righter and the better').)

B. A. O. Williams and R. F. Atkinson, 'Consistency in ethics', *Proceedings of the Aristotelian Society*, supplementary vol. 1965. (Conflict of duties.)

Ousia. See SUBSTANCE.

P

Paradigm. A paradigm for a concept is an ideal instance of it which can be used for assessing other instances. Plato seems sometimes to have thought of his Forms (see IDEA, UNIVERSALS) as paradigms in this sense.

Recently, however, T. S. Kuhn has introduced 'paradigm' in a technical sense, or senses, into philosophy of science. Here a paradigm is basically a way of looking at things, a shared assumption which governs the outlook of an epoch and its approach to scientific problems; or an accepted theory, e.g. Ptolemaic or Copernican astronomy. These have remained the most important of the Kuhnian senses, though in his later work *disciplinary matrix* is used for approximately these senses, and paradigms become standard forms of solutions to problems (e.g. they become equations, formulae, etc.). These solutions are then used for solving further problems, and so govern the forms these further solutions take. Kuhn is largely concerned with how shifts of paradigms occur as science develops.

T. S. Kuhn, *The Structure of Scientific Revolutions*, Chicago UP, 1962, 2nd edn with postscript, 1970.

M. Masterman, 'The nature of a paradigm', in I. Lakatos and A. Musgrave (eds), *Criticism and the Growth of Knowledge*, Cambridge UP, 1970. (Extracts twenty-one senses of 'paradigm' from Kuhn and discusses, reducing to three groups. Cf. Kuhn's reply (ibid, § 6, and 'postscript' (above). For further discussions see bibliography to SCIENCE.)

Paraconsistency. The view that there are important logical theories that do not allow (as classical logic does) that a contradiction

Paradigm case argument

has every proposition among its logical consequences. A system containing contradictory propositions is inconsistent, but if it does not contain every proposition, it avoids being trivial. It is claimed that various scientific and mathematical theories are in fact of this nature, and so can be logically analysed by paraconsistent logics, and also defended as they stand, in that we need not assume that the inconsistencies in them are merely aberrations that must be removed before they can be properly studied. See also DIALETHEISM.

G. Priest, R. Routley and J. Norman (eds), *Paraconsistent Logic: Essays on the Inconsistent*, Philosophia Verlag, Munich, 1989.

Paradigm case argument. A type of argument claiming that certain things must exist or be real because certain expressions have a standard correct use in our language. It is claimed that there must be such a thing as freewill because there are standard situations, paradigm cases, where it is generally agreed to be correct to say, 'He did it of his own freewill'. Without such situations, it is argued, the word 'freewill' would have no meaning. An example seeming to support this is that only because red things exist or have existed can 'red' have the meaning it has. The argument is that certain things must exist because certain expressions have a meaning and therefore a correct use.

The argument has been attacked on various grounds. Even for 'red' to mean what it does, perhaps there need only *seem* to be red things. This assumes that there could seem to be red things though there were in fact none. If a certain expression is to have meaning, does this imply that something exists, or only that it could exist, or neither? And are there relevant differences between terms like 'red' and 'freewill'? Also how much can the argument show? Even if 'freewill' means what it does because situations exist where we are not subject to external constraint, hypnotism, etc., does this show that we have freewill in a philosophically interesting sense?

Appeal to the paradigm case argument is closely associated with linguistic PHILOSOPHY. See also TRANSCENDENTAL ARGUMENTS.

P. Edwards, 'Bertrand Russell's doubts about induction', *Mind*, 1949. (Applies the argument to legitimize induction, as does P. F. Strawson, *Introduction to Logical Theory*, Methuen, 1952, chapter 9).

O. Hanfling, 'What is wrong with the paradigm case argument?', *Proceedings of the Aristotelian Society*, 1990–91. (Defends the argument.)

J. Passmore, *Philosophical Reasoning*, Duckworth, 1961, chapter 6. (Critical of this and related argument.)

R. J. Richman, 'On the argument of the paradigm case', *Australa-*

Paradox

sian Journal of Philosophy, 1961. (Attacks argument. Cf. discussions by C. J. F. Williams (ibid.) and Richman (ibid., 1962.)

J. W. N. Watkins, 'Farewell to the paradigm case argument', *Analysis*, vol. 18, 1957–8. (Cf. discussions in same volume.)

Paradox. Etymologically, 'against belief'. Full-blooded paradoxes which affect the basis of logic exist when some statement needed for logic can apparently be both proved and disproved. Among them, paradoxes depending on purely logical or mathematical terms are called *logical paradoxes*, or *paradoxes of set theory* (e.g. RUSSELL'S PARADOX) while paradoxes depending on notions like meaning, designation, etc., are called *semantic paradoxes* (e.g. LIAR PARADOX); these are sometimes distinguished from the logical ones. In *pragmatic paradoxes* there is a contradiction not in what is said but in what is done in saying it. 'It's raining, but I don't believe it is' is not contradictory for both parts could be true. But uttering the second part frustrates the normal intention of uttering the first. *Strategic paradoxes* offer problems for how it is rational to act, claiming that each of two inconsistent policies can be defended as preferable to the other (NEWCOMB'S PARADOX, PRISONER'S DILEMMA). Other paradoxes claim e.g. that apparently indispensable notions are inconsistent (e.g. ZENO'S PARADOXES), or that apparently possible situations are impossible (e.g. PREDICTION PARADOX). Loosely speaking a paradox may be little more than something odd or unexpected (e.g. material and strict IMPLICATION paradoxes). But how significant a given paradox is is often disputed. See also theory of TYPES.

T. Baldwin, *G. E. Moore*, Routledge, 1990. (See pp. 226–32 for discussion of 'Moore's paradox', a pragmatic paradox.)

A. Pap, *Semantics and Necessary Truth*, Yale UP, 1958, chapter 9C (Types of paradox, especially pragmatic.)

*R. M. Sainsbury, *Paradoxes*, Cambridge UP, 1988 (revised 1995). (General introduction.)

Parenthetical verb. See BELIEF.

Parmenides. See ELEATICS.

Particularism. The view that only particulars (see UNIVERSALS) exist, and more specifically that the properties and relations of particulars are themselves particulars, not universals (see TROPES).

Particularism resembles NOMINALISM, but a particularist might accept abstract particulars like numbers, seen as abstract objects. They would be particulars rather than universals because they do not have instances (there are instances or twoness, but not of the number two). Nominalists, however, would normally reject numbers seen as abstract objects.

For *moral particularism*, see ETHICS.

Particulars. See UNIVERSE, INDIVIDUALS.

Pascal's wager. If God and an afterlife exist we could face *infinite* suffering in Hell. Therefore it must be rational to act as though they do exist, however low the probability (above zero), since the resulting sacrifice of pleasure is only finite.

P. T. Landsberg, 'Gambling on God', *Mind*, 1971.

Peirce, Charles S. 1839–1914. Born in Cambridge, Mass.; he worked as an astronomer, government physicist, and university teacher in America. He is especially famous as the first main PRAGMATIST, but he also developed an elaborate system of logic. This contributed to modern mathematical logic in many ways, notably by his development of a logic of relations, including the distinction between monadic, dyadic and polyadic relations (see MONAD). He also developed a metaphysics based on three categories which he called firstness, secondness and thirdness. Peirce published no books in his lifetime, but apart from his *Collected Papers*, 8 vols, 1931–58, some selections exist: *Chance, Love and Logic*, 1923. *The Philosophy of Peirce*, 1940. See also UNIVERSALS, SYNECHISM.

Perception. The faculty of apprehending the world specifically through the senses, or the general exercise of it, or particular cases of its exercise. Perception raises problems which form an important branch of epistemology.

The analysis of perceiving is complicated by the variety of its objects (cf. SEEING). How is perceiving the redness of Smith's face related to perceiving that his face is red, that he is angry, that he is subconsciously afraid? And can one perceive an object without perceiving facts about it?

Usually 'perceive' is a 'success' or 'achievement' word (cf. EPISTEMOLOGY on 'factive'), i.e. we can only perceive what is there or is true. But this may not always hold, if we allow that Macbeth perceived a dagger, and it does not apply to 'perceive as' (cf. SEEING). We can misperceive, i.e. make mistakes about what we perceive.

Perception is thus a complex notion, and two main and connected problems concern its relations to sensory experience, and to intellectual notions like belief, judgment, inference.

Sense-perception obviously involves the senses, but exactly how?

Perception

Very often we perceive things otherwise than as they are, sometimes knowingly and sometimes not. The penny seen from one side looks elliptical, the candle seen out of focus looks double, the whistle seems to change pitch as the train passes. All this has suggested, by the *argument from illusion*, that what we 'directly' or 'immediately' perceive or are aware of (often called SENSE DATA, etc.) sometimes or always differs from what is 'out there' in the world: we perceive objects by interpreting or inferring from these sense data. More radically, the fact that we sometimes seem to perceive when we are not strictly perceiving at all, as when we dream or hallucinate, suggests SCEPTICISM about how we can know that an external world exists at all. The former position may be reinforced because we know scientifically how the physical and physiological processes involved inevitably affect the information we get through our senses. (But if the presence of such processes means that we *never* perceive objects, even when the processes are not distorted, what is it that we never do? What would it be to 'really perceive' an object?)

If we do attempt to start from a basis limited to 'pure experience', it is difficult, as empiricists from Locke and Hume onwards have found, to get beyond it. The sense data, etc. supposed to serve as a bridge between us and the world end up as a drawbridge that keeps us from the world. This attempt has been attacked in two ways. Firstly, the arguments for it are suspect, and seem self-defeating. We can only contrast appearance with reality if we already have independent knowledge of reality, and the fact that we may be deceived on any occasion does not imply that we may, or even could, be deceived on every occasion. Secondly, it seems impossible to isolate and describe any 'pure experience' (the GIVEN). Not only does all describing involve language, and so memory, but experience is ineradicably affected by context and knowledge. The retinal image has two dimensions, but we see the world as having three, even with one eye closed. The penny looks round, as much as it looks elliptical (has 'looks' two senses here?), and continues to look so while being turned or moved (*object constancy*. We select part of what we see as foreground, seen against a background (the *figure/ground* theory emphasized by *Gestalt psychologists*), and there is the duck/rabbit phenomenon (see SEEING). As artists know, *perceptual reduction*, abstracting a basic 'pure experience' from our perceptions, is difficult or impossible.

Yet the facts remain that perception involves the senses, that perceptions are normally the basis for beliefs, and that illusions do occur. Any theory of perception should answer questions like these: Is there direct or immediate awareness or pure experience, and if so, has it special objects? If it has, how are these related to physical objects or parts of them, including their surfaces? Do words like 'looks', 'seems', 'appears', always imply doubt, or are they ambiguous between a sense that does and a sense that does not? Is perception something unitary, or has it two parts, a sensory part involving this 'direct' awareness and some process of interpretation or judgment based on this? If two parts, are they successive or simultaneous? Does a single account hold for different modes of perception such as seeing, hearing, etc.? Do we in fact perceive physical objects at all? Or do we only infer their existence? Or do we treat them as LOGICAL CONSTRUCTIONS (cf. PHENOMENALISM)? If we do perceive physical objects (and shadows, etc.), under what conditions do we do so? Must we know we are doing so? Must we notice or pick out the object? Are there really such things as unconscious and subliminal perception? What features of an object can we perceive? Its colour? Shape? Nature? Behaviour? Causal properties? Beauty? Suitability for this or that? Does the object play a causal role, and if so, what does it cause, our having an experience or our perceiving the object? And does this role enter the analysis of what we *mean* by saying we perceive the object, so that to say we perceive something is to say, among other things, that it causes us to do something? Or is it merely that our perceptions of it, or our accompanying experiences, are always in fact caused partly by it? And why does it matter by what route the causal chain operates (cf. MEMORY on deviant causal chains)?

Views giving causation a role in one of these ways are among *causal theories of perception*. *Representative (representational) theories* say either that what we perceive is not the object but something else (sense data, etc.) representing it, or that we do perceive the object but only by being directly aware (etc.) of such representatives which may or may not he *parts* of the object. Causal and representative theories often go together. *Realist theories* say that whatever it is that is perceived exists independently of being perceived. *Naïve realism* is properly the view, attributed to the 'plain man', that we not only perceive ordinary objects but normally perceive them as they are, by a direct relation without sense data, interpretations, etc., and with 'as they are' raising no problems. There is a paradox in attributing any philosophical view to the 'plain' non-philosophical man, and in practice 'naïve realism' often starts by meaning whatever the plain man would say without reflection (i.e. discounting illusions, etc.), and ends, as the argument develops, by meaning simply realism.

Perceptual usually applies to things as they appear to the perceiver. Thus *perceptual consciousness* is the total conscious experience of the perceiver qua perceiver. *Perceptual objects* are whatever it is one perceives, be it sense data, physical objects, or whatever,

Perception

considered as having just those characteristics they are perceived as having. These are *perceptual characteristics* (what these are may be unclear, as in the penny case above). *Perceptible characteristics*, however, are those accessible to perception (e.g. colour but not magnetism). The *perceptual field* is the total of a person's perceptual objects at a given moment, not necessarily distinguished as separate objects. *Perceived object* refers usually to the physical or public object (or shadow, etc.) perceived, considered as having the characteristics it really has. *Percept* is similar to 'perceptual object'. It sometimes refers to sense data, but sometimes to the contents of perceptual consciousness for those *not* holding a sense datum theory (Firth). See also SENSES, SENSATION, SENSE DATA, SEEING, FEELING, PHENOMENALISM.

T. Crane (ed.), *The Contents of Experience*, Cambridge UP, 1992. (Essays, mainly specially written.)

J. Dancy (ed.) *Perceptual Knowledge*, Oxford UP, 1988. (Reprinted essays, more recent than Swartz.)

R. Firth, 'Sense-data and the percept theory', *Mind*, 1949–50, reprinted with important addendum (p. 270) in Swartz. (Develops and discusses 'percept theory' as against sense datum theory, and discusses perceptual reduction).

E. H. Gombrich, *Art and Illusion*, Phaidon, 1960. (Argues against isolatability of experience in perception, from point of view of art and with plentiful illustrations.)

J. Heil, *Perception and Cognition*, California UP, 1983. (Perception involves acquiring belief in a certain way, but belief need not involve language and cannot be analysed in terms of internal representations (see also COGNITIVE PSYCHOLOGY).)

*R. J. Hirst, *The Problems of Perception*, Allen and Unwin/Humanities Press, 1959. (Introduction, advocating one view.)

F. Jackson, *Perception*, Cambridge UP, 1977. H. Robinson, *Perception*, Routledge, 1994. (Two defences of sense data theories).

M. Martin, 'Sight and touch', in Crane. (Brings out differences between these).

D. Owens, *Causes and Coincidences*, Cambridge UP, 1992. (See pp. 143–58 for defence of a causal theory.)

C. Peacocke, *Sense and Content*, Oxford UP, 1983, chapters 1 and 2. (Rehabilitates sensation as having a role in question about perception, distinguishing sensational and representational properties of experiences.)

*P. Smith and O. R. Jones, *The Philosophy of Mind: an Introduction*, Cambridge UP, 1986. (Chapter 7 attacks view that perception involves inner objects. Chapter 8 defends view that perception is

Person

acquisition of beliefs for which see Heil (above) and Armstrong in Dancy.)

P. Snowdon, 'How to interpret "direct perception" ', in Crane. (Defends version of direct realism, taking sense data and argument from illusion seriously, though without accepting them.)

R. J. Swartz (ed.), *Perceiving, Sensing and Knowing*, 1965. (Reprinted essays with bibliography.)

J. J. Valberg, 'The puzzle of experience', in Crane. (see esp. pp. 18–32 for statement of argument from illusion. Cf. also his book *The Puzzle of Experience*, Oxford UP, 1992, from which this extract is reprinted.)

Perdurance. An ordinary object, like a table, is usually thought to be made up of spatial parts, and if it endures for say a week, it and each of its parts are said to be present on each day. But philosophers sometimes think of such objects as made up of temporal parts, say a Monday part, a Tuesday part, and so on. In that case, the object is never present as a whole and its Monday part is present only on Mondays, and so on. The object is then said to *perdure*. An object which either endures or perdures can be said to *persist*.

D. K. Lewis, *On the Plurality of Worlds*, Blackwell, 1986, p. 202.

Perfection (principle of). See SUFFICIENT REASON.

Performatives. See SPEECH ACTS.

Peripheric. See JAMES–LANGE THEORY.

Perlocutions. See SPEECH ACTS.

Person. Certain modern writers use 'person' in a technical way to stand for a type of entity different from material objects and disembodied spirits. P. F. Strawson insists that persons are not reducible to these other things. He distinguishes *M-predicates*, applying to both material bodies and persons (e.g. weighing ten stone), from *P-predicates*, applying only to persons (e.g. thinking, going for a walk). Others have made a similar distinction. Some P-predicates, however, may apply to persons only because they have bodies (e.g. going for a walk). See also IDENTITY, philosophy of MIND.

T. Forrest, 'P-predicates', in A. Stroll (ed.), *Epistemology*, Harper and Row, 1967.

B. Smart, 'How can persons be ascribed M-predicates?', *Mind*, 1977.

P. F. Strawson, *Individuals*, Methuen, 1959, chapter 3.

Personalism

Personalism. Any of a wide variety of views emphasizing the primacy, in the universe, of persons (non-technical sense), whether human or divine.

P. A. Bertocci, 'The perspective of a teleological personalistic idealist', in John E. Smith (ed.), *Contemporary American Philosophy*, 2nd series, Allen and Unwin, 1970.

R. T. Flewelling, 'Personalism', in D. D. Runes (ed.), *Twentieth-Century Philosophy*, 1943. (General survey.)

Perspectivism. The theory that there can be radically different and incommensurable conceptual schemes or perspectives, one of which we must, consciously or unconsciously, adopt, but none of which is more correct than its rivals; see RELATIVISM.

Perspectivism was named by J. Ortega y Gasset (1883–1955) and versions of it have been held by Nietzsche, E. Sapir (1884–1939), B. L. Whorf (1897–1941) and T. S. Kuhn (1922–).

Phase terms, phrase universals. See IDENTITY.

Phenomena. See NOUMENON, PHENOMENOLOGY.

Phenomenalism. Literally, a theory based on appearances. Earlier phenomenalists analysed physical objects in terms of actual and possible sensations (Mill treated matter as a permanent possibility of sensation). More recently phenomenalism has taken a linguistic form. Its main claim has been that sentences about physical objects can be analysed without residue into sentences about SENSE DATA, which Moore and Russell distinguish from SENSATIONS. Its point, in both versions, is that we can only know appearances, but need not postulate unknowable objects lurking behind them, because belief or talk about such objects is really only a disguised form of belief or talk about the appearances themselves. The phenomenalist goal of providing detailed translations of statements about physical objects, vigorously pursued until just after the Second World War, is now widely regarded as unattainable, even in principle.

Like subjective IDEALISM, from which perhaps it developed, phenomenalism makes appearances central. Subjective idealism says physical objects are unreal. Phenomenalism says they are real, but are not what they seem – they are appearances, actual or possible. BERKELEY is hard to classify. Though usually called a subjective idealist, he held that physical objects were real but were ideas and not *material* objects. See also PERCEPTION, PHILOSOPHY.

Primarily phenomenalism is a doctrine about physical objects.

Phenomenology

More broadly, any view can be called phenomenalist which uses LOGICAL CONSTRUCTIONS.

A. J. Ayer, *Foundations of Empirical Knowledge*, Macmillan, 1940. (Defence of modern phenomenalism. Cf. his later view in 'Phenomenalism', *Proceedings of the Aristotelian Society*, 1946–7, reprinted in his *Philosophical Essays*, 1954.)

A. C. Grayling, *Berkeley: the Central Arguments*, Duckworth, 1986. (Generally sympathetic introduction to Berkeley).

*J. Hospers, *Introduction to Philosophical Analysis*, RKP, 1956, chapter 8. (Discusses phenomenalism in relation to other theories.)

R. Le Poidevin, 'Fables and models', *Proceedings of the Aristotelian Society*, supplementary vol., 1991. (See p. 73 for a way of distinguishing phenomenalism from idealism.)

J. S. Mill, *An Examination of Sir William Hamilton's Philosophy*, 1865, chapter 11, appendix to chapter 12. (Early version of phenomenalism.)

Phenomenology. Literally, the description or study of appearances. Any description of how things appear, especially if sustained and penetrating, can be called a phenomenology. The close attention given by linguistic PHILOSOPHY to the actual workings of language is sometimes called *linguistic phenomenology*. But more specifically 'phenomenology' refers to a movement starting with Brentano and associated especially with Husserl. This at first emphasized the description of human experience as directed onto objects, in the sense in which thoughts or wishes have objects, even if unreal ones ('intentional objects'; see INTENSIONALITY). In Husserl the emphasis shifted away from the mere description of experience towards a description of the objects of experience, which he called phenomena. Phenomena were things which appear. He saw them in fact as essences which the mind intuited, and the task of phenomenology was to describe them. This, however, was not an empirical task, but an a priori one. It resembled in fact what was later called conceptual analysis (see PHILOSOPHY), though it insisted that the essences were real things, not, for example, ways in which words were used. (We can still think of unreal things like unicorns; the essence of unicorn is real on this view). Phenomenology also led on to the study of being, associated with EXISTENTIALISM. Husserl thought that studying essences as they were intuited involved laying aside various preconceptions derived from science; this laying aside was called *reduction, epoche*, or *bracketing* the world.

D. Bell, *Husserl*, Routledge, 1990. (General discussion of his philosophy.)

Philosophy and analysis

E. Husserl, *Cartesian Meditations*, 1931 (French), 1950 (German), Nijhoff, 1960 (English). Cf. also his *The Idea of Phenomenology*, 1907, Nijhoff, trans. 1964, and *The Paris Lectures*, 1929, trans. 1964.

G. Ryle, *Collected Papers*, vol. 1, Hutchinson, 1971. (Includes several relevant items. Chapter 10 brings out some connexions with conceptual analysis, and chapter 12 some with existentialism.)

H. Spiegelberg, *The Phenomenological Movement*, Nijhoff, 1960. (Extended history, ending with philosophical summary.)

M. Warnock, *Existentialism*, Oxford UP, 1970. (Includes chapter on Husserl.)

Philosophy and analysis. An embarrassment for professional philosophers is that they cannot produce any succinct, or even agreed, definition of their profession. 'What is philosophy?' is itself a philosophical question.

Literally meaning 'love of wisdom', 'philosophy' came to stand for knowledge in general about man and the universe. The Stoics and Epicureans (c. 300 BC) divided knowledge into logic (including also what is now called epistemology), physics (including all that we now call science), and ethics (including also what we now call philosophy of mind and psychology). *Natural philosophy*, dealing with the world of nature, and *moral philosophy*, dealing with humanity, were the descendents of physics and ethics, respectively, in these senses. 'Natural philosophy' is now, when used at all, limited to physics while 'moral philosophy' is normally limited to ETHICS. Metaphysics, which the Stoics and Epicureans had largely assimilated into physics, became assimilated to natural theology, and became the centre of philosophy, after Aquinas had separated natural from revealed or dogmatic theology.

Only in the last century or two have the sciences become so specialized that philosophy appears as simply one discipline among others. There are two main ways of distinguishing it, by its subject-matter or its methods. Many have held that its subject is in some way 'ultimate things', either about the universe as a whole or about matters affecting human fate and conduct in the most basic way. Now, however, philosophy is more commonly distinguished by certain methods, its subject being whatever is most suitably studied by them. In particular, philosophy avoids using the senses and relies on reflection. It is an a priori study. In developing from its older to its modern form it has shed the sciences one by one as they became amenable to systematic empirical study rather than armchair speculation – first physics and chemistry, and then the human sciences (economics, psychology, sociology). But philosophy also lacks any

Philosophy and analysis

definite and systematic procedures for proving results. Mathematics has therefore always lain rather outside philosophy, and mathematical LOGIC, though needed more than ever as a tool by philosophy, is itself now becoming a separate subject, allied to mathematics.

All this circumscribes the subject-matter of philosophy. Science tells us what particular things the world contains, but philosophy asks about the different ways in which we can classify *whatever* the world, or any world, contains (cf. CATEGORIES, METAPHYSICS). Science gives us knowledge, but philosophy asks what we *can* know, and how (EPISTEMOLOGY).

One role, then, of philosophy is to look behind or after (*meta-*) the sciences and analyse the concepts (notions, ideas) and methods they use. A given science X, often has an associated 'philosophy of X' (or 'meta-X') which fulfils this role. METAPHYSICS, where 'physics' means the study of nature in general, is the most general of these studies, though questions of scientific *method* now fall under a separate study, philosophy of SCIENCE.

Analysis, in some sense, is always therefore an important part of philosophy. Under the influence of POSITIVISM and allied trends, much twentieth-century English-speaking philosophy (to which the rest of this entry is confined; for other kinds cf. EXISTENTIALISM, PHENOMENOLOGY, IDEALISM) has assumed that substantive results in subjects like ethics, politics and aesthetics could not be reached by rational argument. These subjects were matters of attitude and persuasion. Philosophy, it was often thought, should simply analyse concepts (*conceptual analysis*). It should become *analytical philosophy*, using *philosophical analysis*.

Analysis, however, is ambiguous. It can mean simply the explication of concepts like *substance, cause, good, material object*, asking, for example, what things count as material objects and what they all have in common. In this ordinary sense all philosophy involves analysis. There are, however, various kinds of analysis. One kind claims that what is being analysed is 'really' something else at a deeper level, which replaces it (cf. PHENOMENALISM and LOGICAL CONSTRUCTIONS); the original thing may or may not somehow survive the analysis rather than being eliminated (cf. REDUCTIONISM). Another kind, sometimes called *logical analysis* claims simply to show the correct logical form of ordinary sentences (cf. theory of DESCRIPTIONS), making no metaphysical claims about what really exists, etc. But even this is in fact reductive, since it condemns some ways of speaking and replaces them.

After the Second World War a reaction against the restrictions of logical positivism, and the failure of phenomenalism, suggested that any consistent outlook or set of concepts (e.g. in ethics or religion) was prima facie as good as any other, and that philosophy

Philosophy and analysis

should analyse what is involved in everyday ways of speaking and thinking, without trying to judge between them. This emphasizes ways of speaking, but it is no longer reductive. It does not condemn some ways of speaking as fundamentally unjustified and seek to replace them. It is called *linguistic* or *ordinary language philosophy*, using *linguistic analysis*, and was often condemned as evading the real problems; though ordinary language philosophy need not, as its enemy Russell thought, be done *in* ordinary language, i.e. without technical terms. Philosophy of LANGUAGE is different from linguistic philosophy, being a subject, not an outlook.

The term *analytical philosophy* sometimes carries the implication that philosophy should confine itself to conceptual analysis and not claim to answer any substantive questions. In this sense it has come under attack in recent decades, especially since some philosophers, like Quine, would say that, since no clear account can be given of 'ANALYTIC', we cannot coherently seek the analytic truths about concepts that conceptual analysis demands. But there is a wider sense of 'analytical philosophy' in which it denotes the attempt to tackle philosophical problems piecemeal by analyzing the problems themselves into manageable parts rather than trying to construct grand overall systems from which solutions to these problems emerge. In this second sense analytical philosophy is still the dominant outlook in English-language philosophy (despite a growing tolerance of large systems: see METAPHYSICS), and indeed is growing on the European continent in various countries on both sides of the old Iron Curtain.

Nevertheless analytical philosophical is now bolder in making substantive claims, and is much less isolationist. But it still, like linguistic philosophy, feels discomfort, if no more, at outraging common sense. It relies heavily on the techniques of formal logic, but is more sensitive to its debt to the empirical sciences, e.g. physics and cognitive science (see COGNITIVE PSYCHOLOGY). This has blurred the edges between philosophy and science, though the philosopher must still have an eye for the difference between questions for reflection and questions for observation; observation may stimulate, but can never solve, philosophical problems. Partly for this reason and partly because of its own internal development, involving constant refinement and sophistication, philosophy has become much more technical than it used to be at the mid-century; philosophy of mind and philosophy of language have been particularly influenced in this respect and are both growth areas.

Since the late 1960s much of philosophy has been under the influence of a debate between REALISM and antirealism. The influence of Wittgenstein has been particularly strong on antirealist thinking. There has been a revival of interest in essentialism and innate ideas (the latter largely under the influence of Chomsky), while at the same time Berkeley's idealism has been taken more seriously than it used to be. The influence of language is still great, but not overriding.

See also AESTHETICS, EPISTEMOLOGY, ETHICS, LOGIC, METAPHYSICS, POLITICAL PHILOSOPHY, PROCESS PHILOSOPHY, SOCIAL PHILOSOPHY, Philosophies of EDUCATION, HISTORY, LANGUAGE, LAW, MATHEMATICS, MIND, RELIGION, SCIENCE.

*M. Hollis, *Invitation to Philosophy*, Blackwell, 1985. (Brief elementary introduction.)

T. Honderich and M. F. Burnyeat (eds), *Philosophy As It Is*, Penguin, 1979. (Reprints of notable articles, with introduction to each by editors. Cf. also T. Honderich (ed.), *Philosophy Through Its Past*, Pelican, 1984, modern articles on earlier thinkers.)

*T. Nagel, *What Does It All Mean?*, Oxford UP, 1987. (Brief elementary introduction.)

*A. O'Hear, *What Philosophy Is*, Pelican, 1985. (Brief elementary introduction.)

J. A. Passmore, *100 Years of Philosophy*, Duckworth, 1957, revised and expanded, 1966. (Full, documented and readable. Tends to conflate important and unimportant.)

Philosophical Review, 1992. (The January issue is devoted to four survey articles, with many references, covering developments in various fields in philosophy from 1950 to 1990. See pp. 195–209 for discussion of relations between philosophy and its own history.)

R. Rorty (ed.), *The Linguistic Turn*, Chicago UP, 1967. (Essays on relations between language and philosophy in mid-twentieth century, with long introduction and full bibliography.)

R. Rorty, J. B. Schneewind and Q. Skinner (eds), *Philosophy in History*, Cambridge UP, 1984. (Specially written essays covering both theoretical questions and specific examples.)

*B. Russell, *The Problems of Philosophy*, Home University Library, 1912. (Dated in detail but still standard as introduction.)

B. Russell, *My Philosophical Development*, Allen and Unwin, 1959. (Final chapter attacks linguistic philosophy.)

G. Ryle (ed.), *The Revolution in Philosophy*, Macmillan, 1956. (Philosophy as it saw itself about 1950.)

*R. Scruton, *Modern Philosophy: An Introduction and Survey*, Sinclair-Stevenson, London, 1994.

*N. Warburton, *Philosophy: The Basis*, Routledge, 1992.

Phrastic and neustic. Sentences like 'The door is shut', 'Shut the door!', 'Is the door shut?' seem to have something in common as

Physicalism

well as differences. R. M. Hare called what they had in common the *phrastic* (roughly, what is said, or the content) and what was peculiar to each of them the *neustic* (from the Greek for assenting or subscribing). The phrastic might be represented as 'The door being shut' and the respective neustics as 'Yes', 'Please', 'Query'. Thus the first sentence would be analysed as, 'The door being shut: yes.' Later Hare distinguished also the *tropic*, or sign of mood (from the Greek for 'mood'), from the neustic, which he kept for assent or subscription. See also SENTENCES, SPEECH ACTS.

R. M. Hare, *The Language of Morals*, Oxford UP, 1952. (See index. Original distinction. For tropics see his 'Meaning and speech acts'. *Philosophical Review*, 1970, pp. 19ff., reprinted with appendix in R. M. Hare, *Practical Inferences*, Macmillan, 1971, pp. 89 ff.)

Physicalism. See POSITIVISM.

Physico-theological argument. See DESIGN.

Plato. 427–348/7 BC. Earliest European philosopher of whom substantial works survive. Pupil of SOCRATES, founder of Academy (probably c.385 BC), teacher of ARISTOTLE. Lived mostly in Athens, with occasional visits to Sicily where he tried unsuccessfully to put into practice the ideal state of his dialogue *Republic*. Contributed to all the main branches of philosophy, notably with his theory of 'FORMS' or 'IDEAS'. Wrote some thirty-four dialogues, which all survive. See also ALBERT, BEING (bibliography), DIALECTIC, EDUCATION (bibliography), EMPIRICISM, IDEALISM, LANGUAGE (PHILOSOPHY OF), MEANING, METAPHYSICS, NEOPLATONISTS, PLEASURE (bibliography), POLITICAL (bibliography), PYTHAGORAS, SCEPTICISM, SOPHISTS, SUBSTANCE (bibliography), THIRD MAN ARGUMENT, UNIVERSALS.

Platonism. See UNIVERSALS, MATHEMATICS.

Pleasure. An agreeable quality of experiences or the experiences themselves. An ambiguity exists between 'pleasure' in general and 'pleasure' in the sense of a pleasant activity or experience, a source of pleasure in the first sense. 'Pleasure' can also mean something like 'will' as in 'at the king's pleasure'.

Philosopher's discuss primarily the first sense, and start by asking what pleasure is. It has often, especially in connexion with HEDONISM, been regarded simply as 'agreeable feeling'. But competing accounts have been offered, especially recently. Pleasure has been thought to be a process, or a kind of activity, or to be essentially connected with attention or desire. *Adverbial theories* make pleasure a modification of activity, so that 'experiencing pleasure' means something like 'living pleasurably'. The relations between pleasure and enjoyment, liking, pain, etc., are also topics for discussion. Special problems concern asceticism and masochism: Does anything count as disliking or failing to like pleasure, or as liking or failing to dislike pain?

Discussions of hedonism have raised the question whether pleasure can be measured. Can pleasures, or amounts of pleasure, whether of the same or different people, be compared and added together, or arranged in order of magnitude, as some versions of UTILITARIANISM demand? What would it be that was being measured? Are there any bad pleasures? Can pleasure itself be bad, or only its source? *Qualitative hedonism*, a form of ethical HEDONISM, says pleasures differ in quality as well as quantity, and some are better than others. How pleasure relates to happiness is also important for hedonism and utilitarianism.

A particular set of problems concern pleasure and belief, and the notion of being pleased that.... How is pleasure related to what one is pleased at, by, etc., especially when the object is illusory? How are the object and the cause of a pleasure related? And can pleasures themselves ever be false, as against merely resting on false beliefs? Can one be mistaken about whether one is pleased, etc.? See also UTILITARIANISM.

J. Annas, 'Aristotle on pleasure and goodness', in A. O. Rorty (ed.), *Essays on Aristotle's Ethics*, California UP, 1980, esp. pp. 292–8. (Are pleasures commensurable? Are they subjective?)

Aristotle, *Nichomachean Ethics*, book 7, chapters 11–14, book 10, chapters 1–5. (Aristotle's two discussions of pleasure. The relations between them are disputed.)

J. Dybikowski, 'False pleasure and the *Philebus*', *Phronesis*, 1970. (False pleasure and Plato. Fairly difficult, with occasional Greek, but refers to other literature.)

R. B. Edwards, *Pleasure and Pain*, Cornell UP, 1979. (Defence of qualitative hedonism.)

J. C. B. Gosling, *Pleasure and Desire*, Oxford UP, 1969. (Discusses hedonism in light of modern treatments of pleasure.)

J. C. Hall, 'Quantity of pleasure', *Proceedings of the Aristotelian Society*, 1966–7. (Can pleasure be measured?)

D. A. Lloyd Thomas, 'Happiness', *Philosophical Quarterly*, 1968.

M. A. McCloskey, 'Pleasure', *Mind*, 1971. (Asymmetries between pleasure and pain.)

J. S. Mill, *Utilitarianism*, 1861, chapter 2. (Qualitative hedonism.

Plenitude (principle of)

See J. Plamenatz, *The English Utilitarians*, 1949, p. 137; this volume includes Mill.)

D. L. Perry, *The Concept of Pleasure*, Mouton, 1967. (General discussion of what pleasure is, and how it relates to neighbouring concepts and expressions.)

Plato, *Philebus*, esp. §§ 31–55. (Extended discussion, including on whether there are false pleasures.)

Plenitude (principle of). Principle that the universe, to be as perfect as possible, must be as full as possible: must contain the greatest possible diversity of kinds in the greatest possible profusion compatible with the laws of nature. Cf. the idea that existence is a perfection (cf. ONTOLOGICAL ARGUMENT). An alternative version is that nothing can remain a real but unactualized possibility throughout eternity.

Aristotle and Hobbes (see bibliography to MODALITIES).

J. Hintikka, *Time and Necessity*, Oxford UP, 1973, chapter 5. (Discusses principle in Aristotle, criticizing Lovejoy. Cf. review in *Journal of Hellenic Studies*, 1977, pp. 183–6. Cf. also under SUBSTANCE (bibliography), R. S. Woolhouse, p. 196 for brief discussion of some later views.)

A. O. Lovejoy, *The Great Chain of Being*, 1936.

Plotinus. See NEOPLATONISTS.

Poisson's theorem. See NUMBERS (LAW OF LARGE).

Polar concepts. Concepts which allegedly only have application if their opposites have application, e.g. *good* and *evil*, if it is true that there could be nothing good in the universe unless there were something evil for it to contrast with, and vice versa.

C. K. Grant, 'Polar concepts and metaphysical arguments', *Proceedings of the Aristotelian Society*, 1955–6. (Cf. also Heraclitus, fragments B23, 111 (in the standard Diels–Kranz numbering).)

Polish notation. Notation for propositional CALCULUS dispensing with special symbols. 'p', 'q', etc., stand for propositions. 'A' means 'or'. 'C' means 'materially IMPLIES'. 'E' means 'is materially equivalent to'. 'K' means 'and'. 'N' means 'not'. Constants precede the VARIABLES they govern. Punctuating is done entirely by ordering symbols (supplemented all too rarely by spacing). E.g. 'Apq' means 'p or q'; 'NApKqr' means 'neither p nor both q and r'. Convenient for typesetters but not for readers, beyond very short expressions.

Political philosophy

Political philosophy. Political philosophy studies both substantive questions and concepts used in them, the former having returned to favour recently, as in ETHICS. The basic concern is with authority and sovereignty in groups of people not subject to further authority (sovereign states), and with associated organizational questions.

The notions of authority and obedience lead to two groups of questions. The first concerns the nature and purpose of the state, its ultimate justification or dispensability, and the relations between it and its citizens. Is the state a real entity with a life of its own? Is it founded on divine right, natural law, utility, or social contract – a contract whereby its citizens or their ancestors have somehow, perhaps by not emigrating, pledged themselves to behave in certain ways? Or might the contract be purely hypothetical (Rawls)? Does the state exist for its own sake? Or to promote the real or supposed interests of its citizens, or of some of them? Or to guarantee its citizens maximum freedom from mutual interference? Are there limits to the power it should have over its citizens, and can its citizens ever properly disobey, secede, or engage in revolution?

The second group of questions, which is not independent of the first, concerns different types of constitution, and where sovereignty lies within them. Should only some citizens or inhabitants of the relevant area have the right to participate politically, and if so, which? By what methods may the sovereign body justifiably reach its decisions, and in particular, especially in modern times, what are the forms of direct and representative democracy, and how acceptable are they? How should the representatives be elected? How may a constitution be changed? What rights should belong to minorities and those excluded from participation? What are the basis and limits of property and privilege?

The two groups come together in questions about ideal states or utopias and ideals in general, like the various forms of liberty and equality, and the relations between them.

Further questions concern the use of force by the state and its citizens, internally and externally, the relations of sovereign states with each other, and transfers of sovereignty within and between sovereign states.

Political science studies actual past and present political institutions, and explains rather than justifies them. Political philosophy is often called *political theory*, especially when studied in departments of political science.

Aristotle, *Politics*. (Books 4–6 discuss different constitutions, books 7–8 ideal state, while book 2 criticizes Plato.)
S. I. Benn and R. S. Peters, *Social Principles and the Democratic*

Polyadic

State, Allen and Unwin, 1959; American edn. 1964, entitled *Principles of Political Thought*. (Full-scale general introduction.)

P. Laslett *et al.* (eds), *Philosophy, Politics and Society*, Blackwell, 5 vols, 1956, 1962, 1967, 1972, 1979. (Miscellaneous essays, reflecting development of subject since the war.)

R. Nozick, *Anarchy, State and Utopia*, Blackwell, 1974. (Argues for very slimmed-down version of state, based on just exchange of goods justly acquired. Influential on development of Thatcherism in UK. See also discussion in J. Wolff, *Robert Nozick: Property, Justice and the Minimal State*, Polity Press, 1991.)

Plato, *Crito* (obedience), *Republic* (ideal state), *Statesman* (or *Politicus*: different constitutions; cf. *Republic*, book 8), *Laws* (second-best state).

A. Quinton (ed.), *Political Philosophy*, Oxford UP, 1967. (Essays, with annotated bibliography.)

J. Rawls, *A Theory of Justice*, Oxford UP, 1972. (Influential version of contract theory.)

Polyadic. See MONAD.

Polymorphous. Literally, having many forms. Concept introduced by Ryle and applied, in particular, to THINKING, though little referred to now. The general idea is that there is no particular action we must be engaged in to be thinking, and perhaps also that there is no overt action we could not engage in without thinking; but the detailed interpretation of polymorphousness is controversial.

D. L. Mouton, 'The concept of thinking', *Nous*, 1969. (Includes criticism of Ryle.)

J. O. Urmson, 'Polymorphous concepts', in O. P. Wood and G. Pitcher (eds), *Ryle*, Macmillan, 1970. (Cf. also ibid., pp. 77–8).

Popper, Sir Karl R. 1902–94. Austrian philosopher of science, and also political philosopher, born in Vienna. He was connected with the Vienna Circle (see POSITIVISM) in his youth but later migrated to New Zealand and then to England where he worked in London. He asserted that if a statement is to be scientific rather than metaphysical it must be falsifiable, but he did not, as the logical positivists did, dismiss metaphysical statements as meaningless. He then based his philosophy of science on the hypothetico-deductive method, claiming that enumerative INDUCTION is invalid, and indeed does not in fact occur, while verification and CONFIRMATION (as opposed to his own 'corroboration') are impossible. As his philosophy of science said we should aim to eliminate the false rather than establish the true, so, rather analogously, his political philosophy said we should aim to eliminate the bad rather than establish the good, and he opposed utopianism and any appeal to historical inevitability. *Logik der Forschung*, 1934–5, trans. with additions as *The Logic of Scientific Discovery*, 1959. *The Open Society and Its Enemies*, 1945. *The Poverty of Historicism*, 1957. *Conjectures and Refutations*, 1963. *Objective Knowledge*, 1972. See also BASIC STATEMENTS, CONCEPT, CONVENTIONALISM, EVIDENCE, FREEWILL, HISTORICISM, INSTRUMENTALISM, PROBABILITY.

Positivism. Doctrine associated with COMTE who adopted the term 'positive' to convey six features of things: being real, useful, certain, precise, organic, relative. He used it of his philosophy, which insisted on applying the scientific attitude not only to the sciences but also to human affairs. He saw the sciences as forming a natural sequence resting on mathematics and developing, both in order of logic and historically, through the physical and biological sciences to sociology (whose name he invented) and morals. Thought, he said, evolved from the theological attitude, explaining things by introducing gods, etc., through the metaphysical attitude involving a search for things-in-themselves and causes, to the scientific attitude stressing the observable. He emphasized synthesis, both of reason, feeling and action, which the two earlier attitudes had failed to balance, and of the various sciences, and even of the three attitudes, since the superseded ones still had their merits. This is why his list of features includes 'relative' and 'organic'. Positivism continued ever after to emphasize the unity of the sciences, and to confine science to the observable and manipulable. The evolutionary approach fitted well with nineteenth-century biological developments and with systems extending these to human affairs, like that of Herbert Spencer (1820–1903).

Comte, however, was more concerned to expound and apply scientific method than to examine it and ask what it presupposes. More critical, in the sense of stressing the limitations of what science can do, was MACH. For him, science aims at the most economical description of appearances, i.e. ultimately of our sense-experience, or sensations. Appearances are explained in the sense of being described in familiar terms, but no hidden entities or causes are postulated. Atoms, being unobservable are treated as a mere façon de parler (cf. PHENOMENALISM). This goes beyond the earlier positivism by criticizing notions (e.g. those of physical object and atom) that seem proper to science itself, not merely to metaphysics. Mach's outlook, and the similar one of R. Avenarius (1843–96), are sometimes called *empiriocriticism*.

Logical positivism is primarily associated with the *Vienna Circle* of the 1920s, whose most famous members were M. Schlick, Carnap,

Positivism

O. Neurath and Waismann. Wittgenstein and Popper were on its fringes. C. Hempel and H. Reichenbach in Berlin, and later Ayer in England, were its allies. It also influenced philosophy in America, Holland and Scandinavia. Schlick preferred the name *consistent empiricism*, and *logical empiricism* has a similar sense. The prefix 'logical' indicates partly that the topic for enquiry is meaning, partly that the doctrine is regarded as true as a matter of logic, and partly that logic is seen as the basic tool of philosophy. Under the influence of Mach, and also of Hume, the Circle concentrated on the general problem of MEANING, and developed the *verification* or *verifiability principle*. This said that something is meaningful if and only if it is either verifiable empirically, i.e. ultimately (not necessarily directly) by observation through the senses, or is a TAUTOLOGY of logic or mathematics, in which case it does not assert anything. The *verification theory* either *identifies* meaning with method of verification, or simply says that the verification principle is to be accepted.

Positivists have always tried to limit enquiry and belief to what can be firmly established. Following the empiricist tradition they have usually taken this to be primarily what we learn immediately from the senses. Metaphysics and theology they dismissed. Ethics and aesthetics they usually tried to assimilate as far as possible to sciences like psychology, later distinguishing different kinds of meaning (emotive, evaluative, prescriptive, etc.: see NATURALISM) to deal with what was left of them. But they found it difficult to deal with science, and most of everyday discourse (e.g. about material objects, other people, or the past), without letting metaphysics and other nonsense through. They sometimes required only verifiability in principle, not in practice. But then meaning can hardly be identified with the 'method' of verification, especially if in the end a statement is verifiable simply if we 'know what it would be like' for it to be true. And must verification be conclusive ('strong') or will mere provision of evidence ('weak' verification) suffice? Since few, if any, statements are conclusively verifiable, much energy was devoted to elaborating 'weak' forms of the principle and a theory of CONFIRMATION, especially by Ayer and Carnap.

'Verify' may mean either 'show to be true' or 'test for truth'. Carnap substituted 'test' for 'verify'. But Popper used the first sense, and argued that with universal affirmative statements like 'All swans are white', which he thought important for science, it is easier to falsify false ones than to verify true ones. He therefore emphasized falsifiability, not, however, as a criterion of meaningfulness but as demarcating scientific statements from metaphysical ones. He accepted both as meaningful.

Neurath and others thought that sentences could only properly be compared with sentences, not with the world. They therefore sympathized with the coherence theory of TRUTH. This sympathy was reinforced by the difficulty of showing general laws to be true.

Carnap emphasized the unity of science, and his *physicalism* claimed that all scientific statements could be translated into statements about physical objects, or space-time points (as against electrons, desires, social systems, etc.). He also insisted that meaningful statements must be verifiable publicly, not just by one person. 'Physicalism' is also used for the doctrine that all meaningful statements can be translated into the language of physics, and for the IDENTITY THEORY OF MIND; cf. MATERIALISM.

Among questions facing the verification principle is whether it is itself a tautology, empirical or meaningless. One answer treats it as a recommendation. Other problems concern necessary statements (see MODALITIES): if, as logical positivists think, they assert nothing, of what use are they?

Logical positivism itself has long been superseded (see PHILOSOPHY AND ANALYSIS), but its spirit has to some extent been revived during the last third of the twentieth century in the form of antirealism (see REALISM).

Operationalism or *operationism* stems from P. Bridgman and treats concepts rather as one version of logical positivism treats statements: concepts must be defined in terms of the operations employed in applying them, e.g. length can be defined only in terms of techniques of measurement, so that length may be a different concept when applied to football pitches and stellar diameters. Cf. PRAGMATISM.

Legal positivism names a complex variety of doctrines, only partly connected with positivism as above considered. The main connecting threads are emphasis on law as what is commanded or 'posited', and emphasis on law as it is (positive law) rather than as it should be (e.g. natural law). See also MEANING, REDUCTIONISM, CONFIRMATION, BASIC STATEMENTS, ANALYTIC.

*A. J. Ayer, *Language, Truth and Logic*, Gollancz, 1936, 2nd edn with important 'Introduction', 1946. (Classic statement in English of logical positivism.)

A. J. Ayer (ed.), *Logical Positivism*, Free Press, 1959. (General Essays, including famous one by Hempel, and long bibliography.)

A. C. Benjamin, *Operationism*, Thomas, Springfield, Ill., 1955. (General treatment.)

P. Bridgman, *The Logic of Modern Physics*, Macmillan, 1927. (Operationalism.)

R. Carnap, *The Unity of Science*, Kegan Paul, Trench, Trubner, 1932,

Possibilism

transl. with Introduction by M. Black, 1934. (Classic statement of one form of physicalism.)

*A. Comte, *Introduction to Positive Philosophy*, Bobbs-Merrill, 1970, Hackett, 1988. (Translation of first two chapters of his *Cours de philosophie positive* of 1830, also translated with further selections from the *Cours* in *The Essential Comte*, Croom Helm/ Barnes and Noble, 1974.)

J. L. Evans, 'Meaning and verification', *Mind*, 1953. (Critical discussion of development and presuppositions of logical positivism, and different versions of verification principle.)

H. L. A. Hart, *The Concept of Law*, Oxford UP, 1961, esp. p. 253. (Legal positivism.)

C. Hempel, 'On the Logical Positivists' theory of truth', *Analysis*, vol. 2, 1935.

C. Hempel, 'A logical appraisal of operationism', *Scientific Monthly*, 1954, reprinted in his *Aspects of Scientific Explanation*, Free Press, 1965. (Sympathetic discussion. Popper (below), p. 440, briefly criticizes operationalism. Cf. also C. Taylor, *The Explanation of Behaviour*, RKP, 1964, chapter 4, and for some further references D. H. Mellor, *The Matter of Chance*, Cambridge UP, 1971, p. 76.)

D. Hume, *Enquiry concerning Human Understanding*, 1748. (Last paragraph is famous forerunner of verification principle.)

*L. Kolakowski, *Positivist Philosophy*, Penguin, 1966, trans. 1968. (Elementary introduction, mainly on earlier forms and related outlooks.)

*E. Mach, *Popular Scientific Lectures*, Open Court, 1898, chapter 9: 'The economic nature of physical inquiry'. (Popular exposition.)

D. Makinson, 'Nidditch's definition of verifiability', *Mind*, 1965. (Difficulties in formulating verifiability principle. Moderately technical. Nidditch himself, in *Mind*, 1961, is revising Ayer's formulation.)

K. R. Popper, *The Logic of Scientific Discovery*, Hutchinson, 1959 (German original, 1934). (Standard statement of Popper's falsificationist position.)

H. Putnam, 'Pragmatism', *Proceedings of the Aristotelian Society*, supplementary vol., 1995. (Assesses favourably a pragmatist version of verification.)

M. Schlick, 'Meaning and verification', *Philosophical Review*, 1936, reprinted in H. Feigl and W. Sellars (eds), *Readings in Philosophical Analysis*, Appleton-Century-Crofts, 1949. (Exposition and applications of verification theory, equating meaning with method of verification.)

Possibilism. See ACTUALISM.

Possible worlds

Possible. See MODALITIES.

Possible worlds. A device going back to Leibniz but brought to prominence recently, especially by D. K. Lewis, for analysing necessity and possibility and related notions (see MODALITIES). Each of the infinitely many logically possible states of affairs is regarded as a 'world'. A proposition can then be called logically necessary if it is true in all possible worlds, and logically possible if it is true in at least one. Counterfactuals can be analysed in terms of possible worlds (see CONDITIONALS), and so can propositions themselves: a proposition can be defined as a set of possible worlds, namely the set of those worlds in which it is true; see SENTENCE.

One problem arising concerns the status of possible worlds. Are they merely abstract possibilities, or have they some sort of reality of their own? The latter view is *modal realism*, and is represented in an extreme form (sometimes called *concrete* as opposed to *abstract modal realism*) by Lewis, for whom possible worlds are as real as the actual world (and *are* actual for themselves, though not for us), but they are spatiotemporally disconnected from the actual world and from each other, so that even in principle we cannot travel from one to another. (Sometimes 'modal realism' is confined to Lewis's view.) See also ACTUALISM.

But if possibilities have a reality of their own like this, how is it that we can come to know of them? And how can they concern or be about the things in our world? This latter problem is that of transworld identity. This is most acute for Lewis's version, and he has suggested that everything in the actual world has a *counterpart* in every possible world in which (speaking intuitively) 'it' exists at all. *Counterpart theory* then deals with the relations between these counterparts in the relevant different worlds.

A further problem concerns the use of possible worlds in analysing counterfactuals: this involves judgments of comparative similarity between them, so how are these to be made?

D. K. Lewis, *On the Plurality of Worlds*, Blackwell, 1986. (Develops his version of modal realism.)

M. J. Loux (ed.), *The Possible and the Actual*, Oxford UP, 1979. (Essays, mainly reprinted, on possible worlds and transworld identity.)

A. McMichael, 'A problem for actualism about possible worlds', *Philosophical Review*, 1983. (Includes expositions and discussions of various views about possible worlds.)

G. H. R. Parkinson, 'Philosophy of logic', in N Jolley (ed.), *The Cambridge Companion to Leibniz*, Cambridge UP, 1995 (See pp. 212–16 for brief discussion of Leibniz on possible worlds:

Pour soi

for more extended discussion, see B. Mates, *The Philosophy of Leibniz*, Oxford UP, 1986, chapter IV.)

A. Plantinga, *The Nature of Necessity*, Clarendon, 1974. (See chapter 5 for possible worlds.)

R. C. Stalmaker, 'Propositions', in A. F. MacKay and D. D. Merrill (eds), *Issues in the Philosophy of Language*, Yale UP, 1976, followed by critical 'Comments' by L. Powers, and developed in Stalmaker's *Inquiry*, MIT Press, 1984. (Propositions as sets of possible worlds. See also Stalmaker's 'Possible Worlds', *Nous*, 1976, reprinted in Loux, and (with editorial introduction) in T. Honderich and M. F. Burnyeat (eds), *Philosophy As It Is*, Penguin, 1979, for his view of possible worlds themselves.)

Pour soi. See BAD FAITH.

Pragmatics. See SEMIOTIC.

Pragmatism. Originally developed as a theory of meaning by Peirce who was concerned with the meaning of concepts affecting the intellect, especially scientific concepts, rather than those confined to the senses (like *red*) or emotions. He thought the meaning of such concepts, and of statements in which they appeared, was exhausted by the effects they could have on our experience and actions. When the name became widely used for various related theories he used *pragmaticism* for his own particular version. This theory can be thought of as a looser form of operationalism (see POSITIVISM), and Peirce expressed an affinity for positivism.

Pragmatism is also often thought of as a theory of truth. Peirce made truth 'the opinion which is fated to be ultimately agreed to by all who investigate'. He seems to mean that truth is what would be believed if investigation continued indefinitely, whether or not it does continue; it is the limit where belief is finally stabilized. This side of pragmatism was developed by W. James, who differed from Peirce by including, and emphasizing, the effect of concepts on our senses and emotions. Truth, for James, is agreement with reality, but this means that it is what works or satisfies us, in the sense that it is whatever we ultimately find believable or consistent. But he allowed that our emotions might well, and properly, influence what we do ultimately so find.

Other philosophers who have been labelled pragmatists include Dewey, F. C. S. Schiller (1864–1937), C. I. Lewis (1883–1964) and F. P. Ramsey (1903–30). 'Pragmatism' is also sometimes used as a general label for views like CONVENTIONALISM and INSTRUMENTALISM, though these (especially instrumentalism) perhaps replace truth, at

least in certain contexts, rather than define it. See also
SUPERASSERTIBLE.

B. Aune, *Rationalism, Empiricism, and Pragmatism*, Random House, 1970. (Chapters 4 and 5 discuss modern versions of pragmatism. Cf. also D. H. Mellor (ed.), *Prospects for Pragmatism*, Cambridge UP, 1980, essays written in honour of F. P. Ramsey.)

A. J. Ayer, *The Origins of Pragmatism*, Macmillan, 1968. (Treats Peirce and James.)

J. Buchler (ed.), *The Philosophy of Peirce*, RKP, 1940. (Selections from Peirce. See especially chapters 2, 3 and 17, and for the quotation p. 38.)

W. B. Gallie, *Peirce and Pragmatism*, Penguin, 1952.

W. James, *Pragmatism*, 1907.

W. James, *The Meaning of Truth*, 1909. (Selected essays, issued to clarify *Pragmatism*.)

H. Putnam, 'Pragmatism', *Proceedings of the Aristotelian Society*, supplementary vol., 1995. (Assesses favourably a pragmatist version of verificationism.)

A. Rorty (ed.), *Pragmatic Philosophy*, 1966. (Anthology.)

Predicate. What is said of (predicated of) a subject. In 'Grass is green' *grass* is the subject and *is green* is the predicate. (But in traditional formal logic, and loosely elsewhere, the predicate would be *green*, not *is green*.) A *subject/predicate sentence* is a sentence in which something is predicated of a subject as in 'Grass is green', as against, for example, conditional or existential sentences such as 'There are lions in Africa'. There is in certain contexts, notably in discussions of whether existence is a predicate, a certain ambiguity between whether a predicate is linguistic (a set of words) or non-linguistic (what the words in some sense stand for, or a property). Also 'logical predicate' has sometimes been used for what would be the grammatical predicate of a sentence when it is expressed in its proper logical form (cf. theory of DESCRIPTIONS). See also MONAD for some kinds of predicate, and for *M-predicate* and *P-predicate* see PERSON.

Predicative. See ATTRIBUTIVE.

Prediction paradox. Some boys are told they will be examined next week, but will not know on which day until it arrives. It cannot be Saturday, or they would know on Friday night. But if Friday is the last possible day, it cannot be Friday either, or they would know on Thursday night. By repeating the argument the other days too

Preface paradox

are eliminated. Apparently, therefore, the examination cannot occur, under the conditions stated. Many other examples are used.

D. J. O'Connor, 'Pragmatic paradoxes', *Mind*, 1948, followed by discussions (over many years) in subsequent issues of *Mind*.

W. V. O. Quine, *Ways of Paradox and other Essays*, Harvard UP, 1966, chapter 2. (Claims paradox is unreal.)

R. M. Sainsbury, *Paradoxes*, Cambridge UP, 1988. (See pp. 94–106 (pp. 91–103 in second edition, 1995) for elementary introduction.)

Preface paradox. It seems paradoxical for an author to assert things in his book, and modestly add in his preface that his book probably contains errors. Can one coherently say, 'Some of my beliefs are false'?

C. New, 'A note on the paradox of the preface', *Philosophical Quarterly*, 1978.

Prescriptivism. See NATURALISM.

Presupposition. See IMPLICATION.

Price, Richard. 1723–91. Welsh philosopher and economist, born in Glamorgan, who worked as a clergyman in London. He supported the American and French revolutions. He was a leading representative of the 'intuitionist' school of moral philosophy, which opposed the 'MORAL SENSE' theory of HUTCHESON and others. He insisted that our knowledge of right and wrong was derived from reason, and that right and wrong themselves were 'real characters of actions', not 'only qualities of our minds'. *A Review of the Principle Questions in Morals*, 1758.

Price, H. H. (1899–1984) was an epistemologist and metaphysician who wrote on PERCEPTION, BELIEF, THINKING and UNIVERSALS, and also on psychical research. See also SENSE DATA, SIDGWICK.

Primitive. In philosophy, 'basic', 'undefined', 'taken for granted'.

Principle. See LAWS.

Prisoner's dilemma. Two prisoners are told that if both confess both will be gaoled for two years; if neither confesses both will be gaoled for one year; if one alone confesses he will be freed and the other gaoled for three years. What will rational prisoners do? Many variants are possible, but in general a prisoner's dilemma situation exists when it is better for each if each does A than if each does B, but better for each if he does B than if he does A. An example of the dilemma is disarmament negotiations, and it is important in general for game theory (see DECISION THEORY) and ethics. See also NEWCOMB'S PARADOX.

D. P. Gauthier, 'Morality and advantage', *Philosophical Review*, 1967, reprinted in J. Raz (ed.), *Practical Reasoning*, Oxford UP, 1978. (Uses dilemma to explore relations between these notions. Cf. also his (more technical) 'Reason and maximization', *Canadian Journal of Philosophy*, 1975).

D. Parfit, 'Prudence, morality, and the prisoner's dilemma'. *Proceedings of the British Academy*, 1979, published separately, 1981. (Discusses some ramifications of dilemma. Cf. also his *Reasons and Persons*, Clarendon, 1984.)

*R. M. Sainsbury, *Paradoxes*, Cambridge UP, 1988. (See pp. 64–70 (pp. 66–72 in 2nd edn, 1995) for elementary introduction.)

Private language. Anyone can invent a private Esperanto for their diary, but can languages, or parts of languages, be private in a more radical sense? In particular, can a language contain elements which it is logically impossible for anyone but its speaker to learn or understand, e.g. can a language contain words which have meaning by standing for objects only accessible to the speaker? The importance of the question is that sensations, pains, etc., have been thought to be such objects, so that words which had meaning by standing for them would be private in the relevant sense. Three questions therefore are whether such a private language is possible, and, if not, how words like 'pain' do have meaning, and in what sense, if any, pains are private.

Wittgenstein seems to have argued that to use a language is to do something one may do correctly or incorrectly. One must therefore be able to check, at least in principle, that one is doing it correctly. But with a private language no such checking would be possible. It is disputed whether this argument is sound, and also whether the alternative account that Wittgenstein himself gave of how words like 'pain' have meaning commits him to some form of behaviourism. The issue is important in connexion with various kinds of scepticism. See also ACCESS.

M. Budd, *Wittgenstein's Philosophy of Psychology*, Routledge 1989. (see esp. chapter 3.)

O. R. Jones (ed.), *The Private Language Argument*, Macmillan, 1971. (Includes much of the important literature.)

S. Kripke, *Wittgenstein on Rules and Private Language: An Elementary Exposition*, Blackwell, 1982. (One famous though controversial interpretation of Wittgenstein.)

J. T. Saunders and D. F. Henze, *The Private-Language Problem*,

Probability

Random House, 1967. (Presents opposing attitudes in dialogue form, finally offering solution.)

Probability. *Probability theory* or the *calculus of chances* or *probabilities* is the mathematical theory underlying probability arguments and most (though not all) theories of induction with a mathematical basis. (See CONFIRMATION, where the relation between confirmation and probability is also discussed.) This calculus contains elementary rules governing results to be expected from tossing dice or drawing marbles from a bag. It also covers BAYES'S THEOREM, and topics like the law of large numbers (see NUMBERS (LAW OF LARGE)). Results within this theory are purely mathematical, and are not predictions about what actual dice, etc. will do. Use of the theory simply draws out the logical implications of assumptions already made.

Various theories have been offered about the nature of probability. The *classical theory* defines an event's probability as the proportion of alternatives, among all those possible in a given situation, that include the event in question. There are 36 possible results of tossing two dice, of which 11 include at least one six, so the probability of getting at least one six in a throw of two dice is 11/36. But the alternatives must be equiprobable (equally probable) – or equispecific, if 'equiprobable' seems question-begging in an analysis of 'probable'. This is hard to ensure. Attempts to ensure it have often used the principle of INDIFFERENCE. Other difficulties concern the probability of theories, such as Darwinism, and cases where the alternatives are not obviously finite and definite in number, e.g. the probability that all swans including future ones are white; since we can breed swans the number of future swans could depend on our very probability calculations. Also BERTRAND'S PARADOX and BERTRAND'S BOX PARADOX become relevant here. Kneale's 'range' theory attempts to answer some of these difficulties. *Range* is used elsewhere too. For Carnap a proposition's range is the set of state-descriptions compatible with it. See CONFIRMATION.

The *frequency theory* defines probability in terms of the ratio of times something happens to times it might happen. If the proportion of smokers who die of cancer remains steady at 10 per cent then the probability of smokers dying of cancer is 10 per cent. Since most of the classes we are concerned with are open classes, the probability is defined as the limit, in the mathematical sense, to which the frequency tends in the long run. We often talk of the probability of single events, e.g. that Smith will die of cancer, and it is disputed how, if at all, the frequency theory can account for this. Also the notion of a limiting frequency raises a problem because in an infinite or open-ended series, such as tosses of a coin, any limiting frequency is compatible with any result in a finite run. If a penny falls heads a million times running the limiting frequency of heads could still be a half it it fell tails the next million, or indeed if it merely behaved normally the next million times. Therefore in applying the theory we seem to have to say things like '*Probably* the limiting frequency is this' or '*Probably* present trends of cancer among smokers will continue', where 'probably' is unexplained.

The *propensity theory*, substituted by Popper for the frequency theory, defines probability as a propensity of objects themselves, e.g. of a die to show a six. Popper claims propensities are no more 'mysterious' than gravitational fields, but one can still ask just what propensities are and how wide an area the theory covers. The word 'chance' can also be used for 'propensity', and for objective probability when this is distinguished from subjective degrees of belief (see below).

The *logical relation* theory makes probability a logical relation between evidence and a conclusion, rather like entailment (see IMPLICATION) only weaker (cf. CONFIRMATION). Probability is therefore always relative to evidence. Apart from the difficulty of finding such a relation, one defect of this theory as an analysis of 'probably' is that if we know a true proposition, p, which entails another, q, we can 'detach' q, i.e. assert it on its own, but if p only makes q probable, we can at best say 'Probably q', which leaves 'probably' unanalysed – and even that we cannot say if we know there is another true proposition which makes q improbable.

The *subjectivist theory* analyses probability in terms of degrees of belief. A crude version would simply identify the statement that something is probable with the statement that the speaker is more inclined to believe it than to disbelieve it. Degrees of belief may be measured in terms of the bets the believer would be willing to place, and more refined versions of the theory say one is only entitled to use 'probably' if one's bets are 'coherent', in the sense that one does not bet on contradictory propositions in such a way that one is bound to lose whatever happens, which can be expressed by saying that one does not let oneself have a 'Dutch book' made against one. This, however, still bases probability on the attitudes of the believer. Because 'coherence' is required, subjectivism is sometimes described as the view that probability is the degree of the rational man's belief. However, when this means that calling something probable is saying that it is rational to believe it, it is not subjectivist, since it no longer analyses probability in terms of beliefs actually held. It then has no special name.

Another version of the subjectivist theory is the *speech act theory*. To call something probable is not to describe one's belief but to express it. To say war is probable is to say, but only tentatively, that

Probability

war will occur. Like other SPEECH ACT analyses (e.g. of 'good', 'true') this faces the objection at least prime facie (cf. GOOD), that it ignores cases like 'If war were probable we would emigrate', where it is not being even tentatively asserted that war will occur. It has never in fact been popular, and perhaps applies better to sentences like 'It may happen' than to 'It is probable that it will happen', or even 'It will probably happen'.

Between them these theories try to account for the ideas that probability is objective and not of our choosing, and yet is somehow relative to our knowledge, since things in the world are either so or not so, and not probably so (though quantum physics may provide an exception to this). Problems also arise over when to say something *was* probable, especially if eventually it never happened.

Many recent writers think that there is more than one kind of probability. They often distinguish between probability as a logical relation, where probability statements are true or false as a matter of logic (Carnap's *probability*$_1$), and probability as relative frequency, where probability statements are empirical statistical statements which form the material for the mathematical calculus of chances (Carnap's *probability*$_2$). Some, like the frequency theorist Reichenbach, hold the *identity conception of probability*, saying that these two kinds are really one. Surely, however, one should distinguish at least three kinds of statement: empirical statistical statements, like 'The probability of an Englishman being a Catholic is 10 per cent', where this just means that 10 per cent are so; purely mathematical statements, like 'The probability of a double six with two throws of a true die is 1/36', where this makes no prediction about any actual dice; and 'ordinary' probability statements, like 'The probability of Smith being a Catholic is high', 'Smith is probably a Catholic', 'The probability of a six with this die is low', 'This die will probably not show six', 'The probability of rain tomorrow is high', 'The probability of Darwinism being true is high'. These 'ordinary' statements may of course themselves be of various kinds, and may rest on statistical or mathematical statements.

Probabilities are called *absolute, a priori* or *prior* if they are considered as relative either to nothing or to the general background of knowledge rather than to some real or assumed set of evidence statements; otherwise they are *relative* or *conditional*. When a certain probability is assumed, e.g. the probability of an *a* which is *b* being *c*, the probability of an *a* which is *c* being *b* is called the *inverse* probability (cf. BAYES'S THEOREM). This notion raises no problems itself, but has been put to controversial uses, as a result of which LIKELIHOOD has been introduced.

Probabilism is the view that scientists can and should seek to attach probabilities to their hypotheses, i.e. to confirm them. Popper's opposing view that this is impossible and that the scientist should seek the most improbable, i.e. the most easily falsifiable (though not yet falsified), hypothesis is sometimes called *improbabilism*. See also BAYES'S THEOREM, CONFIRMATION.

A. J. Ayer, *The Concept of a Person*, Macmillan, 1963. *Miscellaneous Essays*. (Chapter 7 discusses logical relation theory, and single events. Criticized by C. G. Hempel, *Aspects of Scientific Explanation*, Free Press, 1965, pp. 65–6).

R. Carnap, 'The two concepts of probability', *Philosophy and Phenomenological Research*, 1945, reprinted in H. Feigl and W. Sellars (eds), *Readings in Philosophical Analysis*, Appleton-Century-Crofts, 1949, and in H. Feigl and M. Brodbeck (eds) *Readings in the Philosophy of Science*, Appleton-Century-Crofts, 1953. (Cf. also his book *Logical Foundations of Probability*, 1950, and, for another version, J. O. Urmson, 'Two of the senses of "probable" ', *Analysis*, vol. 8, 1947, reprinted in M. Macdonald (ed.), *Philosophy and Analysis*, Blackwell, 1954).

B. de Finetti, 'Foresight: its logical laws, its subjective sources', translated from 1937 French original in H. E. Kyburg and H. E. Smokler (eds), *Studies in Subjective Probability*, Wiley, 1964. (De Finetti is main representative of subjectivist theory.)

I. Hacking, *The Emergence of Probability*, Oxford UP, 1975. (Historical.)

J. M. Keynes, *A Treatise on Probability*, Macmillan, 1921. (Chapter 1 defends logical relation theory. See also chapter 4 for principle of indifference.)

*H. E. Kyburg, *Probability and Inductive Logic*, Macmillan, 1970. (Part I gives basis of calculus of chances and discusses various theories of probability. Includes exercises and bibliographies. Other elementary accounts of the calculus of chances include B. Mates, *Elementary Logic*, 2nd edn, Oxford UP, 1972, chapter 2, §5, H. C. Levinson, *The Science of Chance: From Probability to Statistics*, Faber and Faber, 1952, I. Copi, *Introduction to Logic*, Macmillan, 6th edn, 1982, chapter 14, R. Fogelin, *Understanding Arguments*, Harcourt, Brace, Jovanovich, 1978, 4th, revised, edn (with W. Sinnott-Armstrong), 1991, chapter 10.)

K. R. Popper, 'The propensity interpretation of probability', *British Journal for Philosophy of Science*, 1959. (Propensity theory. Cf. D. H. Mellor, *The Matter of Chance*, Cambridge UP, 1971, chapter 4, and A. O'Hear's review of Popper in *Mind*, 1985, pp. 463–9.)

H. Reichenbach, *Experience and Prediction*, Chicago UP, 1938, (§ 33 advocates identity conception, and discusses single events.)

R. Swinburne, *An Introduction to Confirmation Theory*, Methuen, 1973. (First two chapters discuss kinds of probability.)

Problematic

*R. von Mises, *Probability, Statistics and Truth*, William Hodge, 1939, revised (Allen and Unwin/Macmillan), 1957 (German original, 1928). Non-technical account of one version of frequency theory (first chapter), followed by discussion and applications.

Problematic. See MODALITIES.

Process philosophy. An approach traceable back as far as Heraclitus (fifth century BC) whereby the basic reality is process rather than static substance.

D. Browning (ed.), *Philosophers of Process*, Random House, 1965. (Selections, with introductions, from nineteenth- and twentieth-century writers.)

Proof theory. See METAMATHEMATICS, LOGIC.

Proper. It is convenient to allow a whole to count as one of its parts, a class as one of its subclasses, etc. 'Proper' is used to exclude these special cases, e.g. a proper part is a part smaller than the whole, as a proper fraction is a fraction less than one.

Property. (i) Any characteristic. (ii) A characteristic relevant for the indiscernibility of identicals (see LEIBNIZ'S LAW). Tully is the same as Cicero, but 'Tully is hereby named by a five-letter name' is true, while 'Cicero is hereby named by a five-letter name' is false. So *being hereby named by a five-letter name* is not a single property in this sense. It may, however, be doubted whether it is a characteristic at all, when the 'hereby' is unspecified (in which case we need not posit characteristics not subject to Leibniz's law). (iii) A positive, as against negative, characteristic, e.g. *being red*, but not *being not red* (which is too indefinite in its application: does it apply to abstract things?). (iv) A non-relational characteristic, e.g. *being red*, but not *being a brother*. (v) The Aristotelian and medieval *proprium*: a characteristic following from, and unique to, the essence of a species, but not part of its definition. *Able to laugh* is a proprium of a man, if only man can have it but man is not defined as a laughing animal. Other senses exist.

S. Shoemaker, *Identity, Cause, and Mind*, Cambridge UP, 1984, chapter 10. (Discusses sense near to (iv).)

Propositional acts, attitudes, verbs. See SENTENCES, CONTENT (on attitudes).

Propositions. See SENTENCES.

274

Psychologism

Proprium. See PROPERTY.

Protocol statements. See BASIC STATEMENTS.

Psycholinguistics. General term for the study of language from the point of view of psychology, though applied particularly to the movement which since the 1950s has involved intense study of *generative grammar* (roughly, what mental processes underlie the generating of sentences in natural languages, taking account of both syntax and semantics (see SEMIOTIC)).

*J. Caron, *An Introduction to Psycholinguistics* (trans. T. Pownall), Harvester Wheatsheaf and Toronto UP, 1992 (French original, 1989).
*D. D. Steinberg, *An Introduction to Psycholinguistics*, Longman, 1993. (Partly philosophical, including exposition and discussion of Chomsky, and partly empirical study of language-learning.)

Psychologism. See NATURALISM. In general terms psychologism is the appeal to psychological arguments to solve philosophical problems. Sometimes this is made through confusion and sometimes explicitly. Something may depend on whether the appeal to psychology is intended to answer or simply to replace a philosophical problem; was Hume a psychologizer in his treatments of causation and the external world? Psychologism has often, and especially in the first half of the twentieth century, been regarded as a mistake. For instance Frege attacked the view that the concept of number, which mathematics is concerned with, can be analysed in terms of the mental processes by which we arrive at arithmetical judgments. Recently, however, as explained under NATURALISM, this attitude to psychologism has been modified.

'Psychologism' and also 'mentalism', can alternatively refer to the view, as against eliminative MATERIALISM and certain kinds of BEHAVIOURISM, that there are inner mental states. ·

Popper sometimes uses 'psychologism' for the view that 'Social laws must ultimately be reducible to psychological laws'.

N. Block, 'Psychologism and behaviourism', *Philosophical Review*, 1981. (Second sense of 'psychologism', defined as 'the doctrine that whether behaviour is intelligent depends on the internal information processing that produces it', p. 5.)
G. Frege, *The Foundations of Arithmetic* (trans. J. L. Austin from German original of 1884), Blackwell, 1950. (Often referred to by the German title *Grundlagen*. See pp. 33–9 for attack on psychologism about numbers.)
K. R. Popper, *The Open Society and its Enemies*, RKP, 1945, vol.

Psychology (philosophical)

2, chapter 14. (See p. 90 for quotation. Elsewhere, Popper uses 'psychologism' more in the first sense above.)

Psychology (philosophical). See MIND.

Psychophysical parallelism. Doctrine that mental events and physical (in particular, bodily) events form separate chains, with causal relations holding or not holding within each chain, but not between the chains. The apparent connexions between the chains can be attributed to God. Associated in one form with Leibniz. See also OCCASIONALISM.

Putnam, Hilary. 1926–. Born in Chicago, he has worked mainly at Harvard. Like KRIPKE, he came to philosophy from mathematics; their causal theories of MEANING have much in common, with Putnam concentrating mainly on 'natural kind terms' (such as 'lemon' or 'water'). This has led him to an EXTERNALIST view of thinking and similar notions, with his slogan that ' "meanings" just ain't in the *head*!', and to a realist approach to the philosophy of science. More recently he has widened his philosophical sympathies, adopting a still rigorous but less science-based approach. His publications include *Mind, Language and Reality*, 1975; *Philosophical Papers*, 3 vols (*Mathematics, Matter and Method*, 1975; *Mind, Language and Reality*, 1975; *Realism and Reason*, 1983); *Meaning and the Moral Sciences*, 1978; *Reason, Truth and History*, 1981 (chapter one of this is the locus classicus for the 'brain in a vat' image); *The Many Faces of Realism*, 1983; *Representations and Reality*, 1988; *Realism with a Human Face*, 1990; *Renewing Philosophy*, 1992; *Words and Life*, 1994.

Psychosemantics. Term associated especially with Fodor for the study of meaning from the point of view of what is going on in the mind when we use language meaningfully or have propositional attitudes (believing, desiring, etc., which have a meaningful content). See also LANGUAGE OF THOUGHT.

J. A. Fodor, *Psychosemantics: the Problem of Meaning in the Philosophy of Mind*, MIT Press, 1987, partly revised in his *The Elm and the Expert: Mentalese and its Semantics*, MIT Press, 1994. (Cf. his *A Theory of Content and Other Essays*, MIT Press, 1990 (mainly reprints), and also, B. Loewer and G. Rey (eds), *Meaning in Mind: Fodor and his Critics*, Blackwell, 1991, for critical discussions of his position, with replies by him and bibliography of works by and about him.)

Pythagoras

Pythagoras. Late sixth century BC. Born in Samos, he migrated to south Italy and founded Pythagorean 'brotherhood' whose doctrines, even centuries later, were often attributed to him. Traditionally he was the first to see the connexion between musical harmonies and ratios of string lengths, and he and his followers developed arithmetic and geometry (including 'Pythagoras' theorem'), and in various ways tried to explain reality itself in terms of numbers. They may have originated the ideas (though without providing compelling evidence) that the earth is spherical and not the centre of the universe. They also developed religious ideas about the soul and reincarnation, together with rules for a 'way of life'. Both their mathematical and their religious ideas are said to have influenced Plato. Recently, however, much scepticism has been expressed about their alleged mathematical and scientific contributions. See also METAPHYSICS, NIETZSCHE.

J. A. Philip, *Pythagoras and Early Pythagoreanism*, Toronto UP, 1966. (Balanced discussion taking account of scholarship later than Schrödinger.)

E. Schrödinger, *Nature and the Greeks*, Cambridge UP, 1954. (Contains sympathetic appreciation by famous modern physicist, though predating recent scholarship.)

Q

Quale. Plural: 'qualia'. A quale, such as red, is a quality considered as it appears to consciousness rather than as science might define it. Qualia are like SENSE DATA, but universal, not particular. Etymologically 'quale' is to 'quality' as 'quantum' is to 'quantity'. Two associated problems concern 'absent qualia' (more accurately, the absence of qualia: might someone have no *experiences* at all but live like a human while really being a ZOMBIE?), and 'transposed qualia' (or 'the inverted spectrum': whenever we both see something we both *call* red, might you be having an experience I would call green if I had it?). Accounting for these possibilities raises problems especially for FUNCTIONALISM (see Shoemaker reference in bibliography there). Occasionally 'quale' is used for something like 'TROPE'.

J. Bennett, 'Substance, reality, and primary qualities', *American Philosophical Quarterly*, 1965, reprinted in C. B. Martin and D. M. Armstrong (eds), *Locke and Berkeley*, Macmillan, n.d. (See part 2, §55, for how far transposed qualia problem can extend.)

E. Conee, 'The possibility of absent qualia', *Philosophical Review*, 1985. (Could there be ZOMBIES?) R. Kirk, *Raw Feeling*, Clarendon, 1994. (Includes extended treatment of transposed qualia problem, and claims there is no unbridgeable explanatory gap between qualia and brain states. Cf. A. Clark, *Sensory Qualities*, Clarendon, 1993, claiming that we can 'explain qualitative facts in terms that do not presuppose other qualitative facts' (p. vii).)

J. Levine, 'Materialism and qualia: the explanatory gap,' *Pacific Philosophical Quarterly*, 64.4, 1983. (Claims that there is an

Quantification

unsolved epistemological problem in explaining why certain qualia are associated with certain neural states.)

S. Shoemaker, 'Qualia and consciousness', *Mind*, 1991. (Qualia are indispensable.)

M. Tye, 'Visual qualia and visual content,' in T. Crane (ed.), *The Contents of Experience*, Cambridge UP, 1992. (Claims there are no visual qualia.)

Qualities (primary and secondary). A distinction as old as the Greeks, but first elaborated by Locke, between qualities like shape or velocity, which seem to belong to things independently of observers (primary), and those like colour or taste, which seem to depend on the existence of observers (secondary); the terms 'primary' and 'secondary' stem from the seventeenth century chemist R. Boyle. The distinction proves hard to elaborate in detail though is widely agreed to exist in some form. For *tertiary qualities* see SUPERVENIENCE.

J. Bennett (see bibliography to QUALE).

J. Locke, *An Essay concerning Human Understanding*, 1690, book 2, chapter 8.

C. McGinn, *The Subjective View*, Oxford UP, 1983. (Compares secondary qualities with indexicals (see TOKEN-RELEXIVES).)

A. D. Smith, 'Of primary and secondary qualities', *Philosophical Review*, 1990. (General historical survey, defending secondary qualities but claiming 'primary quality' should be either dropped or kept for whatever qualities are fundamental for current science.)

M. D. Wilson, 'History of philosophy and philosophy today; and the case of sensible qualities', *Philosophical Review*, 1992. (See exp. pp. 209–33 for assessment of recent interpretations of Locke and others on primary and secondary qualities, and pp. 234–43 for effects on that topic of recent scientific and philosophical developments.)

Quality-word. See METAPHYSICS

Quantification. Literally, specification as to quantity. Two kinds of proposition are very important for formal logic, those saying something about everything, or everything of a given kind, and those saying something about at least one thing, or at least one thing of a given kind. So there are two main *quantifiers*. (In what follows, *x* is an individual VARIABLE.) The *universal quantifier* 'binding' (see VARIABLE) *x* is read 'For all (any, every) *x*', and is symbolized '(x)' or '$(\forall x)$', sometimes (Πx)'. The particular (or *existential*)

Quantifier shift fallacy

quantifier is read 'For some (i.e. at least one) x' or 'There exists at least one x such that', and is symbolized '$(\exists x)$', sometimes '(Σx)'. (Except with '(x)' the brackets are sometimes dropped.) Thus, using 'Rx' for 'x is red', typical sentences might be '(x) (Rx)' meaning 'For all x, x is red', i.e. 'Everything is red', and '$(\exists x)$ (Rx)' meaning 'For some x, x is red', i.e. 'There is at least one red thing'. The x in the first bracket in each case may or may not be counted as part of the quantifier. The bracket immediately following a quantifier ('(Rx)' in the above examples) defines its *scope*, i.e. how much of the ensuing discourse it governs, or how much of what follows is being said of the variable in it. (Precise conventions about brackets, etc. again vary.) Either of these quantifiers can be defined in terms of the other plus negation.

Other quantifiers exist, such as 'For most x', 'For exactly one x' (the *singular quantifier*), 'For exactly $2x$,' etc. These can be symbolised by subscripts: '$(\exists_2 x)$' would mean 'For exactly two x'.

The values of a VARIABLE bound by a quantifier are *quantified over*. In the above examples objects in general are quantified over, but sometimes the range of objects quantified over (the *universe of discourse*) is limited: see MANY-SORTED LOGIC. When predicates are quantified over, f or F usually replaces x; '$(\exists f$ means 'There is at least one f such that.'

Quantification is *objectual* (or *referential*) if it is taken to imply the existence, as 'real objects', of the values of the variable (cf. the views of Quine). Otherwise it is *substitutional*. Consider 'John is tall.' Can we infer '$(\exists f)$ (John is f)'? To those who interpret quantification substitutionally this is harmless, and merely says that for some replacement for f, the sentence 'John is f' is true. But those who interpret it objectually may reject the inference because it seems to imply a realist view of universals like tallness, which they reject on other grounds.

J. A. Faris, *Quantification Theory*, RKP 1964. (Semi-elementary. See also any modern introduction to logic, e.g. I. Copi, *Introduction to Logic*, Macmillan 6th edn, 1982.)

R. B. Marcus, 'Interpreting quantification', *Inquiry*, 1962. (Objectual and substitutional quantification. See also W. V. O. Quine, *Philosophy of Logic*, Prentice-Hall, 1970, pp. 91–4, and for his views on logic and metaphysics, his 'On what there is' (see bibliography to BEING).)

Quantifier shift fallacy. The fallacy of arguing from 'Every nice girl loves a sailor' to 'Some (one) sailor is loved by every nice girl', i.e. of confusing 'For all x there is a y such that . . .' with 'There is a y

such that for all *x* . . .' (see QUANTIFICATION). The latter implies, but is not implied by, the former.

Quantifier words. A group of words including 'all', 'any', 'each', 'every', 'some', 'no', 'a', all concerned in various ways with the notion of quantity (cf. QUANTIFICATION).

Traditional formal logic dealt mainly with four kinds of proposition, *universal affirmative* (called *A propositions*: 'All cats are black'), *universal negative (E propositions*: 'No cats are black'), *particular affirmative (I propositions*: 'Some cats are black'), and *particular negative (O propositions*: 'Some cats are not black'). These were pictured as the corners of the *square of opposition*, whose sides and diagonals represented logical relations between the propositions (provided all four had the same subject and the same predicate, 'cats' and 'black' in the above examples). *Singular propositions* ('This cat (or Tiddles) is black') were traditionally treated as universal, though complications arise. The affirmative/negative distinction is called one of *quality*, the universal/particular distinction one of *quantity* (cf. QUANTIFICATION).

Both in the square of opposition and in the SYLLOGISM it was assumed that 'All cats are black' entails (see IMPLICATION) 'Some cats are black'. 'Some' can mean 'Some and perhaps all' on the inclusive interpretation, or 'Some but not all' on the exclusive interpretation, Nearly all logicians have found the inclusive interpretation more convenient because simpler. It is also assumed that 'some' means 'at least one', i.e. 'Some cats are black' is still true if only one is. In 'Some tea is undrinkable' it means 'not none'. In the last century, however, a problem arose, known as that of *existential import*, about which, if any, of the above four propositions entail that there exist any cats (or any black things, though this was less emphasized). It appeared that no otherwise acceptable answer could preserve intact the square of opposition and the traditional list of valid syllogisms, though for purposes of formal logic it was, and still is, found convenient to interpret. 'All cats are black' as *existentially negative*, i.e. as saying that nothing is a cat and not black. This is true if there are no cats, and so does not imply that there are any. But 'Some cats are black' was interpreted as *existentially affirmative*, i.e. as saying that there exists at least one thing which is both a cat and black. Clearly 'All cats are black' no longer then entails 'Some cats are black'.

To call 'All unicorns are black' true simply because there are no unicorns seems odd. One solution (Strawson) is to say that 'All unicorns are black' does not entail, but does presuppose, that there are unicorns (for this and related distinctions see IMPLICATION). If there are none it will then fail to be true, but in a way that need

Quantifier words

not upset the square of opposition (since it will not be false either, and the square only applies to what is true or false).

However, let us compare the following sentences: 'All coins in my pocket are silver.' 'All (of) the coins . . .' 'Some coins . . .' 'Some of the coins . . .' 'No coins . . .' 'None of the coins . . .' The cases containing 'the' imply (i.e. entail or presuppose) that coins exist in my pocket. ('The' may be implicit, as in 'All John's children', i.e. 'All the children of John'.) But these cases say nothing about coins that might be, but are not, in my pocket. The other cases, however, are rather ambiguous. 'All coins . . .' is perhaps most naturally taken to mean 'Were you to find any coins in my pocket (which you might or might not) they would be silver (I throw coppers away on principle)'. (Cf. LAWS for some issues relevant here.) 'Some coins . . .' could either mean 'Some of the . . .' or could be used in the same way as in the 'foxes' example below, according as 'some' is stressed or not. But 'some' does not mean 'some of the' in 'There are some unicorns' or 'Some water is needed', – nor in 'Some foxes entered my garden last night', where it is what is said about them that implies their existence; contrast: 'Some foxes would be useful to clear this field of rabbits.'

All this raises the question whether some or all of the quantifier words, in at least some of their uses, form part of referring expressions. Does 'No cats are black' refer to all cats and say of them that they are not black? Does 'Some cats are black' refer to all cats and say that they are not all not black, or does it perhaps refer only to those that are black? All these views have difficulties, and some writers say quantifier words never have a referring role (cf. DISTRIBUTION, REFERRING).

It seems that one role of 'any' is to make clear that what is being said is more like a law than a factual statement. 'Any body unacted on by forces moves in a straight line' carries less suggestion that there are such bodies than 'All bodies . . .' 'Any', however, can imply existence when combined with 'the', as in 'Any of the ones in that box would have done', and has ambiguities of its own: Compare 'Is any (at least one) member ready to vote?' and 'Is any (old) member entitled to vote?' Only the latter can be answered with 'Yes, any member'.

Another main role of 'any' is to emphasize randomness or choice: 'Any you choose, no matter which.' This may explain why 'any' is allied to 'some' as well as to 'all', for choice may be relevant in either case. But it only partly explains the substitution of 'any' for 'some' in many negative, interrogative and conditional contexts: 'Have you any matches (I don't mind which, or of what kind)?' 'If I had any matches', 'I haven't any matches (no matter what kind you choose)', 'I have some matches (but I have no choice about which, or what kind they are)', – but why 'I want some matches' and not (by itself) 'I want any matches'? ('I want *any* matches' (stressed) means 'I want as many as you've got, no matter what they're like'.) The negation, etc., may be only implicit: 'It was too smooth to have any effect', 'I was ashamed to take any' (but: 'glad to take some'), 'The question whether (condition that) there is any'.

'Any' tends, more than 'all', to focus attention on the individuals rather than the mass. Suppose we know that nearly all swans are white but a few are black. Then 'All swans are probably white', on its most natural interpretation, will be false, while 'Any swan (you choose) will probably be white' may be true. Note too that, though 'Any swan is white' implies 'All swans are white', 'Any of the candidates may win' does not imply 'All of the candidates may win; but 'any of the swans is white (choose which you like)' does imply they all are.

'Each' too, emphasizes that the things in question are taken one by one, or distributively, while 'all' can be interpreted distributively ('All the soldiers were conscripts') or collectively (I doubt if *all* the soldiers could defeat that enemy (much less each of them)'). 'They each gave a pound and presented him with a clock' is normally elliptical. The role of 'any', as against 'each', in selecting is seen by comparing 'I will take any of you on' with 'I will take each of you on'.

'Every' (from 'ever each', and apparently peculiar to English) is like 'each' in many respects. They both imply existence, and do not, like 'any', cover hypothetical cases. But whereas 'each' emphasizes taking the items separately, 'every' sometimes does not, but rather resembles 'all'. 'I told everybody to come', but not 'I told each person to come', is true if I told a crowd in which everybody was present. Similarly 'I will take every one of you on', like 'I will take all of you on', is ambiguous about whether I mean together or separately.

'A' is rather like 'any', though it only goes with the singular, and only with words that *can* be in the plural. Like 'any', though with these limitations, it can approximate to 'all' ('A whale breathes air') or to 'some' ('A man met me'). When approximating to 'all' it often signifies typicality rather than universality ('A cat usually likes fish'; in 'Any cat usually likes fish' the 'usually' limits the number of occasions, not the number of cats (unless there are commas round 'usually'), while in the former case it may limit either). 'A' also may or may not imply existence. 'I am looking for a dog' may or may not mean I have a definite dog in mind.

Other quantifier words include 'many', 'most', 'few', 'a few', 'several', 'one' (and numbers generally), and even 'the' in some uses ('The whale is a mammal'). 'The' perhaps gets its generalizing

Quine, Willard V. O.

use from referring to species ('The species whale is a species of mammal').

Finally, this entry, after its first four paragraphs, illustrates an approach to philosophical questions typical of the movement known as linguistic PHILOSOPHY.

T. Czezowski, 'On certain peculiarities of singular propositions', *Mind*, 1955. (The place of singular propositions in traditional logic. Cf. J. L. Mackie, ' "This" as a singular quantifier', *Mind*, 1958, L. Gumanski, 'Singular propositions and "this" as a quantifier', *Mind*, 1960.)

P. T. Geach, *Reference and Generality*, Cornell UP, 1962. (Contains discussions of quantifier words in connexions with reference, and also with conjunction and disjunction, and with scope. Draws on medieval discussions.)

*J. N. Keynes, *Formal Logic*, 1884, 4th (revised) edn, 1906. (Standard account of traditional formal logic.)

E. S. Klima, 'Negation in English' in J. A. Fodor and J. J. Katz (eds), *The Structure of Language*, Prentice-Hall, 1964. (Elaborate and technical, but see p. 294 for 'too' and p. 314 for 'ashamed' and 'glad'.)

W. V. O. Quine, *Word and Object*, Wiley, 1960, § 29. (Quantifier words and scope.)

P. F. Strawson, *Introduction to Logical Theory*, Methuen, 1952. (Chapter 6 discusses existential import.)

*Z. Vendler, 'Each and every, any and all,' *Mind*, 1962. (Cf. also his article 'Any and all' in P. Edwards (ed.), *The Encyclopedia of Philosophy*, Crowell, Collier and Macmillan, Free Press, 1967, where he connects the topic with the philosophy of science.)

Quine, Willard V. O. 1908–. American mathematical logician, born in Akron, Ohio, and working in Cambridge, Mass. He has elaborated a system of logic, following RUSSELL, where singular terms can be eliminated, and has cast doubt upon the ANALYTIC/synthetic distinction and similar distinctions, and on the extent to which determinate TRANSLATION is possible between, or even within, languages. He denies the possibility of a formalized INTENSIONAL logic. His slogan 'To be is to be the value of a variable' offers a criterion for distinguishing between realists and nominalists (cf. BEING, METAPHYSICS). *Methods of Logic*, 1950 (part 4 eliminates singular terms). *From a Logical Point of View*, 1953 (contains 'On What There Is', 1948 (the slogan), 'Two Dogmas of Empiricism', 1951 (analytic/synthetic), and articles relevant to meaning and intensional logic). *Word and Object*, 1960. *Ontological Relativity and other Essays*, 1969. *Philosophy of Logic*, 1970. *The Roots of Refer-*

Quine, Willard V. O.

ence, 1973. See also AMBIGUITY (bibliography), CONDITIONALS, INSCRIPTION (bibliography), INTUITIONISM (bibliography), LEIBNIZ'S LAW, MEANING, MODALITIES, QUANTIFICATION, QUANTIFIER (bibliography) REFERRING (bibliography), SATISFY (bibliography), SENTENCES, TOKEN-REFLEXIVES.

R

Radical interpretation and translation. See TRANSLATION.

Ramsey sentence. A device for showing what a theory is committed to. Suppose a theory T introduces certain new terms, $a, b, c \ldots$ where these are considered as names, whether of objects, properties, classes, etc.; e.g. if the theory introduces a predicate '... is a' we let a stand for the property a-hood. We can then represent the theory in the form T $(a, b, c \ldots)$ i.e. as 'theory T, containing terms $a, b, c \ldots$'. The relevant Ramsey sentence will then replace these terms by variables $x, y, z \ldots$, which are existentially quantified (see QUANTIFICATION): $\exists x \, \exists y \, \exists z \ldots [T(x, y, z, \ldots)]$.

D. Lewis, 'How to define theoretical terms', *Journal of Philosophy*, 1970 (using ideas from F. P. Ramsey's 'Theories', reprinted in D. H. Mellor (ed.), *Philosophical Papers*, Cambridge UP, 1990.

Range. See PROBABILITY, VARIABLE.

Rationalism. Any view appealing to reason as a source of knowledge or justification. Reason can be contrasted with revelation, in religion, or with emotion and feeling as in ethics, but in philosophy it is usually contrasted with the senses (including introspection, but not intuitions). 'Rationalist' is to 'A PRIORI' somewhat as 'EMPIRICIST' is to 'empirical', though the empiricist is more likely to apply his view to *all* knowledge. Rationalism is an outlook which somehow emphasizes the a priori and also the INNATE. 'Rationalist' has a variety of interpretations corresponding to those of 'empiricist'. A philosopher can be both rationalist and

Realism

empiricist, in different though important respects (e.g. Kant); but such philosophers are often thought to be best classified as neither.

'Continental rationalists' is a traditional label for Descartes, Spinoza and Leibniz, with various lesser figures of that period who are regarded as sharing their general outlook.

*J. Cottingham, *The Rationalists*, Oxford UP, 1988.

D. W. Hamlyn, *The Theory of Knowledge*, Macmillan, 1970. (Chapter 2 briefly discusses basis of rationalism as it appears in Descartes, Leibniz and Bradley (and then discusses empiricism).)

W. von Leyden, *Seventeenth-Century Metaphysics*, Duckworth, 1968. (Chapter 3 has general introduction to rationalism and empiricism.)

A. O. Lovejoy, *The Great Chain of Being*, Harvard UP, 1936; Harper and Row, 1960. (Chapter 5 brings out some features and conflicts of some developed rationalist philosophies (Leibniz and Spinoza). See also A PRIORI, EMPIRICIST.)

*J. Lyons, *Chomsky*, Fontana, 1970, expended, 1977. (Elementary introduction to influential thinker who has revived some rationalist ideas in the sphere of language-learning.)

G. Ryle (see bibliography to EPISTEMOLOGY (second Ryle item)).

Realism. Like 'real', 'realism' gets its senses largely from what it is contrasted with. Any view can be called realist which emphasizes the existence, reality or role, of some kind of thing or object (e.g. material objects, propositions, UNIVERSALS), in contrast to a view which dispenses with the things in question in favour of words (nominalism), ideas (idealism, conceptualism), or LOGICAL CONSTRUCTIONS (pheomenalism). Cf. PERCEPTION, IDENTITY, DEFINITION. For *naive realism* see PERCEPTION.

A question much debated recently is whether it makes sense to talk of truths that are real but can never be verified, and so are inaccessible to our knowledge. *Realists*, of the relevant kind, see no objection to this, and so allow that the meanings of individual sentences can be given simply in terms of TRUTH CONDITIONS (see MEANING). *Antirealists* refuse to accept unverifiable sentences, asking how we could acquire an understanding of them, or manifest it by asserting them on suitable occasions. They therefore insist on replacing truth conditions by assertibility conditions. Antirealism differs from traditional verificationism (see POSITIVISM) in not insisting on sense experience as the only means by which verification or assertibility can be achieved; it is not committed to saying, with the logical positivists, that a priori statements don't really say anything. Dummett in particular emphasizes the greater role allowed to infer-

Reason

ence in antirealism, and follows Quine in blurring the ANALYTIC/ synthetic distinction.

Putnam distinguishes *internal* from *external* or *metaphysical realism*. The latter is ordinary realism and postulates, in any relevant sphere, a fact of the matter independent of all theories; the former is weaker and only allows such postulations within a given theory.

'*Irrealism*' is sometimes used for the view that, 'of a given region of discourse . . . no real properties answer to the central predicates'.

In aesthetics realism emphasizes the nature of things as they are in themselves, not as we see them. A realist art-form aims to portray things as they are, not as mediated by some attitude, etc. of the artist; cf. NATURALISM.

For *modal realism* see POSSIBLE WORLDS.

P. A. Boghossian, 'The status of content', *Philosophical Review*, 1990. (Irrealism, which he argues against. For quotation see p. 157.)

D. Davidson (see para. beginning with him in bibliography to MEANING for the realism/antirealism debate. Cf. also M. A. E. Dummett, *Truth and Other Enigmans*, 1978, esp. its Preface, and M. Platts (ed.), *Reference, Truth and Reality*, 1980, esp. item by C. McGinn. For Dummett on antirealism and logical positivism see G. Evans and J. McDowell (eds), *Truth and Meaning*, 1976, p. 111. The intelligibility of realism is defended against Dummett by A. H. Goldman, 'Fanciful arguments for realism', *Mind.*, 1984).

Midwest Studies in Philosophy, vol. 12, 1988. (Single-topic journal issue entitled *Realism and Anti-Realism*. Also covers that topic in ethics.)

H. Putnam, *Reason, Truth and History*, Cambridge UP, 1981, chapter 3. (Internal and external realism. See also his *Meaning and the Moral Sciences*, RKP, 1978, part 4.)

C. Wright, *Realism, Meaning and Truth*, 2nd edn, Blackwell, 1993. (Chapters 9 and 10 discuss antirealism and verificationism, favouring them in limited area.)

Reason. A general faculty, common to all or nearly all humans and sometimes regarded, either seriously or by poetic licence, as a sort of impersonal external power ('the dictates (truths) of reason'). This faculty has seemed to be of two sorts, a faculty of intuition by which one 'sees' truths or abstract things ('essences' or universals, etc.), and a faculty of reasoning, i.e. passing from premises to a conclusion (*discursive reason*). The verb 'reason' is confined to this latter sense, which is now anyway the commonest for the noun too, though the two senses are related (to pass from premises to conclusion is to intuit a connexion between them).

Kant contrasts reason, which is concerned with mediate INFERENCES, and understanding and power of judgment, which are concerned with acquiring concepts and passing judgments, respectively.

Practical reason has been distinguished from *theoretical* or *speculative reason* since Aristotle, and raises problems: Is reason in the practical sphere 'the slave of the passions' (Hume), i.e. is it limited to showing us means to ends which the passions dictate?

How far can reason be distinguished from feeling, emotion, etc.? (This problem parallels that of relating theoretical reason to the senses: cf. PERCEPTION.) Can reason mediate between morals and self-interest ('A sacrifice beyond all reason')? Also how many kinds of reasoning are there apart from deductive reasoning? (Cf. LOGIC.)

A second group of uses of 'reason' allows the plural and involves expressions like 'a (the, his) reason'. A reason may be a cause as in 'the reason for the explosion', or a factor in an explanation as in 'the reason why there are infinitely many prime numbers', and again problems arise over the practical sphere: how are reasons for believing related to reasons for acting? Only the former are evidence, but Smith's honesty may be a reason for believing him, and also for rewarding him.

Can the reason why someone acts be a cause of his acting? This depends on whether actions can be caused but it is a further question whether *his* reason can be the cause. 'The' reason might be something he is unconscious of, which 'his' reason cannot be (cf. FREEWILL).

'He has a reason to act' may mean that acting would promote some purpose he has, or some interest he has, or some purpose he should morally have. An interest is perhaps a purpose he would or should rationally have if he knew certain facts. One can have a reason, even consciously, and act as it prescribes, without acting *from* it. Also *the* reason why Smith acted, whether or not it coincides with *his* reason, need not be *a* reason for acting, not even a poor reason. See also INCONTINENCE.

Aristotle, *De Anima (On the Soul)*, (III, 4–8 (theoretical reason), III, 9–10; *Nicomachean Ethics*, VII, 1–10; *De Motu (Movement of Animals)*, 701a, 7–25 (all these treat practical reason). (Classic though difficult discussions.)

H. I. Brown, *Rationality*, Routledge, 1988. (Criticizes view that rationality consists in evaluating evidence by rules. Also criticizes FOUNDATIONALISM and social relativism.)

R. Edgley, *Reason in Theory and Practice*, Hutchinson, 1969.

Recursive

(Defends practical reason, discussing its relations with theoretical.)

D. Gauthier, 'Reason and maximization,' *Canadian Journal of Philosophy* 1975. (How is maximizing utility related to rationality?)

D. Hume, *A Treatise of Human Nature*, 1739–40, book 2, part 3, § 3. (Reason as slave of passions; see p. 415 of edition by L. A. Selby-Bigge (Clarendon, 1888), and see also the indexes of this and Selby-Bigge's edition of Hume's *Enquiries* (Clarendon, 2nd edn, 1902) under 'reason' and 'reasoning' for Hume's general treatment of reason both theoretical and practical.)

I. Kant, *Critique of Pure Reason*, 1781, 1787. (See 'reason', 'understanding', 'judgment' in index to N. Kemp Smith's translation, 1929.)

J. Kemp, *Reason, Action and Morality*, RKP, 1964. (The place of reason in morals and conduct. Includes historical material.)

J. Raz (ed.), *Practical Reasoning*, Oxford UP, 1978. (Readings.)

Recursive. Said of a procedure which can be applied to a starting point to get a certain result, and then re-applied to that result to get a further result, and so on. Adding one is a recursive procedure for generating the natural numbers from zero. *Recursion theory* is a branch of mathematical logic studying FUNCTIONS definable by such procedures. See also DEFINITION, INDUCTION.

A set is *recursively enumerable* if there is a procedure for generating its members (not necessarily in any given order). If both a set and its complement (i.e. the set containing just those items in the relevant domain that are not members of the original set) are recursively enumerable then the set itself is called recursive. In that case there is a DECISION PROCEDURE for whether candidates for membership are or are not members: since there is a process for generating both members and non-members, we wait to see in which list the candidate item appears. With a merely recursively enumerable procedure we can prove that something is a member, if it is, but cannot prove it is not a member, if it is not. The predicate calculus, for instance (i.e. the set of its theorems), is recursively enumerable but not recursive.

Reduction. See PERCEPTION, PHENOMENOLOGY.

Reductionism. Also called *reductivism*. Tendency to reduce certain notions, whether everyday ones, like *physical object*, or theoretical ones in science, like *electron*, to allegedly simpler or more basic notions, or more empirically accessible ones, e.g. one might claim to dispense with the word 'electron' and talk only of vapour trails in cloud chambers. To reduce a theory or a science to another is to show that the latter can in principle yield all the results of the former, e.g. that everything psychology tells us we could in principle learn from physiology. Reductionism is a feature especially of PHENOMENALISTS, and other empiricists, and of POSITIVISTS in philosophy of science. See also PHILOSOPHY.

But reduction can also, and in recent discussions usually must, be distinguished from elimination. 'Water is H_2O' reduces water to H_2O but does not say there is no water, while 'Demons are (really) viruses' does say that there are no demons. In reduction we get a straight definition of water, whereas demons are not, or not straightforwardly, defined in terms of viruses. Rather the phenomena once attributed to demons are now thought to be caused by viruses. Similarly MATERIALISM may take a reductive or an eliminative attitude to mental phenomena. A third outlook, however, appeals to SUPERVENIENCE.

To sum up, we might *reduce* (say) A to B by saying that A is real, but *what* it is is B – there is only one thing there, which is both A and B, B having explanatory priority; or we might *eliminate A*, so that there is only B; or we might say that A is real and distinct from B, but *supervenes* on it.

D. Charles and K. Lennon (eds), *Reduction, Explanation, and Realism*, Oxford UP, 1993. (Specially commissioned essays. See its 'Introduction' for relations between reduction, elimination and supervenience.)

T. Horgan, 'From supervenience to superdupervenience', *Mind*, 1993. (See esp. p. 575 for reductive and eliminative materialism, and the possibility of a third kind, with many references.)

Reduction sentences. A technical device introduced by Carnap, to avoid a difficulty that arises over definitions like ' "is soluble" means "dissolves if immersed" '. With 'if' interpreted in terms of material IMPLICATION, as is usual in logic, this definition would make anything soluble that was never actually immersed. The general idea is to avoid giving a definition, but to give instead conditions under which something is soluble, and conditions under which it is not, which do not imply that everything which is never immersed is soluble.

R. Carnap, 'Testability and meaning', *Philosophy of Science*, 1936 and 1937, § 8.

Reference. See REFERRING, MEANING.

Referent. See REFERRING.

Referring

Referring. There is a group of terms, including 'refer', 'denote', 'name', 'designate', 'stand for', 'mention', 'be about', 'talk about', 'say of', 'apply to', 'be true of', which somehow seem to connect language with objects in the widest sense. Some of these terms are used varyingly, and sometimes interchangeably, but all have peculiarities.

Referring is done primarily by people. Words and sentences refer only in so far as people use them to do so, and therefore often differently on different occasions. (Cf. MEANING for referring and denoting, and for sense and reference. A sentence can 'refer' in this derivative way, by containing a term that refers, without having a 'reference' in the technical sense, i.e. without referring as a whole and in its own right.)

When does referring occur? 'Smith is tall' is true of many people. But if I say the words 'Smith is tall' I normally refer only to some Smith I have in mind. The context shows which. Suppose, however, I intend to refer to Smith, and in fact say things true only of him, but mistakenly use the name 'Jones'. Have I referred to Smith? If my audience realize the mistake, perhaps I have, although I referred to him as 'Jones'. But suppose they are deceived? Certainly I have not mentioned Smith, whereas I perhaps have mentioned one of the Joneses, at any rate if there is exactly one reasonably relevant in the context. (*Mentioning* something involves at least using some name or description which actually applies to it – or would apply to it if it existed; see 'Alaska' example below.) A further case is when I deliberately use 'Jones' because I know (or believe) my audience wrongly thinks of Smith as 'Jones'. In general must I, to refer, secure uptake? These and other problems occur also when I use not names but descriptions, or words like 'someone' (cf. also QUANTIFIER WORDS).

So much for subject expressions, but do we refer in using predicates, and in identity statements? Suppose I say, perhaps mistakenly, 'That is my doctor': have I referred to, and have I mentioned, my doctor? Again we can mention and refer to universals ('Tallness is becoming commoner') but do I mention or refer to tallness in saying 'Smith is tall'. Confusions in this area may contribute to referential theories of MEANING. That we *can* refer to tallness, and that 'tall' as a predicate has *some* relation to tallness, may suggest that 'tall' always refers to tallness and has meaning by doing so. An ambiguity of *stand for* may also cause confusion here: ' "Tall" stands for tallness' may mean ' "Tall" refers to tallness', or ' "Tall" is the term to use when applying the concept tallness'. Other questions bearing on referential theories of meaning are how we can understand propositions which involve reference to objects we are not acquainted with, and whether we must be in some way causally related to things if we are to refer to them, i.e. whether we should accept a causal theory of reference (see also MEANING).

Many of these problems recur with *about*. 'Talk about' resembles 'refer to'. Talking *about* something may seem to involve more than 'merely referring to' it, but perhaps one can refer to something without talking about it only if one is interrupted in mid sentence, etc. Of course talking about something here may amount simply to asking questions etc. about it. 'Be about' applies mainly to statements, problems, etc., rather than people, and has a more technical air. It is not obvious where to draw the line between what a statement is and is not about, and there is a danger of any statement being about everything (Goodman).

So far we have distinguished referring from related notions, and have considered the effects of things like the role of the speaker's intentions and mistakes, and of the speaker's and hearer's beliefs. A special group of problems concern referring and existence. How can we refer to or talk about what does not exist, be it fictional (Pickwick), future (one's own death), a LOGICAL CONSTRUCTION (the average man), or simply a muddle (the round square)? Do such things have some sort of BEING SO (Meinong), or do we not 'really' refer to them (Russell. Cf. theory of DESCRIPTIONS)? Or is referring not, or not always, a relation (which requires real terms to relate)? Is the use of the 'objects' mentioned in the first sentence of this entry simply a linguistic device? Perhaps 'The king of Alaska is tall' mentions that non-existent king, but does this simply mean that a certain phrase is used – a phrase suitable for mentioning a real king if there were one?

The 'king of Alaska' example introduces a further group of problems: how far are notions like referring essential to language? Does the fact that the phrase is suitable for mentioning a real king if there were one mean that 'mentioning the king of Alaska' is a phrase we can only understand because we understand phrases like 'mentioning the Queen of England', where this is one? Are non-designative names possible only because we have designative names? We have asked whether it is only because their objects are sometimes real objects that referring etc. are possible. One can ask whether at least some of these objects must be particulars and not UNIVERSALS. But one can further ask whether referring, etc., could be dispensed with, either in a language spoken by people who already knew a language containing them, or (more radically) in a people's first language. Could other devices in language, like predicating, be understood without these notions? Quine claims that we can eliminate singular terms in favour of found VARIABLES; but could we understand the role of these without first understand-

Reflective equilibrium

ing that of singular terms? Could there be a language with quite different devices altogether.

A *referent* is what is referred to. A *reference class* (probability theory) is the population serving as a basis for statistical statements. In '10 per cent of Englishmen are Catholics' Englishmen form the reference class; in 'The probability of a double six is 1/36' the reference class may be throws of a die, or of a double die, according to context. For *divided reference* see MEANING.

K. Donnellan, 'Reference and definite descriptions', *Philosophical Review*, 1966. (Often reprinted. Influential distinction between attributive and referential ways of interpreting definite DESCRIPTIONS.)

G. Evans, *The Varieties of Reference*, 1982. (Thorough but difficult.)

P. T. Geach, *Reference and Generality* Cornell UP, 1962. (Referring and allied notions, including discussion of QUANTIFIER WORDS. See especially 'denoting' in index. Cf. also his *Mental Acts*, 1957.)

N. Goodman, 'About', *Mind*, 1961. (Mainly rather technical, but § 2 is good introduction to paradox concerning 'about'. Cf. also D. Holdcroft, 'A principle about "about"', *Mind*, 1968, M. Hodges, 'On "being about"', *Mind*, 1971, which both concern 'about' and existence. See Holdcroft, pp. 515–17 for whether sentences have references.)

L. Linsky, *Referring*, RKP, 1967. (Discusses referring in connexion with existing and describing. More historical than Meiland, discussing Meinong, Frege, Russell, Strawson.)

G. McCulloch, *The Game of the Name: Introducing Logic, Language, and Mind*, Clarendon, 1989. (Introduction to many aspects of contemporary philosophy based on the topic of proper names. Presupposes elementary logic and some general appreciation at undergraduate level of aims of analytical philosophy. Each chapter has annotated bibliography.)

J. W. Meiland, *Talking about Particulars*, RKP, 1970. (General discussion of nature of referring.)

W. V. O. Quine, *Methods of Logic*, RKP, 1952. (Part 4 tries, following Russell, to eliminate singular terms, i.e. to eliminate referring except by bound variables (see QUANTIFICATION).)

P. F. Strawson, *Individuals*, Methuen, 1959. (Part 2 distinguishes referring and predicating. Stresses role of particulars and discusses eliminability of referring. Fairly difficult. Cf. I. Hacking, 'A language without particulars', *Mind*, 1968, claiming that a certain Amerindian language is such a language.)

Reflective equilibrium. The goal of a process of reconciling our native intuitions in a given area with a set of principles which we take to govern that area. The intuitions and the principles are balanced against each other, with the result that discordant intuitions are exposed as such and discounted, while the principles are adjusted and sophisticated to take account of and systematize as many of the intuitions as possible. In particular, moral and political philosophy, scientific reasoning, and questions about personal identity have provided fields for this process.

S. Darwall, A. Gibbard and P. Railton, 'Toward *fin de siècle* ethics: some trends', *Philosophical Review*, 1992. (See pp. 168–74 for some relevant discussion.)

N. Goodman, *Fact, Fiction and Forecast*, Athlone Press and MIT Press, 1954; revised in later edns (see chapter 3, and section 2).

J. Rawls, *A Theory of Justice*, Oxford UP, 1972. (See its index.)

H. Sidgwick, *The Methods of Ethics*, Macmillan 1874 (7th edn and final version, 1907). (Balances utilitarianism and other systems against the moral intuitions of common sense.)

Reflexive. A relation is reflexive if a term which has it at all must have it to itself (*as old as*). It is *irreflexive* or *aliorelative* if a term cannot have it to itself (*older than*), and *non-reflexive* if it may or may not have it to itself (*fond of*).

Refute. Successfully show to be false. But it is not necessary for hearer to be convinced. Not synonymous with 'reject' or 'rebut'.

A. Flew, *An Introduction to Western Philosophy*, Thames and Hudson, 1971, revised edn, 1989, pp. 21–3.

Reid, Thomas. 1710–96. Born at Strachan, he worked mainly in Aberdeen and Glasgow. He is generally known as the founder of the 'Scottish school of common sense', which reacted against the sceptical conclusions of the 'British EMPIRICISTS'. Reid, like KANT, was particularly influenced by HUME (whom some scholars think he misinterpreted.) Being unable to accept Hume's sceptical conclusions, he attacked the basis from which Hume began, and substituted one based on our common-sense assumptions. *Essays on the Intellectual Powers of Man*, 1785 (epistemology). *Essays on the Active Powers of Man*, 1788 (psychology and ethics).

Relations (external and internal). A relation is internal to the things it relates (its terms) when they would not be the things they are unless related by it. Otherwise it is external. 'Orange is between red and yellow' expresses an internal relation, presumably, because these colours would not be what they are unless related in this way. Alternatively a relation is internal if without it its terms would not

Relativism

have the qualities they have. If crimson is a dark colour and pink is a light colour, *being darker than pink* is internal to crimson, for if crimson were not darker than pink it would not be a dark colour. In a looser sense whether a relation is internal may depend on how its terms are described. *Being married* is internal to a husband, described as such, but not, presumably, to Smith. For the husband would not be a husband unless married, but Smith could be Smith whether married or not. Some philosophers, notably Bradley, held the *doctrine of internal relations*, that all relations are internal in one or both of the stricter senses. Bradley added that ultimately relations are unreal.

F. H. Bradley, *Appearance and Reality*, 2nd edn, 1897, Appendix B. (Cf. also chapter 3.)

G. E. Moore, *Philosophical Studies*, Kegan Paul, Trench, Trubner, 1922, chapter 9. (Criticizes doctrine).

Relativism. Any doctrine could be called relativism which holds that something exists, or has certain properties or features, or is true or in some sense obtains, not simply but only in relation to something else. Some form of relativism seems plausible for statements like 'Strawberries are nice' (for whose palate?), 'The angles of a triangle sum to two right angles' (in Euclidean or non-Euclidean geometry?), 'I am at rest' (relative to my car? the earth? the sun?). In practice two forms of relativisism have been popular: cognitive and moral.

Cognitive relativism, so called as applying to knowledge claims in general rather than simply to claims about value, etc., can take the extreme form that all beliefs are true. If no proposition can be both true and false, then when A believes what B disbelieves we can call their disagreement merely apparent and say they are really thinking of different propositions; if A Says 'X is red' and B says 'X is not red' they must really be saying (e.g. 'X looks red to me'. This could be avoided by saying they are talking of the same proposition, but each saying that it is true to him, not simply true; 'true' is replaced by 'true for'. This second doctrine can be called *subjective relativism*, and Plato attributes it to Protagoras (second half of fifth century BC).

Cognitive relativism is more plausible when applied not to individuals but to societies, cultures, or 'conceptual schemes' (*cultural relativism*). Individuals can then hold false beliefs if they misapply their own principles, as a Euclidean geometer could wrongly think the angles of a triangle sum to three right angles. Cultural relativism can also apply to principles of reasoning as well as to propositions believed, but a standard objection to all these relativisms is that

296

the claim that relativism is true, or the argument by which it is supported, is itself surely put forward as being absolutely true or valid; do not the very notions of asserting and arguing involve those of absolute truth and absolute validity? Is not to assert something, or put forward an argument, to present it as being absolutely true or valid?

Could one then limit relativism to certain spheres? It has seemed especially plausible in science, partly because scientific theories seem to become accepted without their predecessors being straight-forwardly refuted, and partly because it is claimed that different scientific systems are simply incommensurable (Kuhn) and scientific terms are THEORY-LADEN: 'mass' and 'time' mean something differ-ent for Einstein from what they meant for Newton, so that Einstein couldn't show Newton was wrong in what he said. Relativism is encouraged by the holistic approach of Quine and others, where we can call any statement true or false if we make enough adjustments elsewhere in our theory (we can insist that the sun goes round the earth by making enough adjustments to our dynamics etc.) But the related doctrine of the indeterminacy of TRANSLATION is differ-ent from incommensurability, and they may even be inconsistent (Hacking). Relativism may also seem inevitable if we cannot avoid taking for granted some background of theory or set of concepts (*conceptual scheme*) or PARADIGM; we cannot criticize everything at once. (But see Davidson on conceptual schemes.) But if we adopt relativism in science, will not the same reasons make us adopt it elsewhere, with the problems discussed above? Can we stop halfway?

Moral relativism, encouraged in both ancient and modern times by anthropological reports of cultural diversity, applies relativism to statements of value or duty, etc. As cognitive relativism may replace 'true' by 'true for', so moral relativism may replace 'right' by 'right for', saying, e.g., that cannibalism is right for certain primi-tives but wrong for Europeans. But relativism here must be distin-guished from saying that cannibalism is thought by Europeans to be (absolutely) wrong, and from saying that cannibalism is (absolutely) wrong for Europeans but right for primatives, as someone might say it is right for the starving, or that smacking children is right for parents but wrong for teachers. Obviously one's role or circum-stances can affect what it is right for one to do, and some doctrines are only improperly called relativism. Also one who thinks *all* moral judgments are relative to societies, etc. must not conclude it is (absolutely) right to live and let live (see Williams). We must distin-guish saying something is (absolutely) right for those in certain circumstances and saying that 'right' has no meaning and must be replaced by a different term, 'right for' or 'right by such-and-such

Relevance logic

standards'; a relativist might say nothing can be right except by reference to some standard, and standards can only be judged by reference to other standards. How does 'right' compare with 'true' here? Another question is whether the relativist means that any act can only be judged by the standards of the agent or his society, or that any appraisal can be judged only by the standards of the appraiser or his society (Lyons). This may affect (e.g.) our assessment of one society's appraisal of another society. Suppose A approves and B disapproves of C's abortion: on the former view only that appraisal will be correct which accords with the norms of C's society; on the latter view both appraisals can be correct if they accord with the norms of A's and B's societies respectively.

Relativism is not the same as SUBJECTIVISM, in any sphere. Some relativism may be subjectivist, but a relativist need not say that what seem to be assertions of the relevant kind are really disguised commands or expressions of attitude, etc., nor that they are really about the speaker's or someone else's beliefs or attitudes.

See also PERSPECTIVISM.

M. Giaquinto, 'Science and ideology', *Proceedings of the Aristotelian Society*, 1983–4. (How they differ and why science is better.)

M. Krausz and J. W. Meiland (eds), *Relativism: Cognitive and Moral*, Notre Dame UP, 1982. M. Hollis and S. Lukes (eds), *Rationality and Relativism*, Blackwell, 1982. (Two sets of readings, both with introduction and bibliography. First includes Davidson, Williams and Lyons: second includes Hacking.)

T. S. Kuhn, H. Putnam (see bibliography to SCIENCE).

Plato, *Theaetetus*, §§ 152–86. (Discussion of Protagoras. Cf. also Plato's dialogue, *Protagoras*.)

W. V. O. Quine, 'Two dogmas of empiricism' in his *From a Logical Point of View*, Harper and Row, 1953. (Classic source for his holistic approach.)

G. Sher, 'Moral relativism defended?', *Mind*, 1980 (Criticizes views of G. Harman in Krausz and Meiland (above).).

F. E. Snare, 'The diversity of morals', *Mind*, 1980. (Defends version of moral relativism.)

Relevance logic. See IMPLICATION.

Reliabilism. See EPISTEMOLOGY.

Religion (philosophy of). The study of general philosophical problems about religion and God. Particular religious doctrines belong rather to *revealed* or *dogmatic theology* or to *comparative religion*, though their logical, metaphysical, etc. implications belong to philosophy of religion.

An initial question is, what counts as a religion? Must there be one or more gods involved? What counts as a god, and in particular as the God of monotheism?

Natural theology is a part of philosophy of religion. Without using revelation it examines the existence, nature, properties and abilities of God, and His relations to the world. Are there limits to His power? Can He perform logical impossibilities, or set Himself problems that He cannot solve (*paradox of omnipotence*)? Can He be omniscient compatibly with human, or indeed His own, freewill (*paradoxes of omniscience*)? Can He be both omnipotent and benevolent, the world being as it is (*problem of evil*)? Concerning His nature one can ask whether He exists necessarily, how His essence relates to His existence, and whether He has His predicates in the ordinary sense or analogically. An important question is whether God exists in time. If so, must He not in some way develop? And how does His existence fit in with relativity theory? If He is timeless, in what sense can He be a person or can He act? And can His omniscience include knowledge of facts involving temporal TOKEN-REFLEXIVES (see Sorabji)?

Arguments for God's existence include the ONTOLOGICAL ARGUMENT, the COSMOLOGICAL ARGUMENT, the argument from DESIGN, and the argument from religious experience. The last has it that there is a special religious experience which guarantees or lets us infer the existence of God as its object.

On God and the world one can ask: Did He create the world, and if so, in what sense? Does He determine laws of nature, or of logic, or of morality? Does He intervene in the world with miracles, and what counts as a miracle?

Religious questions have been affected by the recent dominance of logic and semantics. How do religious words and discourse have meaning? Are religious statements to be interpreted literally or in some other way (the modern version of the medieval problem about analogical predication; see above)?

The field of religious experience suggests questions about mysticism, awe, the numinous, and also faith: what is faith, how is it related to rational evidence and superstition, and can it be justified? Can there be a duty to believe? Religions promising immortality engender questions shared with philosophy of MIND. Problems peculiar to Christianity arise over concepts like the Trinity, the Incarnation, transubstantiation, salvation, grace and prayer, and their bearings on substance, causality, freewill again, and responsibility.

B. Davis, *An Introduction to the Philosophy of Religion*, Oxford

Remembering

UP, 1982. (Mainly covering God's existence and nature, evil, morality, miracles, survival of death.)

P. Helm (ed.), *Divine Commands and Morality*, Oxford UP, 1981.

*J. Hick, *Philosophy of Religion*, Prentice-Hall, 1963. (General introduction.)

A. Kenny, *The Five Ways*, RKP, 1969. (Aquinas' proofs for God's existence.)

J. L. Mackie, 'Evil and omnipotence', *Mind*, 1955. (Problem of evil and paradox of omnipotence. Cf. discussions in succeeding volumes, and in Schlesinger (below). See also Mackie's *The Miracle of Theism*, Clarendon, 1982, discussing this and other arguments about God's existence.)

*B. Mitchell (ed.), *The Philosophy of Religion*, Oxford UP, 1971. (Introductory anthology.)

A. O'Hear, *Experience, Explanation and Faith*, RKP, 1984. (Discusses arguments about God's existence falling in these areas.)

G. Schlesinger, *Religion and Scientific Method*, Reidel, 1977. (Offers new solution to problem of evil and claims that theism can be scientifically confirmed.)

N. Smart, *Philosophers and Religious Truth*, SCM Press, 1964. (Early chapters have good points on miracles, freedom, God's existence. Fifth chapter contrasts mystical and numinous.)

R. K. Sorabji, *Time, Creation, and the Continuum*, Duckworth, 1983. (See chapter 16 on timelessness and omniscience, based on discussion of ancient writings.)

Remembering. See MEMORY.

Resemblance. See UNIVERSALS.

Resultance. See SUPERVENIENCE.

Results. See CAUSATION.

Richard's paradox. One of what are sometimes called the semantic PARADOXES (cf. RUSSELL'S PARADOX, TYPES). Take all decimal numbers between 0 and 1 specifiable in finitely many words. Each will have infinitely many digits. Those which apparently terminate are followed by endless 0's. Arrange these numbers in some order in a table, so that each number occupies a row and its digits appear in successive columns. Take the number formed by the diagonal of the table, starting from the top left. For any n, the n-th digit of this diagonal number will be the n-th digit of the n-th row in the table. Replace each digit in this diagonal number by its successor.

Russell, Bertrand A. W.

(Assume the successor of 9 is 0.) The resulting number cannot appear in the table, yet is specifiable in finitely many words (we have just specified it).

This *diagonal procedure* was originally used by G. Cantor (1845–1918) to prove that there must be more decimal numbers than can be put in a table as above, even though such a table has infinitely many rows. Since the infinite number of decimals thus exceeds the infinite number of rows in such a table, in the sense that these numbers cannot be paired off with each other, there must be more than one 'transfinite' (i.e. infinite) number. This last result is not affected by solutions to Richard's paradox, which only concerns numbers specifiable in finitely many words.

E. Teensma, *The Paradozes*, Van Gorcum, 1969, pp. 32–4.

Rousseau, Jean-Jacques. 1712–78. Political philosopher and philosopher of education, he was born in Geneva and lived largely in France, often under patronage (including that of HUME in England). He emphasized the corrupting effects of society on man in his natural condition. He thought that society must be considered to be founded on a social contract between men, and he elaborated a notion of the 'general will', which would be represented in the decisions made in a properly ordered society. The sovereign's decisions were legitimate only when they represented this general will, not (as with HOBBES) whenever the sovereign had effective power. He also set forth principles of education in line with his other views. *Discours sur les sciences et les arts*, 1750. *Discours sur l'origine et les fondements de l'inégalité parmi les hommes*, 1755. *Du Contrat social*, 1762. *Émile*, 1762 (on education).

Russell, Bertrand A. W. 1872–1970. Born at Ravenscroft, Glos., he worked mainly in England (especially Cambridge), sometimes in America. His early fame rested on two main contributions to logic, the theory of DESCRIPTIONS and the theory of TYPES. He taught Wittgenstein at Cambridge before the First World War. His later work concentrated mainly on EPISTEMOLOGY, metaphysics and philosophy of mind, where he based himself mainly on the empiricist tradition of HUME, MILL, etc., though he was notorious for changing his views. He also stressed the importance to philosophy of modern scientific developments. A prolific writer, Russell was also famous for his great political and social commitment. *The Principles of Mathematics*, 1903, revised, 1937. 'On Denoting', *Mind*, 1905 (theory of descriptions). *Principia Mathematica*, 1910–13 (with WHITEHEAD. Theory of types). *Our Knowledge of the External World*, 1914. 'The philosophy of logical atomism', *Monist*, 1918. *The*

Russell's paradox

Analysis of Mind, 1921. *An Inquiry into Meaning and Truth*, 1940. See also BROAD, CALCULUS, CATEGORIES, CAUSATION, CLASS, FREGE, IMPLICATION, INDUCTION, INTENSIONALITY AND INTENTIONALITY, LANGUAGE (PHILOSOPHY OF), LOGICAL ATOMISM, LOGICAL CONSTRUCTIONS, MATHEMATICS (bibliography), MEANING, MONISM, PARADIGM CASE, PARADOX, PHENOMENALISM, PHILOSOPHY, QUINE, REFERRING, RUSSELL'S PARADOX, SENSE DATA, SENTENCES, STRAWSON, SUFFICIENT REASON, TOKEN-REFLEXIVES, TRUTH, UNIVERSALS, VARIABLE

Russell's paradox. Most classes are not members of themselves (the class of cats is not a cat), but some classes are members of themselves (the class of classes is a class). Is the class of all classes that are not members of themselves a member of itself? If yes, no. If no, yes. This is the most famous of the logical PARADOXES. Russell invented his theory of TYPES in order to answer it.

R. M. Sainsbury, *Paradoxes*, Cambridge UP, 1988, revised, 1995. (Chapter 5 gives brief introduction.)

Ryle, Gilbert. 1900–76. British philosopher born at Brighton and working in Oxford, who was one of the early protagonists of 'linguistic PHILOSOPHY'. His main work was in philosophy of MIND and in philosophical LOGIC. He was particularly famous for criticizing the 'ghost in the machine' view of mind and body, which he attributed primarily to DESCARTES, and he analysed various mental concepts in terms of dispositions to behave in certain ways. In his youth he felt some affinity for PHENOMENOLOGY. *The Concept of Mind*, 1949. *Dilemmas*, 1954. See also CATEGORIES, CONDITIONALS (bibliography), DIALECTIC (bibliography), EPISTEMOLOGY, FEELING, FREEWILL (bibliography), HETEROLOGICAL, INFERENCE, LIAR, MATHEMATICS, NEGATION, POLYMORPHOUS, RATIONALISM, SCEPTICISM, SEEING, SENSATION, SENTENCES, THINKING, TOPIC-NEUTRAL.

S

Salva Veritate. See INTENSIONALITY.

Santayana, George. 1863–1952. Born in Madrid, he worked at Harvard and then in Europe, dying at Rome. An apparently paradoxical figure, a Catholic agnostic who attacked broadchurchmanship and religious and political liberalism, an aesthetically minded Platonist who called himself a materialist, a rejector of modern ideas of inevitable progress who admired the pragmatist William James, he accepted our impulses for what they were but treated reason as a further impulse, a neutral integrator of the rest. He believed in essences, but not as a superior realm. The ordinary world exists, and we must start from ordinary beliefs, and not seek the illusory foundations sought in vain by the sceptic. How far his philosophy changed in his later works is controversial. *The Sense of Beauty*, 1896. *The Life of Reason* (five volumes), 1905–6. *Winds of Doctrine*, 1913 (criticisms). *Scepticism and Animal Faith*, 1923. *Realms of Being* (four volumes, on Essence, Matter, Truth, Spirit), 1927–40, in single volume with new introduction, 1942. *Dominations and Powers*, 1951 (social philosophy).

Sartre, Jean-Paul. 1905–80. Born in Paris, he worked mostly in France, with some study in Germany. Famous both as a writer of novels and plays and as a philosopher, he represented one form of EXISTENTIALISM, though his later work tended towards Marxism. He was the most explicitly atheistic of existentialists, and took an active part in politics. *Esquisse d'une théorie des émotions*, 1939. *L'Être et le néant*, 1943. *L'Existentialisme est un humanisme*, 1946 (popular, but often regarded as not representing his main thought).

Satisfice

Critique de la raison dialectique, 1960 (Marxist in tendency). See also BAD FAITH, MARCEL, MERLEAU-PONTY.

Satisfice. As an optimizing policy gets, or aims to get, the best results possible so a satisficing policy gets, or aims to get, results sufficient but not necessarily the best possible. The notion derives from the economist H. A. Simon (1916–).

M. Slote and P. Pettit, 'Satisficing consequentialism', *Proceedings of the Aristotelian Society*, supplementary vol., 1984. (Some philosophical implications Cf. also M. Slote, *Common Sense Morality and Consequentialism*, RKP, 1985, chapter 3.)

Satisfy. A notion introduced by Tarski to help construct his semantic definition of TRUTH for formalized languages. Consider a sentential FUNCTION 'x loves y' and suppose that John loves Mary. Then 'x loves y' is satisfied by any ordered sequence of objects whose first two terms are John and Mary taken in that order. In general, suppose a certain sentential function contains n different free VARIABLES (some of which may be repeated: 'x loves x' has only one.) Then take any sequence of objects and assign its first n terms, taken in order, to the n variables respectively, also taken in some order (usually alphabetical). Then the sequence satisfies the function if the first n terms of the sequence are related as the resulting sentence says they are. To ensure the sequence is long enough, it is convenient to take only infinite sequences and ignore all superfluous terms, i.e. all after the first n. A sentence, or closed sentential function, contains no free variables, so that all the terms in all sequences are superfluous. 'John loves Mary', therefore is (vacuously) satisfied by all sequences if he does, and by none if he doesn't. Tarski therefore defines truth by calling a sentence true if all sequences satisfy it and false if none do. The limitation to formalized languages has to do with problems like the LIAR PARADOX.

W. V. O. Quine, *Philosophy of Logic*, Prentice-Hall, 1970, esp. chapter 3. (Priority of satisfaction over truth.)
A. Tarski, 'The semantic conception of truth and the foundations of semantics', *Philosophy and Phenomenological Research*, 1944, reprinted in H. Feigl and W. Sellars (eds), *Readings in Philosophical Analysis*, Appleton-Century-Crofts, 1949. (See also the account by M. Black, 'The semantic definition of truth', *Analysis*, 1948, reprinted in M. MacDonald (ed.), *Philosophy and Analysis*, Blackwell, 1954.)

Saturated. See CONCEPT.

Scepticism

Scepticism. Any view involving doubt about whether something exists, or about whether we can know something, or about whether we are justified in arguing in certain ways. Throughout the ages many philosophers have held that unless we know some things for certain we cannot know anything at all, or even legitimately think anything probable (cf. FOUNDATIONALISM). Many of them, especially the Greek sceptics and Descartes, have therefore sought a sure mark or 'criterion' of when a proposition is true.

One can doubt whether knowledge can he had in certain spheres, or whether it can be had by certain methods. An extreme rationalist like Plato, sometimes, may doubt if we can ever get knowledge through the senses. An extreme empiricist like Hume may doubt if we can ever get it through reason, or through any reasoning except deductive (Hume again; see INDUCTION). Particular arguments may attack the reliability of particular kinds of alleged knowledge, e.g. memory, precognition, intuition.

The sceptic may doubt whether we can know something, or even have any reason to believe it (cf. agnostics). Less often he may deny that certain things exist, or that they could exist, even though he must then claim to know negative propositions (dogmatic scepticism; cf. atheists). He may deny or doubt the existence of God, of objects when not experienced (Berkeley), of any objects at all beyond our experiences themselves, i.e. beyond our SENSATIONS or SENSE DATA (Hume; cf. PERCEPTION), and that subjects like ethics contain any truths to be known (logical POSITIVISTS; cf. NATURALISM). Sceptics have asked how we could know of the past (Russell asked how we know we did not spring into existence, complete with 'memories', five minutes ago), or of minds other than our own. Descartes even tried, unsuccessfully, to doubt his own existence. Milder forms of scepticism allow that we can know something but only by certain methods: perhaps we can know that ordinary objects, or others' feelings, exist, but only by inference, not by direct observation.

The views that nothing exists outside one's own mind, or that nothing such can be known to exist, are called *solipsism* (literally, 'only-oneself-ism'). A weaker version of solipsism concerns merely the existence of other minds (one form of the *other minds problem*, though this problem also concerns what we can know, and how, *about* other minds, e.g. what others are thinking and feeling).

One particular question that the sceptic asks is how I can know that I am not now dreaming.

Methodological scepticism is the adoption of sceptical views not to defend them but as a starting point, departures from which are to be justified. Thus Descartes' *method of doubt* involves doubting

Scepticism

everything until something necessarily undoubtable is found, on which knowledge can be built. See also METHODOLOGICAL SOLIPSISM.

Radical forms of scepticism have often been unpopular on the grounds that they cannot coherently be stated without presupposing their own falsity (cf. TRANSCENDENTAL ARGUMENTS). See also PRIVATE LANGUAGE ARGUMENT, ACCESS, INCORRIGIBLE, PERCEPTION, SEXTUS EMPIRICUS.

J. L. Austin (see bibliography to SENSE DATA).

J. Bogen and M. Beckner, 'An empirical refutation of Cartesian scepticism', *Mind*, 1979. (Attacks Descartes' argument from dreaming. For an earlier and different attack see M. Macdonald, 'Sleeping and waking', *Mind*, 1953).

M. F. Burnyeat (ed.), *The Skeptical Tradition*, California UP, 1983. (Historical essays, half on ancient scepticism and half on modern reactions.)

A. P. Griffiths, 'Justifying moral principles', *Proceedings of the Aristotelian Society*, 1957–8. (Tries to rescue morals from the sceptic.)

D. Hume, *Treatise*, 1739, and *Enquiry concerning Human Understanding*, 1748. (Nearest among great philosophers to scepticism.)

A. A. Long, *Hellenistic Philosophy*, Duckworth, 1974. (Includes treatment of Greek sceptics.)

G. E. Moore, *Philosophical Papers*, Allen and Unwin/Macmillan, 1959. (Several items attack scepticism.)

H. Putnam, 'Brains in a vat', chapter 1 of his *Reason, Truth and History*, Cambridge UP, 1981. (How far can scepticism be coherently stated?)

G. Ryle, *Dilemmas*, Cambridge, UP, 1954, chapter 7. (Scepticism and perception.)

B. Stroud, *The Significance of Philosophical Scepticism*, Clarendon, 1984. (Sympathetic treatment of scepticism, emphasizing need to ask how the problem arose and what the significance of philosophical scepticism is.)

P. Unger, *Ignorance: a Case for Scepticism*, Clarendon, 1975. (Defends scepticism because of high standards required for knowledge.)

M. Williams (ed.), *Scepticism*, Dartmouth Publishing Company, 1993. (Reprinted essays on issues connected with scepticism and the external world.)

M. D. Wilson, 'Skepticism without indubitability', *Journal of Philosophy*, 1984. (Significance of seventeenth-century scepticism. This and the adjacent article by Stroud are summarized by R. J. Fogelin in the same issue, p. 552.)

J. Wisdom, J. L. Austin and A. J. Ayer, 'Other minds', *Proceedings of the Aristotelian Society*, supplementary vol., 1946, Wisdom

Science (philosophy of)

reprinted in his *Other Minds*, Blackwell, 1952, and Austin in A. Flew (ed.), *Logic and Language*, 2nd series, Blackwell, 1966.

Schopenhauer, Arthur. 1788–1860. Born in Danzig and educated partly in France and England, he worked mostly in Germany. He admired KANT, but, like KIERKEGAARD, reacted against the prevalent philosophy of HEGEL. He saw his chief contribution to philosophy as the identification of the Kantian thing-in-itself with the will, and emphasized the role of will in the world, both animate and inanimate. His treatment of unconscious willing partly anticipated Freud. He combined this with an ethic of pessimistic resignation strongly influenced by Indian thought. *Über die vierfache Wurzel des Satzes vom zureichenden Grunde* (*The Fourfold Root of the Principle of Sufficient Reason*), 1813, revised, 1847. *Die Welt als Wille und Vorstellung* (*The World as Will and Idea* (or *Representation*)), 1819. *Parerga und Paralipomena* 1851 (miscellaneous essays).

Science (philosophy of). The study of science in the broadest sense, its nature, aims, methods, tools, parts, range, and relation to other subjects.

The study of how science works is normally taken as a fair guide to how it should. This study is often called *methodology*, a term which can also be relative, e.g. methodology of history. Literally 'methodology' means 'study of method'; a method is not itself a methodology. *Inductive logic*, or *the logic of induction*, is normally limited to the study of INDUCTION as a mode of reasoning. Whether strictly there is any inductive *reasoning* is a question philosophy of science shares with philosophy of logic. But philosophy of science itself studies the process, taken as a whole, whereby we start from premises about the world and reach, by rational means, conclusions about the world which cannot be reached from those premises by deduction alone. Everyday thinking also uses such a process, but science is more systematic and method-conscious, and so more often studied.

The 'mathematical' sciences, especially physics, need special mathematical techniques, but scientific argument in general is often taken to presuppose a mathematical apparatus for applying the notions of PROBABILITY and CONFIRMATION, both of which themselves raise many problems. The calculus of chances (see PROBABILITY), which underlies probability, is often, but not always, taken as the basis for scientific procedure.

When studying the nature of scientific reasoning we naturally ask how it can be justified, and what are its purposes. In what circumstances can a scientific statement properly be accepted? In particular what role does simplicity play, and when is one hypothesis

Science (philosophy of)

simpler than another? Apart from prediction and control the main purpose of science is perhaps EXPLANATION, and an important part of philosophy of science concerns what this is and how it is achieved. LAWS of nature, CAUSATION and scientific necessity (see MODALITIES) are important concepts here: what are they, and are they real or should they somehow be explained away or reduced to other notions?

The difficulties about acceptability, and about what laws of nature are, lead to questions about the nature of scientific systems. Are they perhaps abstract systems which we fit to the world as we might choose between alternative geometries (see SPACE)? Just as there are problems about a system as a whole, so there are about the terms in it. What sort of meaning and definition can they have? (Cf. POSITIVISM for operationalism.) Should so-called theoretical entities such as electrons, which cannot be directly observed, be postulated as really existing things, or should they be treated as LOGICAL CONSTRUCTIONS? These problems about the terms and structures of scientific hypotheses lead one to ask about the properties a good hypothesis should have, and about the respective roles of observation and experiment, and the nature and types of measurement (see MAGNITUDES).

Moreover, how does science develop? Is it through the orderly replacement of hypotheses found to be false by better ones, or in some other way? Does it progressively approach an absolute truth? And how far does science extend? Do geology, astronomy, psychology, sociology, even history, have equal claims with physics, chemistry and biology to be called sciences (cf. SOCIAL PHILOSOPHY, philosophy of HISTORY), and can they be reduced to a common basis, as physicalism (in one of the senses of that term: see POSITIVISM) asserts?

L. W. Beck (see bibliography to LOGICAL CONSTRUCTIONS).

R. Boyd, P. Gasper and J. D. Trout (eds), *The Philosophy of Science*, MIT Press, 1991. (41 collected essays, divided into sections with introduction to each.)

L. J. Cohen, *The Implications of Induction*, Methuen, 1970. (Develops alternative to calculus of chances as basis of confirmation.)

M. Giaquinto, 'Science and ideology', *Proceedings of the Aristotelian Society*, 1983–4. (Defends rationality of science against various irrationalist approaches without making this a mere matter of definition.)

*D. A. Gillies, *Philosophy of Science in the Twentieth Century: Four Central Themes*, Blackwell, 1993. (The themes are inductivism, conventionalism, observation, demarcation (of science as such).)

Scotus, John Duns

*I. Hacking (ed.), *Scientific Revolutions*, Oxford UP, 1981 (Essays stemming from the work of Kuhn.)

I. Hacking, *Representing and Intervening: Introductory Topics in the Philosophy of Natural Science*, Cambridge UP, 1983. (Discusses scientific objectivity ('representing') and experimental method ('intervening').)

T. S. Kuhn, *The Structure of Scientific Revolutions* Chicago UP, 1962, 2nd edn with postscript, 1970. (One, controversial, view of how science develops. For criticism see I. Lakatos and A. Musgrave (eds), *Criticism and the Growth of Knowledge*, Cambridge UP, 1970, and Hacking (ed.) (above). See also P. Horwich (ed.), *World Changes: Thomas Kuhn and the Nature of Science*, MIT Press, 1993 (conference papers reflecting Kuhn's influence and with 'Afterwords' by him).)

P. Lipton, *Inference to the Best Explanation*, Routledge, 1993.

Midwest Studies in Philosophy, vol. 19, 1993. (Issue devoted to philosophy of science.)

H. Putnam, 'What is "realism"?', *Proceedings of the Aristotelian Society*, 1975–6. (Science and truth. Explained in his *Meaning and the Moral Sciences*, RKP, 1978.)

Scientism. A general term, usually pejorative, emphasizing the value or self-sufficiency of science in a certain area, e.g. the view that philosophical problems require none but scientific techniques for answering them.

T. Sorell, *Scientism*, Routledge, 1991. (Treats the subject both inside and outside philosophy.)

Scope. See QUANTIFICATION.

Scotus, John Duns. c. 1266–1308. Born probably at Duns near Anglo-Scottish border. Scottish theologian and philosopher who probably worked in Cambridge, Oxford and Paris. His interests were in the same general area as those of AQUINAS, though somewhat less closely tied to ARISTOTLE. He held distinctive views on such questions as the nature of being, of matter, of relations, of transcendentals (see BEING), and on how individual members of a species are distinguished (where he introduces his notion of *haecceitas* ('thisness'); see HAECCEITY). He also introduced a fresh proof for God's existence. Among his authentic works are the *Opus Oxoniense* (a commentary on the *Sentences* of Peter Lombard), *Quaestiones Quodlibetales* (miscellaneous questions), *De Primo Principio*, and commentaries on Aristotle's metaphysics and logic.

John Scotus Erigena

His philosophy, with that of his followers, is called *Scotism*. See also OCKHAM.

A. B. Wolter (ed. and trans.), *John Duns Scotus: a Treatise on God as First Principle*, Franciscan Herald Press, 1961. (Has Latin text and English tradition.)

A. B. Wolter (ed. and trans.), *Duns Scotus: Philosophical Writings: a Selection*, Nelson, 1962, Hackett, 1987. (Has Latin text and English translation. Bobbs-Merrill published the English without the Latin in 1964.)

John Scotus Erigena (ninth century) was an Irish theologian and philosopher whose *De Divisione Naturae* shows NEOPLATONIC influence, and develops (following earlier Greek thinking) an idea similar to that of the analogical predication discussed by later thinkers.

Seeing. Cf. PERCEPTION throughout. In general, seeing is having sight. We normally use eyes, but sight cannot be defined as perception through eyes if we allow that we might see with artificial eyes, or none. Would a man without eyes count as seeing if he consistently knew the colours of surrounding objects? An interesting problem here concerns *blindsight*, where certain brain-damaged people can accurately report certain features of their environment apparently only accessible to sight but disclaim having any visual experiences. This leads on to the question whether seeing something involves noticing and identifying it. *Seeing as* is important here. We can switch from seeing a certain ambiguous drawing as a picture of a duck to seeing it as a picture of a rabbit. Does this involve a change in belief, or in judgment, or what? How are seeing X, seeing X as Y (which may or may not be the same as X), judging X to be Y, and taking X to be Y, related together? The role of judgment or inference arises in other cases too. Our retinal image is two-dimensional. Must we therefore use inference in seeing the world as three-dimensional? We judge that a pillar-box looking grey in sodium light is red. But when the sun looks larger at sunset than at noon, though we know that even the visual image it subtends is not, is any judgment involved? And is there any *non-epistemic seeing*, i.e. seeing that does not involve belief in any way?

The things we see include objects, shadows, flashes, properties like 'the blue of her dress', relations, events, states of affairs, facts. Does this variety throw any light on whether seeing is a unitary notion, and if it is, what the conditions are for its occurrence? We may see literally or metaphorically ('the point of the joke', 'that his wits were failing'), and these can be hard to distinguish, when our evidence is largely visual.

Normally what we see must exist, though we see pink rats and

Seeing

'see in the mind's eye' (see below). It is disputed whether we see whole objects in the same sense in which we see the parts of their surfaces in our line of vision.

Sometimes 'see' means 'catch sight of' or 'come to see', and so means something momentary ('suddenly he saw it'). But, as 'come to see' suggests, in another sense we can go on seeing something. This raises the question how far 'see' is a 'success' or 'achievement' word, i.e. a word which does not, or not simply, refer to an activity, like 'run', but refers to a success or achievement, like 'win'.

Is visualizing a sort of inner seeing? If so, what is seen? Does it involve seeing or having mental images, and how, if so, are these related to what is visualized (which may be real or imaginary)?

Seeing differs from some of the other SENSES in certain ways. Colours seem to be 'in' objects in a way sounds or smells are not. Is the feel of velvet in the velvet? We 'catch sight of', or 'like the look of', something, but 'sights' and 'looks' are not things we see, in the way sounds are things we hear. How analogous is seeing the colour of something to hearing the sound of it? (Cf. SENSATION.)

Many of the questions about seeing might be summed up by asking how far seeing is a kind of experience and how far it is a source of knowledge.

T. Clarke, 'Seeing surfaces and physical objects', in M. Black (ed.), *Philosophy in America*, Allen and Unwin, 1965.

F. Dretske, *Seeing and Knowing*, RKP, 1969. (Relations between them. On seeing and believing see also M. Alcock and H. Jackson, 'Seeing and acquiring belief', *Mind*, 1979, D. Close, 'What is non-epistemic seeing?', *Mind*, 1976, 'More on non-epistemic seeing', *Mind*, 1980, J. Heil, 'Seeing is believing', *American Philosophical Quarterly*, 1982.)

C. L. Hardin, *Color for Philosophers*, Hackett, 1988. (Emphasizes the relevant scientific facts, along with philosophical discussion. Cf. also E. Thompson, *Colour Vision: a Study in Cognitive Science and the Philosophy of Perception*, Routledge, 1995, claiming to analyse colours as relations between persons and objects, avoiding extremes of objectivism and subjectivism.)

D. Lewis, 'Veridical hallucination and prosthetic vision', in J. Dancy (ed.), *Perceptual Knowledge*, Oxford UP, 1988.

E. J. Lowe, 'Experience and its objects', in T. Crane (ed.), *The Contents of Experience*, Cambridge UP, 1992.

M. G. F. Martin, 'Sight and touch', in T. Crane (ed.), *The Contents of Experience*, Cambridge UP, 1992.

J. M. Shorter, 'Imagination', *Mind*, 1952, reprinted in O. P. Wood and G. Pitcher (eds), *Ryle*, Macmillan, 1970. (Seeing and visualizing, and the relation between imagination and mental images.)

Self-deception

M. Tye, *The Imagery Debate*, MIT Press, 1992. (Contains material relevant to both seeing and imagining. See esp. chapter 7 on visual qualia.)

G. N. A. Vesey, 'Seeing and seeing as', *Proceedings of the Aristotelian Society*, 1955–6, reprinted in R. J. Swartz (ed.), *Perceiving, Sensing, and Knowing*, Doubleday, 1965.

L. Wittgenstein, *Philosophical Investigations*, Blackwell, 1953, II, xi, pp. 193–214. ('Duck/rabbit', etc. Cf. review by P. F. Strawson in *Mind*, 1954, pp. 95–7, reprinted in G. Pitcher (ed.), *Wittgenstein*, Macmillan, 1966, pp. 59–61.)

Self-deception. See BAD FAITH.

Self-regarding. Attributed to desires or actions if aimed at affecting oneself. If aimed at affecting others, these are other-regarding. Self-regarding aims need not be selfish (e.g. improving one's own moral character is not), nor need other-regarding aims be altruistic (e.g. sadism is not). Actions may also be divided, irrespective of their aims, into *self-affecting* (affecting only the agent) and *other-affecting* (affecting others too); both individual actions and types of action may be so divided.

C. D. Broad, 'Egoism as a theory of human motives', *Hibbert Journal*, vol. 48, 1949–50, reprinted in his *Ethics and the History of Philosophy*, 1952, and in D. Cheney (ed.) *Broad's Critical Essays in Moral Philosophy*, 1971; cf. also chapter 12 in this last.

J. S. Mill, *On Liberty*, 1859. (Advocates self-affecting/other-affecting distinction as basis for state interference with individual, but calls it self-regarding/not self-regarding.)

Semantic ascent. See FORMAL MODE.

Semantics. See SEMIOTIC.

Semiotic. Literally, 'theory of signs'. A generic term covering three important species. In each case philosophers study the notions in general and from an abstract point of view, while linguists study their application to particular languages and adopt an empirical approach to the more general questions, as in the case of semantics. *Syntax* or *syntactics* studies signs independently of their interpretation. In philosophy it studies some of the properties of logical systems (see AXIOM). In linguistics it studies the formal aspects of natural languages (e.g. why it is that 'the man runs' is a well-formed string of words while 'the runs man' is not). (This usage is rather different from that where syntax, as the study of sentences, contrasts with grammar, as the study of individual words.) *Semantics* studies signs in relation to what, or how, they signify. It is the general study of meaning. *Pragmatics* studies signs in relation to what we do with them, given that they have the meaning they have (cf. pragmatic IMPLICATION). It also studies meaning itself in so far as this depends on what we do with the signs (e.g. SPEECH ACT theories of meaning); here it fuses with semantics. (In this entry SIGN is used in its wide sense.)

N. Chomsky, *Aspects of the Theory of Syntax*, MIT Press, 1965. (Important source for his ideas at that time.)

T. Crane, 'The language of thought: no syntax without semantics', *Mind and Language*, 1990. (Claims that if there is a LANGUAGE OF THOUGHT it must have semantics as well as syntax, so that there cannot be a 'syntactical theory of the mind'.)

J. D. Fodor, *Semantics: Theories of Meaning in Generative Grammar*, Harvard UP, 1979.

H. P. Grice, *Studies in the Way of Words*, Harvard UP, 1989. (Collected essays on semantics and pragmatics by important contributor, especially to pragmatics.)

*R. K. Larson and G. M. A. Segal, *Knowledge of Meaning: Introduction to Semantic Theory*, MIT Press, 1995. (General introduction.)

C. W. Morris, *Signs, Languages and Behaviour*, Prentice-Hall, 1946, chapters 8 § 1. (Source of the distinctions.)

W. V. O. Quine, *Elementary Logic*, Ginn and Co., Boston, New York, 1941. (One of many text-books introducing basic ideas of formal logic.)

Sensa. See SENSE DATA.

Sensation. Either a kind of experience or a faculty, the latter including, in philosophy, the faculty of having 'pure experiences' (see PERCEPTION). Usually SENSE DATUM means an alleged object of experience distinct from the experiencing, while 'sensation' means the experience itself, but it is controversial how far there is a clearcut distinction here. We hear sounds, but 'have' auditory sensations. Is this because sounds can exist independently of being heard? When we 'have' or 'feel' a sensation, 'sensation' is perhaps an 'internal accusative', like 'blow' in 'strike a blow'; whatever the case with sense data, sensations must presumably be had by some subjects. All this raises the question of what sensations are. Are they objects of some sort? Or properties of the subject which has them? Must the subject be conscious of them, or could (say) a pain exist without being present to consciousness, e.g. because the subject was distracted? Is pain representation of damage to the body?

Sensationalism

Also are sensations located? Is a pain in the leg really in the leg – even a 'phantom' pain felt when the leg has been amputated? And how do we know the location of a sensation, if it has one? Experiences seem to be called sensations primarily when either they have no external correlate, or they are of something rather general or obscure. Hearing a ringing in the ears is an auditory sensation. 'Seeing stars' and being dazzled, and perhaps being hallucinated, having after-images, and seeing a pure blue sky, are visual sensations, but we seldom talk of visual sensations of colour; cf. SEEING on the nature of colour. 'Sensation of' usually means 'consisting of' as in 'sensation of pain, giddiness, nausea', but it can mean 'apparently, or as if, caused by' as in 'sensation of hardness, falling,' 'sensation of warmth' may be of the 'consisting of' kind as in fever or of the 'caused by' kind as when extending a hand to fire. 'Sensation' can apparently refer to a *kind* of experience like 'the sensation of falling' or to something datable such as 'the sensation I had just now', but phrases like 'I keep feeling that sensation' suggest that the 'datable' cases should really be analysed as 'kind' cases where 'had' means 'had an instance of'. This affects the question whether several people can have the same sensation. (For a related important problem concerning sensations see PRIVATE LANGUAGE.)

Most sensations seem to be bodily, but some, like the sensation of being followed, are hard to classify. See also PERCEPTION, FEELINGS, SEEING.

D. W. Hamlyn, *The Theory of Knowledge*, Macmillan, 1970. (Chapter 6 has general discussion of sensation, sense data and perception.)

F. Jackson, 'The existence of mental objects,' in J. Dancy (ed.), *Perceptual Knowledge*, Oxford UP, 1988. (Defends it.)

C. Peacocke, *Sense and Content*, Oxford UP, 1993, chapter 1.

G. Ryle, 'Sensations,' in H. D. Lewis (ed.), *Contemporary British Philosophy*, 3rd series, 1956, reprinted in R. J. Swartz (ed.), *Perceiving, Sensing, and Knowing*, Doubleday, 1965. (One view of ambiguity of 'sensation' and role of sensations.)

*P. Smith and O. R. Jones, *The Philosophy of Mind: an Introduction*, Cambridge UP, 1986. (Chapters 14 and 15 defend functionalist account of pain.)

G. N. A. Vesey, 'Berkeley and sensations of heat', *Philosophical Review* 1960. (Why we can call both objects and sensations hot.)

Sensationalism. Also called *sensationism*. An extreme form of EMPIRICISM whereby all our knowledge rests ultimately on SENSATIONS or on SENSE DATA, which initially are given to us free from any element of interpretation or judgment.

Sense data

P. Alexander, *Sensationalism and Scientific Explanation*, RKP, 1963.

Sense. See MEANING.

Sense data. Generally, entities which exist only when, and because, they are sensed. Many philosophers throughout history have thought that perception shares with memory, imagination, dreams, hallucinations, etc., a basis in 'pure experience' that is free from interpretation and error. This was usually treated as a special and infallible direct or immediate awareness, recently often called *sensing*, of things variously described as impressions, ideas, perceptions or sensations until Moore and Russell popularized the term 'sense data' (plural of 'sense datum', literally 'given to sense'). *Sensa*, plural of 'sensum', is also used (but see Price, p. 19). Usually it is held that sense data have all the properties they appear to have, and no others, and can only be sensed by one subject. Colour patches, sounds, smells, tastes, feelings of hardness or heat are typical examples. After-images, dream images, mental images, pains, kinaesthetic sensations, feelings of nausea, etc., are sometimes included, sometimes not.

In practice, however, it is hard to pick out and describe sense data, and to base our knowledge of physical objects on them (cf. PERCEPTION), and so conceptions of them vary. Often for sense data, as for Berkeley's ideas, to exist is to be sensed or perceived. But sometimes they are said to be public, and parts either of objects or of the surfaces of objects (Moore attacked Berkeley's 'To be is to be perceived'). They may then lack some properties they seem to have, or have others as well, discoverable on further inspection. Or they may be intrinsically vague in some respects. When one catches a quick glimpse of a speckled hen, does one's sense datum have a definite number of speckles? Those who try to connect sense data with physical objects sometimes suppose there could be merely possible sense data (*sensibilia*, plural of 'sensibile'), and that objects, even when not being perceived, consist of these. It is also hard to individuate sense data, i.e. say where one ends and the next begins, and hard to say if they can change. And are they substances, qualities, events, or what?

The *act/object view* of sensing so far discussed, where sensing is an act directed upon sense data as objects, is sometimes replaced by the allegedly less objectionable *adverbial view*, where 'I am sensing a red sense datum' is replaced by 'I am sensing redly'. Another view is that talk of sense data is a mere linguistic convenience, providing a noun for talking about appearances, so that on seeing a red dress in sodium light one says 'I sense a grey sense datum' instead of 'I seem to see something grey'.

Sense data

Recently sense data, after being unpopular for some time, have undergone a certain rehabilitation.

See also SENSATION, PHENOMENALISM, QUALE.

J. L. Austin, *Sense and Sensibilia*, Oxford UP, 1962. (Attacks sense datum theory held by A. J. Ayer in his *Foundations of Empirical Knowledge*, Macmillan, 1940, who replies in 'Has Austin refuted the sense-datum theory?', *Synthèse*, 1967, reprinted in Ayer's *Metaphysics and Common Sense*, Macmillan, 1969, and (with discussions) in K. T. Fann (ed.), *Symposium on J. L. Austin*, 1969.)

A. J. Ayer, *The Central Questions of Philosophy*, Weidenfeld and Nicolson, 1973. (See pp. 70–2 for some terminological points.)

T. Crane (ed.), *The Contents of Experience*, Cambridge UP, 1992. (Contains partial rehabilitation of sense data. See pp. 2–5 of its Introduction, and E. J. Lowe's paper 'Experience and its objects', pp. 86–7.)

R. Hall, 'The term "sense-datum" ', *Mind*, 1964. (Origin of the term.)

R. J. Hirst, *Problems of Perception*, Allen and Unwin/Humanities Press, 1959. (First four chapters criticize arguments for sense data.)

G. E. Moore, 'The refutation of idealism', *Mind*, 1903. (Attacks Berkeley's 'To be is to be perceived'. For his own view of sense data cf. his 'A defence of common sense', in J. H. Muirhead (ed.), *Contemporary British Philosophy*, 2nd series, Allen and Unwin, 1925, reprinted in Moore's *Philosophical Papers*, Allen and Unwin, 1959, and discussed by Bouwsma in Warnock (below).)

*H. H. Price, *Perception*, Methuen, 1932, 1950, Greenwood Press, 1981. (Chapter 1 introduces and defends sense data, which form basis for rest of book.)

*B. Russell, *The Problems of Philosophy*, Home University Library, 1912.

T. L. S. Sprigge, *Facts, Words and Beliefs*, RKP, 1970, chapter 1. (Defends sense data. Cf. also F. Jackson, *Perception*, Cambridge UP, 1977, H. Robinson, *Perception*, Routledge, 1994. Jackson is criticized by C. L. Hardin, *Color for Philosophers*, Hackett, 1988, pp. 96–112.)

R. J. Swartz (ed.), *Perceiving, Sensing and Knowing*, Doubleday, 1965. (Part 2 contains relevant articles, including G. A. Paul, 'Is there a problem about sense data?', *Proceedings of the Aristotelian Society*, supplementary vol., 1936 (defending linguistic view), and Quinton (below).)

G. J. Warnock (ed.), *Philosophy of Perception*, Oxford UP, 1967.

Sensing

(Various relevant articles. See esp. those by O. K. Bouwsma, R. J. Hirst, R. Wollheim, A. M. Quinton.)

Senses. Normally the faculties of sight, hearing, touch, taste, smell. Occasionally the sense organs are called 'senses'. The kinaesthetic sense, sense of muscular movement, can be included, though not normally the sense of balance, nor the MORAL SENSE, nor things like a sense of rhythm, beauty, responsibility, etc.

Should the senses be distinguished and defined in terms of their objects, or of their organs, or of how they operate? How far do they parallel each other?, e.g. do we hear and smell objects as directly as we apparently see them? How can they apparently trespass on each other's territory? How can ice which *feels* cold, *look* cold? (Cf. SEEING.)

Because of problems like 'trespassing', various philosophers since Aristotle have distinguished the senses' *special* or *proper objects* (or *special* or *proper sensibles*; but for 'sensibilia' see SENSE DATA) from others. Various views of these proper objects are possible. They may be (i) those primarily accessible only to one sense, such as tastes, sounds, etc.; or (ii) those a sense cannot be mistaken about; or (iii) those a sense must perceive if it perceives anything (perhaps we cannot see without seeing shapes, though shapes can also be felt); or (iv) those a sense perceives directly, without interpretation or inference. (i) is the commonest view. Those objects accessible to more than one sense, as shape is accessible to sight and touch, are then called *common sensibles*. Aristotle postulated a *common sense (sensus communis)* for them to be the proper objects of. The nature and roles of this 'common sense', which has no connexion with shrewdness, etc., are disputed. It seems to have been a sort of unifying general sense which acted through all the sense organs.

T. Crane (ed.), *The Contents of Experience*, Cambridge UP, 1992. (See esp. an article in it by M. G. F. Martin, 'Sight and touch'.)

D. W. Hamlyn, *Sensation and Perception*, RKP, 1961. (Proper objects, etc. See index under 'sense-objects'.)

B. J. O'Shaughnessy, 'The sense of touch', *Australasian Journal of Philosophy*, 1989. (Argues for primacy of touch among the senses.)

R. Sorabji, 'Aristotle on demarcating the five senses', *Philosophical Review*, 1971.

Sensibilia. See SENSE DATA.

Sensing. See SENSE DATA

Sentences, propositions, statements

Sentences, propositions, statements. A *sentence* is a set of one or more words in a natural or artificial language, provided the set is constructed according to the grammatical rules and can be used by itself for asserting, asking, commanding, etc., so far as its structure goes, though it need not be meaningful: 'Saturday is in bed' is a sentence. Sentences may be individuated syntactically (so that 'I saw wood' is one sentence with two meanings, that I cut or sighted it) or semantically (so that 'I saw wood' becomes two sentences). One sentence, as syntactically defined, may play different roles: 'The company will parade at noon' may be a prediction or an order. In artificial languages of the kind used in formal logic, sentences (including open ones: see below) are often called *well-formed formulae* (see AXIOM), and the grammatical rules are called *formation* or *syntactical rules*. Such languages are normally designed to exclude as ungrammatical the meaningless, and also the paradoxical (e.g. 'This sentence is false': cf. LIAR PARADOX). An *open sentence* is a sentential FUNCTION. An *eternal sentence* (Quine) is one without tenses and other TOKEN-REFLEXIVES, and having its verbs in the 'timeless present' ('Chaucer comes before Shakespeare'), so that if anyone using it on a certain occasion speaks truly, anyone else using it on any other occasion will also speak truly. (Contrast 'The weather is hot', which may be true today and false tomorrow.) Philosophers have in fact been mainly concerned with indicative or *declarative sentences*, i.e. those fitted for making assertions.

In natural languages, sentences have usually been defined and distinguished in ways allowing them to suffer from various kinds of ambiguity and meaninglessness. *Propositions* have therefore been introduced. They have provided something common to sentences, in the same or different languages, which mean the same ('I am hot' and 'J'ai chaud'), or to utterances which do not mean the same, but say the same thing ('I am hot' said by me and 'You are hot' said to me by you), or to an assertion and the corresponding question or command, etc. ('The door is shut'/'Is the door shut?'/ 'Shut the door!') In this last use propositions resemble PHRASTICS, but are expressed in the indicative, and so, unlike phrastics, can represent what is assertible but unasserted ('Snow is white' can be asserted, but is unasserted in 'If snow is white . . .'). Whether propositions can similarly represent unasked questions, uncommanded commands, etc., is another question. Propositions have also served as what can be true or false, and what logical relations like entailment relate. Finally they have served as what is believed, wished, judged, etc. (Believing and wishing, etc. are *propositional attitudes*. Things like judging, which occur at a definite time, are *propositional acts*. All these verbs are *propositional verbs*.)

A big difficulty with propositions is how they are to be individu-

Sentences, propositions, statements

ated, i.e. when do we have one and when another? This difficulty can be avoided, or at least mitigated, if we take a proposition to be a sentence in one of its meanings, assuming it is clear when a sentence has one meaning and when another. This is how propositions were usually treated before the problems they were later supposed to solve became urgent. It makes them less useful for explaining things like translation and wordless thoughts where either more than one sentence, or no sentence, seems to be involved. Another difficulty concerns how many roles propositions can play at once. To take the above examples, can they provide both something common for 'I am hot' and 'J'ai chaud', and something common for 'I am hot' and 'You are hot', when the latter is said to me by you?

Various views have been held about the nature of propositions. Ayer has treated them as LOGICAL CONSTRUCTIONS out of synonymous sentences. For Russell, at one time, the constituents of a proposition were the actual objects it was about, which anyone believing the proposition must be acquainted with; propositions apparently about nonexistent things, or things the believer could not be acquainted with, were really about something else (e.g. sense data or universals). Frege introduced his notion of 'sense' to account for how propositions mentioning the same object twice could be informative (see MEANING), and held that the constituents of a proposition (or thought – *Gedanke* as he called it) were the senses of the terms in it. More recently too propositions have been often regarded as structured entities whose constituents are either the objects and properties they are about or modes of presentation of these. Sometimes propositions are called *coarse-grained* if they are interpreted in a *de re* or *transparent* way (see MODALITIES; INTENSIONALITY), so that if terms in them are replaced by other terms referring to or describing the same things, or true of the same things, we still have the same proposition. If they are interpreted in a *de dicto* or *opaque* way, so that such substitutions cannot be made without getting a different proposition, they are *fine-grained*. Propositions are also sometimes equated with sets of POSSIBLE WORLDS, namely those in which they are true, so that those propositions which are true in exactly the same possible worlds are the same proposition, and so too are propositions which entail (see IMPLICATION) one another.

Propositions are standardly represented by 'that'-clauses ('That all cats are black'), and are often treated as the CONTENT of propositional attitudes (see BELIEF). But 'that'-clauses themselves raise problems about their interpretation (Davidson).

Some of these difficulties have led to the introduction of *statements* either instead of or in addition to propositions. Statements,

Sentences, propositions, statements

which are usually thought to be what is true or false, are either datable statings which are fairly easy to individuate ('His statement was made before lunch'), or they are the content of such statings, or what is stated ('That statement has been often made'). The flavour of the 'datable statings' view shows itself in the feeling that something assertible but unasserted (cf. 'Snow is white' above) is better called a proposition than a statement, and in the fact that statements, rather than propositions, are contrasted with questions, commands, etc. One way of accepting both statements and propositions is to treat statements as what is common to 'I am hot' and 'You are hot', said of the same person, and propositions as what is common to 'I am hot' and 'J'ai chaud', or 'I am hot' said by different people (Lemmon).

Individual uses of 'proposition' and 'statement' are legion (for a further use of 'statement' see Ayer), but it is largely in connexion with natural languages that they need to be distinguished from each other and from 'sentence'. This is because of TOKEN-REFLEXIVES, whereby a sentence may not only be ambiguous, but may be true or false, or neither, according to who utters it when. Therefore the distinctions are not needed in formal systems (see AXIOM), nor in discussing ordinary language so far as we can assimilate this to formal systems by translation, or ignore the differences. For many purposes the three terms, and especially 'proposition' and 'statement', are used interchangeably (as often in this dictionary).

Singular statements or propositions predicate something of a single subject as in 'Socrates is wise', 'Socrates is not wiser than Plato', and are contrasted with *general* ones, which may be *universal*: 'All cats are black' ('All John's cats . . .' is universal for most but not all purposes), or *particular*: 'Some cats are black', 'There exist black cats' (cf. QUANTIFIER WORDS). A *multiply general* statement contains each of the two main quantifiers (see QUANTIFICATION) or their defined equivalents ('Every man has some faults'). 'General' is sometimes used for 'universal'. For *atomic* and *molecular* see LOGICAL ATOMISM. See also JUDGMENT, FACTS, SPEECH ACTS.

A. J. Ayer, *Language, Truth and Logic*, Gollancz, 1936. (See index to 1946 edition.)

R. Carnap, *Introduction to Semantics*, Harvard UP, 1942, § 37. (Ambiguity in 'proposition'.)

A. Church, 'On Carnap's analysis of statements of assertion and belief', *Analysis*, vol. 10, 1950, reprinted with Carnap's reply, 'On belief sentences', in M. Macdonald (ed.), *Philosophy and Analysis*, Blackwell, 1954. (Pro substantial propositions.)

D. Davidson, 'On saying that', *Synthèse*, vol. 19, 1968–9, reprinted in D. Davidson and J. Hintikka (eds), *Words and Objections*, Reidel, 1969 (with Quine's comment at pp. 333–5), and in Davidson's *Inquiries into Truth and Interpretation*, Clarendon, 1984.

G. Frege, 'The thought: a logical inquiry', *Mind*, 1956 (German original, 1918–19), reprinted in Salmon and Soames.

P. Horwich, *Truth*, Blackwell, 1990. (See pp. 94–6 for brief exposition of Frege and Russell on propositions, in context of treating them as the CONTENT of BELIEF, to which the believer is related.)

E. J. Lemmon, 'Sentences, statements and propositions', in B. A. O. Williams and A. Montefiore (eds), *British Analytical Philosophy*, RKP, 1966. (Criticized by R. T. Garner, 'Lemmon on sentences, statements and propositions', *Analysis*, vol. 30, 1970.)

R. B. Marcus, 'Rationality and believing the impossible', *Journal of Philosophy*, 1983. (Includes discussions, with references, of various views of propositions.)

G. E. Moore, *Some Main Problems of Philosophy*, Allen and Unwin, 1953, Collier Books, 1962, written much earlier. (Contains important discussions of propositions. See pp. 262–6 for a difficulty over false propositions.)

W. V. O. Quine, *Word and Object*, Wiley, 1960. (See p. 35–6 for accounts of *occasion* and *standing sentences*.)

B. Russell, *Logic and Knowledge*, Allen and Unwin, 1956. ('The philosophy of logical atomism' and 'On propositions' in this volume discuss propositions, the latter giving his later view. See pp. 222–4 for difficulty over false propositions.)

G. Ryle, 'Are there propositions?', *Proceedings of the Aristotelian Society*, 1929–30. (Pros and cons of substantial propositions.)

N. Salmon and S. Soames (eds), *Propositions and Attitudes*, Oxford UP, 1988. (Important collection with accessible introduction.)

R. C. Stalmaker (see bibliography to POSSIBLE WORLDS).

A. Stroll, 'Statements' in A. Stroll (ed.), *Epistemology*, Harper and Row, 1967.

Serial relation. Relation which is CONNECTED, TRANSITIVE and asymmetric (see SYMMETRIC), thus uniting a series. *Less than* is a serial relation which unites the natural numbers into a single series.

Set. See CLASS.

Set theory. See CALCULUS.

Sextus Empiricus. Wrote c.200 AD in unknown location. Generally considered the main representative of ancient SCEPTICISM, of an agnostic rather than dogmatic kind (i.e. he rejected the view that knowledge was demonstrably impossible, and insisted on keeping an open mind on this as on other questions). He was influenced by the earlier sceptic Pyrrho of Elis (wrote c.300 BC) and used logical modes of argument ('tropes') deriving from Aenesidemus of Knossos (1st century BC). He is also a major source for our knowledge of STOIC logic (which he opposed). His main works are the *Pyrrhonian Hypotyposeis* (*Outlines of Pyrrhonism*) and *Adversus Mathematicos* (*Against the Learned*, with variously titled subdivisions).

Shaftesbury, Third Earl of. 1671–1713. Also called Anthony Ashley Cooper, he was born in London, lived mostly in England, and died at Naples. His early education was entrusted to LOCKE. He was an early representative of the MORAL SENSE school, believing in a 'natural sense of right and wrong'. He emphasized the existence of altruistic sentiments, and gave a utilitarian basis for morality, which could be reinforced by religion but was not dependent upon it. *An Inquiry concerning Virtue or Merit*, 1699. *Characteristics of Men, Manners, Opinions, Times*, 1711 (collected treatises, including the *Inquiry*). See also HUTCHESON.

Sidgwick, Henry. 1838–1900. Born in Yorkshire, he worked in Cambridge, and is best known as a leading UTILITARIAN. He claimed that a kind of HEDONISTIC utilitarianism underlies common sense morality. He also wrote on economics, the nature of philosophy, and the philosophy of Kant, and was interested in psychical research (cf. BROAD, H. H. PRICE). *The Methods of Ethics*, 1874 (7th edition and final version, 1907). *The Principles of Political Economy*, 1883. *The Elements of Politics*, 1891. See also INTUITION.

Sign and symbol. Some distinguish these, saying that signs operate through a natural or causal connexion as in 'Clouds are a sign of rain', while symbols are conventional as in 'A broken line is a symbol for a footpath'. The convention need not be explicit. Symbols may be chosen, or arise, because of their causal associations: a scarifying bang may be used as a danger-warning. Symbols relying on resemblance are sometimes called *icons*. But 'sign' is often used in a wide sense to include symbols.

H. H. Price, *Thinking and Experience*, Hutchinson, 1953, esp. chapter 6.

Sinn. See MEANING.

Slingshot. See FREGE ARGUMENT.

Social philosophy

Smith, Adam. 1723–90. Moral philosopher and economist, who was born at Kirkcaldy and worked mainly in Scotland, including Glasgow University. Though primarily known for his economic theory based on an individualistic system of free enterprise, he also developed a system of moral philosophy in his first book. This system was primarily founded on that sympathy which, he said, we feel for the motives of moral agents and for the gratitude or resentment of those affected by the actions of such agents. He also criticized the 'moral sense' theory of his teacher HUTCHESON. There is some dispute about how far a single view of human nature underlies Smith's two main books. *The Theory of Moral Sentiments*, 1759. *An Inquiry into the Nature and Causes of the Wealth of Nations*, 1776.

Social contract. See POLITICAL PHILOSOPHY.

Social philosophy. The study of philosophical problems arising from economics, anthropology, sociology and social psychology. It borders on philosophy of mind since it studies concepts involved in action like motive, intention, freewill, responsibility. However, it emphasizes the agent's role as a member of a group, and the group as itself an agent. Hence it considers ethical problems like that of collective responsibility, and metaphysical and methodological problems concerning the nature of groups and features of their behaviour. How far can group behaviour be caused or predicted, or described in terms of general laws? How far can it be reduced to the play of economic forces, and what kinds of EXPLANATION can be given of it? How does a social scientist form the concepts he uses? What counts as a society or social behaviour, and how are these related to individuals and individual behaviour? How far can one be objective in collecting and assessing evidence in the social sciences, and in general how far can or should these sciences resemble the natural sciences?

The 'rational man' is often used as a model in economics. This leads to problems about his behaviour, especially in competitive situations (game theory, DECISION THEORY). The notions of preference and voting behaviour can be studied by means of logical systems which formalize these notions. Such systems show how various electoral procedures work and study problems like the VOTING PARADOX and variants of it.

Social philosophy shares with ethics and political philosophy problems about things like the rights of a group acting in self-defence against members or outsiders, what constitutes the interests of a group as such, how these interests relate to members' and

Socrates

outsiders' interests, how it is legitimate to achieve them, and how decisions are to be taken.

The methodological, as against ethical, political and psychological, parts of the subject are often called the *philosophy of the social sciences*. See also HISTORY.

M. Brodbeck (ed.), *Readings in the Philosophy of the Social Sciences*, Macmillan and Collier-Macmillan, 1968.

J. Feinberg, *Social Philosophy*, Prentice-Hall, 1973. (Mainly on freedom, rights, justice.)

D.-H. Ruben, *The Metaphysics of the Social World*, RKP, 1985. (Criticizes versions of individualism in social philosophy.)

R. S. Rudner, *Philosophy of Social Science*, Prentice-Hall, 1966. (Emphasizes classificatory questions, objectivity, functionalism.)

A. Ryan, *The Philosophy of the Social Sciences*, Macmillan, 1970. (Emphasizes connexions with general methodology.)

Socrates, c. 469–399 BC. Mentor of PLATO and of several so-called 'Socratic schools' (Megarians, Cynics, Cyrenaics). Probably scarcely left Athens except on military service. Executed for 'corrupting the youth and introducing strange gods'. He apparently wrote nothing, and is known to us mainly through Plato and Xenophon (and a caricature in Aristophanes' contemporary comedy, *The Clouds*). ARISTOTLE, who never met him, regards him as mainly interested in ethics, but as laying the basis for Plato's theory of 'Forms'. See DIALECTIC, INCONTINENCE, SOPHISTS.

Socratic paradox. See INCONTINENCE.

Solipsism. See SCEPTICISM.

Sophists. A movement of itinerant professional lecturers on many topics, including philosophical ones, who flourished in Greece, mainly in the last half of the fifth century BC. They differed widely in outlook, though many shared a tendency to scepticism. They emphasized the study of human affairs rather than natural science or abstract metaphysics, and they were responsible for many initiatives in ethics and political philosophy, and also philosophy of language, philosophy of mind and epistemology. They were accused, especially by PLATO, of logic-chopping and subversiveness, but also of pandering to popular tastes. Leading sophists, all active in this period, include Protagoras of Abdera, Gorgias of Leontini, Prodicus of Ceos, Hippias of Elis, Antiphon of Athens. After the fifth century the movement continued but declined in quality.

W. K. C. Guthrie, *A History of Greek Philosophy*, Cambridge UP, vol. 3, 1969. (Covers Sophists and Socrates in two sections, which are also published separately.)

G. B. Kerferd, *The Sophistic Movement*, Cambridge UP, 1981.

J. De Romilly, *The Great Sophists of Periclean Athens*, Clarendon, 1992, French original, 1988. (Balanced discussion from point of view of history of ideas rather than philosophy and emphasizing both destructive and reconstructive sides of sophists.)

Sorites. See HEAP.

Sortal. A UNIVERSAL which provides a principle for distinguishing, counting and reidentifying particulars (see UNIVERSALS), i.e. for saying of what sort they are. If a sortal applies to an object at any time, then it applies to that object throughout its existence. *Cat* is a sortal. *Thing, red thing, snow*, are not sortals (but *patch of snow* perhaps is: Strawson, p. 202). Cf. COUNT NOUN.

P. F. Strawson, *Individuals*, Methuen, 1959. (See 'universals' in index. Cf. also M. Dummett, *Frege: Philosophy of Language*, Duckworth, 1973, p. 76. For potentially wider usage cf. J. Locke, *An Essay concerning Human Understanding*, 1690, 3.3.15. See also N. Griffin, *Relative Identity*, Oxford UP, 1977, chapter 3.)

Sosein. See BEING.

Sound. See VALID.

Space and time. Some problems concern space or time individually, while others concern both. These latter have become more prominent recently.

How are space and matter related? Parmenides (see ELEATICS) thought that to say empty space exists would be to say that what is not exists. Aristotle and Descartes too, among others, rejected it. Modern physics blurs the issue by allowing matter and energy to be intertransformed in certain circumstances, and emphasizing fields of force. General relativity theory treats gravity as a property of space rather than of matter, and quantum mechanics complicates the distinction between space and matter.

Until about two centuries ago Euclidean geometry was thought to be unique, and so *the* geometry of space. It relied on the *axiom of parallels*, that through a given point not on a given straight line exactly one straight line could be drawn parallel to the given one. But then it was realized that not only was this independent of the other axioms, but consistent systems could be developed if it were replaced by an axiom saying either that more than one such line,

Space and time

or that none, could be drawn. These replacements yield geometries often called hyperbolic or Lobachevskian (N. I. Lobachevsky, 1793–1856) and elliptic or Riemannian (G. F. B. Riemann, 1826–66) respectively. In these systems space is regarded as curved, negatively in Lobachevskian and positively in Riemannian geometry, because it has in three dimensions properties analogous to those of the surfaces of a saddleback and sphere, respectively, in two dimensions. It now becomes an open question what kind of geometry applies to real space, and geometries can be developed for imaginary spaces, which need not be limited to three dimensions. Real space evidently has three, but is this logically necessary (cf. MODALITIES, ANALYTIC)? And what makes a dimension specifically spatial as against merely a parameter or independent variable for some measuring system? Spaces studied by mathematics are *metrical* if they allow of measurement and *topological* if they do not. Some transformations of spatial things affect shape and size, and so disturb measurements, but leave relations of betweenness undisturbed: if *b* was between *a* and *c* before the transformation, it remains so afterwards. Topology studies these transformations. The topological transformations of a rubber ball, for example, are those possible with stretching and squeezing but without tearing.

Logical space is a term used by Wittgenstein in his difficult discussion of logical possibility. A place in logical space is given by the sense of an atomic sentence (see LOGICAL ATOMISM), which then describes that place. A rough example: the question whether my cat is black constitutes a place in logical space. When I say that it *is* black, I describe that place as being of a certain sort. The logical relations between propositions and between the terms in them can then be treated as having some analogy with spatial relations. Later this 'mapping' of relations between concepts was often called *logical geography*. This use of 'space' is metaphorical but it suggests the question what makes the analogy an apt one (cf. the above question about dimensions).

The notion of empty space suggests that of time without change. This, however, has been more generally rejected (but see Shoemaker), presumably because there seems to be no analogue here of the effects of perspective. Would the progressive fading of memory serve as an analogue? But this is unreliable and seems to depend in fact, though not in principle, on changes.

Time, more than space, seemed not to be real or measurable because most, if not all of it so far as it consists of periods rather than moments, seems not to exist at any given moment, and what fails to exist *now* has seemed less real than what merely fails to exist here (Augustine).

A famous attack on the reality of time was made by McTaggart, who distinguished two series of temporal positions. The *A series* contains notions like *past, present, future*, which apply to different events at different times. The *B series* contains notions like *earlier than, simultaneous with, after*, which permanently link whatever events they do link. He then argues that the B series by itself, without the A series, cannot account for change, and so for time, while the A series involves either a contradiction or a vicious regress. Some try to make the B series basic by defining 'present' as 'simultaneous with this utterance' (cf. discussion by Broad in Smart, pp. 334–8).

It is hard to describe the 'passing of time', for whether time itself flows or we move in time, how fast do these things happen? They seem to need second-order time to occur in (Dunne), but this makes doubtful sense, and only leads to a regress. A further problem arises over our consciousness of change, if we can only experience the present and this is strictly momentary (cf. Augustine's problem about measuring time when only one instant of it is there to measure). To deal with this, the *specious present* was used by various psychologists who claimed empirical evidence for it, and philosophers. 'Specious' suggests it only appeared to be present. It was usually claimed that the specious present was some short period ending at the present and forming the object of an act of awareness occurring at the present instant. The awareness itself was momentary, but it was awareness of a period of time. The stream of experience was then founded, in complex and controversial ways, on such acts. It has been argued, however, that the whole idea of analysing experience into successive units is mistaken; perhaps the momentary present is only a myth. There still remains the general question of how we acquire our ideas of time and space – e.g. are memory and perception involved? Bergson distinguishes time as viewed by science, which is 'spatialized' into a series of moments, like cinema frames albeit mathematically dense, from '*duration*' as experienced by consciousness, which cannot be so split up.

Time, unlike space, has only one dimension (but see MacBeath), and an apparently irreversible direction. This topic is controversial, but on one view this irreversibility is connected with the second law of thermodynamics, which says that entropy, or lack of organization, tends towards a maximum in isolated systems. For time to be reversed would thus be for this law to be broken. This law can be analysed as an effect of the statistical probabilities governing matter in motion: of all the possible configurations of a set of particles that can follow after a given state the vast majority correspond to a higher degree of disorder than exists in that state. Therefore it seems that the irreversibility of time is guaranteed by, and is simply a reflection of, a mathematical law of probability. But

Space and time

a difficulty arises because this law is symmetrical with respect to time: the above statement of it will hold equally if we replace 'follow after' by 'precede'. Another view analyses the direction of time in terms of that of causation.

Einstein's special theory of relativity treats space and time together as space-time. The main point of this is that in certain cases whether one event precedes another depends on the observer's motion relative to the two events, and motion involves both space and time.

A different and historically earlier, though not completely separate, issue is whether space and time are absolute or relational ('relative' is also used, but often kept for the Einstein view). Are space and time independent of the objects in them, as the absolute view says, or are they merely sets of relations between objects, so that it does not make sense to talk of absolute directions or absolute motion? The questions mentioned above about empty space, and time without change, are relevant again here. The question about motion has largely centred round rotation and centrifugal force, i.e. the relations between force and acceleration.

Also, are space and time parallel, in the sense that all, or nearly all, that can be said of the one can be said of the other, e.g. can a thing move around in time as it can in space? This raises questions about the relations between objects and events.

A question that has had some discussion recently is whether space and time are necessarily unique. Could there be a set of objects spatially and temporally related to each other but not to us? (For a different use of the same idea cf. D. K. Lewis's treatment of POSSIBLE WORLDS.) And could there be duplicate universes in space or time? If we went off in a rocket, travelling in what by all available tests was a straight line, and eventually reached what appeared to be a second earth, could we decide whether it really was another one or whether we had somehow come back to this earth? Similarly, could there be a 'mirror universe', i.e. could the universe contain a point or axis of symmetry? (Cf. INCONGRUENT.) The 'duplicate universe' question was asked earlier about time than about space (cf. METAPHYSICS for the doctrine of eternal recurrence, and in general cf. LEIBNIZ'S LAW). Finally could time be closed or circular? And could it have a beginning or an end?

On the infinite divisibility of space and time see ZENO'S PARADOXES.

H. G. Alexander (ed.), *The Leibniz–Clarke Correspondence*, Manchester UP, 1956. (Clarke defended Newton's absolute view in a series of letters to Leibniz, who defended the relational view. Alexander's introduction discusses later writers too.)

Space and time

Aristotle, *Physics*, IV. (Place, void and time.)

H. L. Bergson, *Time and Free Will*, Allen and Unwin, 1910 (French original, 1899), chapter 2. (Duration. His later works ascribe it to the world itself as well as to consciousness.)

J. W. Dunne, *An Experiment with Time*, 1927, 3rd (revised) edn, Faber, 1934, revised edn, Macmillan, 1981.

R. Flood and M. Lockwood (eds), *The Nature of Time*, Blackwell, 1986. (Series of lectures, taking account of modern physics.)

Paul Horwich, *Asymmetries in Time*, MIT Press, 1987. (Offers a unified treatment of various areas where asymmetries of time arise.)

*R. Le Poidevin and M. MacBeath (eds), Oxford UP, 1993. (Mainly reprinted essays, including McTaggart, Quinton and Shoemaker. Has annotated bibliography.)

M. MacBeath, 'Time's square' in Le Poidevin and MacBeath. (Could time have more than one dimension?)

D. H. Mellor, *Real Time*, Cambridge UP, 1981. (Defends McTaggart's attack on A series, and rejects tensed facts, but keeps B series.)

*W. Newton Smith, *The Structure of Time*, RKP, 1980. (General introduction.)

G. Plumer, 'The myth of the specious present', *Mind*, 1985. (Discussion, with references. Cf. also R. M. Gale, 'Has the present any duration?', *Nous*, 1971.)

A. Quinton, 'Spaces and times'. *Philosophy*, 1962, reprinted in Le Poidevin and MacBeath. (Are space and time unique? Cf. also K. Ward. 'The unity of space and time', M. Hollis. 'Box and Cox', *Philosophy*, 1967.)

C. Ray, *Time, Space and Philosophy*, Routledge, 1991. (Introduction to various problems arising from modern science.)

F. Reif, *Statistical Physics*, McGraw Hill, 1965 (vol. 5 of Berkeley Physics course), chapter 1. (Elementary account of the view that irreversibility of time is related to statistical physics.)

W. C. Salmon, *Space, Time and Motion: a Philosophical Introduction*, Minnesota UP, 2nd edn, 1980. (Moderately elementary introduction to issues from modern physics.)

L. Sklar, *Space, Time and Spacetime*, California UP, 1974. (Extended introduction to effects of modern science on philosophy of space and time. Requires some fairly elementary mathematics.)

*J. J. C. Smart (ed.), *Problems of Space and Time*, Macmillan, 1964. R. Gale (ed.), *The Philosophy of Time*, Macmillan, 1968. (These two volumes contain, with some overlap, many relevant discussions, with editorial introductions. Several of the authors mentioned above are included, including McTaggart in Gale.)

Specious present

R. K. Sorabji, *Matter, Space, and Motion*, Duckworth, 1988, chapter 10. (Could time be circular?)

R. Swinburne (ed.), *Space, Time and Causality*, Reidel, 1983. (Discussions, often technical, of absolute versus relative, time and causation, quantum mechanics, the Einstein–Podolski–Rosen paradox.)

R. Taylor, 'Spatial and temporal analogies and the concept of identity', *Journal of Philosophy*, 1955, reprinted in Smart. (Defends parallelism of space and time. Cf. also J. M. Shorter, 'Space and time', *Mind*, 1981. On objects and events see F. I. Dretske, 'Can events move?', *Mind*, 1967. A. Quinton, 'Objects and events', *Mind*, 1979, P. M. S. Hacker. 'Events and objects in space and time'. *Mind*, 1982.)

L. Wittgenstein, *Tractatus*, 1921, trans. D. F. Pears and B. F. McGuinness, RKP, 1961. (Logical space. Very difficult.)

Specious present. See SPACE.

Speech acts. When we speak there are many things we may be doing. We are normally saying something meaningful. We may be stating, ordering, promising, etc. And we may hope to achieve certain ends such as frightening someone. The systematic study of what we do in or by speaking dates mainly from J. L. AUSTIN, who distinguished three main levels of what he called 'speech acts': *Locutionary acts*, or *locutions*, are acts of uttering meaningful sentence. *Illocutionary acts*, or *illocutions*, are what we do *in* saying things, e.g. stating, promising. *Perlocutionary acts*, or *perlocutions*, are what we do *by* saying things, e.g. persuading, frightening. (The words 'in' and 'by' are only rough guides: Austin, chapter 10.) Austin thinks illocutions rely on conventions and can usually be made explicit with 'hereby': 'I hereby warn (order) you . . . .' Perlocutions depend on natural or causal processes. etc.' we cannot say, 'I hereby persuade you.'

These distinctions grew out of the breakdown, or apparent breakdown, of an earlier distinction between *constatives*, or utterances which state something, and so can be true or false, and *performatives*, or utterances which do something other than stating. To say 'I promise' is to promise, not to say *that* one is promising.

The related notions of performatives and illocutions have been used to try and explain the meaning of certain terms like GOOD, TRUE, PROBABLE, by reference to the 'force' of utterances containing them, i.e. what these utterances normally achieve (cf. NATURALISM). To explain a term's meaning in this way is to offer a *speech act analysis* of its meaning.

Of Austin's three main terms 'illocution' is the most important, but whether meaning can ever be explained in terms of illocutionary force is disputed. Whether illocutionary force is something distinct from meaning, and whether there are locutions, as distinct from illocutions, have also been disputed. Other problems concern how successful a speech act must be to count as a speech act, and what the speaker must intend. Must the hearer hear and understand the speaker? Must the speaker intend the hearer to believe or understand something, and if so, what? (Cf. REFERRING.) The use of 'act' in this way has been objected to as a term of art which here rests on confusion (Cerf, § IV, in Fann).

J. L. Austin, *How to Do Things with Words*, Oxford UP, 1962.
K. T. Fann (ed.), *Symposium on J. L. Austin*, 1969, part 4. (Six relevant discussions.)
H. Fingarette, 'Performatives', *American Philosophical Quarterly*, 1967. J. D. B. Walker, 'Statements and performatives', *American Philosophical Quarterly*, 1969. (Both these defend Austin's earlier constative/performative distinction.)
J. R. Searle (see bibliography to GOOD. Cf. also his 'Austin on locutionary and illocutionary acts', *Philosophical Review*, 1968, criticizing notion of locution.)
J. R. Searle (ed.), *The Philosophy of Language*, Oxford UP, 1971. (First four items are relevant).

Spinoza, Baruch (Benedict). 1632–77. Jewish philosopher who was born and lived in Holland, working as a lens-grinder. He is usually counted among the 'Continental RATIONALISTS', and his main work is his *Ethics*. In this he sets out to give a systematic exposition of philosophy in general on the model of Euclid, culminating in ethics. The result concerns metaphysics at least as much, and shows much Cartesian influence, though he replaces DESCARTES' body/mind dualism by a monism in which there is but a single SUBSTANCE, known as 'God or nature'. He was also a rigid determinist. *Tractatus Theologico-Politicus*, 1670. *Ethica Ordine Geometrico Demonstrata*, 1677. *Tractatus de Intellectus Emendatione (Treatise on the Improvement of the Understanding)*, 1677. See also DOUBLE ASPECT, IDENTITY THEORY.

E. M. Curley (ed. and trans.), *The Collected Works of Spinoza*, vol. 1, Princeton UP, 1985. (Includes *Ethics* etc. For political work see R. H. M. Elwes (ed. and trans.), *The Chief Works of Benedict de Spinoza*, vol. 1, Dover, 1951, vol. 1.)

Square of opposition. See QUANTIFIER WORDS.

Stadium. See ZENO'S PARADOXES.

Stand for

Stand for. See REFERRING.

State-description. See CONFIRMATION.

Statements. See SENTENCES.

Stochastic. Concerning or involving conjecture or randomness.

Stoics. Movement founded by Zeno of Citium (c.336–c.264 BC; different from Zeno the ELEATIC), and named from the porch ('stoa') in Athens where he taught. Stoics treated knowledge under three heads: logic, physics, ethics. They developed propositional LOGIC and the theory of IMPLICATION, and tried to discover a sure mark ('CRITERION') of truth. They developed a thoroughgoing materialism, treating matter as a continuum (as opposed to Epicurean atomism), but added a rather nonmaterial flavour with their pantheism and notions such as the 'tension' ('tonos') that matter was subject to. In ethics (to which the later Stoics largely confined themselves) they held determinist views and advocated acceptance of fate, based on self-sufficiency and a realization that 'virtue' was the only ultimate value. Leading Stoics include also Chrysippus (c.280–c.206 BC), Posidonius (c.135–c.51 BC), Seneca (c.4 BC-AD 65), Epictetus (c.AD 50–c.138), Marcus Aurelius (AD 121–80). Cicero (106–43 BC), though not a Stoic himself, is an important source for their views. See also CATEGORIES, DIALECTIC, EPICUREANS, IDEA, METAPHYSICS, NIETZSCHE, PHILOSOPHY, SEXTUS.

A. A. Long, *Hellenistic Philosophy*, Duckworth, 1974.
A. A. Long and D. N. Sedley, *The Hellenistic Philosophers*, , Cambridge UP, 1987. (Vol. 1 contains translated texts and vol. 2 Greek and Latin texts with commentary.)

Strawson, Peter F. 1919–. British philosopher born in London and working in Oxford, who has been a leading member of the later phase of 'linguistic philosophy'. He has both earned the strictures of RUSSELL for his attention to 'ordinary language' in criticizing Russell's theory of DESCRIPTIONS, and has cautiously led linguistic philosophy back to METAPHYSICS along lines laid down by KANT. He has also made notable contributions to the theory of truth and to the mind/body problem (cf. MIND, NO-OWNERSHIP, PERSON). 'On Referring', *Mind*, 1950 (criticizes Russell). *Individuals*, 1959 (return to metaphysics). *The Bounds of Sense*, 1966 (commentary on Kant). *Subject and Predicate in Logic and Grammar*, 1974. See also CATEGORIES, CONDITIONALS, CONJUNCTION, FACTS, FEATURE-PLACING,

332

Subjectivism

Structure (deep and surface). The *surface structures* of a phrase or sentence, studied by *surface grammar*, are its grammatical analysis or analyses as it stands. Its *deep structures*, studied by *depth grammar*, are the abstract structures underlying given interpretations of it and determining them, e.g. 'Pretty little girls' camp' has two surface structures (according to whether 'pretty' is adjective or adverb (cf. 'fairly')) but five possible deep structures: it has five interpretations, two with 'pretty' as adverb and three with it as adjective (see AMBIGUITY). See also GRAMMARS.

N. Chomsky, *Cartesian Linguistics: a Chapter in the History of Rationalist Thought*, Harper and Row, 1966, pp. 31 ff. (See n. 80 for deep structure and logical FORM. Later, however, he revised his views in *Reflections on Language*, Fontana, 1976, pp. 81–4, where he abandons the term 'deep structure', as unduly conflating syntactic and semantic considerations; cf. also pp. 93–105, on logical form, and his later *Knowledge of Language: its Nature, Origins and Use*, Praeger, New York, 1986.)

G. Harman (ed.), *On Noam Chomsky: Critical Essays*, Doubleday Anchor, 1974. (For logical form, etc. see index under 'Logical analysis', and also J. D. Atlas, 'On presupposing', *Mind*, 1978 (criticizing equation of logical form with deep structure).)

L. Wittgenstein, *Philosophical Investigations*, Blackwell, 1953, § 664.

Structure-description. See CONFIRMATION.

Sub-contraries. See CONTRADICTION.

Subjectivism. View or views which claim that what appear to be objective truths or rules in certain spheres, notably ethics, are really disguised commands or expressions of attitude, etc., e.g. 'Lying is wrong' would be regarded not as stating an objective fact, but as really being the command 'Never lie!', or an expression of the speaker's hostility to lying, like 'Lying! Grr!' (cf. NATURALISM). An alternative version of subjectivism says that the utterances in question do express objective truths, but only about human minds, wishes, beliefs, experiences, etc., whether these be of the speaker or of people in general. 'Lying is wrong' would then mean 'I, or perhaps people generally, disapprove of lying'. Berkeley's IDEALISM is called 'subjective' because it holds that physical objects are really ideas in the mind, even though the mind in question may be that of God.

Subsist

Objectivist views, by contrast, claim of certain things that they exist independently of the mind, or that there are, in the relevant sphere, truths independent of human wishes and beliefs, or that there are similarly independent ways of establishing certain truths or answering certain questions (e.g. on how to act, or how to argue rationally). See also INTERSUBJECTIVE, RELATIVISM, PROBABILITY, COGNITIVISM.

F. Jackson, G. Oppy and M. Smith, 'Minimalism and truth aptness' *Mind*, 1994. (Claims that one cannot defend the status of various ethical and other utterances as true or false by watering down the notion of truth.)

Subsist. See BEING.

Substance. Parmenides (cf. ELEATICS) gave an apparent logical demonstration that reality must be one. He seems to have thought that anything real must exist at all times and in all places, and there were many attempts in the next century or so to distinguish between the real, which obeyed one or both of these demands, and the merely apparent or derivative. In the atomism of the late fifth century BC, as in the EPICUREAN system which derived from it, the atoms of which things were made were real, while their shifting colours and temperatures were merely attributed to them by us. Against this background, the notion of substance as one of the CATEGORIES is first explicitly discussed by Aristotle. 'Substance' is the traditional translation, followed here, for the Greek *ousia*. Some scholars, however, think 'substance' a bad translation, partly because of its later treatment by Locke (see below). They prefer terms like 'being' or 'entity' or 'essence'.

Aristotle seems to use 'substance' in two main senses (though some see instead two *kinds* of sustance here). In the first sense a substance is a particular concrete object, like Socrates or this horse, while in the second sense it is the FORM or essence which makes a substance in the first sense the thing it is. Socrates is what he is because the flesh of which he is made has taken on the form of man and not, say, that of horse. In his *Categories* Aristotle uses *primary substance* for the former sense of 'substance' and *secondary substance* for the latter sense (or rather for something approximating to that). Socrates is a primary substance and *man* is a secondary substance. There is, however, a problem about this second sense of 'substance', where a substance is a form, for it is not clear how forms are related to UNIVERSALS. Aristotle denies, in his *Metaphysics*, that anything universal can be a substance. The modern sense

Substance

of 'substance' as 'stuff' (water, iron, etc.), though uncommon in philosophy, seems to be an amalgam of these two senses.

There is, however, a third possible sense of 'substance', which Aristotle mentions but dismisses, namely matter, or what remains when one removes the form or properties of something. For Locke, as traditionally interpreted, the substance of something is the *substrate* which remains when we remove *all* its properties, a rather mysterious 'something . . . we know not what' which underlies the 'accidents' or properties of things. We can only know something by describing it, i.e. giving its properties, which is impossible if it itself has none. But this interpretation of Locke has been challenged, and anyway substances (plural) for him were the things themselves, including their properties.

Descartes defined substances as what can exist without depending on anything else, except God, who alone can create or destroy them and who Himself is the only substance in the strictest sense. For Descartes therefore, as for Parmenides, substance was permanent, so that the material world formed but a single substance, since only it, not things in it, was permanent (once God had created it). Properties, or attributes and modes, as they were called, depended for their existence on the substances in which they inhere. A substance therefore is a substrate for properties, but for Descartes it is not something isolated somehow from all its properties and so unknowable. *Modes* are, roughly, ways in which an attribute can be possessed, rather like the DETERMINATE of a determinable. Leibniz, who thought of substances as living things, connected substance with the notions of actuality and activity. These thinkers disputed about the number and kinds of substances, the main classification being into material and spiritual substances, though Spinoza claimed that there could be only one substance, generally known as 'God or nature'.

This notion of a substance as what exists in its own right or independently raises certain difficulties. Firstly, what things are distinguishable and definite enough to count? Cloud? Rainbows? Shadows? Secondly, what sort of independence is in question? Is a hand a substance although it must be a hand of someone? Is a father a substance when described as 'father', or only when described as 'man', since a father must be the father *of* children? In other words, do fathers as such form one kind of substance as men or horses do? Or is the independence not logical, as here, but of some other kind – perhaps metaphysical, as Descartes thought in calling God the only substance in the full sense, other things being only derivatively so because they owe their existence to God? In what sense is substance prior, since one can no more have a substance without attributes than attributes without a substance? How indeed is *sub-*

Substance

stance related to *attribute*? Is a substance a mere bundle of attributes? If so, what binds the bundle together? Or does a substance underlie all its attributes, which leads back to the unsatisfactory view of an unknowable substrate? If substrate are what attributes apply to, what can be said about attributes of attributes? Surely we can say of an attribute, as well as of a substance, that it is desirable, or rare, or say that scarlet is brighter than crimson.

These considerations suggest a further ambiguity in the term 'substance'. Is there perhaps an absolute or metaphysical sense where the contents of the world are divided into substances and other things (attributes, relations, etc.), and a relative or logical sense where whatever we are talking about is the substance and what we say about it are the attributes? (Cf. CATEGORIES.) Some philosophers have rejected the metaphysical sense and supposed that substance is at bottom a linguistic notion (cf. METAPHYSICS. This is one form of *nominalism*). But if we accept the metaphysical notion of substance, should we count among substances any abstract things like UNIVERSALS or propositions (see SENTENCES)?

See also PROCESS PHILOSOPHY.

Aristotle, *Categories*, (trans. with commentary by J. L. Ackrill in Clarendon Aristotle series, 1963, translation but not commentary reprinted in J. Barnes (ed.), *Oxford Translation of Aristotle*, 2nd edn, Princeton UP, 1984), esp. chapter 5 but cf. chapter 7, *Metaphysics*, books 7 (or Z), 8 (or H), 12 (or Λ).

M. Ayers, 'Substance: prolegomena to a realist theory of identity', *Journal of Philosophy*, 1991. (Defends a notion of substance based on six criteria.)

Descartes, *Principles of Philosophy*, part I, §§ 51–3, 56. Cf. also § 5 of appendix to *Replies to Objections*, II. (For substance as permanent see J. Bennett, *Kant's Dialectic*, Cambridge UP, 1974, § § 19–21.)

W. C. Kneale, 'The notion of a substance', *Proceedings of the Aristotelian Society*, 1939–40. (General historical discussion, followed by tentative defence of substance.)

J. Locke, *Essay*, book 2, chapter 23. (For challenge see M. R. Ayers, *Locke*, Routledge, 1991, vol. 2, part 1, and also J. Bennett, 'Substance, reality, and primary qualities', *American Philosophical Quarterly*, 1965, reprinted in C. B. Martin and D. M. Armstrong (eds), *Locke and Berkeley*, Macmillan, n.d.)

D. M. MacKinnon, 'Aristotle's conception of substance', in R. Bambrough (ed.), *New Essays on Plato and Aristotle*, RKP, 1965.

G. Martin, *Leibniz: Logic and Metaphysics*, Manchester UP, 1960, trans. 1964, § 28. (Leibniz on substance.)

Sufficient reason (principle of)

A. Quinton, *The Nature of Things*, RKP, 1973. (Extended modern treatment of four relevant problems.)

R. D. Sykes, 'Form in Aristotle: universal or particular?', *Philosophy*, 1975. (Can serve as elementary introduction to these topics in Aristotle.)

D. Wiggins, *Sameness and Substance*, Blackwell, 1980. (Fairly difficult modern treatment of substance.)

R. S. Woolhouse, *Descartes, Spinoza, Leibniz: the Concept of Substance in Seventeenth-Century Metaphysics*, Routledge, 1993.

Substrate. See SUBSTANCE.

Sufficient conditions. See NECESSARY AND SUFFICIENT CONDITIONS.

Sufficient reason (principle of). Principle that nothing can be so without a reason, causal or otherwise, why it is so. Nothing occurs by 'blind chance', and, in particular, two apparent alternatives such as our universe and a 'mirror universe' like ours but with right and left interchanged, are not really alternatives unless there is enough difference between them for God to have had a reason to create one rather than the other. The principle is associated mainly with Leibniz, for whom it forms one of the two main principles of reasoning, and governs 'truths of fact'. His other principle is the principle of CONTRADICTION, which governs 'truths of reason'. A third principle, the *principle of the best*, or of *perfection*, explains why one rather than another possibility is actualized by saying that the actual world is the best of all possible worlds.

The principle, however, has far older roots. Democritus (fifth century BC), for instance, is said to have made his atoms come in all possible shapes because it would be arbitrary for them to come in some and not others, and in the Middle Ages Buridan's ass (though not to be found in the works of Jean Buridan (c.1295–1356)) starved to death because equally placed between two exactly similar and equally attractive bales of hay between which it could not choose.

G. W. Leibniz, *Monadology*, 1714, esp. §§ 32–6, 53–4. (Leibniz's 5th paper to S. Clarke, 1716, § 21 (in H. G. Alexander (ed.), *The Leibniz–Clarke Correspondence*, Manchester UP, 1956) derives identity of indiscernibles (see LEIBNIZ'S LAW) from sufficient reason principle.)

N. Rescher, *The Philosophy of Leibniz*, Prentice-Hall, 1967, chapter 2. (Schematizes relations between the three principles.)

B. Russell, *A Critical Exposition of the Philosophy of Leibniz*, 1900, §§ 14–15. (Claims Leibniz only partly distinguishes sufficient

Summum bonum

reason and perfection principles. Cf. G. H. R. Parkinson, *Logic and Reality in Leibniz's Metaphysics*, Clarendon, 1965, pp. 105–6.) Simplicius, *Commentary on Aristotle's Physics*, 28. 25–6. (Democritus on shapes of atoms.)

Summum bonum. See GOOD.

Superassertible. Term introduced by C. Wright for use in the REALIST/antirealist debate. A proposition is superassertible if not only is there a warrant for asserting it available on investigation but any further investigation, no matter how long continued, would still warrant its assertion. Superassertibility thus provides a step beyond mere warranted assertibility towards the realists' truth that can transcend all verification. It is akin to Peirce's idea of truth as what will ultimately be agreed on, especially if 'will' is read as 'would be', but does not presuppose that we know what an ultimate ideal state of knowledge would be like. (See also PRAGMATISM.)

C. Wright, *Truth and Objectivity*, Harvard UP, 1992 (esp. pp. 47–8). (See also review by J. Edwards in *Mind*, 1994, esp. pp. 62–3.)

Supervaluation. A device offered for solving the HEAP paradox. This paradox involves a conditional premise of the form: 'If n grains form a heap so do $n-1$ grains.' The supervaluational account claims to reject this premise by insisting, first, that the predicate 'is a heap' always *can* be arbitrarily sharpened in indefinitely many ways. One way would say that 100 or more grains form a heap while 99 or less do not; another would say that 99 or more do while 98 or less do not; and so on. The account then treats the conditional premise as true (absolutely), if, but only if, it is true for all such sharpenings of the predicate.

But now suppose we have, say, 100 grains before us. We cannot say 'If 100 grains form a heap, so do 99', since there will be a sharpening of 'is a heap' where this will not hold, namely just that sharpening which says that 100 grains or more form a heap while 99 or less do not. The same argument applies of course to whatever number of grains we have before us. We can therefore block the paradox without having to decide on any particular sharpening for 'is a heap', though at the cost of not allowing it to remain as an ultimately vague predicate, and indeed of not allowing any ultimately vague predicates (Sainsbury offers 'is an adult' as a predicate that may be importantly vague in certain social contexts).

R. M. Sainsbury, *Paradoxes*, Cambridge UP, revised edn, 1995, pp. 33–9 (revised from 1st edn, 1988, pp. 31–40).

Supervenience

Supervenience. Supervenient characteristics or properties etc. (in older literature often called *consequential characteristics*; occasionally *tertiary qualities*) are characteristics which in a certain way come along ('-vene') on top of a situation of or in addition to ('super-') certain other characteristics without needing to be logically entailed by them (see IMPLICATION). One or two examples may illustrate some of the complexities that arise. Take *right* and *red*. Two otherwise exactly similar actions done in exactly similar circumstances by exactly similar people (or the same person perhaps) cannot differ by one being right and the other wrong; their rightness or wrongness cannot be the *only* feature that distinguishes them. Two objects exactly similar in all their physical and chemical properties cannot in fact differ *just* by one being red and the other not red. *Right* and *red* are therefore candidates for being supervenient properties, though there are differences between them: it seems to *make sense* to suppose that two otherwise indistinguishable objects should be one red and the other not, even if only by magic, while this does not make sense in the case of *right*. We can always ask of an action 'What's right about it?', while we can't ask of an object 'What's red about it?' (where we are not referring to parts or features etc.). This suggests that supervenience comes in degrees, and weak and strong versions of it have been suggested (along with other distinctions: see Horgan section 5). Yet even with rightness, those properties of the action on which the rightness supervenes (called *subvenient*) do not logically entail that it is right. Different people may hold different views on its rightness (as even more obviously they may on something's beauty or niceness, to take two further candidates for being supervenient properties), but what is necessary is that they must, if they are to be intelligible, make the same judgments about each of the things being compared.

If something's having a certain property at a certain time counts as an EVENT, then the event of its having a certain supervenient property will itself supervene on the event(s) of its having the relevant subvenient property or properties. On other views of events, however, such as Davidson's (see below), there will only be one event here.

As the above examples show, supervenience can be used to classify secondary QUALITIES and various value terms. Supervenience can also be used to relate certain properties to what constitutes them: being water or having water's properties may be said to supervene on being H_2O, if being water is regarded as a different property from being H_2O; but see also REDUCTIONISM.

A particularly important role has been played by supervenience during the last third of the twentieth century in philosophy of mind, to explain how psychological properties (having toothache,

Supervenience

believing that it's raining, envying one's boss, etc.) are related to properties of the body, especially of the brain. A pioneer in this has been Davidson, whose *anomalous* MONISM says that any individual mental event is identical with some physical event, but that the mental properties involved will not be identical with, but will supervene on, the physical properties involved. The point is that two creatures in exactly the same mental state could be in different physical states. However, the distinction between narrow and broad CONTENT raises a difficulty here and has led to a distinction whereby supervenience is *global* or *local* according as it applies only to a whole context or world, or to individual items in that world; cf. INTERNALISM AND EXTERNALISM.

Supervenience then is not the same as identity. Whether mental properties can supervene on physical properties without psychology (as the science of mental properties) being *reducible* to the relevant physical sciences is disputed (see Horgan, especially p. 575.) A further distinction has been made between supervenience, where two things cannot differ merely in a supervenient property, and *resultance*, where one property results from or is somehow grounded in others (e.g. by Dancy, who thinks resultance more important and also discusses the relations between supervenience and universability.)

On some non-COGNITIVIST ethical views, what supervenes on certain ordinary properties is a commitment to certain reactions, e.g. that when confronted with two similar actions one of which one has blamed one must also blame the other (or else point to some relevant difference between them.) When this is not so, but what supervenes is a genuinely objective property or fact, the supervenience can be called *ontological* (Horgan, p. 563), Horgan goes on to insist that if supervenience is to support a materialist view of the mind (in the way outlined above), it must be ontological and its being so in that relevant area must admit of explanation (in which case it can be dubbed superdupervenience: p. 566 and section 8; cf. Dancy's emphasis on resultance.)

S. Blackburn, 'Supervenience revisited', in I. Hacking (ed.), *Exercises in Analysis*, Cambridge UP, 1985, reprinted in Blackburn's *Essays in Quasi-Realism*, Oxford UP, 1993. (Discusses significance of a strong and a weak sense of supervenience in connection with his rejection of moral realism's claim that there are objective moral truths independent of any of our attitudes. Fairly difficult.)

J. Dancy, 'On moral properties', *Mind*, 1981. (Distinguishes supervenience from resultance and universability, concentrating on ethics.)

Supremum bonum

D. Davidson, *Essays on Actions and Events*, Clarendon, 1980. (Reprinted essays which include his main contributions to philosophy of mind. Cf. esp. essays 11 and 13. Some of the essays are criticized, with Davidson's replies, in B. Vermazen and M. B. Hintikka (eds), *Essays on Davidson: Actions and Events*, Clarendon, 1985.)

J. Griffin, 'Values: reduction, supervenience and explanation by ascent', in D. Charles and K. Lennon (eds), *Reduction, Explanation and Realism*, Clarendon, 1992. (Doubts the supervenience of values: what exactly supervenes on what?)

*R. M. Hare, 'Supervenience', *Proceedings of the Aristotelian Society*, supplementary vol., 1984. (General discussion of it and its applications by a leading representative of its non-ontological use in ethics. Cf. brief discussions in *Mind* by A. J. Dale (1985) and H. Spector (1987).)

*T. Horgan, 'From supervenience to superdupervenience: meeting the demands of the material world', *Mind*, 1993. (Full discussion, tracing the notion's historical development from 'emergentist' scientific views, and discussing various types and applications of it, and prospects for its usefulness. Includes extensive bibliography. (*Applies to first 16 pp., after which it gets more technical, discussing applications and complications.)

J. Kim, *Supervenience and Mind: Selected Philosophical Essays*, Cambridge UP, 1993. (Essays on supervenience and its applications in philosophy of mind. On weak, strong and global supervenience see especially chapter 5, chapter 9, section 3. For another definition of weak supervenience, see J. Haugeland, 'Weak supervenience', *American Philosophy Quarterly*, 1982, especially p. 97.)

*G. E. Moore, *Principia Ethica*, Cambridge UP, 1903. (Classic pioneering attempt to apply ontological supervenience, though not so called, in analysing good.)

Southern Journal of Philosophy, supplement to vol. 22, 1984. (Symposium papers on supervenience, with comments.)

Ü. D. Yalçin and E. E. Savellos (eds), *Supervenience: New Essays*, Cambridge UP, 1995. (Discussions covering types of supervenience, their relations to each other, to reduction, and to ontological priority, whether supervenient properties can have causal powers, and whether any *explanation* can be given of how a supervenient property relates to its subvenient properties.)

Support. See CONFIRMATION.

Supremum bonum. See GOOD.

Sustain

Sustain. See CONDITIONALS.

Syllogism. A valid or invalid argument in which a conclusion connecting two terms is deduced from two premises connecting those terms to a third term, called the *middle term*. The subject of the conclusion is called the *minor term*, and is connected to the middle term in the *minor premise*. The predicate of the conclusion, the *major term*, is connected to the middle term in the *major premise*, conventionally written first. Only four types of proposition are allowed (see QUANTIFIER WORDS). In 'All men are mortal; all Greeks are men; so all Greeks are mortal', *men* is the middle term, *Greeks* the minor term, and *mortal* the major term.

The middle term may be either subject or predicate in each premise, giving accordingly four different *figures* of syllogism (Aristotle, who first formalized the syllogism, only recognized three as distinct). Since the three propositions in a syllogism can each be of four kinds, each figure will contain $4^3 = 64$ kinds of syllogism, called *moods*, giving 256 moods for the four figures together.

Only a few moods are valid (the number can be predicted mathematically, given certain assumptions. Cf. also DISTRIBUTION). If some of these are assumed to be valid the rest can be derived from them, or *reduced* to them, in an AXIOM SYSTEM. The gist of the assumed moods, especially the only valid mood with universal affirmative conclusion, exemplified above, can then be given by the *syllogistic principle*. The traditional *dictum de omni et nullo* is one form of this principle; taking two first-figure moods as basic it says that whatever applies to all, or none, of a given class applies to all, or none, respectively, of a given sub-class of it. In the above example *mortal* applies to all men, and so to all Greeks.

All the above syllogisms are *categorical*. 'All' is closely related to the material IMPLICATION sense of 'if'. 'All cats are black' is similar in meaning to 'If anything is a cat, it is black'. *Hypothetical syllogisms* have at least one premise in this hypothetical form (but see Keynes).

Modal syllogisms contain, in at least one premise, or in the conclusion, at least one modal term (see MODALITIES), e.g. '*Necessarily* all cats are black'.

Three main criticisms have been made of the syllogism: that as an argument it begs the question because the conclusion is already contained in the premises (cf. INFERENCE); that it is unclear whether the four allowed kinds of proposition entail the existence of things of the kinds they mention (the problem of *existential import*: does 'All unicorns are black' entail that there are unicorns? Cf. QUANTIFIER WORDS); that it is very limited in scope, and in particular

342

Synechism

ignores the logic of relations by using 'be' as its only verb (cf. LOGIC).

Aristotle's *practical syllogism* is a subject of dispute. It is like an ordinary syllogism but has for conclusion an action, or perhaps an utterance closely related to one, such as a resolve: 'All sweet things are good to eat; this is sweet; therefore let me eat it.' Cf. practical REASON, INCONTINENCE, IMPERATIVE.

J. N. Keynes, *Formal Logic*, 1884, 4th (revised) edn 1906. (Full treatment from traditional viewpoint.)

J. Lukasiewicz, *Aristotle's Syllogistic*, Clarendon, 1951, enlarged 1957. (Treats Aristotle historically and from viewpoint of modern logic. 2nd edn 1957 includes modal syllogisms.)

J. S. Mill, *A System of Logic*, Longmans, Green, 1843, book 2, chapter 3. (Famous attack on syllogism's usefulness.)

M. Nussbaum, *Aristotle's De Motu*, Princeton UP, 1978. (See Essay IV for classic discussion of practical syllogism.)

L. E. Rose, 'Aristotle's syllogistic and the fourth figure', *Mind*, 1965.

G. H. von Wright, *Explanation and Understanding*, RKP, 1971. (Practical syllogism. See its index under 'practical inference'.)

Symbol. See SIGN.

Symmetric. A relation holding from *a* to *b* is *symmetric* if it must hold from *b* to *a* (*sibling of*). It is *asymmetric* if it cannot (*parent of*), and *non-symmetric* if it may or may not (*brother of*). 'Non-symmetric' occasionally includes 'asymmetric'. It is *anti-symmetric* if its holding from *a* to *b* and from *b* to *a* implies that *a* and *b* are the same object. *Not greater than* among numbers is anti-symmetric, but *not older than* among people is not, but only non-symmetric: different people can have the same age, but different numbers cannot have the same size, so if *a* is not greater than *b* nor *b* than *a*, then *a* and *b* are the same number. Sometimes 'weak anti-symmetric' is used for this, with 'anti-symmetric' replacing 'asymmetric'.

Symptom. See CRITERION.

Syncategorematic. See CATEGORIES.

Synechism. Any view emphasizing continuity as against discontinuity or atomism. In particular, a term associated with Peirce.

J. A. Passmore, *A Hundred Years of Philosophy*, Duckworth, 1957, 2nd edn, 1966. (See pp. 104–5 (pp. 103–4 in Penguin edn, 1968)).

Synonymy

Synonymy. See MEANING.

Syntax, syntactics. See SEMIOTIC.

Synthetic. See ANALYTIC.

T

Tacit and implicit knowledge. Two terms associated especially, though not exclusively, with two very different philosophers, M. Polanyi (1891–1976) and M. Dummett. The terms are often used interchangeably, though Polanyi uses 'tacit'.

Polanyi starts from such facts as that we can recognize faces without knowing how we do so, and can be specially trained to respond to certain perceived stimuli without knowing just what we are responding to. He claims that we transfer our attention from e.g. the specific features of a face to the face as a whole (we attend *from* the former *to* the latter, as he puts it), and thereby have tacit knowledge of the former. The idea is then developed to cover the foreshadowing by which a scientist sees first a problem and then a possible solution to it in his data. What matters is not that the tacit knowledge be unconscious but that it be what we attend from.

For Dummett implicit knowledge is that knowledge which speakers must have of a language. The knowledge is the propositions which constitute a theory of meaning for the language (roughly, what the individual words mean and how they combine to form sentences), but such knowledge obviously is not explicit in most speakers, and it would be circular to demand that they can formulate it in the language. Such knowledge, however, does not, for Dummett, consist in some inner psychological state which can causally explain our ability to use the language. Rather it is manifested simply in the speaking itself, and to give the content of what is known is simply to give a detailed account of the language itself. For Chomsky, on the other hand, who also uses the notion, it does consist in an inner psychological state.

Tacit knowledge has also been important recently in connection

Tarski, Alfred

with both descriptionalist accounts of mental IMAGERY and psychological accounts of mental competences.

M. Davies, 'Tacit knowledge and subdoxastic states', in A. George (ed.), *Reflections on Chomsky*, Blackwell, 1989. (See esp. section one for the relation between these terms, and also on Chomsky's views. Davies develops his views in his *Tacit Knowledge*, Blackwell, 1996.)

M. Dummett, 'What is a theory of meaning? (II)', in G. Evans and J. McDowell (eds), *Truth and Meaning*, Oxford UP, 1976. (See esp. pp. 70–2, and cf. also B. Smith, 'Understanding language', *Proceedings of the Aristotelian Society*, 1992, esp. section V. Later, however, Dummett rejected this notion; see the Preface to his *The Seas of Language*, Clarendon, 1993, especially pp. x–xii.)

J. Fodor, 'The appeal to tacit knowledge in psychological explanations', *Journal of Philosophy*, 1968, reprinted in his *Representations*, Harvester Press, 1981. (Defends an 'intellectualist' or rule-following account of mental competences in terms of tacit knowledge.)

M. Polanyi, *The Tacit Dimension*, Doubleday, 1966, esp. chapter 1.

Z. Pylyshyn, 'The imagery debate: analog media versus tacit knowledge', in N. Block (ed.), *Imagery*, MIT Press, 1981.

Tarski, Alfred. 1901–83. Mathematician and logician, born in Warsaw where he worked until 1939, and after that at Berkeley, California. His work relevant to philosophy was mainly in his formalization of semantics. This led to his 'semantic theory' of TRUTH, whose formulation was importantly affected by the LIAR paradox. He also contributed to the formal treatment of logical and mathematical MODELS. 'Der Wahrheitsbegriff in den formalisierten Sprachen', *Studia Philosophica*, 1935 (translated from Polish book of 1933). 'The semantic conception of truth and the foundations of semantics', *Journal of Philosophy and Phenomenological Research*, 1944 (shorter version of above). *Logic, Semantics, Metamathematics*, 1956 (collected logical papers from 1923 to 1938 in translation, including 'Wahrheitsbegriff'). *Introduction to Logic and to the Methodology of the Deductive Sciences*, 1941 (translated and revised from Polish original of 1936).

Tautology. Literally, saying the same thing. Loosely, any ANALYTIC truth. More strictly, and usually, either any logical truth, i.e. any statement true in virtue of its form (see ANALYTIC), or a truth-FUNCTIONAL logical truth, such as 'Snow is white or snow is not white'. (Not 'Everything is white or not white', which is logically true, but is not such that its truth can be inferred from the truth or

Thick and thin concepts

falsity of its parts for it has no relevant parts.) The sense of mere repetition, whereby 'I took his life and killed him' becomes a tautology, does not occur in philosophy.

Teleological. Having to do with design or purpose. See also ETHICS, EXPLANATION, and for *teleological argument*, DESIGN.

Temporal parts. See GENIDENTITY.

Term. Sometimes a word or phrase ('Always define your terms'), and sometimes objects or things, such as the terms of a relation. (If John loves Joan the relation *loving* has the people John and Joan as its terms.)

Tertiary qualities. See SUPERVENIENCE.

Tertium non datur. See EXCLUDED MIDDLE.

Theorem. See AXIOM.

Theory. See LAWS.

Theory-laden. Applied to a term if its use can only be understood in terms of some theory. 'He has an anal-retentive personality', for example, only makes sense against a background of Freudianism. It is sometimes claimed that many more terms are theory-laden or theory-loaded than appear so at first sight.

N. R. Hanson, *Patterns of Discovery*, Cambridge UP, 1958. (See index.)

Thick and thin concepts. Terms used especially in recent ethics. Thick concepts are those which seem to combine a purely descriptive element with an element of evaluation or prescription, such as 'cowardly', 'heroic', 'treacherous', 'loyal', 'brutal', 'lewd', while thin terms embody only an evaluative or prescriptive element, such as 'good', 'evil', 'ought', 'right'. It seems hard for someone who does not accept the relevant values or prescriptions to decide whether to call attributions of the thick concepts true or false. However, the correct analysis of the thick concepts is disputed.

A related contrast is that between concepts of causation according to whether they do or do not go beyond mere regular sequence, and concepts of meaning according to whether they do or do not go beyond mere truth conditions. '*Robust*', and '*modest*' (sometimes

Thing-in-itself

'minimalist') are widely used to make this sort of contrast in various fields.

A. Gibbard and S. Blackburn, 'Morality and thick concepts', *Proceedings of the Aristotelian Society*, supplementary vol. 1992.

B. A. O. Williams, *Ethics and the Limits of Philosophy*, Fontana, 1985, esp. pp. 129–30 with context.

Thing-in-itself. See NOUMENON.

Thing-word. See METAPHYSICS.

Thinking. In the seventeenth century 'thinking' was often used to cover mental phenomena in general, including feeling, with the result that Descartes and others could distinguish between substances according as they had extension or thinking as their defining attributes (giving material objects and minds respectively). This usage is no longer current.

Thinking can take many forms: at least those of believing, imagining, pondering, calculating, deliberating, ruminating, assuming, evaluating; it can be something occurring at a given time or a state we can be in; and it can concern theoretical or practical matters (cf. practical REASON). Whether or not all these cases are equally central (Urmson; see Sibley ref. below), it seems hopeless to try and isolate any one activity as that of thinking. Moreover, it may be thought that thinking is never manifested except in other activities that could occur without it. Kicking a football involves thinking, but the same leg-movements could result from a reflex. Here one can in various degrees be 'thinking what one is doing', but the thinking is not, or need not be, a separate activity. For these reasons thinking has sometimes been called POLYMORPHOUS. This in turn suggests an 'adverbial' view of thinking, whereby there is no activity, or even set of activities, to be called thinking, but activities in general can be carried out thoughtfully or thoughtlessly, intelligently or unintelligently, etc. However, this will hardly cover all cases. One cannot calculate thoughtlessly, except in the sense of 'He thoughtlessly went on calculating while the kettle boiled dry'. This example shows that intelligence or thoughtfulness, like care, deliberation, etc., can be manifested in the fact that something is done, as well as in the manner in which it is done. But it also shows that calculating, even if done hastily or carelessly, essentially involves thinking, while being an activity in its own right (not a mere synonym of 'thinking').

Such activities, and especially silent thought, and occasions when thoughts dawn on one or flash across the mind, have at various times occupied much attention. A recently popular theory is that we have here simply physical events in the brain seen from a certain point of view (IDENTITY THEORY OF MIND). More longstanding are disputes about the role of mental images, language, and behaviour. Behaviour, if it involves overt movements, seems irrelevant in many of the cases we are considering. Hypothetical behaviour might seem to be involved, in the sense that the thinker would behave in certain ways if certain things happened, e.g. would give certain answers if asked certain questions. But this does not explain what does happen at the definite time when the thought occurs. Language seems involved in that anything properly called a thought must presumably be expressible in language. But we often have the thought before finding words to express it. It may be true however that thoughts involving abstract things can only occur to a being possessing a language which could express them. Mental images here need not be full-blooded pictures, but may be confused patches of colour, or sounds, or incipient sensations of moving the vocal chords, or anything that might be called material for experience. It seems hard to conceive of thought occurring without any such elements at all. But it seems equally hard to see what relevance such imagery has if it does occur, since it seems that one could have any amount of such imagery without having the relevant thought. If the topic of *'imageless thought'* has been less discussed recently this seems to be rather through despair at finding an answer than for any other reason.

All this suggests two further questions. First, how is thinking related to time? A train of thought takes time, and can be interrupted and left incomplete, but can any of this happen in the case of a single thought that flashes on one? In expressing a thought one may, for example, first say the subject and then the predicate, but does one think them in this or any order? How, in fact, is the structure of a thought, if it has one, related to that of a sentence expressing it? We must distinguish here a thought as a datable occurrence from a thought as the context common to many such occurrences. But how are they related? Have they a common structure? The second question is how far thoughts, in either sense, can be described. Thoughts as contents can be true, valid, fallacious, misleading, sombre, illuminating, commonplace, though some of these terms will only apply to them relative to a context. Thoughts as occurrences can be dated and put into words, but descriptions of them seem either to borrow from descriptions of the content, or to be peripheral and not reaching the heart of the thought itself. Descriptions like 'hasty', 'sudden', 'unexpected' seem to presuppose other descriptions, which yet are not forthcoming.

The question of the structure of a thought raises the question of

Thinking

how thinking a whole thought or proposition is related to thinking of an object, e.g. something which the thought was about. In particular, which is prior? Does one think thoughts by, for example, thinking of objects and attributes and somehow putting them together, as by thinking of the cat and of black, and putting them together to get the thought that the cat is black? Or is thinking of an object something that can only be abstracted from a whole thought, so that one can only think of an object by thinking something about it?

Another important question about thinking concerns the things we think about. If I think about Caesar, does this constitute a relation between me and him? But perhaps Caesar never existed, so that I could not have been related to him; does my thinking still remain what it was? This raises the question of internalist and externalist analyses (see INTERNALISM AND EXTERNALISM) of mental states, and issues about the nature of their CONTENT. Also what happens if I think something false of Caesar, e.g. that he had a beard when in fact he did not? This, with the fact that Caesar no longer exists to be thought of, may suggest that I must use a representative of him to do my thinking with, e.g. a mental image, which can exist now, and be bearded. But even if such an image were always present on these occasions, how would the image itself be related to Caesar? What would make it an image *of* him? For it is Caesar, not the image, that we are supposed to be thinking about, and we must surely know what we are thinking about (it seems), which would be difficult if there were just the image. This whole question remains wide open. With the idea that thought requires a representative cf. the representative theory PERCEPTION. For further questions about thinking and the objects it has cf. INTENSIONALITY AND INTENTIONALITY (see the 'Cicero' example there), and MODALITIES on the de re/de dicto distinction.

A further question we can ask is what it is that thinks? Must a thought belong to a continuing thinker? When Descartes said 'I think, therefore I am', what sort of an 'I' did he prove the existence of? Could we say with G. C. Lichtenberg (1742–99) 'It is thinking', as we say 'It is raining'? And how are Smith's thoughts related to Smith? Are they properties of him? Do they help to constitute him? Must a thinker indeed be human at all? Could machines or computers think, and if not, what condition is it that they fail to satisfy? How far can mental processes be modelled artificially?

See also JUDGMENT, REFERRING.

R. M. Chisholm, 'Sentences about believing', *Proceedings of the Aristotelian Society*, 1955–6. (Discusses cases like the 'Cicero' example in INTENSIONALITY.)

*T. Crane, *The Mechanical Mind: a Philosophical Introduction to*

Thinking

Minds, Machines and Representation, Penguin, 1995. (Elementary introduction, including such questions as whether computers can think.)

M. de Gaynesford, 'How wrong can one be?', *Proceedings of the Aristotelian Society*, 1996. (Must we know what we are thinking about? See first footnote for many references.)

P. T. Geach, *Mental Acts*, RKP. (Exploration of the analogy between thinking and speaking. Cf. also his *God and the Soul*, RKP, 1969, chapter 3.)

W. J. Ginnane, 'Thoughts', *Mind*, 1960. (Clear exposition of the problem of analysing sudden thoughts. For defence of imageless thought see also G. Humphrey, *Thinking: an Introduction to Its Experimental Psychology*, Methuen, 1951, Wiley, 1963, pp. 122–31, 225–30.)

G. C. Lichtenberg, *Aphorismen, Briefe und Schriften*, Scientia-Verlag, Zurich, 1946. (See p. 69.)

D. L. Mouton, 'Thinking and time', *Mind*, 1969. (Refers to Ginnane and Geach.)

G. Myro, 'Thinking', in H. Robinson (ed.), *Objections to Physicalism*, Clarendon, 1993. (Lecture given about 1980 on nature of thinking and our knowledge of it.)

H. H. Price, *Thinking and Experience*, Hutchinson, 1953. (General study.)

A. N. Prior, *Objects of Thought*, Oxford UP, 1971. (Part I discusses the direct objects ('accusatives'), if any, of thinking (propositions, etc.) and requires a fair knowledge of logic. Part II uses less logic (but with some POLISH NOTATION) to discuss examples like the Caesar one above.)

J. Ross, 'Immaterial aspects of thought', *Journal of Philosophy*, 1992. (Claims thinking cannot be identical with any physical process or any function of one.)

F. N. Sibley, 'Ryle and thinking', in O. P. Wood and G. Pitcher (eds), *Ryle*, Macmillan, 1970. (Thinking and the many uses of 'think'. Cf. J. O. Urmson, 'Polymorphous concepts', in same volume, and also A. R. White, *The Philosophy of Mind*, Random House, 1967, chapter 4.)

*P. Smith and O. R. Jones, *The Philosophy of Mind: an Introduction*, Cambridge UP, 1986. (Chapter 16 gives elementary introduction.)

T. L. S. Sprigge, *Facts, Words and Beliefs*, RKP, 1970. (Complex and sophisticated attempt to analyse thinking in terms of images.)

A. Woodfield (ed.), *Thought and Object: Essays on Intentionality*, Clarendon, 1982. (Essays on the nature, types, structure and roles of the contents of thoughts. D. C. Dennett's 'Beyond belief' is reprinted with afterthoughts in his *The Intentional Stance*, MIT

Third man argument

Press, 1987; see esp. pp. 54ff. (pp. 168 ff. in reprint) for difficulties in de re/de dicto distinction.)

Third man argument. Argument named by Aristotle but deriving from Plato, who offered it as a criticism of his own theory of Forms (see IDEA, UNIVERSALS). The term 'man' can apparently be applied to both Socrates and the Form Man, so we need a third 'man' to explain what these have in common. The term 'man' will then apply to this third entity, and so we shall need a fourth, and so on. The theory of Forms therefore seems to lead on to an infinite regress. The detailed interpretation of the argument is highly controversial (Plato himself uses the example, 'large', which may or may not be significantly different), but the argument can be widened to cover the relations between universals and particulars in general.

D. M. Armstrong, *Universals: an Opinionated Introduction*, Westview Press, 1989, pp. 53–7. (Widens the argument, without explicitly naming it.)

C. C. Meinwald, 'Goodbye to the Third Man', in R. Kraut (ed.), *The Cambridge Companion to Plato*, Cambridge UP, 1992. (Offers a solution to the argument, integrating it with general development of Plato's thought, drawing on her *Plato's Parmenides*, Oxford UP, 1991. See n. 13 for references to literature generated by Vlastos.)

J. A. Passmore, *Philosophical Reasoning*, Duckworth, 1961, chapter 2. (Treats the argument from modern point of view, though again without explicitly naming it.)

Plato, *Parmenides* 131e-3a. (For commentary see e.g. R. G. Allen, *Plato's Parmenides*, Minnesota UP and Blackwell, 1983.)

G. Vlastos, 'The Third Man Argument in the *Parmenides*', *Philosophical Review*, 1954, variously reprinted. (Classic discussion which has generated immense literature.)

Time. See SPACE.

Time-slice. See GENIDENTITY.

Token. See UNIVERSALS, TOKEN-REFLEXIVES.

Token-reflexives. When a sentence contains phrases like 'here', 'now', 'this', 'I', 'last year', 'in January', or tenses of verbs, we cannot fully know what was said by someone uttering the sentence, unless we know something about that particular utterance like its date, place, utterer, etc. Particular utterances of a word or sentence are called *tokens* (see UNIVERSALS), and so these phrases, which as

Topic-neutral

it were point back to the token sentences in which they appear, are called token-reflexives. Alternative names for them include *demonstratives, egocentric particulars* (Russell), *indicator terms, indexicals* (but Putnam calls words for natural kinds, like 'water' indexical, as sharing certain features with ordinary indexicals). An important issue, which affects what propositions (see SENTENCES, are, and what sort of things can be true or false, is whether token-reflexives can be eliminated, i.e. whether sentences containing them can be translated into what Quine calls eternal SENTENCES.

J. N. Findlay, 'An examination of tenses', in H. D. Lewis (ed.), *Contemporary British Philosophy*, III, Allen and Unwin, 1956. (Difficulties in eliminating tenses.)

C. McGinn, *The Subjective View*, Oxford UP, 1983. (Compares indexicals with secondary QUALITIES.)

J. Perry, 'The problem of the essential indexical', *Nous*, 1979, reprinted in N. Salmon and S. Soames (eds), *Propositions and Attitudes*, Oxford UP, 1988. (Difficulties raised by the fact that some beliefs seem to involve indexicals or token-reflexives essentially.)

H. Putnam, 'Meaning and reference', *Journal of Philosophy*, 1973, esp. pp. 709–11.

W. V. Quine, *Word and Object*, Wiley, 1960. (Largely follows Russell. See index under 'indicator word'. See § 36 for tenses, and p. 107n. for terminology.)

B. Russell, *An Inquiry into Meaning and Truth*, Allen and Unwin, 1940. (Chapter 7 claims that 'egocentric particulars' can be eliminated. R. M. Gale (ed.), *The Philosophy of Time*, Macmillan, 1968, pp. 296–8, distinguishes token-reflexives as linguistic entities from egocentric particulars as private entities.)

C. Sayward, 'Propositions and eternal sentences', *Mind*, 1968. (Token-reflexives in general cannot be eliminated.)

P. Yourgran (ed.), *Demonstratives*, Oxford UP, 1990. (Reprinted essays on various relevant topics. See esp. items by Perry and Evans.)

Topic-neutral. Expressions which contribute to the structure of a language rather than to the content of what it is being used to express, so that they are neutral as between different subject-matters. Sometimes they may merely be neutral regarding the subject-matter under discussion. Identifying such expressions raises problems. When understood in the first way they might be called the subject-matter of logic. The notion was introduced by Ryle, and

Topological

used by, e.g. Smart in defending his version of the identity theory of mind. See also FORM.

G. Ryle, *Dilemmas*, Cambridge UP, 1954, chapter 8. (See p. 116 for his own definition.)

J. J. C. Smart, 'Sensations and brain processes', *Philosophical Review*, 1959, reprinted in V. G. Chappell (ed.), *The Philosophy of Mind*, Prentice-Hall, 1962, C. V. Borst (ed.), *The Mind/Brain Identity Theory*, Macmillan, 1970. (See reply to objection 3. Borst reprint has footnote referring to criticisms and Smart's reply.)

Topological. See SPACE.

Total evidence requirement. See CONFIRMATION.

Tracking. Term introduced by R. Nozick, who holds that a belief amounts to knowledge if it 'tracks the truth', i.e. would not be held were it false, would be held were it true, and is in fact true. Nozick uses the notion to overcome certain objections to defining knowledge as justified true belief.

R. Nozick, *Philosophical Explanations*, Harvard UP, Oxford UP, 1981 chapter (ed.), on 'Epistemology' (for abridged version see J. Dancy (ed.), *Perceptual Knowledge*, Oxford UP, 1988).

Transcendental arguments. Primarily, an argument which shows of some proportion, not that it is true but that it must be assumed to be true if some sphere of thought or discourse, especially an indispensable sphere, is to be possible. An early example is Aristotle's argument that the law of contradiction cannot be proved, since any proof involves it, but that it must be assumed by anyone who asserts anything at all, and therefore by anyone asserting that the law is false. Kant thought such arguments could also justify non-formal conditions of objective thought (his CATEGORIES). The law of contradiction is a formal condition: see FORM.

Since Kant, transcendental arguments have been popular as a weapon against various kinds of sceptic. The sceptic, it is claimed, cannot state his position without assuming what he is claiming to be sceptical of. His position is therefore parasitic on that of his opponent.

However, there is much dispute about exactly how transcendental arguments work, how they are to be distinguished from other kinds of argument, how many kinds of them there are, and what sort of things they can be used to establish. They may concern not only whether propositions are true, but whether terms are meaningful, whether concepts have application or usefulness, whether arguments are valid, and whether things of a certain kind exist though we cannot construct instances of those kinds.

Transcendental arguments are perhaps a strengthened form of PARADIGM CASE ARGUMENTS. A transcendental argument for something like the legitimacy of INDUCTION would say that a whole sphere of our thought or language presupposes its legitimacy, whether or not we have even heard of induction. A paradigm case argument for it points simply to the fact that we *regard* some arguments as legitimate inductive ones.

Aristotle, *Metaphysics*, book 4 (or Γ), chapter 4.

P. Bieri, R.-P. Horstmann and L. Krüger (eds), *Transcendental Arguments and Science: Essays in Epistemology*, Reidel, 1979. (Essays, with comments, on nature of transcendental arguments, and their bearing on how far science could attain to absolute truth.)

A. P. Griffiths, J. J. MacIntosh, 'Transcendental arguments', *Proceedings of the Aristotelian Society*, supplementary vol., 1969. (Griffiths defends them with examples. MacIntosh is critical.)

R. Rorty, 'Verificationism and transcendental arguments', *Nous*, 1971. (Moderate defence, but stressing limitations. M. S. Gram, 'Transcendental arguments', ibid., is relevant but difficult.)

Transcendentals. See BEING.

Transformation rules. See AXIOM.

Transitive. A relation holding from *a* to *b* and from *b* to *c* is *transitive* if it must hold from *a* to *c*, whatever *a, b* and *c* may be (*ancestor of*). It is *intransitive* if it cannot (*father of*), and *non-transitive* if it may or may not (*fond of*). 'Non-transitive' occasionally includes 'intransitive'. (The qualification 'whatever *a, b* and *c* may be' is needed to exclude certain rogue cases like *results in less than ten when added to*, which looks transitive if *a, b* and *c* are, respectively, 2, 3 and 4, but is not if they are, respectively, 6, 2 and 7.)

Translation (indeterminacy of). Quine claims that assured translation between any two languages, or even within one language, is impossible in principle. There are certain exceptions, namely certain occasion sentences, which are covered by stimulus synonymy, and also truth-FUNCTIONAL TAUTOLOGIES (but on these see Roth under Quine ref.). To translate, in general, we must construct *analytical hypotheses*, which say that an element in one language is equivalent to, or analysable in terms of, an element in the other. But Quine thinks it is impossible in principle to justify choosing one such hypothesis against another, and our choice may affect the truth of

Transparent

the sentence being translated. Quine claims that this raises fatal difficulties for determinate notions of meaning, synonymy and translation.

Translation of this kind is called *radical translation*. A related, though different, notion is *radical interpretation*, which the truth-conditions theory of MEANING must use in constructing a theory of what a speaker's words and sentences mean on the basis of the contexts in which they are uttered. Such interpretation uses the principles of CHARITY or humanity. It differs from Quine's radical translation because it does not envisage different speakers having incommensurable conceptual schemes (see RELATIVISM), but rather may sometimes make one choose between attributing false beliefs to speakers and taking them to mean something different from what they seem to mean.

D. Davidson, 'Radical interpretation', *Dialectica*, 1973, reprinted in his *Inquiries into Truth and Interpretation*, Clarendon, 1984.

R. Kirk, 'Translation and indeterminacy' and 'Quine's indeterminacy thesis'. *Mind*, 1969. (Critical. Answered by A. Hyslop, 'Kirk on Quine on bilingualism' and R. Harris, 'Translation into Martian', *Mind*, 1972.)

A. C. Lambert and P. D. Shaw, 'Quine on meaning and translation', *Mind*, 1971. (Critical.)

W. V. O. Quine, *Word and Object*, Wiley, 1960, chapter 2 (see pp. 35–6 for occasion sentences, and pp. 32–3, 46 for stimulus synonymy. Cf. discussion in D. Davidson and J. Hintikka (eds), *Words and Objections*, Reidel, 1969, and also P. A. Roth, 'Theories of nature and the nature of theories', *Mind*, 1980.)

Transparent. See INTENSIONALITY AND INTENTIONALITY.

Transposition. See CONTRAPOSITION.

Trope. Property or relation considered as it appears in a single instance, so that it is a particular (see UNIVERSALS). The being brown of this table, which it shares with no other object, would be a trope. If Tom, John and Bill are brothers, the being a brother of Bill that Tom possesses would be a trope, as would that possessed by John, and also the being brothers possessed by the three of them. The name 'trope' has recently become established; other names have included 'individual accidents', 'abstract particulars', 'unit-properties', 'property-instances', and others. The notion goes back to Aristotle, but whether there really are such things, and if so, whether they are additional to or replace universals, are disputed questions.

In Greek philosophy 'trope' (which literally means 'way',

Truth and falsity

'method' or 'mode') refers especially to the ten modes of argument attributed to Aenesidemus, writing probably in the first century BC).

Aristotle, *Categories*, chapter 2.

D. M. Armstrong, *Universals: an Opinionated Introduction*, Westview Press, 1989. (Includes extended discussion of various trope theories.)

J. Bennett, *Events and Their Names*, Oxford UP, 1988. (Chapter 6 analyses events as tropes. See also p. 15 n. 7 for references to further discussions.)

K. Campbell, *Abstract Particulars*, Blackwell, 1990. (Makes tropes the basic building-blocks of a metaphysical system.)

A. A. Long and D. N. Sedley (eds), *The Hellenistic Philosophers*, vol. 1, Cambridge UP, 1987. (See its index of philosophers for Aenesidemus and his modes (as they are called there).)

P. A. Simons, 'Particulars in particular clothing: three trope theories of substance', *Philosophy and Phenomenological Research*, 1994. (Defends a 'nuclear' view of tropes, combining 'bundle' and 'substratum' views.)

Tropic. See PHRASTIC.

Truth and falsity. Truth is something we all approve of, and aim, or should aim, to achieve. But just what is it? What we say may be criticized in many ways, only one of which is for failing to state the truth (see below). But failure to do that seems somehow to be the most basic kind of failure. What then is it that we want to achieve? Is truth a relation between what we say and the subject-matter we say it about? Or between different things we do or could say? Or is to call something true simply a way of repeating it? Or perhaps of expressing a certain kind of approval of it or willingness to endorse it? Or is something true if, in a certain sense, it works or produces satisfaction? Various theories exist corresponding to such views.

The *correspondence theory* is perhaps the commonest theory of truth, partly because 'correspondence' can be interpreted strictly or loosely. In its strictest form, primarily associated with Moore and Russell, this theory involves a relation between two things, that which is true (a proposition, belief, judgment, etc.) and that which makes it true (a fact, or perhaps a state of affairs or event). The fact has a structure which the proposition, etc., copies or pictures. But finding pairs of things which correspond in this way is difficult, especially since the sort of structure that a proposition might have, involving the relations between things like nouns and verbs, or

Truth and falsity

subjects and predicates, seems entirely different from any features of the outer world. Subjects and predicates are different (linguistic) things in a way that objects and properties are not; and how would one distinguish the correlates of 'Snow is white' and 'For snow to be white'? Similar difficulties confront correspondence, or picture, theories of how sentences or propositions have MEANING. Also if all we know is propositions, and propositions picture the world, how can we compare the propositions with the world itself to see if they picture it accurately? (Cf. PERCEPTION on the difficulty of knowing about an external world if we must begin from 'pure experience'.)

There is a less strict form of the theory, which no longer requires that each part of the proposition should correspond to a part of reality. On this view something is true if it can be correlated with a fact and false if not, or if its negation can be correlated with a fact. A still looser form calls something true if it simply 'says things as they are'. This leads naturally to F. P. Ramsey's *redundancy* (also occasionally called *no truth*) theory, whereby to call something true is simply to repeat what it says. On this view truth is not a property of anything, but the use of 'true' provides a shorthand way of referring to things said. A development of this is Strawson's *performative* (occasionally, *ditto*) theory, which is a SPEECH ACT theory. Here when we call something 'true' we perform an act of agreeing to, repeating, or conceding it – we say 'ditto' to it. These theories, which are often called *deflationary*, have been criticized as unable to cover all senses of 'true', and loose correspondence theories have been returned to and defended by Austin and, in a modified form, Hamlyn. Recently deflationism has been revived by Horwich's *minimal* theory.

A recent variant of the correspondence theory is Tarski's *semantic theory*. This is primarily designed for, though not confined to, artificial languages, whose elements or 'words' may be infinitely many but are of definite kinds and have definite roles. Sentences in a given language, L, are called 'true-in-L' (not to be confused with 'L-true', Carnap's symbol for 'logically true': see ANALYTIC, VALID) when their elements are so combined as to state what is the case, e.g. 'Snow is white' is true in English if and only if snow is white. This avoids treating propositions and facts as entities, and is easy to develop in a rigorous and formal way. But there are limits to how far it can be applied without great complication, even to formal languages, for reasons connected with the LIAR PARADOX and GÖDEL'S THEOREMS.

The correspondence theory suits philosophers who make a sharp distinction between knower and known. Those who refuse to do this, notably IDEALISTS, often favour the *coherence theory*. The basic idea of this is that something is true if it coheres or is logically consistent with a wider system than any of its rivals cohere with. This theory presupposes that CONSISTENCY can be defined independently of truth, and also that one of the various possible consistent systems of propositions is wider than any of the others. Idealists who hold this theory, however, say that strictly only the system taken as a whole is true. Single propositions in it give only partial approximations to the truth. Can we really understand 'Caesar crossed the Rubicon', it might be asked, and so be in a position to call it true, until we appreciate all its causes and consequences, even to the end of time? The theory is therefore sometimes called a *degrees of truth* theory. Another reason for thinking truth has degrees is that we cannot know whether something belongs to the widest coherent system, if there is one, without examining every proposition, so in practice we must be satisfied with something less. (See also below.) Moreover, in advanced sciences like cosmology it is often difficult to decide between different but consistent ways of describing the universe. All the known celestial movements *can* be explained on a geocentric theory, if it is sufficiently complex. The coherence theory can be supplemented by devices like adopting the simplest out of several competing hypotheses. It is then attractive in those regions of science where immediate verification is impossible. Perhaps partly for this reason it was favoured by some positivists (Neurath, Hempel). Cf. also CONVENTIONALISM, INSTRUMENTALISM, POSITIVISM.

This sort of consideration also lies behind the *pragmatic theory*, for which see PRAGMATISM.

What sort of things can be true? Is 'true' properly or primarily applied to mental acts and states such as acts of utterance, judgments, beliefs, or to linguistic things, such as indicative sentences, or to certain abstract things such as propositions (see SENTENCES)? 'Statement' can be a convenient non-committal word. How we answer this will affect what we say about how truth is related to time and tense: can something, like the sentence 'I am hot', *become* true?

Is everything which is of the right kind to be true or false actually true or false, as one form of the law of EXCLUDED MIDDLE asserts? Is 'My wife is asleep', said by a bachelor, false (Russell) or neither true nor false (Strawson)? Strawson's view claims that there are 'truth-value gaps', i.e. an absence of TRUTH-VALUES where one might expect them. Some have said certain statements about the future are neither true nor false, since the future is not yet determined. Cf. FREEWILL (for logical determinism).

Compare also cases in fiction and mythology, like 'Unicorns are vegetarian', where the legends give no evidence. There are other

Truth and falsity

things which seem to be of the right kind to be true or false but are sometimes thought to be neither, or to be not really of that kind. Examples include value statements, laws of nature and counterfactual CONDITIONALS. It seems, then, that some things fail to be true or false because they are not of the right kind, while others may be not false but wrong for some other reason ('My wife is asleep', said by a bachelor, 'You are a wog/Canuck' said to a foreigner/Canadian). Metaphors and comparisons, etc., raise again the question of degrees of truth, e.g. should exaggerations be described as nearly true, or fairly true, or containing some truth? The HEAP paradox has also been thought to call for degrees of truth.

Special problems arise in certain cases. What is it for a logical or mathematical statement to be true? How is 'true' related to 'provable'? (Cf. GÖDEL'S THEOREMS, mathematical INTUITIONISM.)

A distinction is often drawn, though also often ignored, between the meaning of 'true' and the CRITERIA of truth. It is sometimes unclear to which of these a given theory is intended to apply.

Another use of 'true' and 'false' is that whereby predicates can be true or false *of* subjects. Linguistic PHILOSOPHERS sometimes ask what significance there is in such facts as that artificial teeth, but not artificial silk, are called false, while no teeth are true. See also SATISFY, TRUTH-VALUE, FACTS, VALID, LIAR PARADOX, philosophy of MATHEMATICS.

*M. Black, 'The semantic definition of truth', *Analysis*, vol. 8, 1948, reprinted in M. Macdonald (ed.), *Philosophy and Analysis*, Blackwell, 1954. (On Tarski. Easier than Tarski though it presupposes elementary knowledge of logic.)

D. Davidson, 'The structure and content of truth', *Journal of Philosophy*, 1990. (Discusses Tarskian truth, and rejects both deflationist and correspondence theories, and also antirealist theories (such as the coherence theory and pragmatism), changing some of his earlier views, and finally proposing a further theory of his own.)

D. W. Hamlyn, 'The correspondence theory of truth', *Philosophy Quarterly*, 1962. (Fairly difficult defence of loose correspondence theory.)

P. Horwich, *Truth*, Blackwell, 1990. (States a deflationary theory, calling it 'minimal', though distinguishing it from redundancy theory at pp. 39–41; then defends it against thirty-nine objections.)

H. Joachim, *The Nature of Truth*, 1905. (Coherence.)

D. H. Mellor, *Real Time*, Cambridge UP, 1981. (See chapter 2 on relations between truth and time: is truth timeless in all cases?)

Truth table

G. E. Moore, *Some Main Problems of Philosophy*, Allen and Unwin, 1953, Collier Books, 1962, written much earlier.

G. Pitcher (ed.), *Truth*, Prentice-Hall, 1964. (Contains papers by J. L. Austin, P. F. Strawson, G. J. Warnock, M. Dummett, with excerpt from F. P. Ramsey. On Dummett cf. bibliography to TRUTH-VALUE.)

*B. Russell, *The Problems of Philosophy*, Home University Library, 1912, chapter 12. (Cf. also Russell in bibliography to LOGICAL ATOMISM.)

R. M. Sainsbury, 'Degrees of belief and degrees of truth', *Philosophical Papers*, 1986. (Defends degrees of truth in connection with heap paradox.)

S. Soames, 'What is a theory of truth?', *Journal of Philosophy*, 1984. (See esp. p. 411 for brief statement of three things a theory of truth has tried to do.)

P. F. Strawson, *Logico-Linguistic Papers*, Methuen, 1971. (Includes several relevant items. For truth-value gaps see chapters 1, 4.)

A. Tarski, 'The semantic conception of truth', *Philosophy and Phenomenological Research*, 1944, reprinted in H. Feigl and W. Sellars (eds), *Readings in Philosophical Analysis*, Appleton-Century-Crofts, 1949.

Truth conditions. Conditions for a given sentence, proposition, etc., to be true; e.g. when p and q represent propositions which we assume must be true or false, the truth conditions of 'Not (p without q)' are that p and q be both true, or both false, or p be false and q true. To call something 'one of the truth conditions' of something else is ambiguous. It may mean that the first thing is adequate by itself to guarantee the truth of the second, but other things would be so too. (In the above example three such alternative truth conditions are given.) Or it may mean that the first thing is one of a set of things which are adequate for this if taken together (e.g. the truth of p is one of the truth conditions for 'p and q').

Truth conditions have also been used to give the meaning of terms like 'now' by those who think there is no property of presentness. See also MEANING.

D. H. Mellor, *Real Time*, Cambridge UP, 1981. (See esp. pp. 74–8 for meaning of 'now' etc.)

Truth table. One among the decision procedures (see DECIDABLE) for the propositional CALCULUS. The TRUTH-VALUE, normally *true* or *false*, of a complex expression in the propositional calculus depends on the truth-values assigned to the VARIABLES in it. A truth table is a systematic exposition of all possible combinations of such assign-

Truth-value

ments for the expression in question. Each combination occupies a row in the table, with the resulting truth-value for the whole expression placed, for example, at one end of the row. These truth-values for the whole expression form a column, from which various properties of the expression can be read off, e.g. the expression is logically true if this column contains no truth-value but *true*.

The following example of a truth table for 'Not (p and not q)' (where p and q represent propositions, and '1' means 'true' and '0' means 'false') is written out at unnecessary length to show how it is constructed. Various alternative presentations are possible. In the present case each row should be read from left to right, and the final column shows that the whole expression is false when p is true and q is false, and true in all other cases.

p	q	not q	p and not q	Not (p and not q)
1	1	0	0	1
1	0	1	1	0
0	1	0	0	1
0	0	1	0	1

Truth-value. *True* and *false* are known as the two main truth-values. For a *two-valued logic* they are in practice the only truth-values, though theoretically any two could be chosen. *Three-valued* and in general *many-valued logics* use three or more values accordingly, adding to *true* and *false* or replacing them. When they add to them, as in the first example below, or as degrees of truth do, they reject bivalence (see EXCLUDED MIDDLE). Examples are *true/false/indeterminate, known to be true/known to be false/unknown, necessarily true/necessarily false/contingent, certainly true/99 per cent probable/ . . ./certainly false* (this last group, like that of degrees of truth, could contain infinitely many values). Sometimes a set of truth-values falls into two groups with important logical properties analogous to those of *true* and *false* respectively. Those analogous to *true* are then called *designated values*, and those analogous to *false* are called *undesignated values*.

M. Dummett, 'Truth', *Proceedings of the Aristotelian Society*, 1958–9, reprinted in G. Pitcher (ed.), *Truth*, Prentice-Hall, 1964, in P. F. Strawson (ed.), *Philosophical Logic*, Oxford UP, 1967, and in Dummett's *Truth and Other Enigmas*, Duckworth, 1978. (Includes explanation of designated and undesignated values).

Truth-value gaps. See TRUTH AND FALSITY.

T-sentence. See MEANING.

362

Turing test

Turing machine. A device due to A. M. Turing for solving any problem which can be solved by computation. An indefinitely long tape extends through a point on the machine which reads symbols on it, normally in the form of noughts and ones, or some equivalent (e.g. negative and positive charge.) The machine can carry out just four operations: move the tape one step to the left; move the tape one step to the right; replace a nought on the tape with a one; replace a one with a nought. It also can be in any of a finite number of possible states, each containing instructions (varying from state to state) for carrying out the operations in the light of what it reads on the tape, and for passing from one state to another. The problem to be solved, together with any relevant data, is then coded on to the tape (the rest of the tape being filled with noughts) and fed into the machine. Different machines will have different repertoires (i.e. sets of possible states), according to the problem to be solved, but there can also be a *universal Turing machine* which can be programmed to take on the repertoires of any given machine and so to replace it. However, since the tape must be indefinitely long, and both the number of possible states and the sequence of operations needed indefinitely large (though finite), a Turing machine must be thought of as an idealized blueprint rather than a practicable construction. The idea is important because it makes precise what a computable function is. Any function (in the mathematical sense) that can be effectively computed by a computer at all can be computed by a Turing machine. This lets us distinguish the sort of problems that can, and the sort that cannot, be in principle solved by a computer.

T. Crane, *The Mechanical Mind: a Philosophical Introduction to Minds, Machines and Mental Representation*, Penguin, 1995, chapter 3. (Elementary introduction).

R. Penrose, *The Emperor's New Mind*, Oxford UP, 1989, chapter 2, esp. pp. 46–56, 67–75.

Turing test. Test devised by A. M. Turing for helping us to answer, or rather to provide a more precise substitute for, the question 'Can machines think?' The test takes the form of an *imitation game*. A human and a machine, both hidden behind a screen, confront an interlocutor who asks them a series of questions to find out which is which. The machine is programmed to deceive the interlocutor for as long as possible by imitating the sort of responses a human would give (its answers need not be true), while the human tries to help the interlocutor. If the machine succeeds over some pre-assigned period, it wins the imitation game and passes the Turing test. Turing thought, overoptimistically, that machines capable of a

Types (theory of)

modest success rate (30 per cent) would be a practical possibility by the end of the twentieth century.

N. Block, 'The computer model of the mind', in D. Osherson and E. E. Smith (eds), *An Invitation to Cognitive Science*, vol. III, MIT Press, 1990, esp. pp. 248–53.

A. M. Turing, 'Computing machinery and intelligence', *Mind*, 1950, reprinted in A. R. Anderson (ed.), *Minds and Machines*, Prentice-Hall, 1964, along with various articles discussing the significance of Turing's article.

Types (theory of). Towards the end of the last century interest revived in the logical PARADOXES, from which the semantic ones were not yet distinguished. To cope with RUSSELL'S PARADOX and others, Russell enunciated the *vicious circle principle*: 'If, provided a certain collection had a total, it would have members only definable in terms of that total, then the said collection has no total', i.e. we cannot talk of the *totality* of its members. Classes form such a collection, for him. There are, he said, first-type, or first-level, classes whose members are ordinary objects, second-type classes whose members are first-type classes, and so on. The class of cats and the class of dogs are animal classes. They are first-type classes themselves, and are members of the second-type class of animal classes. There is a class of all classes of a given type which will itself be one type higher, but no class of *all* classes (see also CATEGORIES). Ordinary objects are of type zero. The hierarchy of types also applies to properties: A property of properties of objects belongs to the second type. *Black* is a property of some cats. It has the property of applying to some cats. *Applying to some cats* is therefore a second-type property of the first-type property *black*.

In 'Napoleon had all the properties of a great general', *having all the properties of a great general* is a property of Napoleon, and so is of the first type. But it refers to properties, so is said to be of the second *order*. It attributes to Napoleon only the relevant first-order properties (on this theory). The addition of the hierarchy of orders to that of types gives us the *ramified* as against *simple theory of types*. (But words like 'second-order' are normally used more loosely.) Propositions too are distinguished into orders. A proposition referring to no other propositions is of the first order. One referring to propositions of the first order (e.g. 'Some first-order propositions are false') is of the second order, and so on. The ramified theory was used to solve the semantic PARADOXES, e.g. the LIAR.

Since the ramified theory invalidates certain mathematical procedures, Russell introduced the controversial *axiom of reducibility*,

Type/token

saying that any higher-order property or proposition could be replaced by some first-order one.

Classes, etc., defined in ways violating the vicious circle principle are said to have *impredicative definitions* (for an example see Carnap, p. 37–8).

One disadvantage of the theory is that many words, e.g. 'class', 'proposition', 'true', become systematically, or 'typically', AMBIGUOUS, with different senses for each type or order.

R. Carnap, 'The logicist foundations of mathematics' in P. Benacerraf and H. Putnam (eds), *Philosophy of Mathematics*, Blackwell, 1964, pp. 31–41. (Elementary but illuminating.)

I. M. Copi, *The Theory of Logical Types*, RKP, 1971. (Fuller treatment.)

A. Whitehead and B. Russell, *Principia Mathematica*, Cambridge UP, vol. 1, 1910. (See Introduction, chapter 2, § 1, for vicious circle principle, repeated (though not there so called) in Russell's *Logic and Knowledge*, Allen and Unwin, 1956, p. 63.)

Type/token. See UNIVERSALS.

U _____

Uncertainty principle. See CAUSATION.

Unexpected examination paradox. See PREDICTION.

Universalizability. An important part of morality seems to lie in the idea that what is right for one person must be right for anyone else in the same position. This can be expressed by saying that a moral judgment must be universalizable. If I say that you ought not to lie. I commit myself to saying that anyone else in your position ought not to lie. Similarly, if I call someone's action a good deed I must allow that anyone else who did the same thing in the same circumstances did a good deed.

Universalizability is not the same as generality. 'Everyone ought to give 1 per cent of his income to blind cripples over sixty' is very specific but quite universal. It refers to *all* who have an income and *all* blind cripples over sixty, since all such cripples are put on a level. In spite of this, 'generalize' is sometimes used for 'universalize', as by Singer.

Judgments may be universal in a stricter or a looser sense. The looser kind may mention individual people, places, etc. Thus 'Everyone should fight for his country' is universal in the stricter sense, since no particular country is mentioned. On the other hand, 'Everyone should fight for England', 'Every Englishman should fight for England,' 'Every Englishman should be kind to animals', are all universal only in the looser sense.

Those who make universalizability important for ethics may hold either of two views. The first view uses universalizability to distinguish the MORAL from the *non-moral*. Someone's principle is a moral

366

principle, on this view, if he is willing to universalize it. In this way universalizability helps to define morality, providing either a necessary condition for it (Hare) or a sufficient condition, or both (see NECESSARY AND SUFFICIENT CONDITIONS). The second view (Kant, Singer) tries to distinguish the moral from the *immoral*, by saying that what makes a principle moral is basically that it is universalizable, in the sense that there is no inconsistency in supposing everyone to act on it. 'Inconsistency' here may mean the kind of inconsistency involved in frustrating one's own ends (it is inconsistent to commit oneself to accepting that all promises should be broken, if they would then no longer be regarded as promises, so that one's purpose in making them would be frustrated, whatever that purpose might be). Or it may mean simply the frustration of something which is, or should be, a general end of human action, e.g. maximizing happiness.

There are difficulties in the notion of universalizing. What counts as universalizing a judgment? Suppose that whatever applies to me must apply to everyone like me: how like me must they be? Can I not describe my case in such a way that no one *is* like me? Remembering that very specific judgments can still be universalized, I might say: 'Although people in general ought not to lie, I myself may lie, because I will allow that anyone may lie if he is just six feet tall, has a scar on his left knee, etc., etc.', listing so many of my characteristics that no one else has them all. Also do desires, etc., count as relevant characteristics? If so, I might say: 'You ought to help the poor, and so ought anyone like you, but I need not because I am not like you. I do not desire to help them, as you do.'

One way of expressing the need for universalizability is by saying that whatever is a reason for one person to act must be a reason for anyone else in the same position to act in the same way. This may give a necessary condition for morality, but it is not peculiar to morality, since it is a mere principle of logical consistency. If danger to health is a reason for Smith not to smoke, it is presumably a reason for everyone like him not to smoke – though again it may be hard to describe how 'like' him they must be.

It has been disputed how many kinds of universalizability there are. Universalizability in the sense of mere logical consistency is, as we have just seen, too wide to define morality completely. Universalizability in the sense of impartiality (in particular, not favouring oneself) seems to be a principle which marks the moral from the immoral, rather than the moral from the non-moral. But this principle too, as we have seen, is not easy to formulate. How far universalizability is relevant to morality, therefore, whether as helping to define it or as contributing to its content, is unclear. (Another notion important here is that of SUPERVENIENCE.)

Universals and particulars

For *moral particularism* see ETHICS.

J. Dancy, 'On moral properties', *Mind*, 1981. (Universalizability and allied notions.)

A. Gewirth, 'Categorial consistency in ethics', *Philosophical Quarterly*, 1967. (Discusses how far universalizability can be used for moral attack on racialism. Criticized by N. Fotion, 'Gewirth and categorial consistency, *Philosophical Quarterly*, 1968.)

R. M. Hare, *The Language of Morals*, Oxford UP, 1952, *Freedom and Reason*, Clarendon, 1963. (Claims universalizability gives necessary condition (not sufficient, but important), for defining morality.)

*W. D. Hudson, *Modern Moral Philosophy*, Macmillan, 1970. (General introduction, including discussions of universalizability in connexion with Hare.)

D. Locke, 'The trivializability of universalizability', *Philosophical Review*, 1968. (Distinguishes several senses of 'universalizability', and claims that most of them are of little importance to ethics.)

D. H. Monro, 'Impartiality and consistency', *Philosophy*, 1961 (cf. his *Empiricism in Ethics*, Cambridge UP, 1967, chapter 16.) (Distinguishes these. Criticized by S. B. Thomas, 'The status of the generalization principle, *American Philosophical Quarterly*, 1968.)

H. J. Paton, *The Moral Law*, Hutchinson, 1948. (Probably best translation of Kant's *Grundlegung*, 1785, earliest and most famous major attempt to base morality on universalizability. Difficult.)

M. G. Singer, *Generalization in Ethics*, Eyre and Spottiswoode, 1963. (Elaborate modern development of Kant's view, claiming that generalization (i.e. universalization) is 'the fundamental principle of morality' (*Preface*). Studies in detail the implications of the question. 'What would happen if everyone did that?' Shorter version in his 'Moral rules and principles', in A. I. Melden (ed.), *Essays in Moral Philosophy*, Washington UP, 1958, stressing difference between rules and principles.)

Universals and particulars. Objects around us share features with other objects. It is in the nature of most such features that they can characterize indefinitely many objects. Because of this the features are called universals and the main problem is to describe their status. Exceptions, such as 'being the tallest of men', can be included for convenience. The objects are called their instances. The problem is often called, especially in Greek philosophy, the *one-many* or *one-over-many problem*.

Traditionally three kinds of answer have been given: realism,

Universals and particulars

conceptualism and nominalism. *Realism* in this sense of primarily associated with Plato, who treated universals as objects (cf. FORM, IDEA), separate from their instances, and faced great difficulties over what they were like and how they related to these instances. Plato's Forms, in so far as they are treated rather as particulars (see below), are often said not to be universals, though doing duty for them. *Platonism* is nowadays any view which treats things like universals, propositions, numbers, etc., as independent objects. Frege is a noted modern Platonist. Another form of realism, often attributed to Aristotle though the interpretation of Aristotle is very controversial, denies that universals are objects or separate from their instances, but nevertheless makes them real things which somehow exist just *by* being instantiated. It is unclear how this view treats things like unicornhood. The labels *universalia ante rem* or *res*: universals prior to the object(s), and *universalia in re* or *rebus*: universals in the object(s), are often applied to Plato's and Aristotle's views respectively. *Universalia post rem* or *res*: universals, after, or derivative from, the object(s), normally applies to nominalism, thought it could apply to conceptualism. The term *substantial universals* is applied, like 'realism', primarily to Plato's view, though sometimes also to Aristotle's. It could, but usually does not, denote universals corresponding to substances, e.g. tablehood, as against qualitative universals like hardness. Realists often limit universals to only some general features.

For *conceptualism*, universals are thoughts or ideas in and constructed by the mind. This view, summarily rejected by Plato, is largely associated with the British EMPIRICISTS. It may explain human thinking and the MEANING of many words, but it can no longer explain why the world itself is as it is (which Plato claimed his Forms explained). The view thus avoids Plato's dilemma that the universal is either outside its instances and so irrelevant to them, or inside them and so split up. But what sort of thing is this thought or idea? Does it involve images, and if so, of what sort? Can the same idea be shared by different people, which splits the universal up again, or have they similar but distinct ideas, which leads to the difficulty associated with PRIVATE LANGUAGES? Some writers include conceptualism under nominalism, e.g. Armstrong, who talks of 'conceptual nominalism'.

For *nominalism*, represented especially by Ockham in the middle ages and so by many recent writers, there are only general words like 'dog', and no universals in the sense of entities like *doghood*. Cf. MEANING, and also below on 'types' and 'tokens'. (For N. Goodman (1906–), nominalism means recognizing only INDIVIDUALS (second sense), which for him may be abstract but cannot include classes.)

There are two ways of defining a class of objects. One can define

Universals and particulars

it *extensionally* or *in extension*, by listing its members, or one can define it as containing all those things which have a certain property or set of properties (called defining it *intensionally* or *in intension*; see INTENSIONALITY). The former way makes it impossible for a class, once it is defined, to acquire new members, and is of little use. The latter way leaves it open how many members, if any, a class has; the class of dogs contains whatever things have the properties necessary for being a dog. Nominalism now faces a difficulty, for if there are no universals, i.e. no properties, what determines whether something belongs to the class of dogs or not? This is another version of Plato's demand for Forms to account for the world's being as it is. The main nominalist answer to this difficulty uses the notion of resemblance. An object is a dog if it resembles some given dog which is chosen as a standard or paradigm. Two disputed objections to this are that resemblance itself seems to be an indispensable universal, and that resemblance involves partial identity, for to resemble something is to have something, though not necessarily everything, in common with it; the common feature is then presumably a universal.

A variant on the use of resemblance is Wittgenstein's notion of *family resemblance*, whereby there need be nothing common to all the members of a class, nor need any member be taken as the paradigm, but the members form 'a complicated network of similarities overlapping and criss-crossing' like the fibres that make up a thread. An example Wittgenstein takes is that of a game: have all games got something in common? A somewhat related notion is that of *clusters* (Gasking).

Particulars, which are not always the same as INDIVIDUALS, cannot be instantiated, and cannot appear as a whole at separated places simultaneously though their parts may be spatially separate. A particular can perhaps appear as a whole at different moments of time (though see GENIDENTITY), but these must normally be linked into a stream – though an intermittent sound may constitute one and the same particular, and see Burke. A particular's parts may be constantly changing, as with a flame, and it need not be 'solid' (shadows, rainbows, clouds, can all be particulars, and perhaps the sky). It must, however, be identifiable and distinguishable from other particulars, so clouds, etc., are not always particulars. Particulars can be abstract, provided the conditions about space and time are preserved (e.g. an action or event, like the Renaissance. Rarely non-spatiotemporal things like numbers are included.) *Bare particulars* are particulars considered as independent of all their properties. It is therefore hard to identify or refer to them.

Particulars are like SUBSTANCES in the first Aristotelian sense of that term, though the emphasis is on being unique in space and

Universals and particulars

time rather than, as with Aristotle, on existing in their own right as the bearers of attributes and subjects of change. Therefore shadows and actions are more easily called particulars than substances, while Platonist universals are more naturally called substances than particulars, especially since particulars cannot be instantiated.

As an adjective 'particular' has its everyday sense, and also that given under SENTENCE.

We have seen that universals are sometimes treated rather as particulars. Idealism's *concrete universal* is also a kind of particular. It is a system of instances, treated as a developing individual, e.g. *man* in 'Man has evolved slowly'. Bradley treats ordinary particulars as concrete universals, since they are developing individuals, though really the universe is the sole individual. He uses 'particular' in a more restricted sense than the present entry.

Universals, like particulars, are of many kinds. Some universals (relations) can only be instantiated in ordered pairs or triplets, etc., of objects. Others, like 'round square', cannot be instantiated at all, even in thought. Some can be instantiated together with their opposites: an object can be both beautiful and ugly, in different respects; or the object may instantiate the universal only if described in a certain way: something may be large if described as a mouse, but not if described as an animal (see ATTRIBUTIVE); and the instances may themselves be universals, for a universal may have universals as its instance: red may have the property of being beautiful. Moreover, stuffs, like water, are not particulars but presumably instantiate universals (though *wateriness* rather characterizes other things resembling water). Logically, then, it is the notion of an instance that is correlative to that of a universal, though instances are no doubt usually particulars.

A distinction closely related to that between universals and particulars, and revealing some of the complications in this field, is that between *types* and *tokens*, introduced by Peirce. The word 'in' appears twice in the present sentence, yet it is only one word. Peirce would call these two appearances in any one copy of the present book, two tokens of a single type. A word as found in the dictionary is therefore a type with indefinitely many tokens (written, spoken, etc.) Only types can be derived from Latin. Only tokens can be illegible. A token may be ambiguous, and then so must its type. A type may be polysyllabic, and then so must all its tokens. The distinction is significant for nominalists, for when they say there are only words and no universals, do they mean types or tokens? Also the distinction is not sufficient by itself, for the words in a speech cannot be types, for types are not limited to a single speech, nor yet tokens, since the same speech, and therefore the same words,

Universals and particulars

can be recorded many times (Cohen). It is disputed how closely this distinction resembles that between universals and particulars. *Word* as a universal has instances (several hundred on this page); as a type it has tokens (each of just four letters). Also to what spheres, apart from words, is it relevant? Is the Union Jack, or the lion in 'The lion is carnivorous', a type or a universal or what? Is the lion a concrete universal? Spheres where the distinction has been used include aesthetics, in the analysis of works of art, and in the IDENTITY THEORY OF MIND. See also REALISM, CONCEPT, IDEA, SENTENCES, TROPE, THIRD MAN ARGUMENT.

R. I. Aaron, *The Theory of Universals*, Clarendon, 1952, revised 1967. (Universals as 'natural recurrences' and 'principles of grouping'. Some history.)

E. B. Allaire, 'Bare particulars', *Philosophical Studies*, 1963, reprinted with discussion in Loux (above).

Aristotle, *Metaphysics*, book 7 (or Z), chapters 13–16, *Posterior Analytics*, book 2, chapter 19. (Cf. also Aristotle references under SUBSTANCE.)

D. M. Armstrong, *Universals and Scientific Realism*, vol. 1: *Nominalism and Realism*, vol. 2: *A Theory of Universals*, Cambridge UP, 1978. (Important modern work. See also his *Universals: an Opinionated Introduction*, Westview Press, 1989, which is shorter than his earlier work but contains important revisions.)

F. H. Bradley, *The Principle of Logic*, 1993, book 1, chapter 2, § 4, chapter 6, §§ 30–6. (Concrete universals. Cf. R. M. Eaton, *General Logic*, Scribner's Sons 1931, pp. 269–72.)

M. B. Burke, 'Cohabitation, stuff and intermittent existence', *Mind*, 1980. (Material objects can exist intermittently.)

W. Charlton, *Aesthetics*, Hutchinson, 1970, pp. 27–9. (Types and universals. Relevance to aesthetics. Cf. also R. A. Dipert, 'Types and tokens: a reply to Sharpe', *Mind*, 1980; Sharpe replies in *Mind*, 1982.)

L. J. Cohen, *The Diversity of Meaning*, Methuen, 1962, pp. 4–5. (Brief discussion of types and tokens.)

D. Gasking, 'Clusters', *Australasian Journal of Philosophy*, 1960.

N. Goodman, 'A world of individuals', in I. M. Bochenski *et al.*, *The Problem of Universals*, 1956, reprinted in P. Benacerraf and H. Putnam (eds), *Philosophy of Mathematics*, Blackwell, 1964 (cf. also ibid., pp. 21–3), and in C. Landesman (ed.), *The Problem of Universals*, Basic Books, 1971. (Goodman's nominalism.)

D. K. Lewis, 'New work for a theory of universals', *Australasian Journal of Philosophy*, 1983. (Discuss Armstrong's earlier work, claiming universals are indeed needed, but for reasons different from Armstrong's. Difficult.)

Utilitarianism

M. J. Loux (ed.), *Universals and Particulars*, Anchor Books, 1970. (Selected readings.)

A. Oliver, 'The metaphysics of properties', *Mind*, 1996. (Extended survey article, with references, on recent views on the nature and role of properties, concentrating especially on Armstrong's treatment of properties as immanent universals.)

Plato, *Phaedo, Republic* § 596, *Parmenides*, esp. down to § 135c. (These are among the important passages. The *Parmenides* includes what seems to be strong self-criticism, including the 'third man argument'.)

H. H. Price, *Thinking and Experience*, Hutchinson, 1953, chapter 1, reprinted in Landesman (above). (Moderate defence of resemblance theory, reconciling it with 'universalia in rebus' theory.)

W. V. O. Quine, 'On what there is' (see bibliography to BEING). (Offers a criterion for deciding whether there are universals or not.)

A. B. Schoedinger (ed.) *The Problem of Universals*, Humanities Press, 1992. (General anthology.)

M. A. Simon, 'When is a resemblance a family resemblance?', *Mind*, 1969. (Critical discussion of family resemblance view.)

*H. Staniland, *Universals*, Doubleday Anchor, 1972. (Elementary introduction, if inevitably a bit dated.)

L. Wittgenstein, *Philosophical Investigations*, Blackwell, 1953, §§ 65–77. (Family resemblance view.)

Universe of discourse. See QUANTIFICATION.

Utilitarianism. Moral theories about what we ought to do are commonly, if not uncontroversially, divided into deontological and teleological ones (see ETHICS). The main, though not the only, teleological (or CONSEQUENTIALIST) theory is utilitarianism, which in its most general form is to the effect that we always ought to do what will produce the greatest good.

But 'utilitarianism' is sometimes restricted to *hedonistic utilitarianism*, which holds that the good is pleasure, or perhaps happiness. Early utilitarians seldom distinguished these. *Ideal utilitarianism*, notably represented by Moore, allows other things to be good, or even to be the main goods (for Moore personal relations and aesthetic experiences). Most early utilitarians were hedonistic, though contemporary ones are harder to classify, and often appeal to preference or satisfaction of desire rather than to pleasure. Utilitarianism has never held, as its name may suggest, that one should pursue only the useful and not the good in itself, nor that one should pursue only 'low-grade' pleasures; when Bentham said that

Utilitarianism

if the pleasure is equal pushpin is as good as poetry, one should not ignore the 'if'-clause.

Though the idea of utilitarianism goes back to the Greeks, its most famous exponents have been Bentham and J. S. Mill. Bentham's *greatest happiness principle* says that one should pursue 'the greatest good, or greatest happiness, of the greatest number'. The formula is imprecise, because if we try to spread happiness to many people we may produce less happiness overall than if we confine it to fewer people. Faced with this difficulty, utilitarians have usually said that one should aim for the greatest happiness overall, however distributed. It is therefore often objected that they cannot account for our intuitions about justice. It is also doubted whether they can account for our normal views on promise-keeping, truth-telling, etc. Also utilitarianism faces difficulties in connexion with such things as the double effect doctrine (see ETHICS) or the distinction between (e.g.) killing and letting die.

Utilitarianism may be attacked in a weak or a strong way. The weak way grants that we always ought to aim for the greatest happiness, but says we have other duties too, e.g. to distribute it in certain ways. The strong attack says that some of our duties not only go beyond utilitarianism, but are inconsistent with it, because they involve producing less happiness than other courses of action would produce.

Recently utilitarians have split into two camps. *Act utilitarians* (also called *extreme* or *direct utilitarians*; notably J. J. C. Smart) say that on each occasion we should do whatever act will produce the greatest good. *Rule utilitarians* (also called *restricted* or *indirect utilitarians*) say that we should obey those rules which would produce the greatest happiness if generally followed. These are other versions of rule utilitarianism. Suppose I ignore a red traffic light and, by some fluke, thereby prevent an accident which would otherwise have occurred. Then, whatever my motive, on act utilitarianism I did right, but on rule utilitarianism I did wrong, assuming that general obedience to the traffic laws produces better results than general disobedience to them.

Motive utilitarianism is the view that 'one pattern of motivation is morally better than another to the extent that the former has more utility than the latter' (Adams).

One difficulty for utilitarianism is how we can ever know what we ought to do. Not only can we never know the total consequences of any act, but much may depend on what others do, and they in turn must take account of what we may do (cf. DECISION THEORY, FREEWILL (on self-prediction)). Rule utilitarianism is partly intended to overcome this difficulty, but has difficulties of its own.

Utilitarianism

The question whether we should aim at what we think best or at what is really best raises a difficulty shared by other theories.

An interesting recent question concerns population policy. Normally utilitarians have concerned themselves with problems about creating goods and distributing them among a given population, but further questions obviously arise when we can decide how large that population shall be, and which of various alternative populations shall exist.

Negative utilitarianism says we should aim only to remove evil, not to produce good. Ordinary utilitarianism says we should both remove evil and produce good, aiming at the greatest overall balance of good.

See also HEDONISM, PLEASURE, UNIVERSALIZABILITY.

H. B. Acton and J. W. N. Watkins, 'Negative utilitarianism', *Proceedings of the Aristotelian Society*, supplementary vol., 1963.

R. M. Adams, 'Motive utilitarianism', *Journal of Philosophy*, 1976, reprinted P. Pettit (ed.), *Consequentalism*, Dartmouth Publishing Co., 1993. (For quotation see p. 470 (p. 74 in reprint).)

J. Annas, 'Aristotle on pleasure and goodness', in A. O. Rorty (ed.), *Essays on Aristotle's Ethics*, California UP, 1980. (Uses Aristotle as basis for attacking some of the fundamental assumptions of utilitarianism. Cf. also in same volume J. McDowell, 'The role of *end* in Aristotle's ethics', and the two articles by D. Wiggins, esp. pp. 258–61; all quite difficult and Wiggins uses some technicalities.)

G. E. M. Anscombe, 'Modern moral philosophy', *Philosophy*, 1958, reprinted in G. Wallace and A. D. M. Walker (eds), *The Definition of Morality*, Methuen, 1970, with additional bibliography, and in W. D. Hudson (ed.), *The Is/Ought Question*, Macmillan, 1969. (Criticizes utilitarianism.)

D. Lyons, *Forms and Limits of Utilitarianism*, Oxford UP, 1965. (Discusses relations between versions of act and rule utilitarianism. Discussed by B. A. Brody, 'The equivalence of act and rule utilitarianism', *Philosophical Studies*, 1967.)

*J. S. Mill, *Utilitarianism*, 1861. (Classic and provocative defence.)

G. E. Moore, *Principia Ethica*, Oxford UP, 1903. (Ideal utilitarianism.)

J. Narveson, 'Utilitarianism and new generations,' *Mind*, 1967. (Population control. Discussed by T. L. S. Sprigge, 'Professor Narveson's utilitarianism', *Inquiry*, 1968 (§2), and H. Vetter, 'Utilitarianism and new generations', *Mind*, 1971.)

D. Parfit, *Reasons and Persons*, Oxford UP, 1984. (Part 1 discusses consequentialism in general. Part 4 discusses questions about population policy.)

Utilitarianism

A. Sen and B. A. O. Williams (eds), *Utilitarianism and Beyond*, Cambridge UP, 1982. (Mainly specially written essays, covering philosophy and economics.)

J. J. C. Smart, 'Extreme and restricted utilitarianism', in P. Foot (ed.), *Theories of Ethics*, Oxford, UP, 1967. (Act utilitarianism. See also J. Rawls, 'Two concepts of rules', ibid.)

*J. C. C. Smart and B. A. O. Williams, *Utilitarianism For and Against*, Cambridge, UP, 1973. (Debate with annotated bibliography).

V

Vacuous. In logic certain statements, notably universal statements (see SENTENCES), and CONDITIONALS, are often interpreted more widely than in ordinary thought. 'All unicorns are black' means 'There are no non-black unicorns', and so is true if there are no unicorns. 'If p then q', where p and q are propositions, means 'Not (p without q)', and so is true if p is false. Statements true simply because their subject terms are empty or (in the case of conditionals) their antecedents false, or for certain other 'irrelevant' reasons, are called *vacuously true*. Their contradictions can be called *vacuously false*. A term *occurs vacuously* in a statement if the truth or falsity of the statement remains unaffected when the term is replaced by any other term meaningfully admissible in that context. 'Red' for instance occurs vacuously in 'This table is either red or not red'. Normally (though not always: see Quine) a term not occurring vacuously *occurs essentially*.

W. V. O. Quine, 'Truth by convention', in H. Feigl and W. Sellars (eds), *Readings in Philosophical Analysis*, Appleton-Century-Crofts, 1949. (Vacuous occurrence.)

Vagueness. To be distinguished from AMBIGUITY and OPEN TEXTURE. Problems about vagueness arise especially from the HEAP (or sorites) paradox, and mainly concern how far it affects TRUTH and the law of EXCLUDED MIDDLE, and whether it is an objective feature of the world, or simply a feature, perhaps unavoidable, of our language, or is an illusion depending on our ignorance.

G. Evans, 'Can there be vague objects?', *Analysis*, 1978. (One-page article raising problem for view that there can. NB: The symbol

Valid

'∇' means 'It is vague whether', and '△' means 'It is definite whether'. Cf. also (difficult) discussion by S. A. Rasmussen in *Mind*, 1986.)

T. Parsons and P. Woodruff, 'Worldly inderminacy of identity', *Proceedings of the Aristotelian Society*, 1995. (Vagueness is an objective feature of the world. Cf. also M. Tye, 'Vague objects', *Mind*, 1990.)

T. Williams, *Vagueness*, Routledge, 1994. (General treatment, including historical material and defending the view that vagueness depends on our ignorance. See also bibliography to HEAP.)

Valid. An inference or an argument is *valid* if its conclusion follows deductively from its premises. The premises may be false, but if they are true the conclusion *must* be true. An inference is *invalid* if it is not valid. It is *contravalid* if an inference from the same premises to the opposite conclusion would be valid. Sometimes, however, a valid argument is simply *defined* as one where it is logically impossible for all the premises to be true and the conclusion false. This raises the same 'paradoxes' as strict IMPLICATION. With inductive, etc., inferences, 'valid' may be used as above, in which case they are all invalid, but it may mean simply 'meeting the standards proper to them'. A formula (propositional FUNCTION, open SENTENCE) is valid if it is true for every value of its VARIABLES. Otherwise it is invalid. It is contravalid if it is false for every value. Logically true propositions, i.e. propositions instantiating valid propositional functions, are sometimes called valid, and logically false ones contravalid. *Sound*, applied to an inference, means either 'valid, and having all its premises true' or just 'valid'. An interpretation of an AXIOM SYSTEM is sound if, under it, all the axioms and theorems are truths. Alternatively, it is sound if whatever is derivable in it from certain premises really follows from those premises. A proof system of any kind can similarly be called sound. Soundness is similar to but not identical with CONSISTENCY.

A. Church, *Introduction to Mathematical Logic*, vol. 1, Princeton UP, 1956, p. 55. (Soundness.)

B. Mates, *Elementary Logic*, Oxford UP, 1965. (See index. Soundness and consistency.)

Value. See VARIABLE.

Variable. Symbol used to stand indefinitely for any one of a set of things or notions. It *ranges over* the members of the set. The members are its *values* and the set as its *range*. *Individual variables, propositional variables*, etc., range respectively over INDIVIDUALS, propositions, etc. *Syntactical* variables range over syntactical (i.e. logical) OPERATORS. A symbol assumed to stand for one thing alone throughout a given context is a *constant*. The thing in question may be unspecified. But with *logical constants* it is specified. The logical constants are terms like 'and', 'or', 'not', 'implies'. They are a subclass of logical operators (which go beyond them by including things like quantifiers (see QUANTIFICATION)). In school algebra, x, y, etc., are numerical variables, ranging over numbers, a, b, etc., are numerical constants; and '+', '×', etc., correspond to logical constants.

A variable is *bound* or, occasionally, *apparent*, if it occurs within the scope of a quantifier containing the same variable (see QUANTIFICATION); a bound variable is rather like a pronoun. Otherwise it is *free* or, occasionally, *real*; though the variable within the quantifier itself is sometimes called bound, sometimes neither. In (x) (Fxy), the second x is bound while the y is free; the first x can be called bound or neither. In mathematics a 'real variable' is one ranging over 'real', as against imaginary or complex, numbers.

For *intervening variables* see LOGICAL CONSTRUCTIONS.

A *hidden variable* is something unobserved but postulated to explain, by its variations, variations in observed phenomena that we cannot otherwise account for.

I. Copi, *Introduction to Logic*, 6th edn, Macmillan, 1982. (Elementary introduction. See its index under 'variable'. For fuller treatment see, with its index, his *Symbolic Logic*, 5th edn, Macmillan, 1979 (treatment differs somewhat in different editions).)

Veil of ignorance. See ORIGINAL POSITION.

Veil of perception. Bennett's name for a doctrine, or perhaps just assumption, which he attributes to Locke in particular. This is that we are in effect separated by a veil from the world outside our minds, so that we can only perceive things outside us by having IDEAS which copy and resemble those things.

J. Bennett, 'Substance, reality and primary qualities', in C. B. Martin and D. M. Armstrong (eds), *Locke and Berkeley*, Macmillan, n.d., esp. part I, section 2.

Verification. See POSITIVISM.

Vicious circle principle. See TYPES (THEORY OF).

Vico, Giambattista. 1668–1744. Born in Naples, he worked mainly there. His main work lay in speculative philosophy of HISTORY, where he elaborated a theory of how civilizations independently undergo a certain kind of development, which occurs under divine providence. He influenced CROCE among others. *Principi di una scienza nuova d'intorno alla comune natura delle nazioni (The New Science)*, 1725 (revised in later editions).

Vienna circle. See POSITIVISM.

Vindication. See INDUCTION.

Virtue. In Greek ethics, virtue (*aretē*) was a dominant concept. Socrates and the Sophists were much concerned with its nature and value, and how it might be acquired. Plato devoted several early dialogues to individual virtues. For Aristotle the human good was to live in accordance with virtue, or with the highest if there was more than one. For the Stoics, virtue was the only unconditional good. Christianity substituted a duty to obey the will of God, and in more modern times, ethical outlooks have largely divided into the deontological, making duty the primary concept, and teleological, emphasizing the pursuit of certain ends; see ETHICS.

Recently, however, there has been a revival of interest in virtue as a basis for ethics, under the name *virtue ethics*. The prescribed aim is to promote the virtues in oneself and others, and the emphasis is on what sort of a person one is. Virtues may or may not be MORAL, and what makes them so when they are is disputed. Are courage, tenacity, prudence, moral virtues? Are laziness, carelessness, stubbornness, moral vices? And what of intellectual virtues like wisdom, intelligence, quick-wittedness? For Aristotle, the main intellectual virtues, at least, ranked higher than the moral ones. Further questions concern whether the nature or value of virtues depends on physical or social conditions (would meekness be a virtue in a caveman?), and how far virtue ethics can cater for all our moral intuitions.

A. Macintyre, *After Virtue*, Duckworth, 1981. (Historical discussion of how Greek ethics was superseded by more modern attempts to justify morality, themselves superseded by Nietzsche's emphasis on the will and by recent developments from that; as a result we are so far removed from Greek ethics as only to half understand it.)

O. O'Neill, *Duty and Virtue*, Dartmouth Publishing Co., 1993.

*G. Pence, 'Virtue theory' in P. Singer (ed.), *A Companion to Ethics*, Blackwell, 1991. (Brief introduction, with short but useful bibliography.); 'Recent work on virtues', *American Philosophical*

Voting paradox

Quarterly, 1984. (Critical survey of various recent books and articles. NB Asterisk only refers to first of Pence's publications.)
M. Slote, *From Morality to Virtue*, Oxford UP, 1992. (See also summary, discussions, and Slote's reply, in *Philosophy and Phenomenological Research*, 1994.)

Voting paradox. Let three issues A, B, C, be voted on by three voters whose respective orders of preference are ABC, BCA, CAB. If the first vote is on two issues, and the second vote on the winner and the third issue, the third issue will always win, so that the winner will depend on the order in which the issues are voted on. This example also shows that majority preference is not TRANSITIVE, even when that of each individual is; for a majority prefers A to B, and a majority prefers B to C, but also a majority prefers C to A. This second feature shows that an electorate can be irrational in a way that none of its members need be. It is sometimes called Arrow's paradox because he used it to prove his 'impossibility theorem', that four plausibly desirable conditions cannot be satisfied together by any voting system.

Another paradox sometimes called the voting paradox, or paradox of democracy, asks how we can consistently hold, when outvoted, both that our favoured policy ought to be enacted and that the policy favoured by the majority ought to be enacted.

K. J. Arrow, 'Values and collective decision-making', in P. Laslett *et al.* (eds), *Philosophy, Politics and Society*, 3rd series, Blackwell, 1967, § IV.

R. Wollheim, 'A paradox in the theory of democracy', in P. Laslett *et al.* (eds), *Philosophy, Politics and Society*, 2nd series, Blackwell, 1962.

W

Waismann, Friedrich. 1896–1959. Austrian logical POSITIVIST who was born in Vienna and migrated to Oxford. He was originally a member of the Vienna Circle, but in Oxford he became a leader of 'linguistic PHILOSOPHY', emphasizing the fuzziness in various respects of ordinary language. In particular, he criticized the sharpness of the ANALYTIC/synthetic distinction, and introduced the notion of OPEN TEXTURE. *How I see Philosophy*, 1968 (articles, including six-part article on 'Analytic', originally published in *Analysis*, 1949–53). See also LOGIC.

Weakness of will. See INCONTINENCE.

Well-formed formula. See AXIOM.

Weyl's paradox. See HETEROLOGICAL.

WFF. See AXIOM.

Whewell, William. 1794–1866. Born in Lancaster, he worked in Cambridge, where he became master of Trinity College. He taught minerology and moral philosophy, but is mainly known for his work in philosophy of science, where he developed the hypothetico-deductive method (see INDUCTION), while accepting also certain fundamental principles which were innate but became self-evident only after reflection. He was opposed by J. S. MILL. In ethics he developed a system based on rights, themselves based on human nature. *History of the Inductive Sciences, from the Earliest to the Present Time*, 1837. *Philosophy of the Inductive Sciences, Founded*

Wittgenstein, Ludwig, J. J.

upon Their History, 1840, expanded in 3rd edition into three parts: *History of Scientific Ideas*, 1858, *Novum Organon Renovatum*, 1858. *On the Philosophy of Discovery*, 1860. *Elements of Morality, Including Polity*, 1845.

Whitehead, Alfred N. 1861–1947. Born in Thanet, he worked mainly in Cambridge, London and Harvard. His early work was in mathematics and logic, in which he taught, and then collaborated with, RUSSELL. Later he turned more to METAPHYSICS, and developed a philosophy based on processes and events rather than on material objects. His work was influenced by developments in physics then current, and was also relevant to philosophy of science on topics such as laws of nature. *Principia Mathematica*, 1910–13 (with Russell, Whitehead concentrating mainly on the mathematical parts, Russell on the philosophical). *Science and the Modern World*, 1925. *Process and Reality*, 1929 (often regarded as his main philosophical book, but difficult). *Adventures of Ideas*, 1933.

Wisdom, A. John T. D. 1904–93. British philosopher born in London, who spent his working life mainly in Cambridge. Working under the influence of WITTGENSTEIN's later philosophy, he was one of the forerunners of 'linguistic PHILOSOPHY'. He thought that, while philosophical problems should be attacked by rational methods, light can often be thrown on them, even when they are insoluble, by examining the deeper philosophical motives that led the protagonists to say what they did. This led him to an interest in psychoanalysis, and was also perhaps responsible for a certain allusiveness in his style of writing. *Problems of Mind and Matter*, 1934. 'Other Minds' (series of articles in *Mind*, 1940ff., collected with other articles in book of same title, 1952). *Philosophy and Psychoanalysis*, 1953 (miscellaneous essays). *Paradox and Discovery*, 1965 (more essays). See also LOGICAL CONSTRUCTIONS, SCEPTICISM.

J. O. Wisdom is a younger cousin of John Wisdom, who shares some of his interests, including that in psychoanalysis, but writes also on philosophy of science. See also NUMBERS (LAW OF LARGE).

Wittgenstein, Ludwig, J. J. 1889–1951. Austrian philosopher, born in Vienna, who taught in Cambridge. Both his main works (the first two mentioned below) were leading contributions to philosophical movements, the first to LOGICAL ATOMISM and the second (influential through oral dissemination before publication) to linguistic PHILOSOPHY. All his works but the first were published posthumously. In the first he tried to preserve an extensionalist logic (see INTENSIONALITY AND INTENTIONALITY), which led him to trace the limits of what could be stated explicitly and what could only be

Wittgenstein, Ludwig, J. J.

shown. The second revolves around his rejection of the view that there can be words which have meaning by standing for inner experiences private to the experiencer; this led him to think that philosophical puzzlement in general grew out of misunderstandings of how language works. *Tractatus Logico-Philosophicus*, 1921, trans. 1922 and (better) 1961. *Philosophical Investigations*, 1953. *Remarks on the Foundations of Mathematics*, 1967. *On Certainty*, 1969. *Remarks on the Philosophy of Psychology* (2 vols), 1980. See also CRITERION, EPISTEMOLOGY, FINITISM, LANGUAGE GAME, MEANING, POSITIVISM, PRIVATE LANGUAGE, SEEING, SPACE, STRUCTURE, UNIVERSALS, WISDOM.

Z

Zeno of Citium. See STOICS.

Zeno's paradoxes. The surviving paradoxes of Zeno of Elea (see ELEATICS) fall mainly into two groups, concerning plurality and motion, though these groups are related. Their interpretation and significance is to some extent controversial.

The idea behind the former group seems to be as follows: to have no size is to be nothing, while to have size is to be divisible (whether in reality or only in principle is left unclear). But the parts resulting from division must themselves either lack size, and so be nothing, or have size, and so be further divisible. Therefore we must end with nothing or with infinitely many parts. If these infinitely many parts lack size they cannot contribute to the whole, which will itself lack size; but if they have size, however small, the whole they form will be infinitely large.

The paradoxes of motion seem intended to argue that space and time can be neither atomic (made of indivisible points and moments) nor continuous. The *Moving Rows* paradox seems to argue that if both space and time are atomic there is a maximum velocity, namely one point per moment – but anything moving at this velocity relative to one object can always be shown to be moving faster relative to some other object, so there is no maximum velocity. The argument can be made to cover the cases where only one of space and time is atomic. Aristotle, however, who is our source for this paradox, treats it as simply confusing relative and absolute motion. The above version, whether or not historically accurate, is stronger than Aristotle's. There are other versions.

The *Achilles and the Tortoise* paradox argues that if space and

Zombie

time are both continuous, then if Achilles allows the tortoise a start in a race he can never overtake it. He takes at least some time to reach the tortoise's start, during which the tortoise moves at least some distance. While Achilles covers this distance the tortoise moves some more. While Achilles covers this 'more' the tortoise moves again. Clearly the argument can be repeated indefinitely: even though the successive stages get shorter and are covered ever more quickly, at the end of any given stage Achilles is still behind the tortoise. How can he reach the end of an endless series of stages? The *Dichotomy* is a variant of the Achilles, saying that one can never cover a distance, because one must first cover the first half, then the third quarter, and so on, constantly bisecting the remaining distance. In a more general form the paradox claims that if two objects are separated by a certain distance at a certain time they can never be separated by a different distance at any other time. The name *Stadium* is ambiguous, sometimes meaning the Dichotomy, sometimes the Moving Rows.

The *Flying Arrow* argues that, since at any moment an arrow occupies a definite position, and since between two moments there is nothing but other moments, the arrow can only be *in* positions and never *move* from one to another.

The *Grain of Millet*, on a different topic, argues that a single grain in falling makes no sound, but a thousand grains make a sound, so a thousand nothings become something, which is absurd. Cf. HEAP.

Modern discussions centre on the Achilles, of which many variants have been developed. Its full solution is still disputed.

R. M. Sainsbury, *Paradoxes*, Cambridge UP, 1988 (revised, 1995), chapter 1.

W. C. Salmon (ed.), *Zeno's Paradoxes*, Bobbs-Merrill, 1970. (Modern discussions, with extensive bibliography. On the Moving Rows cf. also J. Immerwahr, 'An interpretation of Zeno's stadium paradox', *Phronesis*, 1978.)

Zombie. As used by philosophers, creature looking and behaving exactly like a human but having no conscious experiences. See also QUALE.